CAUSES
AND
CONSEQUENCES
OF
WORLD WAR II

CAUSES
AND
CONSEQUENCES
OF
WORLD WAR II

EDITED WITH AN INTRODUCTION BY

ROBERT A. DIVINE

CHICAGO

QUADRANGLE BOOKS

1969

Library of Congress Catalog Card Number: 71-78305

Grateful acknowledgment is made to publishers and individuals
as noted herein for permission to reprint copyrighted materials.

PREFACE

IN LESS than a quarter-century an enormous body of scholarly writing has appeared on the Second World War. In this book I have tried to present a cross-section of the conflicting interpretations of the role of American diplomacy in the origins, conduct, and legacy of this war. My focus is nationalistic; I have made no effort to include equally significant historical literature on British, German, Russian, or Japanese diplomacy. Nor have I selected the work of military historians, except in cases where I think there is an intimate relationship between strategy and diplomacy.

The articles are ones which seemed to me to present the major issues in the ongoing historical debate. I have pointed to other significant articles in the introductions to each selection and in the bibliography. In the introductory essay I have sought to provide a broad historiographical survey of the principal books dealing with American diplomacy before and during the war. I have not included the extensive memoir literature in either the introductory essay or in the bibliography.

I wish to express my appreciation to the authors who so graciously permitted me to reprint their work. I also want to thank Walter Lambert for his help in compiling the bibliography, Clarence Lasby for his comments on the introductory essay, and my wife, Barbara Renick Divine, for her perceptive editorial assistance.

CONTENTS

IV. Consequences of World War II

I
Introduction

Diplomatic Historians
and World War II

THE SECOND WORLD WAR separates an older age of depression and reform from a newer era of affluence and political stalemate. The domestic issues of the twenties and thirties, such as the farm problem, unemployment, conservation of natural resources, and collective bargaining, gave way after World War II to an entirely different set of problems ranging from loyalty and inflation to urban decay and civil rights. The war proved to be an even greater watershed in foreign policy. The isolationist-internationalist dialogue which grew out of the fight over the League of Nations in 1919 reached its climax in the debate over entry into World War II. United States participation in the war enabled the internationalists to humiliate their isolationist opponents and ensure a future role of American world leadership by having the country take the lead in founding the United Nations. The writing of the U.N. Charter in San Francisco and the rapid Senate approval of American membership thus symbolized the nation's commitment to an active world policy.

But the belated fulfillment of Woodrow Wilson's dream did not bring the promised utopia. Instead, the United States soon found itself enmeshed in the Cold War with the Soviet Union. For the next quarter-century the United States moved from crisis to crisis, caught up in a deadly rivalry which quickly spread from Europe to Asia, the Middle East, Africa, and Latin America. Inevitably, the Cold War cast its shadow over the historiography of World War II. Debates between historians over the wisdom of American entry into the conflict and over the nature of wartime diplomacy turned more and more on current dilemmas with the Soviet Union. Critics of American policy not only blamed Franklin Roosevelt for allying the United States with Stalin's Russia, but even accused him of fighting against the wrong enemy. Defenders of the administration often went to extremes in justifying American diplomacy, blaming Hitler and Stalin for all postwar ills. The breakdown of the Cold War consensus in the 1960's added a new dimension to the historiographical debate, with New Left revisionists suggesting that the war culminated in a conscious drive for a *Pax Americana* that compelled the Soviets to pursue an aggressive policy in self-defense.

Although several themes run throughout World War II diplomacy, historians have focused on three separate issues. The first is the question of American entry into the war, particularly the role of isolationism in the 1930's, the impact of Hitler's victories on American security, and the showdown in the Pacific with Japan. The second issue is the conduct of wartime diplomacy. Here writers have concentrated their attention on such diverse matters as the policy of unconditional surrender, the strains and stresses within the victorious coalition (particularly between Britain, Russia, and America), and the critical problem of what to do with a defeated Germany. Closely related but treated quite distinctly is the third issue, the consequences of the war. The decision to use the atomic bomb and the quarrel over Poland and Eastern Europe came while the war still raged, but their primary impact was on the future peace. These were the two events that gave rise to the Cold War.

I

A bitter debate between revisionist and orthodox historians has dominated the literature on American entry into World War II.[1] Virtually without exception, the revisionists were men who opposed American entry into the war from 1939 to 1941 and who thus chose to seek ultimate vindication through a historical counterattack. The earliest and foremost revisionist was Charles A. Beard, the distinguished progressive historian. Beard advocated a policy of continentalism during the 1930's, claiming that what happened abroad was of little consequence to a United States whose mission was to perfect democracy at home. In 1946 he published *American Foreign Policy in the Making, 1932–1940,* in which he accused Franklin Roosevelt of misleading the American people in the 1930's by hewing to an isolationist line in his public statements. Two years later Beard published a second volume, *President Roosevelt and the Coming of the War, 1941.* In this book, far more vindictive in tone than his earlier volume, Beard accused the President of lying the nation into war. Placing great stress on Roosevelt's campaign promise in 1940 not to send American boys into foreign wars, Beard argued that FDR tried

1. Historians have expressed virtually complete agreement on the use of the term "revisionist" to describe those who have taken a critical view of American entry into World War II. I am using the term "orthodox" to describe writers who defend the Roosevelt policies, rather than the pejorative term "court historians" coined by the revisionists and the somewhat misleading label of "internationalist historians" used by Wayne Cole in his article "American Entry into World War II: A Historiographical Appraisal," *Mississippi Valley Historical Review,* XLIII (March 1957), 595–617. By orthodox, I mean those scholars who have put forth the prevailing explanation for American entry into the war. While I disagree with Cole's choice of terms, his article stands out as by far the best analysis of this controversy and I have drawn heavily upon it.

to involve the nation in the European war through a series of secret moves, and when that devious strategy failed he turned to the Pacific and provoked Japan into the attack on Pearl Harbor in order to ensure American entry into World War II. Beard's chief concern was the damage he felt Roosevelt had done to the American constitutional system, and he concluded his 1948 book with an eloquent denunciation of presidential usurpation of congressional power "to conduct foreign affairs and initiate war at will." [2] Beard also pointed out the folly through which a policy designed to destroy Hitler's despotism had smoothed the way for the triumph of the Soviet Union, "one of the most ruthless Leviathans in the long history of military empires." [3]

For the next five years revisionist historians elaborated on Beard's themes. These were the early years of the Cold War, when relations between the United States and Russia were at their worst and when McCarthyism raged inside America. Thus it is not surprising that those who had vainly opposed Roosevelt when he was alive should strive to prove how badly he had served the nation now that the mood had turned against New Deal liberalism. The most massive assault came from Charles C. Tansill, who secured access to State Department files closed to Beard. In *Back Door to War: The Roosevelt Foreign Policy, 1933–1941* (1952), Tansill presented a great deal of evidence indicating the strong aversion American diplomats displayed toward Germany and Japan from the early 1930's on, but he was unable to uncover any direct evidence of a conspiracy with Britain and France to bring on the war. Like Beard, Tansill charged that Roosevelt maneuvered Japan into firing the first shot so that the United States could enter the European war via the Pacific back door. Other revisionists, notably Robert A. Theobald, went further and suggested that Roosevelt deliberately exposed the fleet to attack at Pearl Harbor, thus indirectly accusing the President of treason. [4]

Harry Elmer Barnes furnished the most comprehensive revisionist analysis of American entry into World War II in a book which he edited in 1953, *Perpetual War for Perpetual Peace*. Eight revisionist writers contributed chapters assessing various aspects of FDR's policies in the Atlantic and Pacific. In his introduction Barnes decried the "historical blackout" revisionists had suffered, citing the refusal of well-known pub-

2. Charles A. Beard, *President Roosevelt and the Coming of War, 1941: A Study in Appearances and Realities* (New Haven, 1948), p. 590.

3. *Ibid.*, p. 577.

4. George Morgenstern, *Pearl Harbor: The Story of the Secret War* (New York, 1947); Frederic R. Sanborn, *Design for War: A Study of Secret Power Politics, 1937–1941* (New York, 1951); Robert A. Theobald, *The Final Secret of Pearl Harbor: The Washington Contribution to the Japanese Attack* (New York, 1954). Theobald, a retired admiral, wrote to exonerate the Navy from any responsibility for Pearl Harbor.

lishers to print their books and the unwillingness of scholarly reviewers to treat their work fairly. But his strongest condemnation was for the "suicidal" policy of internationalism which had brought the United States and the world to a "calamitous turning point in the history of mankind." Claiming that Russia and Germany would have fought to a stalemate if left alone, Barnes argued that American entry into the war led directly to "the rise and influence of Communism, military state capitalism, the police state, and the impending doom of civilization." [5]

The books by Tansill, Theobald, and Barnes marked the climax of revisionism. Since the mid-1950's no further revisionist books have appeared, and the influence of earlier writers has steadily declined. Despite evident bias and distortion, the revisionist historians provided some important insights into the causes of American entry into World War II. They revealed the striking incompatibility of Roosevelt's public statements and his private actions, of his campaign utterances and his diplomatic moves. At the very least the revisionists demonstrated that FDR was both inconsistent and devious in the way he conducted diplomacy before December 1941. They failed to prove, however, that the President was guilty of betraying the security of the nation at Pearl Harbor. Their contention that administration policy led to the postwar Russian challenge ignored the fact that it took the combined efforts of the United States, the Soviet Union, and Great Britain to halt the Nazi war machine. Most of all, the revisionists, by their extreme criticisms, provoked an equally emotional response from defenders of administration policy which served to distort rather than clarify the historical record.

The orthodox account of American foreign policy began during the war and reached its full development in the early 1950's. Even before Pearl Harbor, Joseph Alsop and Robert Kintner published *American White Paper* (1940), an account of American policy toward the outbreak of war in Europe in 1939. Relying on conversations with many administration officials, these two journalists maintained that President Roosevelt and his advisers decided soon after Munich that a German victory in Europe would endanger the United States, and that the administration should therefore do all it possibly could to aid the Allies. This same theme ran through another journalistic account, *How War Came,* written by Forrest Davis and Ernest K. Lindley in mid-1942. Praising the administration for pursuing a realistic policy of defending the Western Hemisphere, Davis and Lindley condemned the isolationists for preventing FDR from arousing the American people to their peril.

Two influential postwar books carried forward the portrait of a farseeing President slowly educating a reluctant nation. The first was

5. Harry Elmer Barnes, ed., *Perpetual War for Perpetual Peace: A Critical Examination of the Foreign Policy of Franklin Delano Roosevelt and Its Aftermath* (Caldwell, Idaho, 1953), pp. 6, 7.

Robert Sherwood's classic *Roosevelt and Hopkins* (1948). An active interventionist in 1940 when he joined Roosevelt's speechwriting team, Sherwood started out to write a biography of Harry Hopkins during the war years, but his book centered much more on Franklin Roosevelt and his diplomacy. With access to unpublished White House records, Sherwood was able to give a detailed account of the President's policy from 1939 to 1941. He described the various moves Roosevelt took which brought the United States to the brink of war with Germany, but he noted the President's reluctance to take the final step. Sherwood blamed the isolationists, stating that their "long and savage campaign against the President had exerted an important effect on Roosevelt himself: whatever the peril, he was not going to lead the country into war—he was going to wait to be pushed in." [6] Basil Rauch presented a more positive view of FDR's leadership in *Roosevelt: From Munich to Pearl Harbor*. Writing explictly to refute Beard's charges point by point, Rauch described Roosevelt's refusal to act more boldly as a necessary precaution against a successful isolationist attack on his policy. Rauch stressed the broad influence of the isolationists as late as the fall of 1941 and described Roosevelt as walking a tightrope. "He was determined to take no avoidable risk of an 'irrevocable act' that might destroy his policy," Rauch concluded.[7]

William L. Langer and S. Everett Gleason were more critical of Roosevelt's leadership. In *The Challenge to Isolation, 1937–1940* (1952) and *The Undeclared War, 1941* (1953) they used both White House and State Department records to give the most comprehensive account yet written of American entry into the war. Both authors worked for the State Department during the war, and they made no effort to conceal their belief that the Axis powers directly threatened the security of the United States. They think Roosevelt was unduly sensitive to isolationist criticism and that he consistently overestimated the strength of anti-war sentiment. From their "inside" perspective, Roosevelt's refusal to act boldly stems not from a devious desire to lead the nation into war but rather reveals a weakness in the American democratic system. Roosevelt was so intent on building a consensus for his policy and maintaining his political leadership that he neglected to adopt the forthright measures that would have best served the national interest in a grave world crisis.

Orthodox historians are most sympathetic to Roosevelt in defending him from charges of treason and betrayal in regard to Pearl Harbor. These charges, elaborated on at length later by the revisionists, were first aired at the congressional hearings on the Japanese attack during

6. Robert E. Sherwood, *Roosevelt and Hopkins: An Intimate History* (New York, 1948), p. 299.

7. Basil Rauch, *Roosevelt, From Munich to Pearl Harbor: A Study in the Creation of a Foreign Policy* (New York, 1950), p. 346.

the winter of 1945–1946.[8] Walter Millis sifted through this voluminous testimony in writing *This Is Pearl* (1947). Millis exonerated the President from any complicity in the attack, claiming that rather than welcoming war in the Pacific, Roosevelt did all he could to avoid it. According to Millis, the local commanders, General Short and Admiral Kimmel, were primarily to blame for the Japanese success. Herbert Feis took a more moderate position in *The Road to Pearl Harbor* (1950). Focusing on the question of embargoes on strategic materials, Feis stressed the decision in July 1941 to sever trade with Japan by freezing all Japanese assets in the United States. Feis believes the United States was justified in taking this step in order to deny oil and scrap iron to a potential enemy. In his view, the freezing order merely quickened a showdown between the United States and Japan that had been building since the invasion of Manchuria in 1931. Feis had little to say about the actual attack on Pearl Harbor, but the more recent study by Roberta Wohlstetter, *Pearl Harbor: Warning and Decision* (1962), offers the most convincing explanation of the intelligence failure that permitted the Japanese to achieve such great success. Ignoring the polemical literature, Mrs. Wohlstetter examines the mechanics of intelligence gathering and analysis to show how human frailty, not political maneuvering, set the stage for Pearl Harbor.

In defending Roosevelt against the revisionist charge of betrayal at Pearl Harbor, orthodox historians tended to overlook more responsible criticism of American Far Eastern policy in 1941. In *The Axis Alliance and Japanese-American Relations, 1941* (1958), Paul W. Schroeder pointed out a serious inconsistency in American policy. Despite a decision to give Europe priority, Roosevelt neglected opportunities to work out a temporary détente with Japan and instead backed the Japanese into a corner by issuing the freezing order, by refusing to attend a summit meeting with the Japanese Prime Minister, and by insisting that Japan withdraw its troops from China. Schroeder, noting that Ambassador Joseph Grew urged a conciliatory policy toward Japan in 1941, argues that the United States would have been in a much better position to bring its military power to bear against Nazi Germany if Grew's alternative had been adopted.

The orthodox historians, like the revisionists, have been relatively silent since the mid-1950's. Their view has prevailed in textbooks and in scholarly journals, in part because of the cogency of their interpretation

8. *Hearings Before the Joint Committee on the Investigation of the Pearl Harbor Attack,* 79th Cong., 2nd sess. (39 parts; Washington, D.C., 1946). The committee's findings, divided into a Democratic majority report and a Republican minority dissent, were published separately in *Report of the Joint Committee on the Investigation of the Pearl Harbor Attack,* 79th Cong., 2nd sess. (Washington, D.C., 1946).

and in part because there has been a "blackout" of the revisionists, who never held commanding positions in the historical profession. The revisionists have gradually died off without training a cadre of disciples to carry on their crusade. And, lacking a foe to battle, the orthodox historians have moved on to new topics and new debates.[9]

The present generation of historians is writing on the causes of American entry into World War II with a quite different set of concerns. Some writers have engaged in a sympathetic reassessment of the isolationists of the 1930's. Wayne Cole makes Senator Gerald P. Nye, a demon in earlier works, at least a believable and sincere exponent of agrarian isolationism.[1] Manfred Jonas has written a careful reappraisal of *Isolationism in America, 1935–1941* (1966), in which he treats the isolationists and their ideas with respect. In *The American Revisionists* (1966), Warren Cohen deals with the revisionist writers of the 1930's, especially Tansill and Beard, to show how they arrived at their distinctive view of American foreign policy. There has been an equally strong concern with the relationship between Nazi Germany and the United States. By examining Hitler's view of this country and the conduct of his American policy, such scholars as Saul Friedlander, Alton Frye, and James Compton have offset the ethnocentric character of previous writing and have placed American foreign policy in a more cosmopolitan setting.[2] Both Frye and Compton are convinced that Hitler had hostile designs upon the United States, even though they admit there is no direct evidence of Nazi aggression toward the Western Hemisphere. Friedlander, writing from a European perspective, does not explore the question of Hitler's long-range policy toward the United States, but his

9. Charles Beard died in 1948, Tansill in 1964, and Barnes in 1968. Though Beard was highly respected in the profession, he had not had the opportunity to train graduate students after his departure from Columbia in 1917. Beard's extreme views on Roosevelt's foreign policy exposed him to intense criticism, some quite within the bounds of scholarly fair play, and some quite savage, notably Samuel Eliot Morison's slashing critique, "Did Roosevelt Start the War?: History Through a Beard," *Atlantic Monthly,* CLXXXII (August 1948), 91–97.

1. Wayne S. Cole, *Senator Gerald P. Nye and American Foreign Relations* (Minneapolis, 1962).

2. Saul Friedlander, *Prelude to Downfall: Hitler and the United States, 1939–1941,* translated from the French by Aline B. and Alexander Werth (New York, 1967); Alton Frye, *Nazi Germany and the American Hemisphere, 1933–1941* (New Haven, 1967); James V. Compton, *The Swastika and the Eagle: Hitler, the United States, and the Origins of World War II* (Boston, 1967). For an earlier account of German-American relations, written before all the German records were available, see Hans L. Trefousse, *Germany and American Neutrality, 1939–1941* (New York, 1951). Gerhard L. Weinberg has written a fascinating article on the Fuehrer's distorted and shifting view of America, "Hitler's Image of the United States," *American Historical Review,* LXIX (July 1964), 1006–1021.

account suggests that the German leader sincerely wanted to keep the United States out of the European war and that he only decided to join with Japan when he realized that American involvement was unavoidable.

These more recent studies raise the question of precisely to what degree the Axis powers threatened the security of the United States. The orthodox historians have always rested their case on the assertion that a German victory in Europe and a Japanese triumph in Asia would have led inevitably to the invasion of the Western Hemisphere and the conquest of the United States. The generation that lived through World War II could accept no other explanation; it made the war just and necessary. But those who reached maturity after 1945 are not willing to accept this proposition so easily. Members of the Wisconsin school of diplomatic history, notably Lloyd Gardner and Robert F. Smith, have suggested that it was the German threat to American economic supremacy in the world, not endangered national security, that led to an interventionist policy.[3] A reassessment of isolationism, particularly by a generation repelled by the war in Vietnam, might well lead to a new round of historical interpretation which would challenge the prevailing orthodox view. And it is quite conceivable that future historians will take up Beard's charge of presidential usurpation of congressional power, a far more sensitive issue in the 1960's than in earlier decades, and offer a radically different view of Franklin Roosevelt's leadership.

II

In August 1948 *Life* magazine published a provocative two-part article by William Bullitt, former ambassador to the Soviet Union, entitled "How We Won the War and Lost the Peace." Bullitt, a bitter and frustrated man, charged that Roosevelt had brought on the Cold War through his wartime policy of appeasing the Russians. Though most responsible historians rejected this emotional accusation, one theme which Bullitt set forth runs through nearly all subsequent writing on the diplomacy of World War II. "War is not a prizefight," Bullitt wrote. "The winner does not go home from the ring and receive a purse containing peace and prosperity. Military effort unaccompanied by equal political and moral effort produces no constructive result."[4] Bullitt went on to state that the way a war is fought shapes the future peace, and

3. Lloyd C. Gardner, *Economic Aspects of New Deal Diplomacy* (Madison, Wisc., 1964), pp. 98–99; Robert F. Smith, "American Foreign Relations, 1920–1942," in Barton J. Bernstein, ed., *Towards a New Past: Dissenting Essays in American History* (New York, 1968), pp. 232–262.

4. William Bullitt, "How We Won the War and Lost the Peace," *Life*, XXV (August 30, 1948), 92.

concluded that Roosevelt's great failure was his exclusive concentration on the goal of winning the war without regard to the impact of his policies on the postwar world.

The two comprehensive histories of World War II diplomacy support, in quite different ways, a sophisticated version of Bullitt's theme. The first, William Hardy McNeill's *America, Britain, and Russia: Their Co-operation and Conflict, 1941–1946* (1953), is a brilliant and still underappreciated history of the Grand Alliance. Written by an American scholar under British auspices, the book rises above national bias to offer a genuinely international perspective, telling the story, as Arnold Toynbee notes in the foreword, "from the standpoint, not of any one individual or one country, but of a human race on whose long history these brief transactions seemed bound to make a marked and enduring effect." [5] Writing in the early 1950's, before archival or manuscript materials were available, McNeill viewed the eventual breakup of the coalition as a natural and expected development. Given the history of previous wartime concerts and the fundamental differences between Russia and her Western allies, McNeill comments, "the wonder is not that co-operation soon broke down, but that it was possible for co-operation to become as effective as it was during the later war years." [6] Hitler was the cement holding together this curious partnership; once he was defeated, the alliance was doomed.

Throughout his account, McNeill shows that Roosevelt never understood the inherent limitations of the wartime coalition. Instead, FDR propagated the myth that once fascist aggression was destroyed, the world would move into a new era of international peace and harmony. With this millennial expectation, Roosevelt could blithely ignore the postwar world and concentrate all his energy and attention on winning the war. The future would take care of itself. Reinforcing this approach was the ingrained American belief that military affairs should be divorced from political considerations. McNeill stresses Roosevelt's lack of confidence in his own military judgment and his tendency to accept unhesitatingly the policies presented to him by his military advisers. "Victory in the field became an end in itself," McNeill asserts, and

5. William Hardy McNeill, *American, Britain and Russia: Their Co-operation and Conflict, 1941–1946* (London, 1953), p. vi. McNeill's book is the third volume of the *Survey of International Affairs, 1939–1946*, edited by Arnold Toynbee and sponsored by the Royal Institute of International Affairs. McNeill, then an assistant professor of history at the University of Chicago, wrote the book at Chatham House between November 1950 and November 1951. Though he relied entirely on published material, several British officials read his manuscript and presumably supplied him with firsthand information on wartime policies.

6. *Ibid.*, p. 87.

"technical military efficiency became the sole criterion" in the decision-making process.[7] Thus American diplomacy during World War II was directed exclusively toward winning the war on the naive assumption that a military victory would lead automatically to a lasting peace.

Herbert Feis, in his massive book *Churchill, Roosevelt, Stalin: The War They Waged and the Peace They Sought,* develops the same theme less explicitly. Writing in 1957, and with access both to State Department records and to the private papers of Averell Harriman, wartime ambassador to the Soviet Union, Feis is more intent on recounting the course of Big Three diplomacy at the summit than in offering an interpretive analysis.[8] His point of view is frankly American, and he makes little effort to explain Soviet and British motivations. He treats Roosevelt sympathetically, yet he repeatedly echoes McNeill's point that the President ignored "the way in which military developments could affect political possibilities," refusing ever to adjust strategy to serve political ends. "Roosevelt was trying to fight a coalition war without coalition politics," Feis writes, "lest these hinder the conduct of the war." [9]

Throughout, Feis emphasizes FDR's efforts to reduce the inevitable strains of the coalition and especially to establish a cordial relationship with the Soviets. He recounts Roosevelt's eagerness to have a personal meeting with Stalin early in the war, speculating that the President was "tantalized" by the mystery surrounding the Russian dictator and somewhat miffed that Churchill had flown to Moscow in 1942 for a face-to-face encounter with Stalin.[1] Roosevelt was unable to arrange a similar meeting, but when the Big Three held their first summit conference in November 1943, Feis notes that twice the President set up private conversations with Stalin. "Roosevelt used his whole repertoire in his effort to get on close and trustful terms with Stalin," Feis writes, adding that this even included some sharp digs at Churchill. FDR evidently felt he had succeeded in winning Stalin over, for at the final banquet he gave a toast saying that "the rainbow, the enduring symbol of hope, could

7. *Ibid.,* p. 29.

8. Herbert Feis, *Churchill, Roosevelt, Stalin: The War They Waged and the Peace They Sought* (Princeton, 1957). Though Feis did not play a direct role in formulating American wartime diplomacy, he did serve as economic adviser in the State Department until 1943 and as a special consultant to Secretary of War Henry L. Stimson from 1943 to 1946. At the time he wrote this book, the State Department files for the war years were not open to academic historians, and thus Feis enjoyed privileged access to the sources. *Churchill, Roosevelt, Stalin* covers the period through the defeat of Germany in May 1945. Feis continues the story of wartime diplomacy in two other books, *Between War and Peace: The Potsdam Conference* (Princeton, 1960) and *Japan Subdued: The Atomic Bomb and the End of the War in the Pacific* (Princeton, 1961).

9. Feis, *Churchill, Roosevelt, Stalin,* p. 125.

1. *Ibid.,* p. 132.

now, for the first time . . . be discerned in the sky." [2] Though the strains that eventually broke up the wartime coalition were apparent to Roosevelt by the time of the Yalta conference in 1945, Feis asserts that the President believed until his death that he could maintain the alliance with Russia. "He was going to continue to act on the supposition that by patience, proofs of good will and fair purpose," Feis concludes, "the mistrust of the Soviet authorities could be subdued, and they be converted into good partners for the benefit of all mankind." [3]

Two briefer treatments of wartime diplomacy place much less emphasis on Roosevelt's absorption with winning the war. In *American Diplomacy During the Second World War,* Gaddis Smith views FDR's eagerness to get along with Stalin as the central error of American diplomacy. Depicting Roosevelt as a skillful domestic politician out of his element in foreign policy, Smith claims that his naive efforts to charm Stalin simply convinced the Soviet dictator that "the United States would raise no effective opposition to hostile Russian expansion." [4] Thus Smith asserts that a fundamental miscalculation of Soviet behavior, not just concentration on the war effort, undermined American wartime diplomacy. John Snell offers a radically different explanation in *Illusion and Necessity.* Defending FDR as a pragmatic statesman who believed that failure to establish a sound relationship with Russia would doom the future peace, Snell praises Roosevelt's realism. He contends, moreover, that the President did allow political considerations to influence strategy, notably in the decision to launch the North African campaign in 1942. The reason Roosevelt did not pursue a politically motivated strategy toward Russia in the final stages of the war was that such a course was possible "only if the Western powers had been willing before then to bargain with German and Japanese leaders . . ." [5] Snell concludes that the American people would never have tolerated any such deal with the Axis nations.

The charge that Roosevelt won the war and lost the peace gets its fullest airing from the military historians. Much of their work has little bearing on the diplomacy of World War II, but instead centers on the shifting strategy employed to defeat Germany and Japan. The most controversial issues relate to the conduct of the war against Nazi Germany, and particularly to the bitter dispute between British and American military planners over how best to deploy their armies on the European continent. The essence of the debate at the time, and later in the memoirs and accounts of American and British partisans, was

2. *Ibid.,* pp. 276–277.
3. *Ibid.,* p. 596.
4. Gaddis Smith, *American Diplomacy During the Second World War, 1941–1945* (New York, 1965), p. 11.
5. John Snell, *Illusion and Necessity: The Diplomacy of Global War, 1939–1945* (Boston, 1963), p. 143.

whether to pursue the British strategy of invasion through the Mediterranean into southeastern Europe, or to concentrate exclusively on the American plan for a cross-channel attack into France. The actual course followed was a composite policy, beginning in the Mediterranean with the North African campaign and the invasion of Italy, but reaching its climax with the Normandy landings in 1944. Ever since, the British have argued that if their strategy had been followed to the end, Anglo-American forces would have reached central Europe ahead of the Russians and thus would have allowed the Western nations to limit postwar Soviet expansion.

The most persuasive statement of the British view is Chester Wilmot's *The Struggle for Europe*.[6] Primarily a detailed military history of the cross-channel invasion and the defeat of Germany, Wilmot's book is based on a balance-of-power thesis. The Western allies, he contends, went to war to prevent Germany from dominating Europe, only to end up permitting Stalin to achieve Hitler's goal. Arguing that both American and British interests "demanded the restoration of democratic influence in Central and South Eastern Europe," Wilmot condemns Roosevelt and his military advisers for choking off the Italian campaign in 1943 and blocking Churchill's suggestion of a drive from the Adriatic into central Europe, not as a substitute for the landings in France but as an additional thrust.[7] Wilmot also criticizes FDR's policy of unconditional surrender because it permitted the war to proceed "beyond the stage of military decision to the point of political collapse," and thus enabled Russia to move into the heart of Europe. Wilmot divides the blame for these decisions between Roosevelt, whom he sees as a prisoner of his own belief that he could "handle" Stalin, and General George C. Marshall, the wartime chief of staff, who insisted that victory in the field was the sole legitimate goal of American policy.[8] Thus, even after Roosevelt's death, Marshall backed Eisenhower's decision to stop at the Elbe rather than advance his forces as far to the east as possible.

American military historians, particularly those who contributed to the official history, *United States Army in World War II*, have tended to defend American wartime strategy on purely military grounds, finding their ultimate justification in the effective way in which the war was

6. (New York, 1952). Other British accounts that stress the same themes are John Ehrman, *Grand Strategy* (London, 1956); volumes V and VI of the official British *History of the Second World War*, edited by J. R. M. Butler; and Arthur Bryant, *The Turn of the Tide, 1939–1943* (London, 1957) and *Triumph in the West* (London, 1959), based on the diaries of Field Marshal Sir Alan Brooke, Chief of the Imperial General Staff. In his own first draft of his history, *The Second World War* (6 vols.; Boston, 1948–1953), Sir Winston Churchill sets forth the British case vigorously.

7. Wilmot, *Struggle for Europe*, p. 130.

8. *Ibid.*, pp. 713–715.

won.[9] But the editor of the Army history, Kent Roberts Greenfield, deals more broadly with the political implications of strategic decisions in his book *American Strategy in World War II: A Reconsideration.* He frankly acknowledges that American planners concentrated almost exclusively on one goal, " the total military defeat of their enemies." Given the disparate political interests of the wartime coalition, Greenfield argues that this policy "can be defended as having been the height of political wisdom." [1] Those who claim we should have conducted the war so as to restrain postwar Soviet expansion fail to take into account prevailing public attitudes, Greenfield contends. He quotes General Marshall's statement to Eisenhower in support of his decision to stop at the Elbe in April 1945: "Personally and aside from all logistical, tactical or strategical implications I would be loath to hazard American lives for purely political purposes." Marshall's statement was in accord with the insistent demand of the American people that we quickly "thrash the bullies that had disturbed the peace, and get American soldiers and sailors back home." [2] Greenfield thus maintains that domestic political realities, however misguided they may seem in hindsight, dictated the exclusive American concern for military victory.

The Bullitt theme of Roosevelt's winning the war but losing the peace led revisionist writers to make more extreme charges against the President's wartime diplomacy. Not only did FDR ignore the political implications of his military decisions, but he naively tried to win over the Soviet Union by a policy of appeasement. Throughout the war, according to this view, Roosevelt went out of his way to conciliate Stalin without regard to basic American postwar interests.

The fullest statement of this revisionist critique is William Henry Chamberlin's *America's Second Crusade* (1950). Dealing with both the issues of American entry into the war and wartime diplomacy, Chamberlin argues that Russia, rather than Germany, posed the only long-run threat to American security. He condemns Roosevelt for creating power vacuums in Europe and Asia which opened the way for postwar Soviet

9. Pertinent volumes in the Army series include Maurice Matloff and Edwin S. Snell, *Strategic Planning for Coalition Warfare, 1941–1942* (Washington, D.C., 1953); Maurice Matloff, *Strategic Planning for Coalition Warfare, 1943–1944* (Washington, D.C., 1959); and Forrest C. Pogue, *The Supreme Command* (Washington, D.C., 1954). Other books expressing the American point of view on the strategic debate are Kent Roberts Greenfield, ed., *Command Decisions* (Washington, D.C., 1960); Samuel Eliot Morison, *Strategy and Compromise* (Boston, 1958); and Stephen E. Ambrose, *Eisenhower and Berlin, 1945: The Decision to Halt at the Elbe* (New York, 1967). One American author, Hanson W. Baldwin, sides completely with the British in *Great Mistakes of the War* (New York, 1950).

1. Kent Roberts Greenfield, *American Strategy in World War II: A Reconsideration* (Baltimore, 1963), p. 16.

2. *Ibid.,* pp. 19–20.

expansion, and he suggests that the United States should have aligned itself with Germany and Japan in the 1930's, "when they were too weak to be a threat to us and still strong enough to be useful partners in a coalition against the Soviet Union." [3] In *Roosevelt's Road to Russia* (1959), George N. Crocker goes even further, accusing Roosevelt of deliberately betraying the national interest. "By intention and deed," Crocker asserts, Roosevelt "devoted himself to bringing about a state of affairs in Europe and Asia in which there would be no neighboring powers capable of offering any check to Soviet ambitions." [4] Crocker claims that Roosevelt must have understood Stalin's determination to destroy capitalism and impose a communist dictatorship on the world, yet he did nothing to protect the American people from this threat.

Both Chamberlin and Crocker see the Yalta Conference as the climax of Roosevelt's policy of appeasement. They condemn the concessions to the Soviet Union on Poland and Eastern Europe, viewing the proposed coalition government for Poland and the promise of free elections in Russian-held countries as feeble attempts to disguise Soviet domination. All that Stalin conceded to Roosevelt, according to Crocker, was "a few fine phrases with which to cover himself at home." [5] The revisionist authors are most critical of the agreements on the Far East. The granting to Russia of railway and harbor rights in Manchuria is seen as the repudiation of America's historic Open Door policy. China "was offered up as a sacrifice on the altar of appeasement at Yalta," Chamberlin concludes; Crocker denounces the deal as "a moral debacle of unimaginable evil." [6]

The emotional intensity of these accusations led many writers to rally to the defense of the Roosevelt administration. In *Roosevelt and the Russians: The Yalta Conference* (1949), Edward Stettinius, Secretary of State at the time of the conference, praised the Yalta agreements, claiming that the Russians actually made more concessions than the United States.[7] Others were more moderate in their defense. Robert Sherwood acknowledged that Roosevelt made mistakes at Yalta, but he claimed that they became apparent only with "the considerable

3. William Henry Chamberlin, *America's Second Crusade* (Chicago, 1950), p. 342. The quotation is taken from Chamberlin's report of a conversation with an anonymous foreign service officer.

4. George N. Crocker, *Roosevelt's Road to Russia* (Chicago, 1959), p. 8. Both the Crocker and Chamberlin volumes were published by Henry Regnery Company, which by the 1950's had become the primary publisher of revisionist books.

5. *Ibid.*, p. 274.

6. Chamberlin, *America's Second Crusade*, p. 213; Crocker, *Roosevelt's Road to Russia*, p. 280.

7. This book, essentially a memoir of the Yalta conference by Stettinius, was written with the editorial assistance of Walter Johnson.

advantage of hindsight." Sherwood found the Far Eastern agreements "the most assailable point in the entire Yalta record," and he felt that Roosevelt gave in on this issue because the conference was almost over and "he was tired and anxious to avoid further argument." [8]

Four scholars, John Snell, Forrest Pogue, Charles Delzell, and George Lensen, combined in 1956 to write the most thorough analysis of the Yalta Conference. Using the conference records published by the Eisenhower administration in 1955, they concluded that the Yalta agreements formed a realistic, if somewhat unfavorable, diplomatic settlement.[9] Rebutting the revisionist charges of betrayal, these authors argued that the decisions reached at Yalta were determined by the way the war had been fought. In a concluding essay, Forrest Pogue conceded the moral weakness of the Far Eastern agreements, but he defended Yalta on pragmatic grounds. Russian success in the war had created "a new balance of power in the world at large," and Western statesmen either had to try to reach an accommodation with the Soviets or plunge their countries into a new and greater war.[1] Pogue concluded that the decision to try to live with the Russians rather than fight them was a wise one which placed the onus for the Cold War squarely upon the Soviet Union.

The strains within the Grand Alliance between the United States and Russia dominate the literature of World War II diplomacy, but considerable historical controversy has developed over American relations with two other allies, France and China. The re-emergence of de Gaulle as the leader of France and China's rise as the dominant power in Asia led in the 1960's to a new interest in our wartime relations with these two nations.

The American policy of maintaining diplomatic relations with the Vichy regime after the fall of France, working with Admiral Darlan at the time of the North African invasion, and delaying until late 1944 our recognition of de Gaulle's Free French regime has been

8. Sherwood, *Roosevelt and Hopkins*, pp. 866, 867.

9. Secretary of State John Foster Dulles authorized the publication of this volume in the *Foreign Relations* series, *The Conferences at Malta and Yalta, 1945* (Washington, D.C., 1955), more than a decade before it would normally have appeared. The Yalta agreements had been a campaign issue in the 1952 election, and the Republicans promised to disclose everything about the conference once they were in office. There were few startling disclosures in this volume, and revisionist historians immediately charged that the State Department editors deleted documents that might discredit the Roosevelt administration. See Crocker, *Roosevelt's Road to Russia*, p. 243. In a scholarly article, "The *Foreign Relations* Series: A Centennial Estimate," *Mississippi Valley Historical Review*, XLIX (March 1963), 595–612, Richard W. Leopold praises the editors for making the volume so useful to historians.

1. John Snell, ed., *The Meaning of Yalta: Big Three Diplomacy and the New Balance of Power* (Baton Rouge, La., 1956), p. 206.

the most intensely criticized aspect of World War II diplomacy. At the time, liberal groups within the United States condemned the Vichy policy as immoral, pointing out the inconsistency of dealing with a government which was collaborating with Nazi Germany. In response to these attacks, William Langer began working during the war on a history of the Vichy policy from the fall of France to the North African landings. Langer had the sanction of Secretary of State Cordell Hull and his own agency, the OSS, and was given privileged access to pertinent records. *Our Vichy Gamble* finally appeared in 1947, and though Langer claimed that the book represented his independent scholarly analysis and conclusions, it was a point-by-point defense of American policy. In each case Langer justified the administration's decisions on the basis of expediency, claiming that the policy contributed directly to the winning of the war. He described the dealings with Vichy as "a sensible, purely opportunistic policy," and he flayed the critics for basing their case on sentimental and idealistic factors. ". . . The purely ideological approach to the Vichy problem could never be a realistic or practicable one," Langer concluded. "The task of the State Department is to protect American interests abroad, not to sit in judgment on other governments." [2]

Reviewers were quite critical of Langer's book, but his account remained the standard one until the 1960's.[3] Then two new studies of Franco-American relations appeared: Dorothy S. White, *Seeds of Discord* (1964), and Milton Viorst, *Hostile Allies: FDR and Charles de Gaulle* (1965). Neither author undertook the extensive research in official records that gave Langer's book its scholarly strength, but both reflected the new esteem which de Gaulle had achieved in rescuing France from anarchy. Miss White's book was the more modest, dealing with the triangular relations between the Free French, the United States, and Britain from the fall of France through mid-1942. Sympathetic to de Gaulle and mildly critical of American policy, Miss White tried to tell the story of how the initial strains developed between the Roosevelt administration and de Gaulle's Free French movement. In her conclusions she avoided strong judgments, suggesting simply that in this early period de Gaulle developed a distrust for the United States which later caused him to work for a Europe free from American control.

Viorst wrote a much broader and bolder book. Covering the whole span of Franco-American wartime relations, he treated his theme as

2. William L. Langer, *Our Vichy Gamble* (New York, 1947), pp. 383, 389.

3. The most comprehensive critique of Langer's book was the review by Louis Gottschalk, "Our Vichy Fumble," *Journal of Modern History*, XX (March 1948), 47–56. See page 280 below.

a personal duel between two strong personalities. He saw Roosevelt and de Gaulle as incompatible on both personal and political grounds, and he came down strongly on de Gaulle's side. Viorst criticized the decision to deal with the Vichy government as immoral, claiming that it added "a burden upon the struggle for liberty." [4] He was even more indignant at the Allied failure to have de Gaulle participate in the North African campaign and at Roosevelt's refusal to recognize de Gaulle's French Committee of National Liberation as the legitimate government of France until the fall of 1944. The fundamental weakness in American policy, according to Viorst, was Roosevelt's belief that France was a second-rate nation which would be of little consequence in the postwar world. "It was inexcusable," he wrote, "that Roosevelt did not understand that France, under de Gaulle, was rising up to break its chains. It was indefensible that he should have honored a host of baser Frenchmen whom he could dominate to reject the one whom he could not." Like Miss White, Viorst concluded that the "profound disagreement" between France and the United States in the 1960's "is an extension of the great battle for independence that de Gaulle waged against Roosevelt two decades ago." [5]

An equally spirited historical dispute has also developed over United States wartime relations with China. The communist victory in China in 1949 touched off a violent political attack on the policies pursued by the Roosevelt and Truman administrations in the Far East, culminating in charges that communist sympathizers in the State Department had deliberately betrayed Nationalist China. Herbert Feis set out to provide a more rational explanation of American policy in his book *The China Tangle,* published in 1953 at the height of the anti-communist furor in the United States. Feis, like Langer, was given privileged access to both State Department and military records, as well as the private papers of Henry Morgenthau, Patrick Hurley, and Harry Hopkins. Feis disclaimed any effort to give an official, authorized version, stating instead that he was writing as "a private scholar." His account was much less defensive than Langer's. Instead of attempting to justify each step of American policy, Feis simply described what took place in order to unfold "a tale of crumpled hopes and plans that went awry." [6]

The China Tangle covers American policy from Pearl Harbor to the

---

4. Milton Viorst, *Hostile Allies: FDR and Charles de Gaulle* (New York, 1965), p. 40.

5. *Ibid.,* pp. 241, 246.

6. Herbert Feis, *The China Tangle: The American Effort in China from Pearl Harbor to the Marshall Mission* (Princeton, 1953), pp. v, vi. In his foreword Feis acknowledges his indebtedness to former Secretary of State Dean Acheson for encouraging him to write this book.

eve of General George Marshall's first mission to China in 1946. Feis discusses the difficulties with Chiang Kai-chek caused by American wartime strategy of defeating Germany first, and the various ways in which FDR tried to mollify Chiang. But his major focus is on American determination to head off a military conflict between the Nationalists and the Communists after Japan was defeated. He describes how American foreign service officers in China misjudged the character of Mao Tse-tung, and attributes this not to leftist deceit but to their lack of training and experience with "either Communist dogma or methods." Above all, Feis focuses on the belief that the United States could arrange a peaceful political merger of the Nationalists and Communists and thus create in China "a democratic, constitutional form of government." Although he suggests that such a goal was a "mirage," Feis never takes a firm stand on the wisdom of this objective. [7] He does deal more explicitly with the Yalta agreements on the Far East, criticizing their secrecy and ambiguity, but claiming that if Roosevelt had lived, "he could have turned the Yalta Accord into the triumph of compromise which he conceived it to be." Feis refrains from passing final judgment on American policy, but in his last chapter he suggests that it was a great mistake to withdraw United States forces from China so abruptly at the war's end. "We had realized that it was essential to create a powerful military force to win the war," he writes. "But we had not learned that it was no less essential to maintain an adequate military force in order to secure a satisfactory peace." [8]

Ten years after the publication of *The China Tangle*, two books appeared which offered very different explanations for the failure of American policy in China. The first, Anthony Kubek's *How the Far East Was Lost* (1963), was clearly in the extreme revisionist tradition. Based largely on memoir literature and testimony given at congressional hearings, this book argued that communists and fellow travelers within the State Department "were determined to destroy the Nationalist Government and remove Chiang Kai-shek as head of State." [9] Intent on giving Russia mastery of Asia, they succeeded in China but failed in Japan, where Douglas MacArthur frustrated their designs. Kubek believes that American foreign service officers, "the gravediggers of our

7. *Ibid.,* pp. 90, 184, 373.
8. *Ibid.,* pp. 254, 423.
9. Anthony Kubek, *How the Far East Was Lost: American Policy and the Creation of Communist China, 1941–1949* (Chicago, 1963), p. 229. In the preface Kubek expresses his gratitude to Charles C. Tansill and Harry Elmer Barnes for their assistance and advice. Tansill contributed a foreword in which he praised Kubek for his "unusual candor and clear vision" and defended him in advance against the inevitable criticisms "of the motley hordes that crowded the Roosevelt and Truman bandwagons."

national policy," deliberately spread the foolish notion that the Chinese Communists were agrarian reformers, and he plays up out of all proportion the role of Alger Hiss at Yalta, which he claims "marked the greatest diplomatic defeat in American history." [1] Given this approach, it is hardly surprising that Kubek concludes his book by charging that Roosevelt and other internationalists were really bent on creating a world government which could lead not only to a communist takeover of China but of the entire globe.

In *America's Failure in China, 1941–1950* (1963), Tang Tsou provides a far more cogent and effective critique of the same series of events. At the outset Tsou rejects the accusation that the United States "lost" China to the Communists. "No one can lose something which he has never possessed," Tsou writes. "More than any other single person, Generalissimo Chiang Kai-shek was responsible for what happened in China; for responsibility goes with power, and Chiang was the most powerful figure in China." [2] Yet Tsou believes that an unwise American policy contributed directly to the outcome. He identifies the fatal flaw as American insistence on achieving a peaceful unification of the Nationalists and the Communists. He argues that not just a few misguided foreign service officers but all Americans who dealt with the Chinese problem, including such staunch supporters of Chiang as Ambassador Patrick Hurley and General Albert Wedemeyer, backed the policy of a postwar coalition between these two antagonistic groups. "As a result," he says, "official opinion ruled out an alternative which might have been tried with greater effectiveness: the use of the immense American influence and prestige to force the Nationalist government to undertake long overdue reforms and to remake itself into the nucleus of a broad anti-Communist front." [3] Tsou believes that if the United States had abandoned the idea of peaceful unification in China and had instead committed itself to all-out support of a reformed Chinese Nationalist regime, China might have been saved. As a historian he realizes how difficult the execution of such a policy would have been in light of the persistent American refusal to use "military power purposefully to achieve political objectives." [4] Thus his account lends

1. *Ibid.*, pp. 111, 241.

2. Tang Tsou, *America's Failure in China, 1941–1950* (Chicago, 1963), p. ix. Tsou states in his acknowledgments that his book had its origins in Hans J. Morgenthau's desire to have someone analyze American wartime and postwar policy toward China. Morgenthau's Center for the Study of American Foreign and Military Policy at the University of Chicago sponsored the book, and Morgenthau wrote a foreword in which he praised Tsou for clearing away the myths that shrouded our China policy.

3. *Ibid.*, p. 145.

4. *Ibid.*, p. ix.

an air of tragic inevitability to the failure of American policy in the Far East.

These controversies over American relations with France and China reflect again the dominant concern with the theme of winning the war and losing the peace. No one has suggested that a policy of working with de Gaulle or of backing Chiang Kai-shek all the way against the Communists would have speeded the winning of the war. Indeed, it can be argued quite convincingly that both the Vichy and the China policies helped greatly in bringing about the defeat of Germany and Japan, and that policies calculated to "win the peace" might well have prolonged World War II. Much of the criticism of American wartime diplomacy reflects subsequent preoccupation with the Cold War and therefor... e major wartime decisions were m...................................... he foreign policy pursued by the R...................................... ul. It maintained the unity of the .... nflict, a striking accomplishment w...................................... lity of the Axis nations to coordin...................................... Hopefully, future historians, less obs...................................... War, will be able to make more .... ficant diplomatic achievement.

III

In 1945, at the climax of World War II, two crucial developments took place which have haunted the world ever since. The first was the dropping of the atomic bomb on Hiroshima on August 6, which led to the surrender of Japan and the beginning of the nuclear age. The second occurrence was the breakup of the Grand Alliance and the onset of the Cold War between the United States and the Soviet Union. By the 1960's these two long-run consequences of World War II had fully engaged the attention of historians and produced a lively and continuing debate over their nature and meaning.

The historiographical dispute over the use of the atomic bomb has centered on the question of whether or not the United States was justified in using it to end the war against Japan. In the 1960's a group of historians led by Herbert Feis arrived at an affirmative answer, though there were many differences in emphasis among the various writers. Feis set the tone in his book *Japan Subdued,* published in 1961 and subsequently reissued with slight but significant revisions in 1966 under the new title, *The Atomic Bomb and the End of World War II.* In both editions Feis carefully reviews the three choices the United States considered for ending the war with Japan: military invasion of the Japanese islands, diplomatic negotiations involving a guarantee that Japan could retain the Emperor, and the shock of atomic attack. He believes that the United States could have ended the war before the end of 1945 without invading Japan and without using the atomic bomb—probably without even making a promise concerning the Emperor. Continued American air attacks and a naval blockade, coupled with Russian entry into the war, he suggests, would have enabled the peace advocates in Japan to win an internal debate with the militarists and thus bring about unconditional surrender to the United States.[5]

Even though Feis states that the bomb was not essential to end the war, he concludes that the United States was justified in using it. Insisting that the decision must be understood in the context of the war, Feis states flatly, "There was no good reason to refrain from the use of the atomic bomb, like any other weapon, against Japan." At the time, he argues, American leaders believed the bomb would save hundreds of thousands of American and Japanese lives by bringing the war to a swift end. "The primary and sustaining aim from the start of the great exertion to make the bomb was military, and the impelling reason for the decision to use it was military—to end the war victoriously as soon as possible," Feis explains.[6] Thus Feis ends up in the ambiguous position of stating that while it was not necessary to use the bomb to end the war, American leaders sincerely believed that it was, and therefore the decision was a just one.

Len Giovannitti and Fred Freed, who prepared a script for an NBC television documentary and then expanded it into a book, *The Decision to Drop the Bomb* (1965), give a day-by-day account of the American decision-making process from April to July 1945. They have fewer doubts than Feis about the outcome, concluding that the bomb was used "primarily to bring a quick end to a barbaric war." [7] Robert Butow, a specialist in Japanese history, examined the Japanese side of the issue in *Japan's Decision to Surrender* (1954). Butow demonstrates clearly how the atomic bomb led directly to the Japanese surrender

5. Herbert Feis, *Japan Subdued: The Atomic Bomb and the End of the War in the Pacific* (Princeton, 1961), pp. 169, 178; Herbert Feis, *The Atomic Bomb and the End of World War II* (Princeton, 1966), pp. 177, 191. In both editions Feis states his agreement with the conclusion of the U.S. Strategic Bombing Survey, ". . . that certainly prior to 31 December 1945, and in all probability prior to 1 November 1945, Japan would have surrendered even if the atomic bombs had not been dropped, even if Russia had not entered the war, and even if no invasion had been planned or contemplated."

6. Feis, *Japan Subdued*, pp. 177, 180–181.

7. Len Giovannitti and Fred Freed, *The Decision to Drop the Bomb* (New York, 1965), p. 319. The authors acknowledge in the preface their debt to Feis, who served as chief consultant in the making of the NBC documentary.

by impelling the Emperor to break with tradition and enter directly into the political process to back the peace faction against the militarists. Yet while Butow documents how the bomb ended the war, he contends that if the United States had given the Japanese assurances concerning the future role of the Emperor and entered into diplomatic negotiations, "the war might have ended toward the latter part of July or the very beginning of August without the atomic bomb and without Soviet participation in the conflict." [8] Richard Hewlett and Oscar Anderson offer the most detailed and authoritative account of the bomb decision in *The New World,* the first volume in the official history of the Atomic Energy Commission. They stress the role of scientists, especially Vannevar Bush and James B. Conant, in trying to force a reluctant Franklin Roosevelt to begin considering the question of the ultimate use of the bomb as it was being developed during the war. They focus on Henry Stimson, after Roosevelt's death, as the man most directly responsible for the decision to use the bomb. Hewlett and Anderson raise the issue of whether Hiroshima was necessary, but they refuse to give a categorical answer, stating that the question is "insoluble." Yet after summarizing all the arguments pro and con, they indicate their feelings by stating that as the argument raged down through the years, Stimson would always have the advantage because "It was impossible to prove what might have been." [9]

A good many historians, refusing to be intimidated by this caveat, have insisted on speculating on how the United States might have avoided using the bomb. Some, like Butow, have stressed the missed opportunity for modifying the policy of unconditional surrender. A critic of American diplomacy, Hanson W. Baldwin, contends in *Great Mistakes of the War* that conventional weapons, especially the fire-bomb raids and the naval blockade and shelling of the Japanese islands, could have forced surrender in a very short time. "It is quite possible," Baldwin writes, "that the atomic bombs shortened the war by a day, a week, or a month or two—not more." [1] Baldwin attributes the use of the bomb to military miscalculation, but other writers have seen a far more sinister implication. If the bomb was not necessary to end the war, then perhaps it was used for a diplomatic reason—to restrain an

8. Robert J. C. Butow, *Japan's Decision to Surrender* (Stanford, 1954), p. 133. In his conclusion Butow makes the careful distinction that the bomb did not "produce Japan's decision to surrender" (p. 231) but rather produced the circumstances which allowed the decision, already in embryo, to reach maturity.

9. Richard G. Hewlett and Oscar E. Anderson, Jr., *The New World, 1939–1946,* volume I of *A History of the United States Atomic Energy Commission* (University Park, Pa., 1962), p. 406.

1. Baldwin, *Great Mistakes of the War,* p. 101.

aggressive Soviet Union and impose a *Pax Americana* on the world. Patrick Blackett, a distinguished British physicist, wrote a book in 1949 entitled *Fear, War and the Bomb,* in which he accused the United States of dropping the first atomic bomb in an effort to end the war against Japan before the Russians could enter. Citing the haste with which the bombs were used, Blackett argued that the primary motive was to force Japan to surrender to the United States alone. He wrote with the bitterness of a scientist who felt that a "brilliant scientific work" had been betrayed, and concluded that "the dropping of the atomic bombs was not so much the last military act of the second World War, as the first major operation of the cold diplomatic war with Russia now in progress." [2] Blackett's accusation was echoed by a few historians in the 1950's, notably William Appleman Williams,[3] but it was not until the appearance of Gar Alperovitz's controversial book *Atomic Diplomacy* in 1965 that the political and diplomatic implications of the atomic bomb received a full-scale analysis. Alperovitz was primarily concerned with the impact on American diplomacy of the completion of the atomic bomb, not with the impact of diplomacy on the use of the bomb; nevertheless, he ended his book with a brief discussion in which he sharply challenged the prevailing view. He agreed with Blackett that the bomb was not used essentially for military reasons, citing in particular a statement by General Dwight D. Eisenhower to Stimson in July 1945, expressing "grave misgivings" about the projected use of the bomb to defeat Japan. But Alperovitz went beyond Blackett's analysis to suggest that it was far more than concern for a Soviet advance in Asia that determined American policy. The bomb was dropped, Alperovitz conjectured, in order to impress the Soviet Union with American power and thus to make Russia "more manageable in Europe." [4] Admitting that the evidence was still too sketchy to permit "final conclusions" to be drawn, Alperovitz stated his belief that the United States dropped the bomb on Hiroshima and Nagasaki "to convince the Russians to accept the American plan for a stable peace." [5] Thus diplomatic hopes, not military imperatives, compelled the United States to usher in the nuclear age.

In the 1966 revision of *Japan Subdued,* Herbert Feis took cognizance of this revisionist thesis without ever citing or referring to the Alperovitz

2. P. M. S. Blackett, *Fear, War and the Bomb* (New York, 1949), p. 139.

3. William Appleman Williams, *The Tragedy of American Diplomacy* (2nd ed., New York, 1962), p. 254.

4. Gar Alperovitz, *Atomic Diplomacy: Hiroshima and Potsdam* (New York, 1965), p. 242. The quotation is from Leo Szilard, paraphrasing a comment made to him by James Byrnes in May 1945.

5. *Ibid.,* p. 240.

book.[6] He did this by changing a passage in the original edition in which he had said—warning the reader it was only a matter of conjecture— that Churchill and Truman might have been thinking about the future peace as well as ending the war when they decided to use the bomb. In 1966 Feis wrote that "it is likely" that Churchill and "probably also Truman" made the decision with Russia in mind, and that Stimson and Byrnes "certainly" were thinking of the effect of the bomb on the Soviet Union. But in both editions Feis warns against elevating this insight into a charge of "atomic blackmail" against the United States. It is regrettable, he admits, that the United States did not inform Stalin about the bomb before the Potsdam conference, but he denies that American leaders were moved "by an excited wish to impose our will on the rest of the world by keeping atomic bombs poised over their lives." [7] Thus Feis still believes that the decision to drop the bomb was basically a military one, but the Alperovitz thesis had forced him to admit that diplomatic factors, while not dominant, played a greater role than he had been willing to concede earlier. The controversy thus centers on the relative weight to be assigned to wartime as opposed to postwar considerations. Given the difficulty in finding hard evidence on this sensitive point, it is safe to predict a long life for this historiographical dispute.

The controversy over the atomic bomb, important as it is in its own right, is but a part of the larger issue of the origins of the Cold War. The debate over how the diplomatic conflict between the United States and Russia began is a relatively recent development that grew naturally out of the events of the 1960's. The emergence of a détente with the Soviet Union after the Cuban missile crisis of 1962, the gradual breakdown of the bi-polar international power structure with the arrival of a strong China and a resurgent France, the widespread questioning of the basic assumptions of American foreign policy unleashed by the dissent over the Vietnam War—all these changes contributed to a demand for a new look at how the Cold War began. A group of young historians, unhappy with the world they inherited from their elders,

6. The preface to Feis's book is dated July 1965. Apparently the second edition was in press before Alperovitz's book was published. But Giovannitti and Freed comment in their book, also published in 1965, that they had read Alperovitz's doctoral dissertation, the original version of *Atomic Diplomacy*, at King's College, Cambridge University. In a footnote Feis refers to Patrick Blackett as the 'leading exponent" of a revisionist view on the decision to drop the bomb, and goes on to say, "His rendition of history has made an impression on various Western students of the subject, including a few Americans." Feis, *Atomic Bomb*, p. 195n. Alperovitz wrote a review of the two editions of the Feis work in 1967, in which he carefully analyzed the changes Feis had made. Gar Alperovitz, "The Trump Card," *New York Review of Books*, VIII (June 15, 1967), 6–12.

7. Feis, *Japan Subdued*, pp. 181–182; Feis, *Atomic Bomb*, pp. 194–195.

began to reject the orthodox view that the Cold War was a defensive struggle against communist aggression. Instead they came forth with a far less flattering explanation.

The traditional view they challenged was the product of historians who had lived through the onset of the Cold War and who were inevitably reflecting their own nationalistic feelings. Indeed, the question of the origins of the Cold War seemed so obvious to orthodox historians that they found little need to consider it as a separate subject. Herbert Feis, in his volumes on wartime diplomacy, and John Spanier, who wrote one of the earliest and most influential surveys of the Cold War, dealt with the tension between the United States and Russia as a direct consequence of Stalin's aggressive determination to fill the power vacuums left by the defeat of Germany in Europe and Japan in Asia.[8] These men, and the textbook writers of the 1950's and early 1960's, stressed the conciliatory policies pursued by the United States in the face of Russian expansion and hostility. They pointed out how the United States quickly demobilized its immense military forces, sought through patient diplomacy at foreign ministers' conferences to preserve democracy and self-determination in Eastern Europe, and even offered to submit its monopoly over atomic energy to international control, provided adequate safeguards were established. After two years of forbearance, according to this view, the United States finally woke up to the danger of Soviet aggression and adopted a policy of containment with the Truman Doctrine, the Marshall Plan, and the North Atlantic Treaty Organization. Just in time, the United States rescued Western Europe and the world from communism.

The revisionists offer a radically different explanation for the outbreak of the Cold War. They contend that the United States, not the Soviet Union, is chiefly responsible for the breakdown of wartime unity and resulting international tensions. Denna F. Fleming put the revisionist case most fully and convincingly in a book written in London in 1961, *The Cold War and Its Origins, 1917–1960*, although his two-volume work failed to achieve recognition until the publication of Gar Alperovitz's *Atomic Diplomacy* opened a continuing debate on this subject.[9] Fleming and Alperovitz argue that the United States

8. Feis, *Churchill, Roosevelt, Stalin* and *Between War and Peace;* John W. Spanier, *American Foreign Policy Since World War II* (3rd ed., New York, 1968).

9. Fleming is an exception to the generalization that the revisionist historians are young men. He was in his sixties when this book was published, and he had already achieved a substantial scholarly reputation with books on American policy toward the League of Nations and the World Court. A political scientist by profession, Fleming was an ardent Wilsonian internationalist who felt that the United States had betrayed the cause of collective security by engaging in the Cold War with Russia.

brought on the Cold War by refusing to accept Russian control of Eastern Europe. Instead of acquiescing in this logical consequence of World War II, the United States, emboldened by its possession of the atomic bomb, set out to force the Soviets to give up their dominance of Eastern Europe. At Potsdam, according to Alperovitz, Truman served notice on Stalin that he would contest Russian control of the Balkan countries; three days after Hiroshima the United States began a concerted effort to ensure the election of democratic, pro-Western governments in Hungary, Rumania, and Bulgaria. In Hungary the communists lost out in the early elections, but in Rumania and Bulgaria the Soviet Union refused to back down, and the contest was thus joined between the United States and Russia. Fleming stresses other factors, especially the disagreement over Poland, the abrupt American cessation of lend-lease, and American insistence that Russia agree to international inspection before the United States would share its atomic secrets. But he agrees with Alperovitz that by the fall of 1945 the American challenge to Russian influence in the Balkans had led to the outbreak of the Cold War.[1]

There are two fundamental points at issue in the orthodox and revisionist accounts of the onset of the Cold War. First, the two sides disagree on the issue of change or continuity in American policy. Alperovitz and Fleming argue that Truman departed suddenly from Roosevelt's conciliatory diplomacy and began a hard line toward the Soviet Union which caught the Russians completely by surprise. Idealizing FDR's Russian policy, Fleming writes that "if Roosevelt had been able to finish his fourth term in the White House there would· have been no Cold War." [2] Alperovitz is more specific, stating that Truman decided to compel the Russians to live up to the vague promises they had made at Yalta in regard to Poland and Eastern Europe, even though Roosevelt had never expected the Soviets to honor these deliberately ambiguous pledges.[3] Herbert Feis, on the other hand, argues that Truman made up his mind from the outset that "he would not depart from Roosevelt's course or renounce his ways. . . . He abstained from acts intended merely to pay back the Soviet government

---

1. Other revisionist accounts are David Horowitz, *The Free World Colossus: A Critique of American Foreign Policy in the Cold War* (New York, 1965), which follows Fleming closely, and Walter LaFeber, *America, Russia, and the Cold War, 1945–1966* (New York, 1967), a much more restrained and convincing account. Two recent studies of the Cold War that share some but not all of the revisionist assumptions are Louis J. Halle, *The Cold War as History* (New York, 1967), and John Lukacs, *A New History of the Cold War* (Garden City, 1968).

2. D. F. Fleming, *The Cold War and Its Origins, 1917–1960* (2 vols., London, 1961), I, 215.

3. Alperovitz, *Atomic Diplomacy*, pp. 19–29, 247.

for some refusal or offense. He did not resort to retaliation." [4] Feis points out that Truman resisted Churchill's urging for a firmer policy and instead heeded men who had been Roosevelt's advisers—Secretary Stimson, General Marshall, and Harry Hopkins, whom Truman sent on a crucial mission to Moscow in May 1945. Growing Russian truculence finally compelled a change in Truman's policy, according to this view, and the implication is that if Roosevelt had lived he would also eventually have adopted a firmer line.

The revisionist case is only partially convincing. It does seem likely that the inexperienced Truman was more dependent on his advisers than Roosevelt had been, and many of them were ready for a tougher policy by the time of FDR's death. But Alperovitz and Fleming make some unfounded assumptions about what Roosevelt might have done had he lived. The assumption that the President did not expect the Russians to honor the Yalta agreements on Poland and Eastern Europe cannot be proved. More significantly, there is considerable evidence that FDR did not fully trust the Soviets. In September 1944, when his scientific advisers were urging him to inform the Russians about the atomic bomb as a first step toward eventual international control, Roosevelt signed an informal agreement with Churchill to maintain an Anglo-American monopoly over atomic energy in the postwar world. In a conversation with Vannevar Bush a few days later, the President clearly indicated that he planned to use Anglo-American possession of the bomb as a means "to control the peace of the world." [5] There is every reason to expect that Roosevelt would have executed precisely the same policy of atomic diplomacy as did Truman.

The other basic difference between the two schools of historians lies in conflicting interpretations of postwar Soviet intentions. The revisionists base their case on a defensive explanation of Russian behavior under Stalin. Fleming emphasizes the enormous losses the Soviet Union suffered from the German invasion and the consequent Russian determination to guard its exposed western frontier so that she would never be invaded again. "A determined if not sympathetic comprehension of Russia's security complex is the beginning of all wisdom in the period after World War II," Fleming writes.[6] For the revisionists, Russian domination of the Balkans was a natural consequence of the war and one which the United States ought to have accepted. Above all, it was a defensive move which posed no threat to either Western Europe or the United States. Orthodox historians, on the other hand, have seen the Russian move into the Balkans as the prelude to a Soviet reign over all Europe. Viewing Stalin in the same terms as Hitler in the 1930's, they

4. Feis, *Churchill, Roosevelt, Stalin*, p. 599.
5. Hewlett and Anderson, *The New World*, pp. 327–328.
6. Fleming, *Cold War*, p. 253.

endorsed the official view that unless Russia was challenged she would expand indefinitely. Thus John Spanier writes that if the United States had not moved to aid Greece and Turkey in 1947, "the security of all of Western Europe" would have been endangered, and if Russia broke out into the Middle East, South Asia, and North Africa, "America's survival itself" would be at stake.[7]

On this point the revisionists seem clearly to have the stronger case. Failing to understand the deep-seated Russian fear of invasion from the West and the determination based on national interest, not ideology, to dominate Eastern Europe, American leaders challenged the Soviet Union at the most sensitive point. It is understandable that Americans in the 1940's who believed they had finally learned the lessons of piecemeal aggression after Munich should overreact to Russian supremacy in Eastern Europe; but there is less excuse for historians to accept these fears as proof of hostile Soviet intentions. Future scholars will have a difficult time coming to firm conclusions on the issue of postwar Russian aims, because Stalin left no memoirs and it will probably be decades, if not centuries, before the Soviet archives are open to Western scholars. But for the present it seems reasonable to conclude, as the revisionists have, that the Soviet Union was not bent on carrying out a program of unlimited territorial aggression but was instead engaged in securing its western borders against future invasion.

William H. McNeill, writing in the early 1950's, has given us the most perceptive and convincing explanation of the onset of the Cold War. Viewing the breakup of the Grand Alliance as inevitable, given the differences in tradition, culture, and ideology between Russia and the Western nations, McNeill finds the developing tension between Russia and the United States an unfortunate but predictable occurrence.[8] The real question is not how the Cold War began, but how it could have been avoided. When Germany was defeated, each side was determined to hang on to what it possessed. Russia held tenaciously to the countries her armies overran in defeating Germany; the United States and Britain guarded their secret of atomic power with equal zeal. The ultimate result was the division of Europe into spheres of influence corresponding to the areas liberated by the two sides—a division which has proved remarkably stable—and the start of a nuclear arms race which has forced a whole generation to grow up under the shadow of mass annihilation.

7. Spanier, *American Foreign Policy*, pp. 39–40.
8. McNeill, *America, Britain and Russia*, pp. 747–748.

A Guide to the Bibliography of World War II

I. American Entry into World War II

A. GENERAL

BOOKS

Selig Adler, *The Uncertain Giant, 1921–1941: American Policy Between the Wars* (New York, 1965).

Joseph Alsop and Robert Kintner, *American White Paper* (New York, 1940).

Harry Elmer Barnes, ed., *Perpetual War for Perpetual Peace: A Critical Examination of the Foreign Policy of Franklin Delano Roosevelt and Its Aftermath* (Caldwell, Idaho, 1953).

Charles A. Beard, *American Foreign Policy in the Making, 1932–1940* (New Haven, 1946).

———, *President Roosevelt and the Coming of War, 1941: A Study in Appearances and Realities* (New Haven, 1948).

William Henry Chamberlin, *America's Second Crusade* (Chicago, 1950).

Forrest Davis and Ernest K. Lindley, *How War Came* (New York, 1942).

Robert A. Divine, *The Reluctant Belligerent: American Entry into World War II* (New York, 1965).

Donald Drummond, *The Passing of American Neutrality* (Ann Arbor, 1955).

T. R. Fehrenbach, *FDR's Undeclared War* (New York, 1967).

Lloyd C. Gardner, *Economic Aspects of New Deal Diplomacy* (Madison, Wisc., 1964).

William L. Langer and S. Everett Gleason, *The Challenge to Isolation, 1937–1940* (New York, 1952).

———, *The Undeclared War, 1940–1941* (New York, 1953).

Allan Nevins, *The New Deal and World Affairs* (New Haven, 1950).

Julius W. Pratt, *Cordell Hull* (2 vols.; New York, 1964).

Basil Rauch, *Roosevelt, From Munich to Pearl Harbor: A Study in the Creation of a Foreign Policy* (New York, 1950).

Frederic R. Sanborn, *Design for War: A Study of Secret Power Politics, 1937–1941* (New York, 1951).

Robert E. Sherwood, *Roosevelt and Hopkins: An Intimate History* (New York, 1948).

Charles C. Tansill, *Back Door to War: The Roosevelt Foreign Policy, 1933–1941* (Chicago, 1952).

Summer Welles, *Seven Decisions That Shaped History* (New York, 1951).

ARTICLES

Samuel F. Bemis, "First Gun of a Revisionist Historiography for the Second World War," *Journal of Modern History*, XIX (March 1947), 55–59.

———, "Roosevelt's Internationalism—and Churchill's," *Yale Review*, XL (Autumn 1950), 149–152.

Wayne S. Cole, "American Entry into World War II: A Historiographical Appraisal," *Mississippi Valley Historical Review*, XLIII (March 1957), 595–617.

Frank Freidel, "World War I: Before Pearl Harbor," *Current History*, XXXV (October 1958), 211–215.

Samuel Eliot Morison, "Did Roosevelt Start the War?: History Through a Beard," *Atlantic Monthly*, CLXXXII (August 1948), 91–97.

Dexter Perkins, "Was Roosevelt Wrong?," *Virginia Quarterly Review*, XXX (Summer 1954), 355–372.

Robert F. Smith, "American Foreign Relations, 1920–1942," in Barton J. Bernstein, ed., *Towards a New Past: Dissenting Essays in American History* (New York, 1968), pp. 232–262.

B. ISOLATIONISM AND NEUTRALITY

BOOKS

Elton Atwater, *American Regulation of Arms Exports* (Washington, D.C., 1941).

Mark Lincoln Chadwin, *The Hawks of World War II* (Chapel Hill, 1968).

Warren I. Cohen, *The American Revisionists* (Chicago, 1966).

Wayne S. Cole, *America First: The Battle Against Intervention, 1940–1941* (Madison, Wisc., 1953).

———, *Senator Gerald P. Nye and American Foreign Relations* (Minneapolis, 1962).

Alexander DeConde, ed., *Isolation and Security* (Durham, N.C., 1957).

Robert A. Divine, *The Illusion of Neutrality* (Chicago, 1962).

Donald J. Friedman, *The Road from Isolation: The Campaign of the American Committee for Non-Participation in Japanese Aggression, 1938–1941* (Cambridge, Mass., 1968).

George L. Grassmuck, *Sectional Biases in Congress on Foreign Policy* (Baltimore, 1951).

Fred C. Israel, *Nevada's Key Pittman* (Lincoln, Nebr., 1963).

Walter Johnson, *The Battle Against Isolation* (Chicago, 1944).

Manfred Jonas, *Isolationism in America, 1935–1941* (Ithaca, 1966).

James J. Martin, *American Liberalism and World Politics, 1931–1941* (2 vols.; New York, 1964).

John K. Nelson, *The Peace Prophets: American Pacifist Thought, 1919–1941* (Chapel Hill, 1968).

ARTICLES

Ray A. Billington, "The Origins of Middle Western Isolationism," *Political Science Quarterly*, LX (March 1945), 44–64.

Dorothy Borg, "Notes on Roosevelt's 'Quarantine' Speech," *Political Science Quarterly*, LXXII (September 1957), 405–433.

Richard Dean Burns and W. Addams Dixon, "Foreign Policy and the 'Democratic Myth'; The Debate on the Ludlow Amendment," *Mid-America*, XLVII (October 1965), 288–306.

William G. Carleton, "Isolationism and the Middle West," *Mississippi Valley Historical Review*, XXXIII (December 1946), 377–390.

Wayne S. Cole, "America First and the South, 1940–1941," *Journal of Southern History*, XXII (February 1956), 36–47.

———, "Senator Key Pittman and American Neutrality Policies," *Mississippi Valley Historical Review*, XLVI (March 1960), 644–662.

Alexander DeConde, "The South and Isolationism," *Journal of Southern History*, XXIV (August 1958), 332–346.

John C. Donovan, "Congressional Isolationists and the Roosevelt Foreign Policy," *World Politics*, III (April 1951), 299–316.

Bernard Fensterwald, Jr., "The Anatomy of American 'Isolationism' and Expansionism," *Journal of Conflict Resolution*, II (June and December 1958), 111–139, 280–309.

John McVickar Haight, Jr., "France, the United States and the Munich Crisis," *Journal of Modern History*, XXXII (December 1960), 340–348.

———, "Roosevelt and the Aftermath of the Quarantine Speech," *Review of Politics*, XXIV (April 1962), 233–259.

Marion D. Irish, "Foreign Policy and the South," *Journal of Politics*, X (May 1948), 306–326.

Travis Beal Jacobs, "Roosevelt's Quarantine Speech," *Historian*, XXIV (August 1962), 483–502.

Manfred Jonas, "Pro-Axis Sentiment and American Isolationism," *Historian*, XXIX (February 1967), 221–237.

Gabriel Kolko, "American Business and Germany, 1930–1941," *Western Political Quarterly*, XV (December 1962), 713–728.

Jeannette P. Nichols, "The Middle West and the Causes of World War II," *Ohio State Archaeological and Historical Quarterly*, LXII (April 1953), 122–145.

Ralph H. Smuckler, "The Region of Isolationism," *American Political Science Review*, XLVII (June 1953), 386–401.

Roland N. Stromberg, "American Business and the Approach of War, 1935–1941," *Journal of Economic History*, XIII (Winter 1953), 58–79.

Robert P. Wilkins, "Middle Western Isolationism: A Re-Examination," *North Dakota Quarterly*, XXIV (Summer 1957), 69–76.

C. EUROPEAN POLICY

BOOKS

James V. Compton, *The Swastika and the Eagle: Hitler, the United States, and the Origins of World War II* (Boston, 1967).

Raymond H. Dawson, *The Decision to Aid Russia, 1941* (Chapel Hill, 1959).

Saul Friedlander, *Prelude to Downfall: Hitler and the United States, 1939–*

1941, translated from the French by Aline B. and Alexander Werth (New York, 1967).

Alton Frye, *Nazi Germany and the American Hemisphere, 1933–1941* (New Haven, 1967).

Philip Goodhart, *Fifty Ships That Saved the World* (London, 1965).

Warren F. Kimball, *"The Most Unsordid Act": Lend-Lease, 1939–1941* (Baltimore, 1969).

Samuel Eliot Morison, *Battle of the Atlantic* (Boston, 1947).

Arnold A. Offner, *American Appeasement: United States Foreign Policy and Germany, 1933–1938* (Cambridge, Mass., 1969).

Andrew I. Schwartz, *America and the Russo-Finnish War* (Washington, D.C., 1960).

Robert Sobel, *The Origins of Interventionism: The United States and the Russo-Finnish War* (New York, 1960).

Hans L. Trefousse, *Germany and American Neutrality, 1939–1941* (New York, 1951).

David S. Wyman, *Paper Walls: America and the Refugee Crisis, 1938–1941* (Amherst, Mass., 1968).

ARTICLES

George Fischer, "Genesis of U.S.-Soviet Relations During World War II," *Review of Politics,* XII (July 1950), 363–378.

Daniel S. Greenberg, "U.S. Destroyers for British Bases—Fifty Old Ships Go to War," *United States Naval Institute Proceedings,* LXXXVIII (November 1962), 70–83.

John McVickar Haight, Jr., "Roosevelt as Friend of France," *Foreign Affairs,* XLIV (April 1966), 518–526.

Manfred Jonas, "Prophet Without Honor: Hans Heinrich Dieckhoff Reports from Washington," *Mid-America,* XLVII (July 1965), 222–233.

Warren F. Kimball, "Dieckhoff and America: A German's View of German-American Relations, 1937–1941," *Historian,* XXVII (February 1965), 218–243.

William R. Lindley, "The Atlantic Charter: Press Release or Historic Document?," *Journalism Quarterly,* XLI (Summer 1964), 375–379, 394.

Richard Ullman, "The Davies Mission and United States–Soviet Relations, 1937–1941," *World Politics,* IX (January 1957), 220–239.

Gerhard L. Weinberg, "Hitler's Image of the United States," *American Historical Review,* LXIX (July 1964), 1006–1021.

Gordon Wright, "Ambassador Bullitt and the Fall of France," *World Politics,* X (October 1957), 63–90.

D. FAR EASTERN POLICY

BOOKS

Dorothy Borg, *The United States and the Far Eastern Crisis, 1933–1938* (Cambridge, Mass., 1964).

Raymond A. Esthus, *From Enmity to Alliance: United States–Australian Relations, 1931–1941* (Seattle, 1964).

Ladislas Farago, *Broken Seal* (New York, 1967).

Herbert Feis, *The Road to Pearl Harbor: The Coming of War Between the United States and Japan* (Princeton, 1950).

Waldo H. Heinrichs, Jr., *American Ambassador: Joseph C. Grew and the Development of the United States Diplomatic Tradition* (Boston, 1966).

W. C. Johnstone, *The United States and Japan's New Order* (New York, 1941).

Husband E. Kimmel, *Admiral Kimmel's Story* (Chicago, 1955).

Walter Millis, *This Is Pearl!: The United States and Japan, 1941* (New York, 1947).

George Morgenstern, *Pearl Harbor: The Story of the Secret War* (New York, 1947).

Samuel Eliot Morison, *The Rising Sun in the Pacific* (Boston, 1948).

Paul W. Schroeder, *The Axis Alliance and Japanese-American Relations, 1941* (Ithaca, 1958).

Robert A. Theobald, *The Final Secret of Pearl Harbor: The Washington Contribution to the Japanese Attack* (New York, 1954).

Roberta Wohlstetter, *Pearl Harbor: Warning and Decision* (Stanford, 1962).

ARTICLES

John H. Boyle, "The Drought-Walsh Mission to Japan," *Pacific Historical Review*, XXXIV (May 1965), 141–161.

Robert J. C. Butow, "The Hull-Nomura Conversations: A Fundamental Misconception," *American Historical Review*, LXV (July 1960), 822–836.

Richard N. Current, "How Stimson Meant to 'Maneuver' the Japanese," *Mississippi Valley Historical Review*, XL (June 1953), 67–74.

T. N. Dupuy, "Pearl Harbor: Who Blundered?," *American Heritage*, XIII (February 1962), 64–81.

Raymond A. Esthus, "President Roosevelt's Commitment to Britain to Intervene in a Pacific War," *Mississippi Valley Historical Review*, L (June 1963), 28–38.

Herbert Feis, "War Came at Pearl Harbor: Suspicions Considered," *Yale Review*, XLV (Spring 1956), 378–390.

Robert H. Ferrell, "Pearl Harbor and the Revisionists," *Historian*, XVII (Spring 1955), 215–233.

Percy Greaves, Frank Beatty, and Harry Elmer Barnes, "The Mystery of Pearl Harbor," *National Review*, XXIII (December 13, 1966), 1260–1272.

James H. Herzog, "Influence of the United States Navy in the Embargo of Oil to Japan, 1940–1941," *Pacific Historical Review*, XXXV (August 1966), 317–328.

Norman Hill, "Was There an Ultimatum Before Pearl Harbor?," *American Journal of International Law*, XLII (April 1948), 355–367.

Immanuel C. Y. Hsu, "Kurusu's Mission to the United States and the Abortive *Modus Vivendi*," *Journal of Modern History*, XXIV (September 1952), 301–307.

T. B. Kittredge, "The Muddle Before Pearl Harbor," *United States News and World Report*, XXXVII (December 3, 1954), 52–63, 110–139.

John W. Masland, "Commercial Influences upon American Far Eastern Policy, 1937–1941," *Pacific Historical Review*, XI (October 1942), 281–299.

Sherman Miles, "Pearl Harbor in Retrospect," *Atlantic Monthly*, CLXXXII (July 1948), 65–72.

Louis Morton, "The Japanese Decision for War," *United States Naval Institute Proceedings*, LXXX (December 1954), 1324–1335.

———, "Pearl Harbor in Perspective: A Bibliographical Survey," *United States Naval Institute Proceedings*, LXXXI (April 1955), 461–468.

Robert A. Theobald, "Final Secret of Pearl Harbor," *United States News and World Report*, XXXVI (April 2, 1954), 48–93.

Hans L. Trefousse, "Germany and Pearl Harbor," *Far Eastern Quarterly*, XI (November 1951), 35–50.

Richard W. Van Alstyne, "Before Pearl Harbor," *Current History*, XX (February 1951), 70–76.

II. Wartime Diplomacy

A. GENERAL

BOOKS

A. Russell Buchanan, *The United States and World War II* (2 vols.; New York, 1964).

William Henry Chamberlin, *America's Second Crusade* (Chicago, 1950).

Winston S. Churchill, *The Second World War* (6 vols.; Boston, 1948–1953).

Robert A. Divine, *Second Chance: The Triumph of Internationalism in America During World War II* (New York, 1967).

———, *Roosevelt and World War II* (Baltimore, 1969).

Herbert Feis, *Between War and Peace: The Potsdam Conference* (Princeton, 1960).

———, *Churchill, Roosevelt, Stalin: The War They Waged and the Peace They Sought* (Princeton, 1957).

Wilfrid A. Knapp, *A History of War and Peace, 1939–1965* (London, 1967).

Gabriel Kolko, *The Politics of War: The World and United States Foreign Policy, 1943–1945* (New York, 1968).

William Hardy McNeill, *America, Britain and Russia: Their Co-operation and Conflict, 1941–1946* (London, 1953).

William L. Neumann, *After Victory: Churchill, Roosevelt, Stalin and the Making of Peace* (New York, 1967).

———, *Making the Peace, 1941–1945* (Washington, D.C., 1950).

Harley Notter, *Postwar Foreign Policy Preparation* (Washington, D.C., 1950).

Willard Range, *Franklin D. Roosevelt's World Order* (Athens, Ga., 1959).

Ruth B. Russell, *A History of the United Nations Charter: Role of the U.S., 1940–1945* (Washington, D.C., 1958).

Robert E. Sherwood, *Roosevelt and Hopkins: An Intimate History* (New York, 1948).

Gaddis Smith, *American Diplomacy During the Second World War* (New York, 1965).

John Snell, *Illusion and Necessity: The Diplomacy of Global War, 1939–1945* (Boston, 1963).

Sumner Welles, *The Time for Decision* (New York, 1944).

H. Bradford Westerfield, *Foreign Policy and Party Politics from Pearl Harbor to Korea* (Washington, D.C., 1955).

Llewellyn Woodward, *British Foreign Policy in the Second World War* (London, 1962).

ARTICLES

William C. Bullitt, "How We Won the War and Lost the Peace," *Life,* XXV (August 30 and September 6, 1948), 83–97 and 86–103.

William G. Carleton, "The United States in World War II: 1941–1945," *Current History,* XXXV (October 1958), 216–222.

Foster R. Dulles and Gerald Ridinger, "The Anti-Colonial Policies of Franklin D. Roosevelt," *Political Science Quarterly,* LXX (March 1955), 1–18.

Grace Fox, "The Origins of the UNRRA," *Political Science Quarterly,* LXV (December 1950), 561–584.

Hans Adolph Jacobsen, 'The Second World War as a Problem in Historical Research," *World Politics,* XVI (July 1964), 620–641.

William L. Langer, "Political Problems of a Coalition," *Foreign Affairs,* XXVI (October 1947), 73–89.

Robert E. Riggs, "Overselling the UN Charter—Fact and Myth," *International Organization,* XIV (Spring 1960), 277–290.

Edgar Snow, "Fragments from FDR," *Monthly Review,* VIII (January and March 1957), 316–321, 395–404.

Sumner Welles, "Two Roosevelt Decisions: One Debit, One Credit," *Foreign Affairs,* XXIX (January 1951), 182–204.

B. MILITARY STRATEGY

BOOKS

Stephen E. Ambrose, *Eisenhower and Berlin, 1945: The Decision to Halt at the Elbe* (New York, 1967).

Hanson W. Baldwin, *Great Mistakes of the War* (New York, 1950).

Arthur Bryant, *Triumph in the West* (London, 1959).

———, *The Turn of the Tide, 1939–1943* (London, 1957).

Ray S. Cline, *Washington Command Post: The Operations Division* (Washington, D.C., 1951).

John Ehrman, *Grand Strategy,* Volumes V and VI of the *History of the Second World War* (London, 1956).

Kent Roberts Greenfield, *American Strategy in World War II: A Reconsideration* (Baltimore, 1963).

Kent Roberts Greenfield, ed., *Command Decisions* (Washington, D.C., 1960).

Trumbull Higgins, *Soft Underbelly: The Anglo-American Controversy over the Italian campaign, 1939–1945* (New York, 1968).

————, *Winston Churchill and the Second Front, 1940–1943* (New York, 1957).

Paul Kecskemeti, *Strategic Surrender: The Politics of Victory and Defeat* (Stanford, 1958).

Maurice Matloff, *Strategic Planning for Coalition Warfare, 1943–1944* (Washington, D.C., 1959).

Maurice Matloff and Edwin S. Snell, *Strategic Planning for Coalition Warfare, 1941–1942* (Washington, D.C., 1953).

Rodney G. Minott, *The Fortress That Never Was: The Myth of Hitler's Bavarian Stronghold* (New York, 1964).

Samuel Eliot Morison, *Strategy and Compromise* (Boston, 1958).

Forrest C. Pogue, *The Supreme Command* (Washington, D.C., 1954).

Mark S. Watson, *Chief of Staff: Prewar Plans and Preparations* (Washington, D.C., 1950).

Chester Wilmot, *The Struggle for Europe* (New York, 1952).

ARTICLES

Hanson B. Baldwin, "Churchill Was Right," *Atlantic Monthly,* CXCIV (July 1954), 23–32.

————, "Our Worst Blunders in the War," *Atantic Monthly,* CLXXXV (January and February 1950), 30–39 and 30–38.

John L. Chase, "Unconditional Surrender Reconsidered," *Political Science Quarterly,* LXX (June 1955), 258–279.

Lord Hankey, "Unconditional Surrender," *Contemporary Review,* CLXXVI (October 1949), 193–198.

Gordon Harrison, "Was D-Day a Mistake?," *Harper's,* CCIII (August 1951), 77–81.

Richard M. Leighton, "OVERLORD Revisited: An Interpretation of American Strategy in the European War, 1942–1944," *American Historical Review,* LXVIII (July 1963), 919–937.

John F. McCloy, "The Great Military Decisions," *Foreign Affairs,* XXVI (October 1947), 52–72.

Maurice Matloff, "Was the Invasion of Southern France a Blunder?," *United States Naval Institute Proceedings,* LXXXIV (July 1958), 35–45.

Forrest C. Pogue, "Why Eisenhower's Forces Stopped at the Elbe," *World Politics,* IV (April 1952), 356–368.

Mario Pundeff, "Allied Strategy and the Balkans," *World Affairs Quarterly,* XXIX (April 1958), 25–52.

Martin Sommers, "Why Russia Got the Drop on Us," *Saturday Evening Post,* CCXIX (February 8, 1947), 25ff.

C. RUSSIA AND EASTERN EUROPE

BOOKS

George N. Crocker, *Roosevelt's Road to Russia* (Chicago, 1959).

John H. Deane, *The Strange Alliance* (New York, 1947).

Edward J. Rosek, *Allied Wartime Diplomacy: A Pattern in Poland* (New York, 1958).

John Snell, ed., *The Meaning of Yalta: Big Three Diplomacy and the New Balance of Power* (Baton Rouge, La., 1956).

Edward R. Stettinius, *Roosevelt and the Russians: The Yalta Conference* (Garden City, 1949).

ARTICLES

William H. Hale, "The Road to Yalta," *American Heritage,* XII (June 1961), 34–40, 82–85.

Oscar J. Hammen, "The Ashes of Yalta," *South Atlantic Quarterly,* LIII (October 1954), 477–484.

W. Averell Harriman, "Our Wartime Relations with the Soviet Union and the Agreements Reached at Yalta," *Department of State Bulletin,* XXV (September 3, 1951), 371–379.

G. F. Hudson, "The Lesson of Yalta," *Commentary,* XVII (April 1954), 373–380.

———, "Yalta," *Twentieth Century,* CLVII (May 1955), 393–404.

William D. Leahy, "Notes on the Yalta Conference," *Wisconsin Magazine of History,* XXXVIII (Winter 1954), 67–72, 110–113.

Richard C. Lukas, "The Velvet Project: Hope and Frustration," *Military Affairs,* XXVIII (Winter 1964), 145–162.

Robert McNeal, "Roosevelt Through Stalin's Spectacles," *International Journal,* XVIII (Spring 1963), 194–206.

Clarence Manning, "The Yalta Conference," *Ukrainian Quarterly,* XI (Spring 1955), 145–153.

Louis Morton, "The Military Background of the Yalta Agreements," *Reporter,* XII (April 7, 1955), 19–21.

Phillip E. Mosely, "Across the Green Table from Stalin," *Current History,* XV (September 1948), 129–133.

———, "Hopes and Failures: American Policy Toward East Central Europe, 1941–1947," *Review of Politics,* XVII (October 1955), 461–485.

Stephen Pan, "Legal Aspects of the Yalta Agreements," *American Journal of International Law,* XLVI (January 1952), 40–59.

Raymond J. Sontag, "Reflections on the Yalta Papers," *Foreign Affairs,* XXXIII (July 1955), 615–623.

Richard W. Van Alstyne, "The United States and Russia in World War II," *Current History,* XIX (November and December 1950), 257–260 and 334–339.

John Vloyantes, "The Significance of Pre-Yalta Policies Regarding the Liberated Countries in Europe," *Western Political Quarterly,* XI (June 1958), 209–228.

Warren B. Walsh, "American Attitudes Toward Russia," *Antioch Review,* VII (Summer 1947), 183–190.

Paul Willen, "Who 'Collaborated' with Russia?," *Antioch Review,* XIV (September 1954), 259–283.

Rudolph A. Winnacker, "Yalta—Another Munich?," *Virginia Quarterly Review,* XXIV (Autumn 1948), 521–537.

Stephen G. Xydis, "The Secret Anglo-Soviet Agreement on the Balkans of October 9th, 1944," *Journal of Central European Affairs,* XV (October 1955), 248–271.

D. GERMANY

BOOKS

Anne Armstrong, *Unconditional Surrender: The Impact of the Casablanca Policy upon World War II* (New Brunswick, N.J., 1961).

Allen W. Dulles, *Germany's Underground* (New York, 1947).

———, *The Secret Surrender* (New York, 1966).

Henry Morgenthau, Jr., *Germany Is Our Problem* (New York, 1945).

John Snell, *Wartime Origins of the East-West Dilemma over Germany* (New Orleans, 1959).

ARTICLES

John L. Chase, "The Development of the Morgenthau Plan Through the Quebec Conference," *Journal of Politics,* XVI (May 1954), 324–359.

E. W. Debevoise, "The Occupation of Germany: U.S. Objectives and Participation," *Journal of International Affairs,* VIII (1954), 166–184.

Walter L. Dorn, "The Debate over American Occupation Policy in Germany in 1944–45," *Political Science Quarterly,* LXXII (December 1957), 481–501.

William M. Franklin, "Zonal Boundaries and Access to Berlin," *World Politics,* XVI (October 1963), 1–31.

Melvin J. Lasky, "The Morgenthau Plan in Retrospect," *Nineteenth Century,* CXLVI (September 1949), 137–149.

Henry Morgenthau, Jr., "Postwar Treatment of Germany," *Annals of the American Academy of Political and Social Science,* CCXLVI (July 1946), 125–129.

Phillip E. Mosely, "Dismemberment of Germany: Allied Negotiations from Yalta to Potsdam," *Foreign Affairs,* XXVIII (April 1950), 487–498.

———, "The Occupation of Germany," *Foreign Affairs,* XXVIII (July 1950), 580–604.

Fred Smith, "The Rise and Fall of the Morgenthau Plan," *United Nations World,* I (March 1947), 32–37.

Albert L. Warner, "Our Secret Deal over Germany," *Saturday Evening Post,* CCXXV (August 2, 1952), 30ff.

E. FRANCE

BOOKS

Douglas C. Anglin, *The St. Pierre and Miquelon Affaire of 1941* (Toronto, 1966).

Paul Farmer, *Vichy: Political Dilemma* (New York, 1955).

Arthur L. Funk, *Charles de Gaulle: The Crucial Years, 1943-44* (Norman, Okla., 1959).

William L. Langer, *Our Vichy Gamble* (New York, 1947).

Robert Murphy, *Diplomat Among Warriors* (Garden City, 1964).

Milton Viorst, *Hostile Allies: FDR and Charles de Gaulle* (New York, 1965).

Dorothy S. White, *Seeds of Discord: De Gaulle, Free France and the Allies* (Syracuse, N.Y., 1964).

ARTICLES

Martin Blumenson, "Politics and the Military in the Liberation of Paris," *Yale Review*, L (Winter 1961), 271–286.

Russell Brooks, "Casablanca—The French Side of the Fence," *United States Naval Institute Proceedings*, LXXVII (September 1951), 909–925.

Arthur L. Funk, "The Anfa Memorandum: An Incident of the Casablanca Conference," *Journal of Modern History*, XXVI (September 1954), 246–254.

Louis Gottschalk, "Our Vichy Fumble," *Journal of Modern History*, XX (March 1948), 47–56.

Ellen Hammer, "Hindsight on Vichy," *Political Science Quarterly*, LXI (June 1946), 175–188.

Ernest J. Knapton, "Washington and Vichy: Reflections on American Foreign Policy, 1940-42," *Current History*, XIII (July 1947), 17–22.

F. THE FAR EAST

BOOKS

Herbert Feis, *The China Tangle: The American Effort in China from Pearl Harbor to the Marshall Mission* (Princeton, 1953).

Anthony Kubek, *How the Far East Was Lost: American Policy and the Creation of Communist China, 1941–1949* (Chicago, 1963).

Tang Tsou, *America's Failure in China, 1941–1950* (Chicago, 1963).

Albert C. Wedemeyer, *Wedemeyer Reports!* (New York, 1958).

Theodore H. White, ed., *The Stilwell Papers* (New York, 1948).

ARTICLES

Russell H. Buhite, "Patrick J. Hurley and the Yalta Far Eastern Agreement," *Pacific Historical Review*, XXXVII (August 1968), 343–353.

John K. Fairbank, "Dilemmas of American Far Eastern Policy," *Pacific Affairs*, XXXVI (Winter 1963–1964), 430–437.

Ernest R. May, "The United States, the Soviet Union, and the Far Eastern War, 1941–1945," *Pacific Historical Review*, XXIV (May 1955), 153–174.

Louis Morton, "Soviet Intervention in the War with Japan," *Foreign Affairs*, XL (July 1962), 653–662.

Riley Sunderland, "The Secret Embargo," *Pacific Historical Review*, XXIX (February 1960), 75–80.

Sumner Welles, "Roosevelt and the Far East," *Harper's,* CCII (February and March 1951), 27–38 and 70–80.

John A. White, "As the Russians Saw Our China Policy," *Pacific Historical Review,* XXVI (May 1957), 147–160.

III. Consequences of World War II

A. THE ATOMIC BOMB

BOOKS

Michael Amrine, *The Great Decision: The Secret History of the Atomic Bomb* (New York, 1959).

P. M. S. Blackett, *Fear, War and the Bomb* (New York, 1949).

Robert J. C. Butow, *Japan's Decision to Surrender* (Stanford, 1954).

William Craig, *The Fall of Japan* (New York, 1967).

Medford Evans, *The Secret War for the A-Bomb* (Chicago, 1963).

Herbert Feis, *The Atomic Bomb and the End of World War II* (Princeton, 1966).

———, *Japan Subdued: The Atomic Bomb and the End of the War in the Pacific* (Princeton, 1961).

Len Giovannitti and Fred Freed, *The Decision to Drop the Bomb* (New York, 1965).

Richard G. Hewlett and Oscar E. Anderson, Jr., *The New World, 1939–1946,* volume I of *A History of the United States Atomic Energy Commission* (University Park, Pa., 1962).

Robert Jungk, *Brighter than a Thousand Suns* (New York, 1958).

Fletcher Knebel and Charles W. Bailey, *No High Ground* (New York, 1960).

William Appleman Williams, *The Tragedy of American Diplomacy* (2nd ed., New York, 1962).

ARTICLES

Gar Alperovitz, "The Trump Card," *New York Review of Books,* VIII (June 15, 1967), 6–12.

W. J. Coughlin, "The Great *Mokusatsu* Mistake: Was This the Deadliest Error of Our Time?," *Harper's,* CCVI (March 1953), 31–40.

Wesley R. Fishel, "A Japanese Peace Maneuver in 1944," *Far Eastern Quarterly,* VIII (August 1949), 387–397.

A. S. R. Groom, "United States–Allied Relations and the Atomic Bomb in the Second World War," *World Politics,* XV (October 1962), 123–137.

Kazuo Kawai, "Militarist Activity Between Japan's Two Surrender Decisions," *Pacific Historical Review,* XXII (November 1953), 383–389.

———, "*Mokusatsu,* Japan's Response to the Potsdam Declaration," *Pacific Historical Review,* XIX (November 1950), 409–414.

Samuel Eliot Morison, "Why Japan Surrendered," *Atlantic Monthly,* CCVI (October 1960), 41–47.

Louis Morton, "The Decision to Use the Atomic Bomb," *Foreign Affairs,* XXXV (January 1957), 334–353.

I. I. Rabi, "Playing Down the Bomb," *Atlantic Monthly,* CLXXXIII (April 1949), 21–23.

Alice Kimball Smith, "Behind the Decision to Use the Atomic Bomb: Chicago, 1944–45," *Bulletin of the Atomic Scientists,* XIV (October 1958), 288–312.

Henry L. Stimson, "The Decision to Use the Atomic Bomb," *Harper's,* CXCIV (February 1947), 97–107.

B. ORIGINS OF THE COLD WAR

BOOKS

Gar Alperovitz, *Atomic Diplomacy: Hiroshima and Potsdam* (New York, 1965).

Herbert Aptheker, *American Foreign Policy and the Cold War* (New York, 1962).

William G. Carleton, *The Revolution in American Foreign Policy: Its Global Range* (New York, 1963).

Albert Z. Carr, *Truman, Stalin, and Peace* (Garden City, 1950).

Desmond Donnelly, *Struggle for the World: The Cold War, 1917–1965* (New York, 1965).

Herbert Druks, *Harry S. Truman and the Russians, 1945–1953* (New York, 1968).

Herbert Feis, *Contest over Japan* (New York, 1967).

Denna F. Fleming, *The Cold War and Its Origins, 1917–1960* (2 vols.; London, 1961).

André Fontaine, *A History of the Cold War: From the October Revolution to the Korean War, 1917–1950,* translated from the French by D. D. Paige (London, 1968).

Louis J. Halle, *The Cold War as History* (New York, 1967).

Marvin F. Herz, *Beginnings of the Cold War* (Bloomington, Ind., 1966).

David Horowitz, *The Free World Colossus: A Critique of American Foreign Policy in the Cold War* (New York, 1965).

Joseph Jones, *The Fifteen Weeks* (New York, 1955).

George F. Kennan, *Memoirs, 1925–1950* (Boston, 1967).

Walter LaFeber, *America, Russia, and the Cold War, 1945–1966* (New York, 1967).

John Lukacs, *A New History of the Cold War* (Garden City, 1968).

W. W. Rostow, *The United States in the World Arena* (New York, 1960).

Hugh Seton-Watson, *Neither War nor Peace: The Struggle for Power in the Postwar World* (London, 1960).

John W. Spanier, *American Foreign Policy Since World War II* (3rd ed., New York, 1968).

ARTICLES

Gar Alperovitz, "The Double Dealer," *New York Review of Books,* VII (September 8, 1966), 3–4.

———, "How Did the Cold War Begin?," *New York Review of Books,* VIII (March 23, 1967), 6–12.

John Bagguley, "The World War and the Cold War," in David Horowitz, ed., *Containment and Revolution* (Boston, 1967), pp. 76–124.

Norman A. Graebner, "Cold War Origins and the Continuing Debate: A Review of the Recent Literature," *Journal of Conflict Resolution,* XIII (March 1969), 123–132.

George C. Herring, Jr., "Lend-Lease to Russia and the Origins of the Cold War, 1944–1945," *Journal of American History,* LVI (June 1969), 93–114.

Christopher Lasch, "The Cold War, Revisited and Re-Visioned," *New York Times Magazine* (January 14, 1968), pp. 26ff.

Staughton Lynd, "How the Cold War Began," *Commentary,* XXX (November 1960), 379–389.

Thomas G. Paterson, "The Abortive American Loan to Russia and the Origins of the Cold War, 1943–1946," *Journal of American History,* LVI (June 1969), 70–92.

Arthur M. Schlesinger, Jr., "Origins of the Cold War," *Foreign Affairs,* XLVI (October 1967), 22–52.

Robert D. Warth, "Stalin and the Cold War: A Second Look," *South Atlantic Quarterly,* LIX (Winter 1960), 1–12.

II

American Entry into World War II

DOROTHY BORG

Notes on Roosevelt's "Quarantine" Speech

*The nature of presidential leadership is a central issue in the litera-
ture on American entry into World War II. Many historians
believe that Franklin D. Roosevelt perceived the threat of German
and Japanese expansion to American security by 1937 and began
a campaign to arouse an isolationist nation. They cite the quarantine speech, an address Roosevelt delivered in Chicago in October
1937, two months after Japan invaded China, as FDR's first
major effort to alert the American people to the Axis peril.*

*Dorothy Borg, a specialist in American policy toward East
Asia, offers a different assessment of Roosevelt's motives in making
the quarantine speech. Miss Borg gives a more comprehensive
analysis of American policy toward China and Japan in the
1930's in her book,* The United States and the Far Eastern Crisis
*(Cambridge, Mass., 1964). For other interpretations of the Presi-
dent's speech, see Travis Beal Jacobs, "Roosevelt's Quarantine
Speech,"* Historian, *XXIV (August 1962), 483–502, and John
McV. Haight, "Roosevelt and the Aftermath of the Quarantine
Speech,"* Review of Politics, *XXIV (April 1962), 233–259.*

THE "QUARANTINE" SPEECH which President Roosevelt made at Chicago
on October 5, 1937, is generally assumed to have been a landmark in
our foreign policy, showing the point at which the President made a
definite decision to take a strong stand against the Axis powers. It is
also widely supposed that, because of evidence at every hand of the
country's hostility to the speech, Mr. Roosevelt, quite justifiably, felt
compelled to relinquish his determination to deal firmly with the totalitarian states. Yet the further one examines these assumptions, the
more they seem to invite rethinking.

I

In regard to the speech itself, the most popular interpretations are
that the President was announcing that he had decided: to reverse his
foreign policy, abandoning the isolationism of our neutrality legislation

Reprinted by permission from the *Political Science Quarterly*, LXXII
(September 1957), 405–433.

for a Wilsonian type of collective security; or to use sanctions against Japan to stop the hostilities in China; or to initiate forthwith a program for the application of sanctions against future aggressors—meaning the Axis powers. However, a consideration of the events surrounding the speech and of its text suggests that the President was probably only engaging in a groping and intermittent effort, which he had been making for some time, to find some sort of a plan which would avert war between the dictatorships and the democracies. If so, the "quarantine" speech should not be regarded as an indication that, in the autumn of 1937, Mr. Roosevelt resolved to embark upon some strong and specific policy toward the Axis countries, but rather as indicating that he was still pursuing a variety of nebulous schemes for warding off catastrophe.

In order to discus further both the popular interpretations of the speech and the interpretation just advanced, it is necessary first to look at the two areas where the material lies which make more detailed discussion possible: the President's search for a program to avoid war and the story of the writing of the Chicago address.

As the international crisis deepened in the 1930's, Mr. Roosevelt was intensely concerned over the aggression of the Axis nations. In keeping with a pattern he tended to follow almost instinctively, he seems to have felt that, if he advanced notions of his own about possible means of meeting the crisis, he might stimulate others to build on his suggestions until a solution was found. His first great effort to dramatize the concept of searching for a program to stabilize the world situation was made in connection with the Buenos Aires Conference of 1936. It will be recalled that this conference was convened at his suggestion to strengthen the Inter-American peace system. However, both the President and Secretary Hull proclaimed over and over again that the purpose of the conference was not just to work out a scheme for the maintenance of peace in the Americas but to evolve a program which, speaking in general terms, could be copied by the rest of the world. And it was precisely to draw the attention of as many people as possible to the universal significance of the proceedings at Buenos Aires that Mr. Roosevelt made his own dramatic trip to the conference.

Two features of the developments at Buenos Aires have a special significance in connection with later efforts to formulate a program to deal with the problem of war and peace.[1] One was the over-all character of the Buenos Aires agreements. The sixty-seven agreements

1. Stenographic report of the conference in *The Inter-American Conference for the Maintenance of Peace, Proceedings* (Buenos Aires, 1937); *Report of Delegation of the United States to the Inter-American Conference for the Maintenance of Peace* (Washington, 1937), Department of State Conference Series 33.

arrived at by the Conference constituted a comprehensive plan divorced from any commitments to sanctions. They emphasized the value of a so-called constructive approach to peace, by which was meant an attempt to settle the underlying causes of friction that give rise to wars. They also emphasized the need to develop machinery to adjust disputes by peaceful means or, if this proved impossible, to limit hostilities once they occurred.

The second significant factor was the discussion about plans for organizing, in wartime, the countries that were not parties to the dispute. One idea was that an arrangement should be made so that these nations would adopt a collective neutrality that went further than anything as yet embodied in the Inter-American peace system. This view was vigorously pushed by Secretary Hull in his famous Eight Pillars of Peace speech delivered at the outset of the Conference.[2] It was incorporated in the draft convention presented to the Conference by the United States delegation; for the convention would have committed neutral American countries, in case of war between two or more American republics, to apply laws comparable to the neutrality legislation existing in the United States.[3] While the United States proposal was not adopted, the determination to develop the concept of collective neutrality in the Americas remained a fixed part of our policy.

Another idea was that there should be what, for lack of a better term, may be called a collective nonbelligerency. This concept became a center of discussion at Buenos Aires because the Central American nations introduced a draft treaty based on a plan, advanced by Uruguay during the First World War, for the creation by the American states of a moral front which would adopt measures, such as the severance of diplomatic relations, that were noncoercive but not neutral.[4] In the process of watering down the Central American draft, the closeness of this type of a collective nonbelligerency and a common neutrality was underscored. The purpose of both was to have the nations not parties to the conflict form a community for their own protection and to influence the course of the hostilities. (It was thought that a collective neutrality could, if necessary, be manipulated to favor one side or the other, as was indeed done after the outbreak of war in Europe.)[5] Moreover, both the ideas of collective neutrality and of collective non-

2. *Peace and War: United States Foreign Policy, 1931–41* (Washington, 1943), p. 342; *The Memoirs of Cordell Hull* (New York, 1948), I, 498.

3. *Documents on International Affairs, 1936* (London, 1937), p. 77.

4. Martin, Percy Alvin, *Latin America and the War* (Baltimore, 1925), pp. 361 *et seq.*, 381. *Inter-American Conference for the Maintenance of Peace, Proceedings*, pp. 138, 221, 739.

5. Bemis, Samuel Flagg, *The Latin American Policy of the United States* (New York, 1943), p. 287, chapter xxi. Welles, Sumner, *The Time for Decision* (New York, 1944), p. 204.

belligerency were regarded as preventive in that, if either were incorporated in an agreement, they would serve to deter would-be aggressors.

Following the Buenos Aires Conference, the President continued to look for a program to relieve the international tension, suggesting frequently that the nations of the world might get together to work out something comparable to the achievements reached at Buenos Aires. Secretary Hull spoke similarly, both men often stressing the noncoercive character of the Buenos Aires agreements. When, for example, Prime Minister King of Canada visited Washington in the spring of 1937, Mr. Hull told him that, in his estimation, the only way of stopping the drift toward war was for England to seek the cooperation of other European countries in developing a constructive and comprehensive scheme for the stabilization of peace, like the Buenos Aires program.[6] The President himself discussed at length with Mr. King the possibility of calling an international conference to set up a new world organization which would seek to maintain peace by peaceful means rather than by economic or military sanctions.[7] He suggested that new methods of achieving peace be tried, such as "going after the root causes of war" so as to establish a "collective security based on the removal of war causes." Also wars should be prevented or cured by "public opinion," not by "penalty." A few weeks later the President talked along similar lines to Norman Davis, who was about to leave on a mission to Europe, indicating that Mr. Davis might explore some of these ideas with European statesmen informally.[8]

At the same time the President was groping for other means of getting the dictatorships and the democracies to make a concerted effort to ensure peace. Even before the Buenos Aires Conference, Mr. Roosevelt had spoken to friends of the possibility of stopping the trend toward war by some such dramatic action as inviting the heads of the big European nations to a meeting on board a battleship at sea where they would evolve some plan for a "lasting peace" to be achieved without commit-

6. The memorandum of this conversation was an unusually comprehensive statement of Mr. Hull's views and was sent to the President. See *Foreign Relations of the United States, 1937*, I, 641, and Hull, *Memoirs*, I, 546. Even after the outbreak of the Sino-Japanese war, Mr. Hull was urging Japan to join the United States in the leadership of a peace movement based on the Buenos Aires agreements. See *Foreign Relations of the United States: Japan, 1931–41*, p. 331.

7. *F.D.R.: His Personal Letters, 1928–45* (New York, 1947), I, 664. Based on notes of their discussion written by Mr. King while talking with the President and shown to the latter.

8. Memorandum by Mr. Davis on telephone conversation with the President on March 19. Davis files.

ments to coercion.[9] Word of the President's scheme reached the *New York Times,* which printed a front-page article under a streaming headline: "ROOSEVELT IF ELECTED MAY CALL KINGS, DICTATORSHIPS AND PRESIDENTS TO GREAT POWER CONFERENCE." [10]

The net result of all this talk of a program to resolve the existing crisis was that, by the spring of 1937, there were repercussions even in the European dictatorships. Mussolini, in a highly publicized interview, virtually invited the President to take the initiative in bringing the statesmen of the world together to settle some of the outstanding causes of tension.[11] Hitler was rumored to have said that he would attend a conference for the improvement of the international situation if Mr. Roosevelt convened it.[12]

Perhaps encouraged by signs of possible cooperation from the Axis nations, Mr. Roosevelt, in the spring and summer of 1937, tried to take some concrete steps toward a general international agreement that would make for peace.[13] Norman Davis, on his trip to Europe in May, had long conversations on this subject with various European statesmen, primarily British and French—conversations of which he kept detailed records that have turned up in his files.[14] Mr. Davis spoke first with Mr. Spinasse, then French Minister of National Economy, and with Anthony Eden. All agreed that a comprehensive program should be developed that would tackle the three most important sources of the growing international crisis: political and economic conditions and the race in armaments. It was assumed that the United States would have to take the initiative in starting such a program but that President Roosevelt would want to limit himself to economic and disarmament problems, leaving the European powers to settle their political controversies among themselves. In the end it was agreed that some plan might be launched, probably by calling a large international conference, in a few months—possibly September.

When Mr. Davis approached Neville Chamberlain, the latter proved to be more than sympathetic to the idea that the dictatorships and the democracies should try to adjust their differences but considerably less interested in the American concept of bringing this about through a comprehensive program undertaken by many nations. Mr. Chamberlain

9. Hull, *Memoirs,* I, 546.

10. August 26, 1936, story by Arthur Krock.

11. *Foreign Relations of the United States, 1937,* I, 655.

12. *Ibid.,* pp. 29, 638, 640, 649.

13. Apparently in March, Secretary Morgenthau told Mr. Chamberlain that the United States wanted to help in finding some way of preventing the outbreak of war. For correspondence on this, see *ibid.,* I, 98–106.

14. The following accounts of Mr. Davis' conversations are all based upon his memoranda.

thought it impractical "to do everything at once" and declared that, in his opinion, political appeasement would have to precede economic appeasement and the limitation of armaments. He told Mr. Davis that the British government was doing what it could toward a "beginning of political appeasement" and had just instructed its Ambassador in Berlin to impress upon Hitler that the British wanted to establish "more friendly relations and a sound basis for peace" as soon as they were convinced that Germany genuinely desired the same thing. Mr. Davis indicated that he was quite in favor of England's trying to reach an understanding with Germany; he only wondered whether tackling the problem of peace on a wider scale could await the outcome of Britain's efforts. In addition, Mr. Davis raised the question of the possibility of Mr. Chamberlain's coming to the United States to talk with the President directly.

The President decided, after Mr. Davis' return home, to go on from where the latter had left off. Early in June, Mr. Davis wrote the Prime Minister, in the strictest secrecy, that Mr. Roosevelt would like him to visit the White House around late September.[15] The President, he explained, was ready to make arrangements immediately to have an agenda drawn up for their meeting. Mr. Davis stated also that he thought England and America should pave the way for a "broader move" to ensure peace and hoped that, within a few months, it would be possible to start a "concerted and comprehensive effort to achieve economic rehabilitation, financial stability, a limitation of armaments and peace." The Prime Minister replied that he did not believe the time ripe for a meeting with the President.[16] The British government was, he asserted, still trying to open talks with the Germans and these might provide a "valuable indication" of the direction in which it might be possible to advance, thereby serving as a useful preliminary to discussions between himself and Mr. Roosevelt.

The President was, however, too intent upon his course to drop matters here. At the end of July he wrote personally to the Prime Minister saying that he appreciated his desire to make such progress as was possible along other lines but nevertheless would like suggestions for steps that might be taken to expedite their meeting.[17] Mr. Chamberlain did not answer until two months later, when he informed Mr. Roosevelt that he had no suggestions to make.[18] The international situation, he declared, was changing so quickly that any plans were likely

15. Davis files. Draft in Roosevelt files, P. S. F. Great Britain, 1933–38, Box 7.

16. *Ibid.*

17. *Foreign Relations of the United States, 1937,* I, 113.

18. *Ibid.,* p. 131.

to be obsolete almost as soon as they were made. While the tension in Europe was easing somewhat, things were still a "long way from the resumption of cordial relations between the totalitarian states and the democracies."

It was precisely at the time that the Prime Minister rejected the President's second invitation to open discussions that Mr. Roosevelt delivered the "quarantine" speech. Presumably he felt that, if an advance toward peace was to be made, he would have to try some method less dependent upon Mr. Chamberlain's initiative. Perhaps it was to encourage others to supply the necessary impetus that the President renewed his efforts to dramatize publicly the idea of searching for a plan to avert war. Parts of the "quarantine" speech (for reasons that will be clearer later) appear to have constituted one of these efforts. Another effort was started on the day following the "quarantine" speech, when Sumner Welles wrote a memorandum for the President outlining a new peace program.

So much has been written about Mr. Welles's scheme that it does not seem necessary to do more than recall its essentials.[19] Mr. Welles believed that it would be easier to get the democracies and dictatorships together to seek a solution of political, economic, and armament problems if they first succeeded in reaching an understanding on less explosive issues. He therefore suggested trying to achieve a general agreement on questions such as the fundamental rules which ought to govern international behavior. The President himself proposed holding a dramatic meeting of diplomatic representatives accredited to Washington, in the White House on Armistice Day, at which he would read a message designed to set in motion procedures leading to an agreement of the kind Mr. Welles envisaged. Mr. Welles thereupon put his scheme into more concrete form, but the entire matter was dropped before Armistice Day because of Secretary Hull's objections. It was revived, however, in early January 1938, when it was hoped that it would, among other matters, lend support to Great Britain's continued attempt to arrive at an understanding with Germany.[20] Perhaps the best-known part of the story is that which deals with the submission of the Welles plan to Mr. Chamberlain; the latter's rejection of it during Mr. Eden's absence from England; and Mr. Eden's successful efforts to get the Prime Minister to reverse his stand around the middle of January. In the end the matter was dropped for a number of reasons, but in the Hyde

19. *Ibid.,* pp. 665–70. Mr. Welles's own accounts of his plan are in *The Time for Decision,* p. 64, and *Seven Decisions That Shaped History* (New York, 1950), chapter i. See also discussion in *The Challenge to Isolation* by William L. Langer and S. Everett Gleason (New York, 1952), p. 22.

20. *Foreign Relations of the United States, 1938,* I, 115–26.

Park files there are revised drafts with notations by Mr. Roosevelt which show that the President and Mr. Welles continued working on the scheme until at least mid-February.[21]

It would seem, therefore, that the President was searching for a program to reduce the danger of war over a period which started considerably before and continued for some time after the "quarantine" speech. The programs that Mr. Roosevelt acted upon differed in many respects, but all aimed at getting the various conflicting nations to cooperate in the interests of peace—at the least by entering into some sort of initial agreement. The emphasis was mainly on a constructive approach to maintain peace. But it was also on arrangements which were designed to perevent the outbreak of war by providing for a collective neutrality or nonbelligerency, the mere threat of which would act as a restraint upon aggression, or to make possible the use of pressure, through such a neutrality or nonbelligerency, in case hostilities could not be averted.

This, then, was Mr. Roosevelt's search for a plan which could be used to cope with the international situation. The story of the writing of the speech starts with Mr. Hull. The Secretary, on learning that the President was to make an extensive trip in late September, urged him to deliver an address, in some large midwestern city, for the purpose—according to Mr. Hull's own account—of counteracting the growing trend toward isolationism throughout the country.[22] One may take for granted that Mr. Hull also believed that an expression of the moral outrage felt in the United States against the Axis nations would be welcome at home and have a salutary effect abroad. Mr. Roosevelt, no doubt wholly in sympathy with the Secretary's views on this matter, at once agreed and asked Mr. Hull and Norman Davis to furnish him with the necessary material.

The record—pieced together from the Hyde Park files and what has recently emerged from the Davis files—shows that Mr. Davis sent the President four separate memoranda.[23] Two were mailed from Washington where, judging by a statement in Mr. Hull's *Memoirs,* the Secretary and Mr. Davis wrote them jointly.[24] Mr. Davis appears to have written the other two in New York and read them over the telephone to Mr. Dunn in the State Department before mailing them to the President. It is these four memoranda which the President took on his western tour

21. Roosevelt files P. S. F. State–1938.
22. Hull, *Memoirs,* I, 544–45.
23. The four memoranda are in both the Roosevelt and the Davis files. There is one difference in the texts (noted below) and some differences in the accompanying letters and notations.
24. Hull, *Memoirs,* I, 544.

and, during his journey, put together to make up the "quarantine" speech.

The first two memoranda (those in which the Secretary must have had a hand) contained the familiar opening passages of the speech. Without naming the Axis powers, but obviously referring to them, they described with great forcefulness the brutal chaos being created in parts of the world by certain nations. They went on to make two points repetitiously: that disorder in any segment of the globe could not fail to affect every country; and that peace-loving nations must make a concerted effort to maintain peace. Among the statements in the original draft were:

> There is a solidarity and interdependence about the modern world, both technically and morally, which makes it impossible for any nation to isolate itself from what goes on in the rest of the world or to secure itself through indifference, isolation, or neutrality from economic and political upheavals in the rest of the world. . . .
>
> An overwhelming majority of the peoples and nations of the world today want to be left alone in peace. Nevertheless, the peace, the freedom and the security of these peoples and nations are being jeopardized by the remaining ten per cent, who are threatening a breakdown of international order and law. Surely the ninety per cent who want to live in peace under law and according to moral standards that have received universal acceptance can and must find some way to make their will prevail. . . .
>
> If we are to have a world in which it is possible to breathe freely and live in amity, the peace-loving nations must make a concerted effort to uphold laws and principles on which alone peace can exist.

The President used the whole of the first two memoranda, with the exception of one paragraph which will be referred to later.[25] In places, he altered some of the wording and freely rearranged the sentences. One gets the impression that Mr. Roosevelt was trying to edit the text to conform to his usual terse and brilliantly vivid style of writing. But this is only an impression, and certain changes may have been designed to convey a stronger meaning. The only additions Mr. Roosevelt made were a few relatively brief passages apparently inserted to supply either color or clarity.[26]

25. *The Public Papers and Addresses of Franklin D. Roosevelt, 1937* (New York, 1941), p. 406.

26. The paraphrase of a recent author is from James Hilton's *Lost Horizon;* the quotation from a bishop was taken from a letter written to the President by Bishop Frank W. Sterrett (Roosevelt files); the paragraph beginning "the situation is definitely of universal concern" is quoted from the State Department's instructions to the Minister in Switzerland in regard to the League's consideration of the Far Eastern crisis, September 28. *Foreign Relations of the United States, 1937*, IV, 43.

The other two memoranda, which must have been written by Mr. Davis alone, proclaimed at the outset:

> It is my determination to pursue a policy of peace. . . . We recognize, however, that if we are unable to or unwilling to defend our rights and interests we will lose the respect of other nations and we will also lose our own self-respect.
>
> This nation was dedicated to certain principles which our forebears considered to be of greater value than life itself and without which life would not be worth living. If the time ever comes when we are no longer willing or able to defend to the utmost of our ability the principles which are the foundation of freedom and progress we will sacrifice our great national heritage and will cease to have the vitality and stamina to keep this nation alive.

The President omitted these paragraphs and in their place wrote the famous "quarantine" passage:

> It seems to be unfortunately true that the epidemic of world lawlessness is spreading.
>
> When an epidemic of physical disease starts to spread the community approves and joins in a quarantine of the patients in order to protect the health of the community against the spread of the disease.

The remainder of the Davis draft featured the sentence, "War is a contagion"—a sentence which may have suggested the word "quarantine" to the President [27]—and emphasized that "There must be positive endeavors to preserve peace." It closed with a moving statement that there was a tendency, in the welter of conflicting ideologies battling for control of the modern world, to overlook one basic truth: that "man, the human being is . . . the supreme end of society." But, despite its eloquence, the President discarded this passage and wrote the following ending:

27. There are various stories about the President's use of the word "quarantine." Mr. Ickes thought the President took it from a talk in which he (the Secretary) said that neighbors had a right to "quarantine" themselves against the spread of infection such as existed in the international situation. See *The Secret Diary of Harold L. Ickes* (New York, 1954), II, 221. Mr. Welles has stated that the President used the word "quarantine" in talking to him about the possibility of drawing a line in the Pacific to form a quasi blockade against Japan. See Rosenman, Samuel I., *Working with Roosevelt* (New York, 1952), p. 164. For an account by William Phillips see footnote 34, below.

There must be positive endeavors to preserve peace.

America hates war. America hopes for peace. Therefore, America actively engages in the search for peace.

No doubt some of the reasons for thinking that the popular interpretations of the "quarantine" speech should be reconsidered are already evident. Nevertheless, it seems desirable to discuss briefly these interpretations and the conclusion advanced here, one by one.

1. Those who believe the President planned the speech as an announcement of a decision to revert to the type of collective security embodied in the League Covenant rely mainly on two arguments: that the tone of the address was so threatening it must have been designed to indicate a drastic move of this kind; that the speech conspicuously emphasized the idea of nations maintaining peace by a "concerted effort."

But the tone of the speech existed in the original memoranda, where it was clearly not meant to go beyond fulfilling Mr. Hull's purposes of awakening the American people to the dangers of isolationism and of voicing moral indignation at the destructiveness of the Axis countries. It might be argued, as already suggested, that Mr. Roosevelt strengthened the meaning of the original in places, but he does not seem to have sharpened the tone of the draft as a whole, and, in one very important instance, he moderated it. The passage of the Davis text which Mr. Roosevelt discarded and replaced with his "quarantine" statement could certainly be construed as a warning that, if pushed too far, the United States would fight. The first version was even stronger, for it included, "We recognize, however, that a policy of peace at any price will not ensure peace. . . . This nation was born fighting for certain principles which our forebears considered to be of greater value than life itself. . . ." President Roosevelt may have seen the initial draft but, even if he did not, the interpretation to which the revision opened itself could scarcely have escaped him, and it seems probable that he omitted it as too menacing.[28] This thesis is further supported by the fact that the one paragraph (referred to earlier) which the President did not use out of the memoranda sent from Washington had similar overtones.

The reference to a "concerted effort" was also in the drafts forwarded from Washington and, read in context, clearly meant that peace-loving nations should cooperate to arouse the conscience of the world to ensure the maintenance of high moral standards in the conduct of international relations. The presence of this theme is indeed not sur-

28. The original version of this memorandum is in the Davis files and is marked "N.Y. September 17, 1937" with a further notation, "Phoned to Mr. Dunn." Presumably the State Department suggested the changes which appeared in the revised version in the Roosevelt files.

prising, for, of all themes, it was most frequently used by Mr. Hull at this time and was also often employed by the President.

2. The idea that the "quarantine" speech was an advance notice of a declaration of sanctions against Japan resulted, to a large extent, from the circumstances under which the speech was given. The day after Mr. Roosevelt's appearance at Chicago, the League of Nations blamed Japan for the hostilities which had started in China in July and called for a conference of the Nine Power Treaty nations. Within a matter of hours, the State Department endorsed the League's position. The fact that these events happened hard upon each other gave rise to the belief that they were all part of one piece of political strategy which would culminate in the Nine Power nations adopting sanctions against Japan. However, we know today that there was no such direct connection between the President's Chicago address and the League's actions. And there is no convincing evidence to suggest that the President had decided to use coercive measures against Japan.

Sumner Welles, writing in the 1950's, seemed indeed to supply such evidence.[29] He said that in the summer of 1937 the President was far more preoccupied with the Far East than with Europe and that Mr. Roosevelt had, on several occasions, talked to him about the possibility of stationing units of the American and British navies at certain points in the Pacific to enforce an embargo against Japan. Mr. Welles stated further that, as he was in Europe during most of September 1937, he knew little about the writing of the "quarantine" speech but believed the President had in mind the embargo and quasi blockade he had mentioned earlier.

However, on further inspection, it would seem that Mr. Welles's recollections (in common with those of many others) had altered over the years; for in 1944 he had written:

> Partly because of the issues involved in the Spanish war, and partly because the real nature of Hitlerism was becoming increasingly apparent, the President determined to make a vigorous effort to persuade public opinion that in its own interest the United States should propose some constructive plan for international action to check the forces of aggression before they succeeded in engulfing the world. For this effort he selected the very heart of isolationism—the city of Chicago.[30]

Mr. Welles then went on to quote the "quarantine" speech. His recollection closer to the event does not therefore bear out the thesis that the Chicago address reflected Mr. Roosevelt's determination to use sanctions

29. Welles, *Seven Decisions That Shaped History*, pp. 8, 13–14, 70–75, 91–93; Rosenman, *op. cit.*, p. 164, has a letter from Mr. Welles on the "quarantine" speech.

30. Welles, *The Time for Decision*, p. 61.

against Japan but instead supports the interpretation that the President was thinking of some program to stabilize the world situation.

3. There is a contemporary record which suggests that the President planned the "quarantine" speech to introduce a program involving sanctions against future aggressors (meaning the Axis states) which he expected to launch immediately after his return from Chicago. Secretary Ickes, in his diary entry of September 19, 1937, described a talk with the President in which the latter said he was considering addressing a letter to all the countries of the world, except possibly the "three bandit nations," proposing that all peace-loving peoples isolate those who invaded the rights of others. "What he had in mind," Mr. Ickes wrote, "is to cut off all trade with any such nation." [31] According to the Secretary, Mr. Roosevelt said further that his proposal would not apply to the current situations in Spain and China, as what had been done could not be undone; that he wanted to "evolve a new policy for the future." Mr. Ickes himself commented that "of course, if he should do this, it would be a warning to the nations that are today running amuck." The Secretary wrote further that Mr. Roosevelt asked him whether he should send this letter before or after his trip out west, to which Mr. Ickes replied that he should wait until his return.

It would seem, however, that Mr. Roosevelt could not have settled upon this plan more than momentarily, for he appears to have been considering a variety of other schemes with equal seriousness. Just before his talk with Secretary Ickes, the President told two other members of the Cabinet, Hull and Morgenthau, that he was thinking of publicity declaring his readiness to act as a clearinghouse for peace— a suggestion which on the surface does not sound the same as the one discussed with Mr. Ickes. Further, the day after his talk with Mr. Ickes, the President told Mr. Morgenthau that he had dropped the idea of making such a public declaration and had decided to do nothing that would call for any response or action from any quarter, the whole thing being a matter of long-term education. It should also be recalled that at this time the President was considering still another course, not having as yet received a response from Prime Minister Chamberlain to his proposal for opening discussions which were partly intended to lead to an agreement between the democracies and the Axis countries. Moreover, it is clear that he did not abandon the desire to get the democracies

---

31. This statement leaves open to question whether Mr. Roosevelt actually stated he had in mind cutting off all trade with the aggressor or whether Mr. Ickes thought that was what the President had in mind. The document which indicates most clearly that one of the President's ideas was to find some means of using cooperative economic pressures is cited in footnote 34 below.

and totalitarian states together, for he started working on the Welles plan only three days after his Chicago speech.

4. The theory that the "quarantine" speech was not a vital landmark in Mr. Roosevelt's foreign policy but part of a groping attempt to find some means of forestalling war is based on various pieces of evidence (some already mentioned), including Mr. Roosevelt's statements.

Immediately after the delivery of the "quarantine" speech, Mr. Roosevelt went to Cardinal Mundelein's house in Chicago, where they had a long talk which was—and has remained—confidential. However, there appears in the Roosevelt files a letter written, on the following day, by Cardinal Mundelein to the Apostolic Delegate to the United States, which says in part:

> Yesterday the President of the United States delivered here in Chicago a strong and important address which may affect the future peace and tranquility of the world. Afterwards, in my own house, he continued discussion of the subject to which he had given considerable thought. He asked me whether he might invite participation of the Holy See in the movement and, as it is for the purpose of establishing permanent peace in a war-torn world, I answered him that I thought he should. . . .
>
> His plan does not contemplate either military or naval action against the unjust aggressor nation, nor does it involve "sanctions" as generally understood but rather a policy of isolation, severance of ordinary communications in a united manner by all the governments of the pact.[32]

The rest of the letter indicated that the President hoped such a movement for the creation of a "permanent peace" would arrest the wave of lawlessness already submerging parts of the world.

About two weeks after the "quarantine" speech, Norman Davis, who was about to leave for the Brussels Conference where he was to represent the United States, went to see the President for oral instructions.[33] Mr. Davis' notes show that Mr. Roosevelt used language similar to that of the "quarantine" speech and of his talk with Cardinal Mundelein. They state that the President remarked that, if all other procedures failed at Brussels, the countries wanting to stop the Sino-Japanese conflict and safeguard themselves from its consequences—"or in other words the so-called neutral nations"—should "band together for their own protection against this contagion." The other powers might, for example, give China every facility for acquiring arms; or an alternative might be for "the neutrals to ostracize Japan, break off relations."

32. Roosevelt files.
33. Davis files.

Side by side with his notes on this interview, there is, in Mr. Davis' files, a paper marked: "Handed to me by President as of possible use." This contains what must be an excerpt from an article or book which says, in substance, that the Inter-American principle of neutral cooperation, short of force, would seem to offer a useful formula for the United States in the existing situation; and it urges the President to apply this formula so as to develop a "constructive program" in which a group of neutrals, acting in common, might make their influence felt.

It would seem therefore that, immediately after delivering his address at Chicago, Mr. Roosevelt spoke to Cardinal Mundelein, not as though he had just proclaimed some drastic policy, but as though, as in the past, he were throwing out the germ of an idea with the hope that it might grow. From the tenor of his remarks and the paper he gave Mr. Davis, it appears likely that the President thought the Inter-American concepts of collective neutrality or nonbelligerency contained the seeds of some method for dealing with the worldwide situation. He suggested that "so-called neutrals" might develop a common program, but he seems to have been very vague about the nature of that program. It was not to involve military action nor " 'sanctions' as generally understood." But it might include, among other matters, the "severance of ordinary communications in a united manner" or a "break off" of relations. Perhaps in talking to Cardinal Mundelein, Mr. Roosevelt had in mind the possibility of developing a plan which would provide for the creation, under certain circumstances, of a moral front limited to such matters as the severance of diplomatic relations—a plan which, it might be added, would seem to furnish appropriate grounds for an appeal to the Pope. Or perhaps he was looking for a scheme which would, if necessary, permit the extension of the concepts of collective neutrality or nonbelligerency so that they might embrace a wide range of pressures up to and including economic pressures.[34] The mere

34. The President must have mentioned a plan including economic pressures to Clark Eichelberger in early July 1937. In mid-July Mr. Eichelberger sent the President a memorandum based on a talk which they had had some two weeks earlier. The discussion seems to have centered on the possibility of evolving a comprehensive international program which would provide for far-reaching economic measures, drastic disarmament, and a renovation of the existing peace machinery. In connection with the last, Mr. Eichelberger, evidently recapitulating some of the points which had been made during the course of the conversation, wrote that the principle of consultation among nonbelligerents embodied in the Buenos Aires agreement might be extended to the entire world. Once the world had adopted such principles, he continued, the American people would be willing to accept the idea of denying trade to the aggressor. "Instead of sanctions being voted piecemeal, they would take the form of a denial of the economic benefits of the more nearly just international society to the nation that would make war." Also, at some point during this meeting, the President intimated

existence of arrangements of this character was, as stated earlier, regarded as likely to discourage aggression, so that they might be considered as a sound basis for the establishment of a "permanent peace." It is just possible that the President also thought some technique might be developed whereby, if "neutrals" exercised pressures, which were not regarded as sanctions in the ordinary sense but as measures taken for their own protection against the contagion of war, they would avoid the risk of having to resort to military action inherent in systems like that of the League.[35]

Somewhat curiously, in addition to Cardinal Mundelein's letter and Mr. Davis' notes, a document which has long been familiar to historians seems to support the idea that the President had no definite policy at this stage but was contemplating a variety of possibilities, including ways of embroidering on the Inter-American system. This document is a transcript of the off-the-record press conference he held the day after he spoke at Chicago.[36] It is usually assumed that Mr. Roosevelt, anxious to avoid being questioned, was deliberately confusing in his answers to the correspondents; but it seems quite possible that the President's replies were meant to be taken at their face value.

The reporters, over and over again, asked the President to define the meaning of his Chicago address and especially of the word "quarantine." The President stuck to the following explanation of the speech as whole:

> P: . . . the lead is in the last line, "America actively engages in the search for peace." I can't tell you what the methods will be. We are looking for some way to peace. . . .
>
> Q: Foreign papers put it as an attitude without a program. . . .

---

that he might someday make a dramatic speech which—to quote Mr. Eichelberger—would "lead the world on the upward path." Roosevelt files. O.F. 20 State Department, Box 6.

One further account of a conversation with the President at this time should be mentioned, though the whole tenor of the talk, in addition to the vagueness of the language, makes it hard to evaluate. William Phillips, in his autobiography, describes a visit with Mr. Roosevelt on October 6, and states that he asked the President what he meant in using the word "quarantine" in his speech the day before. The President replied that he had searched for a word which was not "sanctions" and had settled on "quarantine" as a "drawing away from someone." Mr. Phillips adds that as the discussion proceeded, Mr. Roosevelt indicated his willingness to "go very far in drawing away." See *Ventures in Diplomacy* (Boston, 1952), pp. 206–207.

35. Based partly on a remark to this effect said to have been made by Mr. Roosevelt some months later. (Talks with John M. Blum who is working on a book with Mr. Morgenthau based on the latter's diaries [now published as *From the Morgenthau Diaries*].)

36. *The Public Papers and Addresses of Franklin D. Roosevelt, 1937*, pp. 414–425.

P: It is an attitude and it does not outline a program; but it says we are looking for a program.

At the outset, a reporter had asked the President whether he would not admit that a "quarantine" must involve a repudiation of our neutrality legislation. Mr. Roosevelt declared, "Not for a minute. It may be an expansion." The correspondent asked, "Doesn't that mean economic sanctions anyway?" to which the President answered, "No, not necessarily." Later the President remarked that there were many methods of attaining peace which had as yet never been tried. A correspondent asserted that, in his position, to quarantine aggressors was no longer neutrality. The President stated that "On the contrary, it might be a stronger neutrality." The conference ended with this exchange:

Q: Do you agree . . . that sanctions mean war?

P: No. Don't talk about sanctions. Never suggested it. . . . Don't get off on the sanction route.

Q: I meant that in general terms; going further than moral denunciation.

P: That is not a definition of "sanctions."

Q: Is a "quarantine" a sanction?

P: No.

Q: Are you excluding any coercive action? Sanctions are coercive.

P: That is exactly the difference.

Q: Better, then, to keep it in a moral sphere?

P: No, it can be a very practical sphere.

For whatever reasons, Mr. Roosevelt seems thereafter to have shunned entering into any explanations of the "quarantine" speech. But in a Fireside Chat on October 12, he referred to his remarks at Chicago, saying in part that it was the duty of a President to think in terms of peace not only for one but for many generations.[37] Peace, he declared, must be "sound and permanent," built on a "cooperative search" for peace by all nations desiring this end.

To me it would seem that, throughout the period before and after the "quarantine" speech, Mr. Roosevelt was moved by a deep inner feeling that it must be possible to find a formula which would avoid as unthinkable a catastrophe as another world war. In retrospect it may look to many as though nothing could have averted tragedy short of a clear-cut and determined policy against the Axis. But the chances are that the Chicago speech reflected no such policy. What governed Mr. Roosevelt's behavior could be fully understood only by a grasp of the whole history of the times illuminated by that rarest of things, a wise and informed feeling for the President's personality. Nevertheless, one

37. *Ibid.*, p. 429.

influence is blatantly obvious, namely, the political situation in the United States, a matter which prompted the rest of these notes.

II

The second assumption referred to at the outset is that Mr. Roosevelt, with full justification, felt that the American people wholly repudiated the "quarantine" speech and that he therefore abandoned his decision to adopt a firm policy against the Axis powers. If Mr. Roosevelt made no such decision, obviously he did not abandon it. But this does not rule out the possibility that the President, Mr. Hull, and others in the Administration believed that the country almost uniformly rejected the speech and were influenced by their belief. Indeed there is a good deal to suggest that this was the case. Sumner Welles has described the President as "dismayed by the widespread violence of the attacks" following his appearance at Chicago.[38] Mr. Hull has stated in his *Memoirs* that the "reaction against the quarantine idea was quick and violent" and set back by many months the Administration's efforts to educate public opinion away from isolationism.[39] Judge Rosenman has likewise spoken of the nation's response to the speech as "quick and violent—and nearly unanimous." [40] The effect of this evaluation of the country's attitude upon the Administration's policy is inevitably an elusive matter. But certainly during the main international event that followed—that is, the Brussels Conference—the Administration's policy was exceedingly cautious, and cables from Washington to Norman Davis during his conduct of the negotiations at Brussels are marked by a worried preoccupation with public opinion at home.[41] As will be seen later, Mr. Roosevelt himself introduced this note of concern in his original instructions to Mr. Davis.

However, even a limited look (such as that which follows) at the kind of material—mainly leading newspapers and weeklies—which the Administration must have used to assess the popular reaction to the "quaran-

38. Welles, *Seven Decisions That Shaped History,* p. 13. See also p. 73 and Welles, *The Time for Decision,* p. 63.

39. Hull, *Memoirs,* I, 545. One cannot help wondering whether the severely critical attitude which Mr. Hull is known to have developed toward the "quarantine" speech did not arise only after he saw the attacks in the isolationist press. Pierrepont Moffat recorded in his diary on October 5, 1937, that a meeting of State Department officials was being held on that day in the Secretary's office when the ticker service brought in the text of the President's Chicago address. "The Secretary was delighted at the speech," Mr. Moffat wrote, "and the majority thought it would be strongly approved by the public." See *The Moffat Papers* (Cambridge, 1956), p. 153.

40. Rosenman, *op. cit.*

41. Statement based on the writer's study of our Far Eastern Policy during this period.

tine" speech raises a question which may well be worth more intensive study.[42] Were the President and those around him, in fact, justified in concluding that the country reacted with speed, vehemence, and solidarity against the speech; or were they perhaps so responsive to the criticisms of certain isolationists that they equated these with the opinions of the country as a whole?

A reading of a group of leading publications, of the type that members of the Administration must have seen, shows that the controversy over the "quarantine" speech lasted until the end of the Brussels Conference in late November. Because the speech was immediately followed by the League's denunciation of Japan and its call for a Nine Power conference, and because we supported the League's action, many believed that these events had been planned to introduce a new, forceful foreign policy which would be fully revealed at Brussels.

In this group of publications, estimates of the country's reaction to the speech went through two phases. Pierrepont Moffat, writing in his diary, described the initial phase—the immediate response to the speech—as a "burst of applause." [43] A similar impression was recorded in comment after comment in the publications surveyed. On October 6, the *New York Times* printed excerpts from sixteen editorials from all parts of the country and indicated their trend in its headline: "ROOSEVELT SPEECH WIDELY APPROVED." [44] The *Christian Science Monitor,* on the 7th, declared that observers were surprised at the degree of enthusiasm evoked by the speech, with even papers hostile to the Administration finding words of praise.[45] In a review of the week on Sunday (the 10th), the *San Francisco Chronicle* wrote that the average citizen had responded to the President's message like a "cavalry horse to a bugle call." [46] It said that Roosevelt had appealed to the nation much as Wilson had taken the case for the League to the country to "whip a little group of Senators"—only, where Wilson failed, Roosevelt succeeded. *Time* magazine stated at about the same

42. There do not seem to be any polls that show any particular shift in opinion right after the "quarantine" speech. See *Public Opinion, 1935–1946* (Princeton, 1951) which includes exact dates on which polls were issued.

Some of the evidence Mr. Hull cites in his *Memoirs* (p. 545) to prove that the country reacted against the "quarantine idea" is unconvincing. He states, for example, that the A. F. of L. passed a resolution, following the speech, to the effect that "American labor does not wish to be involved in European or Asiatic wars." But he fails to mention that, the day after the "quarantine" speech, William Green, at a convention of the A. F. of L., proposed a boycott of Japanese goods and was, according to all press accounts, overwhelmingly applauded. Moreover, about a week later, the A. F. of L. and the C.I.O. both passed resolutions to boycott Japan.

43. *The Moffat Papers,* p. 155.

44. P. 17.

45. P. 1. Article by the Washington Bureau of the *Monitor.*

46. Magazine section, p. 3.

time that the Chicago address had elicited more words of approval, ranging from enthusiastic to tempered, than anything Mr. Roosevelt had done in many a month.[47] He had regained the support of many whom he had alienated earlier and provided himself with an active peace issue which promised to remain popular unless it threatened to involve us in war. Meanwhile, he kept the country guessing whether his proposed "quarantine" meant diplomatic pressures, voluntary boycotts, or economic sanctions.

The marked tendency to agree that the initial response to the speech was positive disappeared in the second phase. Fundamentally, the question was whether the American people were initially enthusiastic about the speech largely because they were glad to have the President openly express disapproval of the Axis powers; and, if so, whether their enthusiasm had changed after the idea became widespread that the "quarantine" speech would be translated into strong action against Japan at the Brussels Conference. Publications such as *Newsweek* felt that, influenced by increasing cries of alarm from leading isolationists, the tide of opinion soon began to turn.[48] Publications like *Time,* on the other hand, believed that popular sentiment remained firmly behind the President.[49] Most of the comments in other publications ranged between these extremes. In general they agreed that the original enthusiasm for the speech had been tempered by anxiety that, at the Brussels Conference, Mr. Roosevelt's new foreign policy would not stop short of war. This was by no means intended, however, to imply that the country would not support punitive measures against Japan, including economic sanctions. For the view was constantly expressed that boycotts, embargoes, etc., against the Japanese would not involve military action. In short, it would seem that the feeling in this group of journals was that the "quick" reaction to the "quarantine" speech, far from being hostile, was decidedly favorable, and it would seem that, in the long run, their opinions differed too widely to justify any definite conclusion.

As for the question of editorial policies, an expansion of a study by Lawrence Kramer of eight newspapers, selected to represent different parts of the country and different political convictions, shows six approving the speech and two opposing.[50]

47. October 18, p. 19. The article was obviously written before the Fireside Chat of October 12.

48. December 20, p. 11.

49. November 1, p. 17.

50. Lawrence I. Kramer, Jr., then at Harvard, wrote a long manuscript summarizing all the editorials in these papers dealing with the major developments in our Far Eastern policy from 1933 to 1937. The above is based on the section on the "quarantine" speech, with additions and analyses made entirely on my own responsibility.

Among the favorable papers were two published on the west coast: the *San Francisco Chronicle* and the *Los Angeles Times*. The *Chronicle* at the outset welcomed Mr. Roosevelt's statements at Chicago as meaning that he had decided to join in cooperative economic sanctions against Japan. It believed the Navy would have to be held in readiness but that there would be no necessity to use it. But, even before the Brussels Conference, the *Chronicle* stated with considerable bitterness that the hopes placed in Mr. Roosevelt's declarations were apparently unjustified. The President had spoken "brave" words at Chicago but there was no indication that he himself knew what he meant by them.[51] The *Times* went through a similar process of expectation and disillusionment. It first supported the "quarantine" speech on the assumption that it foreshadowed the adoption at Brussels of economic and financial measures against the Japanese; but when no such measures materialized, it asked sharply why the speech had ever been made. What originally looked like a statesmanlike utterance, it said, appeared very different in the light of the lack of any effort to implement it.[52]

In the middle of the country, the *Milwaukee Journal* expressed itself, at the close of the Nine Power Conference, with even greater vehemence. It scathingly described the delegates departing from Brussels utterly beaten, their tails between their legs. "Where do we go from here?" it asked, and declared, "Nowhere. There wasn't any bright new dream when the President spoke at Chicago . . . only rhetoric." [53]

The *Cleveland Press,* a Scripps-Howard paper, while hailing the "quarantine" speech and believing it implied more than moral pressure, pursued a cautious policy, never definitely advocating any course.

On the east coast, the *Christian Science Monitor* at the beginning expected the warm response to the President's message to lead to an arms embargo or possibly economic sanctions. But ultimately it, too, became disappointed and concluded that Mr. Roosevelt had grown more afraid than ever of his isolationist critics. The *New York Times,* on its part, saw in the "quarantine" speech and subsequent events the need for reconsidering its editorial position. While applauding the speech as ushering in a more internationalist foreign policy, the *Times* took no definite stand throughout the Brussels Conference. At the end of November, however, it attracted widespread attention by calling on the Administration to overcome its fear of isolationist groups, in and out of Congress, whom it held responsible for undermining our leadership in world affairs and turning the Brussels Conference into a fiasco. A few weeks later the

51. November 5. The editorials in each newspaper are too numerous to cite except where reference is made to a specific editorial.

52. November 26.

53. November 26.

Times, in a dramatic editorial, came out in favor of withholding raw materials and credits from Japan.[54]

While these six papers seem sufficiently representative to assume that their views, or equivalent ones in similar publications, came to the attention of the Administration, it may be well to mention the editorial policies of the Washington papers which Mr. Roosevelt seems frequently to have scanned.[55] The *News,* being a Scripps-Howard publication, followed the cautious policy already noted. The *Post* issued a sensational front-page editorial on October 6 endorsing the "quarantine" speech as a first step toward economic measures against Japan. The *Star* not only advocated such measures but declared that, unless they were boldly applied, the signatories of the Nine Power Treaty would deserve nothing better than the contempt which they would certainly get from the Axis countries.[56] The *Times* and *Herald,* both Patterson papers, were in favor of a long-range Anglo-American blockade of the Japanese.[57] It cannot be stated too often, however, that no matter what actions were recommended it was believed, with few exceptions, that they would not and must not lead to war.

If the editorial opinions of the above newspapers suggest considerable evidence of support for the "quarantine" speech, so, it should be added, did the President's mail. The great majority of the letters on the Chicago address, which fill several boxes in the Hyde Park files, are messages of appreciation, often written with deep emotion.

The other side of the coin is the nature of the opposition to the speech and its influence upon the Administration, including the President. The two hostile papers in Mr. Kramer's study were the *Chicago Tribune* and a Hearst publication. Nothing demonstrated the attitude of the *Tribune* better than its account of Mr. Roosevelt's appearance at Chicago on October 5. It described thousands of Chicagoans turning out to greet the President, expecting to hear a message of peace, and being plunged by his words into a "world-hurricane of war fright." Throughout October and November the *Tribune* harped upon two themes: that a "quarantine" must mean economic sanctions and economic sanctions

54. These two editorials appeared respectively on November 30 and December 24.

55. Mr. Roosevelt's scrapbook at Hyde Park is full of clippings from the Washington press. Grace Tully lists eleven newspapers which the President looked through customarily for editorial opinion. Of these, four opposed the "quarantine" speech: the *Chiaco Tribune,* a Hearst paper, the *New York Herald Tribune,* and the *New York Sun.* See *F.D.R.: My Boss* (New York, 1949), p. 76.

56. October 7.

57. October 10 and 12 respectively. The *New York Daily News,* also a Patterson paper, had come out for such a blockade on October 3 (magazine section, p. 6).

must mean war; that we were merely puppets of the British, serving as saviors of their Empire in the Far East.

The same themes were emphasized by the Hearst press. But Mr. Hearst went much further. He issued a questionnaire to members of Congress which, leading off from the "quarantine" speech, asked whether we should take sides in the Sino-Japanese conflict or steer clear of all wars. The answers were published in a series of articles which began on October 17 and ran for about two weeks. The introduction stated that congressmen from the "Atlantic to the Pacific, from Canada to the Gulf" had "roared back their determination for today, to-morrow, and forever to keep the United States out of foreign wars."

Many of the published replies came from important political leaders, mainly well-known isolationists.[58] Senator Borah said he was utterly opposed to the United States' participating in sanctions against Japan which would be "just the same as initiating war." Senator Vandenberg declared that any move toward naming aggressors, using sanctions, etc., would lead us in the direction of entangling alliances—the one thing we were determined to avoid. Senator George of Georgia wrote that he would not, under any circumstances, favor action which might risk war with Japan. Senator Richard Russell asserted that, instead of policing the world to maintain peace, we should rely upon our neutrality legisla-tion to "quarantine" us against war. Senator La Follette stated that he was opposed to anything which, by implication or otherwise, might ulti-mately require the United States to use force.

The statement which received the widest publicity was that issued by Hiram Johnson on October 19, the eve of Norman Davis' departure for Brussels.[59] Speaking of the coming conference, the Senator said, "We want no union with welching nations who will . . . tell us we must lead mankind to save the world." Mr. Davis, he insisted, would not be going to Europe unless an agreement had been reached in advance between England and the United States. Mr. Roosevelt had no right to make a mystery of what he meant by a "quarantine" and, unless he intended nothing but words, the inevitable result would be war.

Even a cursory look at the record shows that the Administration ob-served Mr. Hearst's tactics closely from the outset. At his press con-ference on October 6, Mr. Roosevelt made some remarks about excerpts from editorials around the country, presumably those in the *New York Times*. He failed, however, to mention that they were mostly in his favor but concentrated instead upon the editorial written by—to use his own words—"the old man of the seas—old man Hearst." This, he declared, was "the silliest ever . . . perfectly terrible—awful. Says it

58. The references in this paragraph are to articles printed on October 17 and 18.

59. *San Francisco Examiner,* October 20, p. 1.

means this is getting us into war and a lot more of that." A few days later, Mr. Ickes recorded in his diary that the Hearst press was after Mr. Roosevelt "full cry" for his Chicago address and that the President had said he wanted to remind Hearst that he had been responsible for an absolutely unjustifiable war with Spain.[60] At about the same time, Pierrepont Moffat noted in his diary that Hearst was "alleged to be about to start a campaign against the idea of a 'quarantine.' " [61] When the campaign got underway, Mr. Roosevelt clearly showed his concern. On the day Norman Davis sailed, the President issued a statement which was generally accepted as a reply to Senator Johnson's attack.[62] Obviously addressing himself to the accusation that we had an understanding with the British, Mr. Roosevelt asserted that we were "of course" entering the Nine Power Conference without any prior commitments. He also emphasized that the purpose of the meeting was to seek a *peaceable* solution of the Sino-Japanese conflict. Off the record, the President dictated some instructions to guide Mr. Davis in his relations with the British.[63] The British Cabinet, these said, must recognize that there was such a thing as American public opinion. Mr. Davis must make clear, "at every step," that the United States would neither take the lead at Brussels nor be made a "tail to the British kite as is now being charged by the Hearst press and others."

There can be little doubt, therefore, that the "quarantine" speech provoked a barrage from prominent isolationists and that this barrage had its effect upon the Administration. There can also be little doubt that considerable evidence of approval of the speech came to the attention of the Administration but was not accepted as weighing substantially in the balance. Perhaps an extensive study would reveal a wider tide of opinion against the address to support the Administration's view. But until such a study is made, it seems pertinent to continue asking whether the Administration's judgment was not unduly governed by its sensitivity to the attacks of leading isolationists.

60. Ickes, *Secret Diary*, II, 227.

61. *The Moffat Papers*, p. 155.

62. *New York Times*, October 20, p. 15.

63. *Foreign Relations of the United States, 1937*, IV, 85. The memorandum was also sent to Ambassador Bingham in London, who conveyed its contents to Mr. Eden (*ibid.*, p. 114).

JOHN C. DONOVAN

Congressional Isolationists and the Roosevelt Foreign Policy

Isolationist sentiment in the 1930's was strongest in Congress. Revisionist historians have charged Roosevelt with usurping congressional authority in his conduct of an interventionist foreign policy. Writers sympathetic to FDR have countered by suggesting that Congress, slow to reflect the changing public mood of the late 1930's, insisted on the passage and retention of neutrality legislation which shackled the President's diplomacy. If Roosevelt had been free to pursue a more flexible foreign policy, according to this view, the United States might have been able to cooperate with England and France to prevent the outbreak of World War II.

John C. Donovan offers a rebuttal to the revisionist position in an article based on his doctoral dissertation, "Congress and the Making of Neutrality Legislation, 1935–1939," Harvard University, 1949. The most significant books on this subject are Wayne S. Cole, Senator Gerald P. Nye and American Foreign Relations (Minneapolis, 1962); Robert A. Divine, The Illusion of Neutrality (Chicago, 1962); and Manfred Jonas, Isolationism in America, 1935–1941 (Ithaca, 1966).

IN THE 1950's, as in the 1930's, there are Congressional efforts to limit executive discretion in the conduct of foreign affairs. Senators Taft and Wherry have generated a debate over the President's authority to send armed forces abroad which is reminiscent of the debate over the neutrality legislation of the earlier decade. The time has therefore come when a more just appreciation of President Roosevelt's leadership in foreign affairs may be possible and when such an evaluation may be useful.

Before an attempt is made to evaluate the foreign policy of Franklin Delano Roosevelt, some attention should be paid to the Congressional views of isolationism that limited the formulation of American foreign policy in the decade prior to World War II. The efforts of the new revisionist school of American history, under the leadership of the late

Reprinted by permission from *World Politics,* III (April 1951), 299–316.

Charles A. Beard, to assess American foreign policy exclusively in terms of executive responsibility have shown less than adequate appreciation of the role that Congress plays in the making of American foreign policy. Any evaluation of the Roosevelt foreign policy that fails to consider the part played by the Congressional isolationists in the formulation of our foreign policy in the 1930's will leave something to be desired. The following article is an introductory effort, based on detailed analysis of the role of Congress in the making of neutrality legislation, suggesting certain basic information which ought to be weighed by those who are interested in reaching a final evaluation.

I

American isolationism found expression in the 1930's in two very different groups in Congress. One group, in which Senators Hiram Johnson and William E. Borah provided the most effective leadership, firmly opposed American support of the program of collective security, insisting that the end product of the struggle for power in Europe would always be war and that there was nothing United States influence could do to alter the process or the result. Consequently, they argued, the government of the United States should concentrate its attention on the primary problem of making American democracy work at home—with some consideration given, of course, to the problem of continental defense. Since war in foreign areas, and especially in Europe, was an inevitable feature of "power politics," the best opportunity for protecting American interests, according to this view, lay in the field of international law, where a scrupulous adherence to our rights and duties as a neutral would keep the nation from involvement in foreign controversies, the outcome of which had no bearing on the future course of American democracy. John Bassett Moore and Edwin M. Borchard were the outstanding intellectual spokesmen for this view, and their advice was gladly and frequently given to Congressional groups studying the problem of keeping the nation "unentangled" and free from "foreign commitments."

The other Congressional group, led by Senators Nye, Clark, and Vandenberg, while agreeing on the futility of American participation in experiments in international political cooperation, considered it essential that the Congress frame neutrality legislation relinquishing many of the traditional rights of a neutral under international law. The purpose of this neutrality legislation would be to avoid any risks which might be involved in carrying on foreign trade in time of foreign war.

Whereas the Johnson-Borah group wanted to insist on American rights to trade in time of foreign war, the second group was anxious to abandon many of these traditional rights as a means of avoiding political involvement in foreign "quarrels." But both groups shared the popular disillusionment concerning American participation in the First World War. Both groups felt that American participation in that war had been based on an erroneous decision encouraged principally by: (1) huge private loans by American firms to Britain and France; (2) armament firms which were in a position to profit from a bigger war; (3) Allied propaganda; and (4) an unneutral and naive American President who thought (*a*) that the outcome of the war had implications for the future of the United States, and (*b*) that the war might conceivably be turned to constructive ends. In this general atmosphere of disillusionment (in which practically nothing was made of the fact that it was the peace and not the war that had been lost) and encouraged by the Nye munitions investigation, sympathy was developed for the notion that the United States ought to enact legislation which would automatically rule out the mistakes of "last time."

In addition to sharing the general feeling of disillusionment concerning the purposes for which World War I had been fought, by 1935 the two Congressional isolationist groups were united in their suspicion of, and opposition to, the foreign policy of the Roosevelt administration. The abortive efforts of the President to obtain a discriminatory arms embargo in 1933 and adherence to the World Court in January 1935 alerted these groups to guard against the possibility of another "unneutral" President leading the nation down the road to collective security and international cooperation. They wanted no part of a policy which might mean taking sides in the "eternal quarrels" of those foreign nations indulging in the "sordid game of power politics." Hence, the theory developed that legislation restricting executive discretion in the conduct of foreign affairs would help to keep the nation out of foreign wars.

As has been pointed out, the Nye-Clark-Vandenberg theory of isolationism advocated the abandonment of traditional neutral trading rights in time of foreign war as a means of preventing "incidents" at sea and as a means of avoiding economic involvement in foreign wars. It is obvious that the logical extension of this theory would lead to the point where the nation would be asked to give up foreign trade in order to keep free of war. As a matter of fact, however, there were very few isolationists of any variety who were prepared to carry the Nye-Clark-Vandenberg theory that far. First to object—and this might have been expected—was the Johnson-Borah group, also isolationist but extremely proud, which considered it ignoble for a powerful, self-respecting nation so to restrict its own legitimate activities.

Thus, when the Congress of the United States eventually faced the terrible dilemma of how to keep out of war without abandoning foreign commerce, the natural answer was found in the famous "cash-and-carry" formula, whereby it was possible to keep the trade and transfer the risk. This problem was thoroughly aired and debated in Congress and on public platforms during 1936 and 1937, and in the latter year a cash-and-carry compromise resolution was adopted, embodying a principle the Nye-Clark-Vandenberg group favored and the Borah-Johnson group disliked, with much more executive discretion written into the legislation than either isolationist group preferred.

From that time on, both isolationist groups concentrated their efforts on retaining the arms embargo which they considered to be the symbol of American "neutrality." And as the aggressive designs of Nazi Germany became the more explicit and menacing, the Roosevelt administration gradually prepared to press for repeal of the arms embargo as a means of discouraging German aggression and, when that effort failed, as a means of strengthening the armed might of Britain and France in the war against Germany.

II

In any complete and thorough study of the making of American foreign policy from 1935 to 1939 which seeks to shed light on who was responsible for what, it will be necessary to consider the very important role played by Congress in the formulation of legislation designed to keep the nation out of war. It will be imperative in any such study to recognize the fact that the idea of designing this legislation was of Congressional origin. Obviously, the whole effort to restrict executive discretion, which lay at the heart of this legislation, was, and could only have been, a Congressional undertaking.

At the outset of the neutrality experiment in 1935, the Administration tried to outflank the Nye-Clark-Vandenberg isolationist bloc by offering its own proposal for neutrality legislation, the purpose being to secure provision for a *discretionary* arms embargo. But Congress wrote the first neutrality law in 1935, including a *mandatory, non-discretionary* arms embargo provision which the President did not want and said that he did not want. And so the Chief Executive was immediately placed in a defensive position, from which he tried repeatedly to obtain as much leeway as possible for the exercise of executive discretion.

Not until the spring of 1939, however, would the Administration risk an outright frontal attack on the arms embargo, the cornerstone of the Congressional isolationist edifice. Even then, the remainder of the Administration's proposal was composed for the most part of features designed to maximize its appeal to legislators of isolationist persuasions.

It is quite possible, of course, that both the Administration and the Congressional isolationists overestimated the strength of popular sentiment in favor of keeping out of war by means of legislation. We do at least know that the isolationist bloc in the Senate invariably deemed it necessary to resort to the use of the filibuster threat, the minority weapon *par excellence,* in order to win concessions for their point of view. When the voting on neutrality legislation came, as it usually did come, in the midst of a legislative docket already crowded with major proposals (frequently dealing with problems of domestic recovery and reform), the Administration leaders in Congress were understandably sensitive to the threat of filibuster. In such a situation it is not surprising that the Administration was willing to compromise with the isolationist bloc. As a result, until the autumn of 1939 (after general war had broken out in Europe), it was next to impossible to tell whether majority support for the Administration's views was or was not within its reach.

In any case, it is a matter of record that the isolationist groups, within and outside Congress, were strong enough and clever enough and in a sufficiently strategic position to win substantial concessions from the Administration from 1935 through 1939. And, when Congress' responsibility for the theory that we ought to try to keep out of war by means of legislation is evaluated, one of the striking facts is the immense amount of time that was devoted to discussion *within the limits* established by this theory. It is almost as if the Congressional mind had erected a mental block prohibiting serious consideration of any measures that might have been taken to try to prevent the outbreak of war. To anyone who feels at all sympathetic toward this latter objective, the worst feature of the neutrality laws and the whole neutrality debate in the 'thirties is the extent to which they diverted attention from this aspect of the problem. It is ironic that a people who pride themselves on their ability to experiment should have so confined their thinking, on this most challenging of all problems, within such narrow limits.

It is probably useless to speculate on what might have been accomplished if Congress had been able to call a halt and bring about a fundamental reexamination of the whole complex issue. But, of course, it was extremely difficult to call a halt once "neutrality" had assumed the guise of an emotional symbol. Once it had been placed on an emotional level, rational discussion was at a serious disadvantage, and expanding the limits within which rational discussion of the issue might be carried on was probably out of the question.

Psychologically, the existence of neutrality legislation had a decidedly unfortunate effect on popular thinking, which tended to assume that a difficult problem had been solved by means of drastic legislation. The existence of legislation that had as its purpose keeping the nation out of war tended to create the comfortable illusion that Americans were safe over here in their own land despite wars in Europe and Asia. It is hardly too much to say that neutrality legislation became the American Maginot line.

In addition to deluding the American people, neutrality legislation had the further unfortunate effect of misleading potential aggressor nations by giving them reason to assume that the United States was indifferent to the use of war as an instrument of national policy. Henry L. Stimson made the point extremely well in his testimony before the Senate Committee on Foreign Relations in 1939 when he said:

> . . . the American people are not insensible to cruelty and aggression. Nor are they so unintelligent that under conditions of today they cannot distinguish an aggressor nation from its victim. . . . Moreover, they are not a constitutionally timid people, nor are they smitten with such an inferiority complex as to make them wish their Government to avoid decisions which are really necessary to their own future interests. And this is the trouble, that the form of this statute today tends to make the outside world believe each one of these fantastic falsehoods and to guide their own policy in the light of that belief.[1]

III

Finally, in November 1939, after war had broken out in Europe, the Roosevelt Administration succeeded in its effort to remove the arms embargo provision from American neutrality legislation, replacing it with a cash-and-carry provision on arms. Thus, two months after the outbreak of general war in Europe, the President proposed and Congress accepted the revision of neutrality legislation in a manner calculated: (1) to aid that group of belligerents which shared the Western democratic tradition and whose existence was considered essential in the interests of American security; and (2) to reduce the possibility of "incidents" at sea involving American ships, goods, and lives as a means of avoiding entanglement as a belligerent in the European war.

Revisionist historians, unfortunately, are likely to concentrate their attention on this second purpose to the utter exclusion of the first. And, of course, if the 1939 Neutrality Act is considered exclusively in terms of the second purpose, it is perfectly clear that the measure had isolationist aspects which proposed to keep this country from becoming involved in the Second World War for causes which allegedly led us into the First World War. There can be no doubt that the American people in the autumn of 1939 did not want their nation to become a belligerent in the European war.

However, when we look at the same act from the point of view of the first purpose, and specifically when we view the provision that repealed the arms embargo and replaced it with a cash-and-carry provision, the conclusion is inescapable that the President and Congress, apparently supported by majority opinion, had decided to support the cause of

---

1. *Neutrality, Peace Legislation and Our Foreign Policy: Hearings Before the Committee on Foreign Relations,* U.S. Senate, 76th Congress, 1st Session, 1939, p. 7.

Britain and France in the war against aggressive and expanding German fascism. Thus, the decision of November 1939 was equally and significantly a decision *away* from isolationism, and this was a decision made by the President, the Congress, and the American people in the usual manner.

The decision was made in the autumn of 1939, shortly after Germany invaded Poland, to place the extensive productive capacity of the United States behind the cause for which Great Britain and France were already fighting. In this connection the fact is apt to be overlooked by revisionist historians that the isolationists in Congress apparently had no objection to placing all of our commerce, *except* arms and ammunition, on a cash-and-carry basis, although they knew perfectly well that such a policy would benefit Great Britain and France immensely. In the autumn of 1939, most Americans left it to the future to decide what should be done when Britain and France had exhausted their own financial resources, but for the present the American nation consciously, deliberately, and by the normal, democratic procedures, decided to become economically involved in the European war.

IV

Those who intend to make the effort to evaluate the Roosevelt foreign policy will do well to note the strong support which the philosophy of isolationism mustered in "progressive" and "liberal" quarters throughout the 1930's. It is one of the startling paradoxes of this period that many of the most enthusiastic supporters of the New Deal domestic program were outspokenly critical of the Roosevelt administration's foreign policy. Charles A. Beard was, of course, the outstanding intellectual spokesman of this brand of American progressivism, but he certainly did not stand alone. In Congress the Western progressives were lined up against the President's foreign policy almost to a man. When the crucial vote came late in October 1939 to repeal the arms embargo, Senator Norris of Nebraska was the only outstanding Western progressive or independent who voted to repeal the arms embargo. Senators Wheeler, Frazier, Nye, Shipstead, Lundeen, Hiram Johnson, La Follette, and Borah—all of whom in the past on many occasions had helped the President form a majority against the dissident conservative wing of his own party when domestic issues were at stake—were joined in opposition to the Roosevelt foreign policy.

As a matter of fact, it might be rather difficult to understand the strength of American isolationism in the 'thirties unless one were aware of the isolationist predilections of an influential branch of American progressivism during the same period. When one has come in contact with a full-blown version of isolationist-progressive doctrine, one realizes at once the powerful appeal it offered to men who cherished the "democratic dream." Fortunately, the Beards have left us a full statement of the philosophy of "continental Americanism" in *America in Midpassage,* a book that reveals most of the assumptions on which the thinking of the isolationist-progressives was based. In this book, the Beards undertook to define this school of thought, and the definition is worth quoting at some length. At the heart of the continentalist philosophy, the Beards write,

> . . . was the idea that through domestic measures, adopted by the democratic process, vast improvements could be and should be effected in American civilization, where at least one-third of the nation was ill-housed, ill-clothed, ill-nourished, and ill-educated; moreover, that this civilization could be defended in its continental home under prudent policies by small but appropriate military and naval establishments. Associated with the vision was the conviction that American democracy should not attempt to carry the Atlas load of the White Man's Burden in the form of imperialism all over the earth, or assume that it had the capacity, even with the best of good-will, to settle the difficult problems of European nations encrusted in the heritages of their long and sanguinary history. Its theories and sentiments were enclosed in such phrases as: let us keep out of the next world war; mind our own business; till our own garden; create the wealth; substitute abundance for scarcity; establish a sound and efficient domestic economy; make America a work of art.
>
> Although owing to the lack of a precise name, this . . . school of foreign policy was often described as isolationist by its critics, its defenders disowned the connotations of the kind of isolationist creed sponsored by Henry Cabot Lodge, Warren G. Harding, and Calvin Coolidge. They likewise refused to be battened down by the name "nationalist," with its chauvinist and military associations. . . . Surrendering shop-worn reliance upon imperialist pressures, moneylending, and huckstering abroad, they turned to the efficient, humanistic use of national resources and technical skills as a means for making a civilization on this continent more just, more stable, and more beautiful than anything yet realized.[2]

Who can doubt that here was a view for Americans who lived in the light of the democratic dream? This was the kind of thinking that most appealed to a good many American progressives in the decade before the Second World War. And yet, it is quite clear, the view was *restricted* to Americans who lived and worked for the ideal. Beardians might protest that their philosophy was not isolationist and their emphasis on

2. Charles A. and Mary Beard, *American in Midpassage* (New York: Macmillan, 1939), pp. 452–453.

domestic reform was not calculated to win the devotion of a Lodge, a Harding, or a Coolidge. They might also protest that their philosophy was not nationalistic, and who can doubt that it was shorn of its chauvinist and militarist connotations? But, protests notwithstanding, this was preeminently a philosophy of isolationism grounded in the rich soil of American nationalism.

It was certainly a doctrine without appeal to internationalists, with its assumption that America lacked the capacity to solve the difficult problems then facing mankind and, therefore, had no obligation to join in trying to solve them. At this point we need to remind ourselves that, according to the "continentalists," we Americans have a primary obligation to keep democracy alive and flourishing in "our own garden." There was the further assumption, not expressed here by the Beards, that the problems of the rest of the world, whatever their outcome, could not appreciably alter the future course of American democracy. Despite the protests of the Beards and their followers, this was obviously, and indeed, *openly*, a nationalist philosophy, with its challenge to make the American civilization "a work of art." Instead of engaging in the perpetual quarrels of Europe (and the war against Hitlerism was, of course, another in the endless series of foreign quarrels), Americans ought to apply "the efficient, humanistic use of national resources and technical skills" in order to build on this continent a civilization "more just, more stable, and more beautiful than anything yet realized."

This was clearly a vision to inspire Americans of progressive faith. In fact, so passionately was the faith held that men were encouraged to think of it as a dream intended *solely* for Americans. Combined with this faith in national democracy was an equally passionate hatred of war. Pacifism as a strand of American isolationism is a subject deserving careful analysis in its own right. And the normal pacifistic hatred of war for its own sake joined hands in the 'thirties with an equally profound fear of what might happen to our own democracy if we prepared to fight for democracy. Hatred of war, that is, pacifism, was one element in American isolationism, and the fear that war would bring totalitarianism was another. One hated to get involved in a war allegedly waged against totalitarianism when involvement seemed certain to bring about the establishment of totalitarianism at home. This was the worst charge the American progressive-isolationists could hurl at the Roosevelt foreign policy—that fighting totalitarianism would accomplish nothing worthwhile abroad and would precipitate the collapse of democracy at home. It was hard for many liberals in the 'thirties to see that the time might not be far off when they would have to participate in war (inherently an illiberal device) in order to give liberalism a chance to survive.

Charles A. Beard was typical of American progressives in general in his devotion to the objectives toward which the domestic New Deal was moving. Thus we find the following evaluation in *America in Midpassage:*

> It was well within the circle of factual description to say that in his numerous discourses Franklin D. Roosevelt discussed the basic human and economic problems of American society with a courage and range displayed by no predecessor in his office; that he thrust their challenges into spheres hitherto indifferent or hostile; that he set in swift circulation, through the use of the radio, ideas once confined to groups more or less esoteric; that he both reflected and stirred the thought of the nation to the uttermost borders of the land. And in doing this he carried on the tradition of humanistic democracy which from colonial times had been a powerful dynamic in the whole movement of American civilization and culture— economic, political, literary, scientific and artistic.[3]

Eight years later Dr. Beard was to conclude that, when this same President passed on, the way had been paved for an American Caesar to destroy the American democracy, so long in the building. He reached this conclusion after observing and studying Franklin D. Roosevelt as leader of the nation during the Second World War. In *President Roosevelt and the Coming of the War,* Dr. Beard asserts that if the precedents established by Franklin Roosevelt's conduct of foreign relations are to stand unmodified,

> . . . the Constitution may be nullified by the President, officials, and other officers who have taken the oath, and are under moral obligation to uphold it. For limited government under supreme law they may substitute personal and arbitrary government—the first principle of the totalitarian system against which, it has been alleged, World War II was waged—while giving lip service to constitutional government.[4]

3. *Ibid.,* p. 948.
4. Charles A. Beard, *President Roosevelt and the Coming of the War, 1941* (New Haven: Yale University Press, 1948), p. 584. For a detailed listing of the charges against President Roosevelt's conduct of foreign relations, see Chapter XVIII of the same book. A brief observation on Beard's charges may be in order. Professor Beard seems to assume that Franklin Roosevelt created all the precedents for the use of executive power in foreign relations. Actually, when Edward S. Corwin first published *The President's Control of Foreign Relations* (Princeton: Princeton University Press, 1917), thirty years before Beard constructed his criticism, he found ". . . an unlimited discretion in the President in the recognition of new governments and states; an undefined authority in sending special agents abroad, of dubious diplomatic status, to negotiate treaties or for other purposes; a similarly undefined power to enter into compacts with other governments without the participation of the Senate; the practically complete and exclusive discretion in the negotiation of more formal treaties, and in their final ratification; the practically complete and exclusive initiative in the official formulation of the nation's foreign policy" (pp. 205–206).

It is almost as though Dr. Beard were seeking to convince us that the progressive-isolationists were correct in the first place in asserting that intervention in World War II would inevitably lead to the destruction of democracy at home. And, as a result, Dr. Beard has left those who still cherish the vision and share the democratic dream (broadened in its applicability) in a terrible dilemma. Are the survivors of the Second World War to believe that another generation has been duped, misled, and unnecssarily led to slaughter? Are we to believe that Franklin Roosevelt, in pursuing the objectives of American foreign policy, either distorted or destroyed "the tradition of humanistic democracy" which had long been "a powerful dynamic in the whole movement of American civilization and culture"? [5]

For those who would seek to evaluate the Roosevelt foreign policy, the obvious fact has to be faced that American democracy was not destroyed in the process of fighting World War II, as many progressive-isolationists feared that it would be. Instead, the American democracy today shows signs of strength and vigor that would have seemed impossible in, let us say, 1932. More than that, a society of free men exists in Great Britain and France and the rest of Western Europe today, although the future of such a society also was in doubt in 1939 and was even more doubtful in the summer of 1940. So, far from destroying "democracy" at home and abroad, the policies of the Roosevelt administration evidently had something to do with keeping it alive in the world and may also have helped to invigorate it. Those who would undertake to evaluate the Roosevelt foreign policy will find it difficult to be critical of its purposes and accomplishments.

V

The major criticism, then, will probably be raised with respect to the methods used by the Roosevelt administration in formulating and carrying out that foreign policy within a system of democratic controls. And at this point, a study of the making of neutrality legislation in the years 1935 to 1939 will produce valuable evidence. In fact, it will not only throw light on some of the methods used, but it also will

5. The most complete and carefully reasoned refutation of Beard's thesis to appear up to this time is Basil Rauch's *Roosevelt, From Munich to Pearl Harbor* (New York: Creative Age Press, 1950). Rauch is convinced on the basis of his examination of the evidence that Beard's interpretation of the Roosevelt foreign policy is grounded on "omissions, distortions, and falsifications." If this evaluation seems harsh, the writer can only add that his analysis of the 1935–39 period would support essentially the same evaluation of Beard's *American Foreign Policy in the Making, 1932–1940* (New Haven: Yale University Press, 1946). See John C. Donovan, "Congress and the Making of Neutrality Legislation, 1935–1939," unpublished doctoral dissertation, Harvard University, 1949.

illuminate the general setting in which decisions were made, thus increasing our understanding of *why* they were made in the way they were made.

A careful study of the making of neutrality legislation will show, for example, that the President did indeed deliver addresses from time to time that must have been encouraging to American isolationists. The evidence also will show that the President was less than candid in explaining the objectives of American foreign policy on several occasions. On the other hand, the record also includes abundant evidence showing that the Roosevelt administration tried with fair consistency to obtain neutrality legislation which would leave a maximum of discretion in the hands of the Chief Executive in the conduct of foreign relations. And there was nothing very mysterious or secret about the Administration's efforts in this respect, as a reasonably careful reading of the *New York Times* will show.

It was certainly no secret that the Administration tried (and failed) to obtain legislative authorization for a discriminatory and discretionary arms embargo in 1933 and again in 1935. The evidence also is quite clear that the neutrality law of 1935 represented definite acquiescence on the part of the Chief Executive in a policy he did not favor and did not believe would work. It is worth remembering that, in signing the act, the President warned that situations might develop in which the "wholly inflexible provisions" of the act might drag the nation into war instead of keeping us out.

The record also reveals that by 1936 the Roosevelt Administration had discovered that the possibility of additional discretionary authority for the Chief Executive lay within the field of conditional contraband, and that the Administration then tried to obtain legislation embodying the normal-trade quota principle as a means toward the desired end. By 1937 the Administration shifted position slightly to favor the cash-and-carry principle, which was growing in popularity, again in order to retain as much discretion as possible for the Chief Executive in the conduct of foreign affairs.

The record also contains the "Quarantine" speech of October 5, 1937, which was both a candid and clear statement by the President in behalf of collective action against aggressors. The loud reaction to that speech in isolationist quarters suggests one of the major reasons for less frankness in a number of other presidential statements on foreign policy.

Not only was the general orientation of the Administration's foreign policy no great mystery, there was also impressive support for the President's contention that a maximum of discretion was rightfully his in the conduct of foreign relations. The Supreme Court's decision in the case of the *United States* vs. *Curtiss-Wright Export Company* in December 1936 had an immediate effect on Congressional thinking that was helpful to the Administration. The Court's opinion in the *Curtiss-*

Wright case recognized ". . . the very delicate, plenary and exclusive power of the President as the sole organ of the federal government in the field of international relations—a power which does not require as a basis for its exercise an act of Congress." [6] This special power of the President in the area of foreign affairs sprang from the fundamental difference between the powers of the federal government in respect to foreign affairs and those in respect to domestic affairs, the Court explained.

> It is quite apparent [the opinion continued] that if, in the maintenance of our international relations, embarrassment—perhaps serious embarrassment—is to be avoided and success for our aims achieved, congressional legislation which is to be made effective through negotiation and inquiry within the international field must often accord to the President a degree of discretion and freedom from statutory restriction which would not be admissible were domestic affairs alone involved. [7]

But apparently most of the isolationists in Congress retained their faith in a greater degree of legislative control of foreign policy than either the President or the Court was willing to admit. And the constant effort of the legislative branch, and especially of the isolationist group in Congress, to tighten the restrictions on executive discretion doubtless accounts in large measure for the unwillingness of the Chief Executive and the Secretary of State to deal with the question of American neutrality policy always in complete frankness.

On several occasions during 1938, the Administration abandoned opportunities to press for repeal of the arms embargo, evidently not wishing to stir up an acrimonious debate on foreign policy. In the first half of 1939, precious months slipped away before the Administration openly campaigned for repeal of the embargo provision. This was due in part to poor support from Senator Pittman, the supposed leader of the Administration forces in the Senate on this particular issue. This was not the first time that Senator Pittman had proved to be a less than satisfactory legislative lieutenant. And furthermore, the President was still reluctant to risk a divisive Congressional debate in view of the unsettled world situation.

The President and his Congressional supporters were unable to convince at least a determined minority in Congress that there was real danger of general European war in 1939. As a result, the first session of the Seventy-sixth Congress adjourned in the summer of 1939 without modifying the Neutrality Act of 1937, except for the cash-and-carry section which was allowed to expire on May 1, 1939. The Congress

6. 299 US 304 at 320.
7. *Ibid.*

of the United States, relying on its own judgment, was apparently convinced that war in Europe was not imminent, although by that time the President and the Secretary of State had pleaded vigorously that the danger was acute.

After the German invasion of Poland in September 1939, the Roosevelt administration moved swiftly and surely to bring about repeal of the arms embargo. In September 1939 the situation in Europe had clarified enough to make it difficult to accept the notion that Germany only wanted to gather "all the Germans" into the fatherland. By that time, the Administration was so thoroughly convinced of the urgent need to strengthen Britain and France militarily in order to protect the interests of American security that there was no longer a disposition to compromise with Congressional isolationists on the central issue. Furthermore, since Congress had been called into special session, the revision of neutrality legislation was the only task on the docket, and public support for the Administration's program was no longer a question mark.

But even in this case, neither the President nor the Secretary of State frankly and openly stated the reasons for the arms embargo repeal to Congress and the American people. The final evaluation of the Roosevelt foreign policy will almost certainly be critical of the Administration for its failure to clarify the issues behind this key decision in foreign affairs. If it had been in the interests of American security to strengthen Britain and France in a war with German fascism, then the leader of the nation should have made the issue as clear as he could. And yet it is to be hoped that the final evaluation will not be based on the assumption that a kind of cynical Machiavellian cunning prompted this lack of frankness. The evaluation of the Roosevelt foreign policy would be neither complete nor fair if it were to omit the fact that a well-organized, well-led, and extremely vocal opposition stood ready to use any frank statement from the Chief Executive on American foreign policy as ammunition against that foreign policy.

And it would be a mistake to assume that the President was cautious simply because he did not care to lose a debate. Here we must consider the fact that most of the leaders of the opposition were unconvinced even in October and November 1939 that German aggression constituted a threat to American security. On the other hand, the President had certain constitutional obligations and responsibilities as Commander-in-Chief that Congress did not share, and he was convinced in his own mind that such aggression *did* threaten American security. The historian, in weighing the factor of the President's special responsibilities as Chief Executive and Commander-in-Chief, will also note that the President had to assume most of the burden of trying to create a semblance of national unity in a time of grave international upheaval. It was doubtless a matter of grave concern to him that a bitter and prolonged debate on foreign policy might serve to widen the breach at home, a possibility that would be expected to delight the leaders of the German, Italian, and Japanese war machines. Individual congressmen, on the other hand, could be expected to pursue their prerogative to criticize with less sensitivity to the broader implications.

It is important to note, in this connection, that throughout this period the President in his difficult and delicate relations with Congress had to be constantly on guard,

> to avoid what Tolstoy called "the irrevocable act." He now carried a heavy share of the responsibility for the future history of the world. If he were to go before the Congress with a request for action on an issue of international importance and were defeated, it would involve more than gleeful editorials in the *Chicago Tribune* and possible losses for the Democratic party at the next election; it could well involve utter, world-wide disaster.[8]

Finally, attention ought to be paid to the fact that, despite the overwhelming desire of the American people to stay out of war, the decision was freely made in November 1939 by the Congress in the usual manner, and apparently with the majority of American people concurring, to revise our neutrality legislation in a way that would provide assistance to Britain and France against Nazi Germany. It is to be hoped that the future historian, in making his evaluation of American foreign policy, will avoid the temptation to oversimplify the independent creative role that is left to executive leadership in a modern democratic and constitutional setting. A study of the making of American foreign policy in the 1930's will reveal the extent to which such leadership is hedged in by public opinion and by the restrictions imposed on independent executive action by the presence of a national legislature which is jealous of its prerogatives.

Not only public opinion and the legislative branch restrict executive action. Also, the historian must consider the tendencies and traditions, the general consensus (the ideology, if you wish) of the people. The truth of the matter will be more nearly approached if the historian heeds the observation that:

> the men who are popularly said to "make history" are dealing with highly intractable material, that this material which includes the wills of their fellowmen, can be moulded only in accordance with certain existing trends, and that the statesman who fails to understand, and refuses to comply with, these trends dooms himself to sterility.[9]

8. Robert E. Sherwood, *Roosevelt and Hopkins* (New York: Harper, 1948), pp. 132–133.

9. E. H. Carr, *Conditions of Peace* (New York: Macmillan, 1942), p. 6.

Possibly we can make the phrase "tendencies and traditions" less ambiguous in the present case. Briefly, it is extremely doubtful that a future historian would dare to speculate that an "unneutral" President, intent upon foreign adventures as a means of surmounting domestic difficulties, would have had any chance of success in trying to take the United States into the Second World War on the side of Nazi Germany. President Roosevelt left his own great mark on history as an influential world leader, but he was also representative of, and reflected, the wills and efforts of millions of his fellow-countrymen, and he was unable to move except in the direction, and largely at the pace, they wanted to go.

JOHN McVICKAR HAIGHT, JR.

Roosevelt as Friend of France

Another central issue in the historiographical debate over American entry into World War II is whether Roosevelt was devious in his conduct of foreign policy. His detractors claim that he engaged in a policy of subterfuge, secretly aiding England, France, and China while publicly proclaiming his hatred of war and dedication to peace. Defenders of the President argue that he made a realistic compromise by placating isolationists with his public statements while protecting national security by aiding nations that opposed the Axis aggressors.

In this article John Haight shows how Roosevelt carried out this dual policy toward France before the outbreak of the war in Europe. Writing in 1966, Haight is primarily concerned with countering de Gaulle's criticism of prewar American neutrality. There is no general history of Franco-American relations in this period, but important issues are discussed in John McVickar Haight, Jr., "France, the United States and the Munich Crisis," Journal of Modern History, XXXII (December 1960), 340–348, and in Gordon Wright, "Ambassador Bullitt and the Fall of France," World Politics, X (October 1957), 63–90.

PRESIDENT CHARLES DE GAULLE, in discussing current Franco-American relations, often focuses upon the prewar neutrality of the United States as well as upon his wartime differences with President Franklin D. Roosevelt. In doing so he conjures up the image of an unreliable American ally. His recollections have also pushed into the background of public memory the two years before France's tragic collapse in June 1940, when, in the words of former Premier Edouard Daladier, "President Roosevelt was for France a very great and noble friend." As Premier during those years, Daladier witnessed at first hand the American President's efforts to help France order some 4,000 American combat planes to rebuild French defenses against the imminent attack of Hitler's vastly superior air power. Hitherto the details of the story have been wrapped in the secrecy of American and French archives, private papers, and personal memories, but it can now be seen that Roosevelt concentrated his principal effort on that aid because he believed that in

Reprinted by permission from *Foreign Affairs*, XLIV (April 1966), 518–526.

no other way could the United States strengthen France so significantly. Neither Morgenthau's monetary agreements nor the sale of machine tools and raw materials would do so much to increase French capacity to resist Nazi aggression. Roosevelt was ready to go as far as possible, in spite of isolationist opposition to the delivery of planes to France, because of his further conviction that, despite the Neutrality Act, the frontiers of the United States extended to the Rhine.

It was not until late 1937 that France seriously considered the purchase of American combat planes to help offset Germany's overwhelming aerial superiority. Since 1935, when Hitler tore up the Versailles Treaty and began to build his air forces, the German aircraft industry had adopted the latest aluminum construction techniques and turned out planes with heavier engines, higher altitudes, and faster speeds than the wood and canvas planes which still made up the majority of the French and British air forces. By the end of 1937 Germany possessed some 1,000 war planes of the latest type, and a French Senator, Baron Amaury de la Grange, did not exaggerate when he informed his Senate colleagues in late December that "German aviation can fly over our territory with impunity."

Shortly after the Senator made this statement, the French Government requested him to cross the Atlantic and determine how quickly the American aircraft industry could produce 1,000 modern planes. De la Grange was selected because of his broad knowledge of both French and American air power and because of his personal friendship with the President. He had first met Franklin Roosevelt when he married an American in 1913 and had seen him often during a tour of duty in Washington in 1918. As he had kept up this friendship, he easily arranged a visit at the White House for the weekend of January 15–16, 1938.

Senator de la Grange found the American President in a particularly receptive mood. Since his Chicago speech of October 1937, Roosevelt had been seeking ways to implement his plea that the peace-loving nations of the world should quarantine the aggressors. Though he had not named them, he privately lumped Germany, Italy, and Japan together at this time as the "three bandit nations." His concern grew in early November when the three officially joined together in the Anti-Comintern Pact and rumors spread that they were bound by new military agreements. He looked toward the Brussels conference of nations interested in the Far East to restrain Japan's undeclared war against China, but when the conference ended in a fiasco, the President sought other means to bring pressure on the aggressors.

Then in early December Japanese planes wantonly sank the U.S.S. *Panay* in the Yangtze River. Outraged, the President proposed to Britain a joint long-range naval quarantine of Japan and sent a naval officer to London to discuss the project. It was, in effect, laid to rest on January 14, however, when Prime Minister Neville Chamberlain asked the United States to join in recognizing Italy's conquest of Ethiopia. Chamberlain's preference for appeasement had blocked the President's search for a resistance policy. It was two days later that Senator de la Grange arrived to open a new avenue by which the United States might help the European democracies to resist the Fascist dictators.

On that Sunday afternoon, January 16, the President invited his French friend into his study and together they discussed the world situation. Roosevelt outlined his plan for a long-range naval quarantine of Japan running from Hong Kong to Manila and thence to Alaska. The Senator in his turn requested rapid delivery of 1,000 planes of the type then used by the American Army Air Corps. A letter de la Grange wrote immediately after this meeting summarizes his impressions of Roosevelt's reaction:

> It is his conviction that, more and more, Japan will depend on Germany and Italy and that, in order to contain the ambitions of these powers, England, France and America will be obliged to combine their efforts.
>
> The President will thus be completely in favor of all measures that the French Government might believe necessary to reinforce its air formations in time of peace and in time of war.[1]

The President also pointed out, added de la Grange, that the arms embargo embedded in the Neutrality Act would not permit France in time of war to replenish its supplies from the United States "with complete freedom." Nevertheless, after further discussion in Washington, de la Grange stated in his final report: "As long as the White House is occupied by Mr. Roosevelt, who is francophile and fears German expansion," France could expect a broad interpretation of the embargo. The Senator personally thought this might mean "surreptitious delivery via Canada." [2]

Senator de la Grange could not report optimistically about his goal "to harness American industry to the French war machine," for he soon discovered that the production of combat planes lagged even more in the United States than in France. Thus, he was finally forced to reveal, "It is regrettable that we cannot obtain in the United States beginning in 1938 a sufficient number of machines to reinforce our weak aviation." Only one plane appeared to measure up to France's needs, Curtiss-Wright's P-36 fighter. However, as the company's production line was just beginning to turn out the first of the 200 ordered by the American Air Corps, France would have to finance a new assembly

1. Letter from Senator de la Grange to Senator Joseph Caillaux, Jan. 21, 1938. De la Grange Papers, held by the Senator's widow in Paris.
2. Final Report on American Mission, Feb. 15, 1938. De la Grange Papers.

line, from which no more than 100 could be shipped before March 1939.

The need for fighters was so great that the French Government favored ordering the 100 P-36s. However, the threat that delivery might be halted by the arms embargo just when a belligerent France needed them most remained a stumbling block. In late February, Edouard Daladier, then the Defense Minister, discussed this problem with the American Ambassador, William C. Bullitt, who agreed to go to Washington to determine whether President Roosevelt would be as helpful as de la Grange predicted. Bullitt's suggestion that Jean Monnet accompany him as Daladier's representative gave this Frenchman his first opportunity to see the President in action.

Bullitt has recalled for this author that he and Monnet crossed the ocean on the same boat, but in order to avoid attention neither gave any sign of recognition to the other until they arrived in the President's study. There, in answer to Daladier's problem, Roosevelt told Bullitt to assure him that he was already campaigning for repeal of the arms embargo and expecting success. He hoped that the threat to ship American arms to the European democracies would make the Fascist dictators pause before launching a war. However, if war did come before the embargo could be repealed, the President said he would rush through the necessary revision of the Neutrality Act. If worse came to worst and he failed in this final effort, he had one last means of getting around the embargo, which specifically forbade flying planes out of the United States to a belligerent country. He would have the planes pushed across the border into Canada. He told Bullitt to search for areas where planes could land on the American side, and he sketched a map indicating likely places. Before leaving, Monnet requested the map as a memento and, with a characteristic grin, Roosevelt handed it to him. Though the map was later destroyed, it provided Monnet in the spring of 1938 with documentary evidence of Roosevelt's attitude toward the arms embargo.[3]

Obviously, the President had made no official commitment to the French Government; he had stated only his personal intentions. However, Guy La Chambre, who was French Minister for Air from early 1938 until March 1940, remembers that those expressed intentions were accepted for fact. Thus after becoming Premier in April 1938, Daladier decided to run the risk of having the P-36s rust on American docks and approved both the order for 100 and an option for an additional 300. It was in recalling this series of incidents that Daladier wrote recently to the present author, "President Roosevelt was for France a very great and noble friend."

3. When asked recently about this sketch, M. Monnet wrote, "I am very much afraid I cannot find the sketch of the airfield on the New York State–Canadian border. My prewar archives were burnt in Cognac during the war."

Daladier and La Chambre turned to President Roosevelt again that spring of 1938 because widespread opposition to the purchase of American planes had sprung up within France. The Finance Minister, Georges Bonnet, objected to the expenditure of France's limited gold reserves as required by the "cash-and-carry" clause of the Neutrality Act. Criticism also came from the Chamber of Deputies and the French press, as well as from labor and management in the aircraft industry. Most serious of all, technicians within the French Air Ministry doubted whether the export model of the P-36 would meet European combat conditions. Believing that other criticisms would be silenced if this last one were proved erroneous, the Minister for Air decided to send France's leading test pilot, Michael Detroyat, to the United States to fly the plane and make first-hand observations.

Permission for such a flight ran into direct opposition from the U.S. Air Corps. As deliveries of the P-36 had not begun, the Air Corps still wrapped its three prototypes in secrecy. Typical of its position was a memorandum written by General H. H. Arnold, then the Assistant Chief of the Air Corps. After listing some dozen specific reasons why the French should not be permitted to fly the P-36, he concluded: "M. Detroyat is an engineer of unusual ability, a skilled test pilot and a skilled pilot of racing planes. He could learn more in twenty minutes alone in this plane than the average engineer could learn from a week's study of both the plane and its blueprints." [4]

President Roosevelt, who had a broader view of the international situation, provided the French with the first evidence that he could act as well as talk. He ordered the Army Chief of Staff to make secret arrangements for Detroyat to fly a P-36 "for just twenty minutes." As Arnold predicted, that was ample time to convince the French pilot of its merits; he reported to Paris that the Curtiss fighter was equal not only to France's prototypes but also to the operational model of the Messerschmitt 109, Germany's newest front-line fighter. The opposition of the French technicians crumbled and in mid-May France signed a contract for 100 P-36s.

The French Government's original expectations of obtaining 1,000 planes had been frustrated, but it could find some comfort in the fact that a British air mission which toured the United States in the spring of 1938 also concluded that only the P-36 could measure up to Germany's current fighters. Even after this mission had obtained President Roosevelt's special clearance to fly the B-18, the Air Corps' medium bomber, it recommended that Britain order no war planes but rather 200 trainers and 200 transports, the latter being adequate for coastal patrol duty far from the battle lines.

4. Memo from Gen. Arnold to Army Chief of Staff, Gen. Marlin Craig, Mar. 9, 1938, Adjutant General's Office, File 452 (3-9-38). Washington: National Archives, Record Group 94.

Despite the inferiority of American combat aviation, France turned again to the United States for further purchases after the Czechoslovakian crisis of September 1938. At this moment, when Hitler led Europe to the brink of war by demanding the annexation of the Sudetenland, the French Air Force was terribly inferior to the German *Luftwaffe*. According to official records, the French possessed but 17 planes which could match the performance of the hundreds poised on the Rhine frontier.[5] No wonder the French Chief of Staff for Air, General Vuillemin, informed the Government on September 26 that "only with great difficulty and at the price of heavy losses" could his Air Force fulfill its mission. If anyone was bluffing at Munich, it was Premier Daladier.

On September 30 Prime Minister Chamberlain returned to Britain to announce "peace in our time," but the French Premier took a more realistic view. On October 3 he called in Ambassador Bullitt, who subsequently cabled Washington: "Daladier sees the situation entirely, clearly, and realizes fully that the meeting in Munich was an immense diplomatic defeat for France and England." The Premier also requested Ambassador Bullitt to leave as soon as possible for the United States to make another effort to help France build up its air defenses. Bullitt arrived in Washington late in the evening of October 13 and went directly to the White House, where his talk with the President continued into the small hours. Later that morning of October 14, the President electrified a press conference by calling for a vast rearmament of the United States. As reports circulated that the President gave priority to air power and aimed at an American production of 20,000 planes, the suspicion grew that he sought such large quantities of planes in order to divert them to Britain and France and thus strengthen their defenses against Hitler's Third Reich.

The truth of these rumors can now be understood on the basis of a discussion which the President had with Jean Monnet, Ambassador Bullitt, and Secretary of the Treasury Henry J. Morgenthau, Jr., on October 25. Monnet recalls that Roosevelt first spoke forcefully about the Nazi challenge to liberty and the danger that Hitler would resort to force in his drive to rule the world. The President then estimated that Germany had the capacity to turn out 40,000 planes while Britain could produce only 25,000 and France 15,000; he felt the United States should develop a 20,000 capacity in order to achieve overwhelming superiority.

It is significant that the President used exactly the same figures the week before during a discussion at Hyde Park with Arthur C. Murray,

5. "Procès-Verbal de Comité de Matériel," Sept. 29, 1938, filed in Box B/104 in the archives of the Service Historique de l'Armée de l'Air at Versailles.

a member of the House of Commons and a prominent Liberal. The President added that these 20,000 American planes would provide "the necessary overwhelming superiority over Germany and Italy." He went on to discuss with Murray how Britain could obtain its share of the new planes and concluded by sending the assurance to Chamberlain, "I will help all I can." [6]

Monnet's report to the Daladier Government reveals that during the White House meeting President Roosevelt had joined in the discussion as to how many planes could be produced for France. The estimate was that in a year's time the American aviation industry, "with certain but not excessive augmentation," could deliver some 1,000 pursuit planes and 1,000 bombers. There were two conditions: "Such deliveries presuppose that only existing American models would be used and that the types would be limited to one or at the most two for bombers and pursuits." [7]

While Premier Daladier welcomed the prospect of obtaining large quantities of American planes, Prime Minister Chamberlain, despite a Royal Air Force recommendation that the United States be aided in developing production, approved the purchase of only 200 additional trainers. The French Premier spelled out his plans to his National Defense Council on December 5. "We presently have the possibility of receiving about 1,000 planes of the latest model in use by the American Army. The American Government has formally promised delivery but it must be kept absolutely secret." He went on: "Our aerial inferiority is tragic. One thousand American bombers are necessary." [8] The Finance Ministry, now under Paul Reynaud, again opposed the expenditure of gold necessary in the "cash-and-carry" transaction and refused to increase the budget. However, by the end of the week Daladier had juggled the budget sufficiently to provide the required funds and directed Monnet to proceed with his American negotiations.

In mid-December, when Monnet returned to Washington to arrange the purchase of the 1,000 bombers, the White House suggested that he avoid opposition by working quietly through Secretary Morgenthau under the pretense that the sale of planes to France was a commercial matter. Morgenthau shared Roosevelt's conviction about the need to strengthen France, and as one of Monnet's colleagues wrote in early 1939, Treasury officials "never ceased aiding the mission." [9] Opposition came from other

6. Lord Elibank (formerly Arthur C. Murray), "Franklin Roosevelt: Friend of Britain," *Contemporary Review,* June 1955, pp. 364–67.

7. Monnet Memorandum, dated Nov. 14, 1938, filed as #6 in "Commandes Américaines" in the private papers held in Paris by Guy La Chambre, Minister for Air, 1938–1940.

8. Gamelin, "Servir," v. 2, "La Prologue de Drame (1930–août 1939)." Paris: Plon, 1946, pp. 371–78.

9. "Final Report, Air Mission to America," Dec.–Jan. 1938, filed as #9 bis in "Commandes Américaines.'" La Chambre Papers.

sources. First, the French technicians who accompanied Monnet soon concluded that none of the American bombers currently in production and released for foreign sale could survive European war conditions. However, on December 21 they learned from the Treasury that two light bombers were being developed for an Air Corps competition by Glenn Martin and Douglas. Monnet immediately requested clearance for his technicians to study the specifications of these bombers.

Recognizing that this request would run into powerful opposition from the Air Corps, Morgenthau went over to the White House. He forcefully backed the French request by referring directly to the President's own attitude toward aid to the European democracies: "If it's your theory that England and France are our first line of defense . . . let's either give them good stuff or tell them to go home, but don't give them some stuff which the minute it goes up in the air will be shot down. No sense in selling them that which we know is out of date." Roosevelt accepted this argument and wrote the following note on Morganthau's memorandum requesting release of the two bombers: "This is O.K. for reasons of state . . . should be kept as confidential as possible and the French orders filled so as not to interfere with the United States' new orders this spring." [10]

After a Cabinet meeting that afternoon, the President persuaded Secretary of War Woodring to give grudging approval to the release. Trouble came when General Arnold, now the Chief of the Air Corps, was informed. He was convinced that the sale of the bombers to France would upset the Air Corps' new expansion program and fought to retain the Douglas bomber, believing it the better of the two. Air Force archives reveal that from December 21, when the General first heard of the French interest, until mid-January, he threw every possible obstacle into the path of the French negotiations for the Douglas plane. His tactics ended only on January 1, 1939, when the President called a conference of all interested service officials. After Roosevelt reiterated his wish that every effort be made to assist the French air mission, he turned to Ambassador Bullitt, who spoke eloquently of time running out and of the need to aid France in building its air defenses. Secretary Woodring hedged and referred to his isolationist friends in Congress who might embarrass the President if the plane were released. It was a tense meeting and Roosevelt got his dander up. The upshot was that he signed a formal order and addressed it separately to the Secretaries of War, Navy, and Treasury. It included the terse phrase, "You are directed" and implied compliance or resignation.

Under this pressure, General Arnold granted the release and Monnet

10. John M. Blum, *From the Morgenthau Diaries*, v. II, *Years of Urgency, 1938–1941*. Boston: Houghton Mifflin, 1964, p. 65.

sent two French representatives out to California in order to satisfy the Air Ministry's requirement to test the new bomber. After watching a flight demonstration, the French test pilot, Captain Paul Chemedlin, irritated the Douglas test pilot with some caustic observations. The American, as General Arnold later reported, decided to "make the Frenchman eat his words or, in other words, to give the Frenchman a ride," and Chemedlin was invited to climb into the after-section of the bomber. The plane was put through its usual paces, but to provide further proof of its maneuverability the pilot brought the bomber down to 400 feet and feathered one engine. He then made a sharp right turn, with the dead engine on the lower wing, and followed this with a snap roll. The plane, pushed too far, stalled. Tragically, the American pilot was killed when his chute failed to open, but miraculously the Frenchman rode the plane down and survived the crash. A compatriot rushed up and, pushing his way through the crowd of bystanders, began excitedly to speak in his native language. The secret was out.

The publicity given to the crash of the Douglas bomber with a French observer on board thoroughly alerted the American public to the fact that the United States was providing aid to the European democracies. In an effort to upset the isolationist argument that such aid would lead the nation down the road to war, President Roosevelt invited to the White House the Senate Military Affairs Committee, which was investigating the presence of the Frenchman in what one of the Committee members called "the very latest word in American plane construction." According to a contemporary account by Joseph Alsop and Robert Kintner, the President at this meeting on January 31 tried to establish the fact that France and Britain were the first line of America's defense.

> He began by painting the dark picture of Europe, describing the German ambitions in the most lively terms, stating that Hitler would not be thwarted, warning that war was imminent. War, he said, . . . would directly affect "the peace and safety of the United States. The immediate struggle," he went on, "was for the domination of Europe, but so soon as one nation dominates Europe, that nation will be able to turn to the world sphere."

After reviewing the German challenges to eastern and western Europe, the President added:

> "That is why the safety of the Rhine frontier does necessarily interest us."
> "Do you mean that our frontier is on the Rhine?" asked one of the Senators . . .
> "No, not that. But practically speaking if the Rhine frontiers

are threatened the rest of the world is too. Once they have fallen before Hitler, the German sphere of action will be unlimited." [11]

It was too strong medicine for many of the assembled Senators. Instead of persuading them to curtail their investigations and support the sale of planes to France, Roosevelt only fanned the isolationist conviction that he was pushing the nation toward war. The secrecy with which he attempted to surround his comments was broken. The strength of the nationwide outcry against what was called extension of the American frontiers to the Rhine prompted the President to back down. Three days later he issued a denial. From a position of leadership Roosevelt retreated into a waiting position of silence.

Monnet's mission was permitted to sign contracts for the new bombers, but, because of the prospect that delivery would be slow, only 100 of each were initially ordered. At the same time, France exercised its option for P-36s and ordered an additional 100 of these fighters. Once again the limited capacity of the American aircraft industry limited France's efforts to secure American aid.

What was perhaps of prime significance for French leaders that winter of 1938–39 was that their negotiations for American planes had proved the sympathy of President Roosevelt and his closest advisers. Though in public he might feel forced to deny that England and France were the first line for the defense of the United States and that the American frontiers thus extended to the Rhine, the leaders of France knew that this belief was in fact the basis of his European policy. While the Air Corps and the isolationists might continue to oppose the sale of other new planes to the European democracies, Daladier, Guy La Chambre, and Jean Monnet were now assured that the American President would, when the time came, do all in his power to aid France. And this in fact Roosevelt did.

When war broke out in September 1939, a third French air mission rushed to the United States and, even while Congress debated the repeal of the arms embargo, secretly and successfully negotiated the purchase of 1,000 combat planes to be delivered by the end of 1940. Of even greater significance for the expansion of the American aircraft industry, France agreed to invest $10 million, a huge sum in those days, to double production of engines, the current bottleneck. In March 1940, patient and careful persuasion by Jean Monnet led Prime Minister Chamberlain's Government to agree to share equally with France in the purchase of 4,300 American fighters and bombers. The larger order, as Premier Daladier had stated in December 1939, aimed to obtain

11. Joseph Alsop and Robert Kintner, *American White Paper: The Story of American Diplomacy and the Second World War.* New York: Simon & Schuster, 1940, pp. 30–31.

"absolute dominance in the air" over Germany. The Premier had been so determined that France make this purchase that he was ready "to make every French resource available to obtain these planes . . . Versailles or any other possession of the French Government." [12]

The ultimate significance of the French and British orders was underscored by the official Army Air Forces history: "The initial expansion of the American aircraft industry in 1939–1940, and one which was of great benefit to the country, was paid for by Great Britain." [13] Secretary Morgenthau claimed that this investment speeded American production of war planes by a crucial 12 to 18 months. Though the planes did not arrive in time to protect France's frontiers on the Rhine from Hitler, they contributed directly to speeding France's liberation in 1944.

Today many Frenchmen, influenced by President de Gaulle's wartime relations with President Roosevelt, remember him less as "a very great and noble friend" than as an essentially hostile ally. Many persons believe that the wartime incompatibility of de Gaulle and Roosevelt is at the base of current Franco-American differences. To whatever extent this is true, contemporary French feeling against America can perhaps be dissipated by recalling President Roosevelt's aid to France in ordering the planes needed so desperately for defense. Indeed, the memory of that Franco-American cooperation has greatly influenced the policy stressed since the war by Jean Monnet. While President de Gaulle has urged what would in effect be the withdrawal of the United States across the Atlantic, Monnet has argued for the maintenance of Roosevelt's frontiers in Europe in both an economic and military sense. Perhaps Franco-American cooperation on that basis will be aided if people will recognize President Roosevelt's courage, conviction, and foresight in attempting, as early as January 1938, to pry open the American arsenal for the benefit of France.

12. Ambassador William C. Bullitt to the Secretary of State, Nov. 23, 1939, in *Foreign Relations of the United States, 1939,* v. II. Washington: G.P.O., 1956, pp. 520–22.

13. *Army Air Forces in World War II,* v. VI *Men and Planes,* eds. W. F. Craven and J. L. Cate, pt. 2, Alfred Goldberg, "Equipment and Services." Chicago: University of Chicago Press, 1955, p. 191.

CHARLES A. BEARD

"In Case of Attack"
in the Atlantic

Charles Beard leveled the most serious charges against FDR's foreign policy in his book President Roosevelt and the Coming of the War, 1941 *(New Haven, 1948). Beard claimed that Roosevelt had made a moral commitment during the 1940 presidential campaign to keep the nation out of war. Not only had the President run on a platform promising not to send American troops to fight overseas "except in case of attack," but in a speech in Boston on October 30 he had flatly declared, "Your boys are not going to be sent into any foreign wars." Yet throughout 1941, according to Beard, Roosevelt deliberately sought ways to escape from his campaign pledge and enter the war in Europe.*

This selection, taken from Chapter Five of Beard's book, focuses on the Battle of the Atlantic. In the spring of 1941 Roosevelt had extended American naval patrols halfway across the Atlantic to help restrict German submarine attacks on English shipping, but he refused to permit American destroyers to escort British convoys, as many of his advisers urged. More orthodox accounts of Roosevelt's policy in the Atlantic are given in William L. Langer and S. Everett Gleason, The Undeclared War, 1940–1941 *(New York, 1953); Robert E. Sherwood,* Roosevelt and Hopkins *(New York, 1948); and Samuel Eliot Morison,* The Battle of the Atlantic *(Boston, 1947).*

ACCORDING TO President Roosevelt's reports to Congress and the Press, no new commitments had been made at the Atlantic Conference, nor was the country any closer to war. Not even an appearance of retreat from the peace and neutrality pledges of 1940 had been indicated by the President's public announcements on his return home. Americans eager to have their country get into the fight at once were dissatisfied. Clark Eichelberger, distinguished advocate of world peace, speaking for the Committee to Defend America by Aiding the Allies, expressed disappointment "that a plan of action against Hitler had not been made,"

Reprinted by permission from Charles A. Beard, *President Roosevelt and the Coming of the War, 1941: A Study in Appearances and Realities* (New Haven, 1948), pp. 133–149. Copyright © 1948 by Yale University Press.

and then he declared: "We must point out with all possible vigor that the United States will have a right to participate in the building of the future world peace if it will make its full contribution to the defeat of the aggressors. Consequently our participation in the conflict should be speeded up." [1]

The Troublesome "Escape" Clause

It is possible that Mr. Eichelberger, in demanding that "our participation in the conflict be speeded up," was speaking in the name of President Roosevelt; for, during the previous months, managers of the Committee to Defend America by Aiding the Allies had covertly kept in touch with the Administration and, with its approval, had acted as propaganda agents in creating favorable public sentiment for its projects in advance of official announcements respecting them from Washington.[2] In other words, when President Roosevelt wished to make one of his "complicated moves" he sometimes privately cooperated with this committee in the business of stirring up an agitation for the move before he deemed the time ripe to make an official acknowledgment of it.

President Roosevelt, however, was not free to make a public demand, in Mr. Eichelberger's style, for speeding up "our participation" in the conflict. The antiwar plank of the Democratic platform, to which he had committed himself in the campaign of 1940, read: "We will not participate in foreign wars . . . except in case of attack." [3] Under this obligation, if such obligations publicly assumed had any moral force, President Roosevelt could call upon the country and Congress to "participate" in the war only in case of an attack. Of this covenant the President was poignantly conscious, for he repeatedly referred to the word "attack" in his public addresses and statements during the year 1941 and more than once he sought to interpret it out of existence as a restraint upon his powers, by giving it an illimitable definition.

To most members of the Democratic convention at Chicago who accepted and approved this conditional antiwar plank, and probably to most American citizens who read it, the plank had a plain meaning.

1. Walter Johnson, *The Battle against Isolation*, p. 218.

2. The inside story of the committee's secret relations with President Roosevelt, Secretary Hull, and other members of the Administration in "softening up" the people for participation in the war is told with gusto by the historian of the committee, Walter Johnson, *op. cit., passim*. In advertising this work, the University of Chicago Press, as if in a novel interpretation of the functions of scholarship, declared: "Isolationism, which here stands condemned by its own lies, must not have another chance." See the jacket of the book.

3. For origin and nature of the antiwar plank, see Beard, *American Foreign Policy in the Making*, pp. 291 ff.

It meant and could only mean to scrupulous minds that if the Democrats were victorious in the coming election, they would not allow the United States Government to participate in foreign wars, unless American territory, shipping, or other possessions were made the object of an unwarranted, unprovoked attack by the armed forces of some foreign power. In case of such an attack, the President had power, on his own motion, to use the armed forces of the United States to repel the assault or invasion,[4] and could call upon Congress for a declaration of war. In the absence of such an attack, on the other hand, if he deemed war against a foreign government to be necessary and proper owing to changed circumstances or for any other reason,[5] he was bound by his commitment to the plank and by the Constitution to appeal to Congress for a legal sanction to employ the armed forces in war, inside and outside of the Americas.

It is possible, of course, that President Roosevelt entertained a disingenuous view of the conditional clause, "except in case of attack," when he bound himself to the antiwar plank during the campaign of 1940. The words had been added to the original draft of the plank on the insistence of his representatives at the Democratic convention and he may have then thought that thereby the antiwar part of the covenant would be or could be rendered innocuous by explication. In any case, however, during the campaign of 1940, the President made no public interpretation of the conditional clause which indicated that he might, after all, have some *arrière-pensée* in respect of it, that he contemplated reducing it to an absurdity by giving it a capricious definition hitherto unknown to lexicography, international law, or diplomacy.

If the President had in 1940 no reservations respecting the meaning of the term "attack," he acquired them sometime in 1941, certainly as early as May 27, for, in a public address on that day, he declared in effect that an attack calling for defensive action on the part of the United States did not necessarily mean a warlike assault by a foreign power on anything belonging to the United States but could "begin by the domination of any base which menaces our security—north or south":

> *I have said on many occasions that the United States is mustering its men and its resources only for purposes of defense—only to repel attack. I repeat that statement now.* But we must be realistic when we use the word "attack"; we have to relate it to the lightning speed of modern warfare.

2 Black, 635 (1863).

5. See *President Roosevelt and the Coming of the War*, Chapter I, pp. 3 ff.

4. See, for instance, the opinion of Mr. Justice Grier in the Prize Cases,

Some people seem to think that we are not attacked until bombs actually drop on New York or San Francisco or New Orleans or Chicago. But they are simply shutting their eyes to the lesson we must learn from the fate of every nation that the Nazis have conquered.

The attack on Czechoslovakia began with the conquest of Austria. The attack on Norway began with the occupation of Denmark. The attack on Greece began with occupation of Albania and Bulgaria. The attack on the Suez Canal began with the invasion of the Balkans and North Africa. The attack on the United States can begin with the domination of any base which menaces our security—north or south.

Nobody can foretell tonight just when the acts of the dictators will ripen into attack on this hemisphere and us. But we know enough by now to realize that it would be suicide to wait until they are in our front yard.

When your enemy comes at you in a tank or a bombing plane, if you hold your fire until you see the whites of his eyes, you will never know what hit you. Our Bunker Hill of tomorrow may be several thousand miles from Boston.

Anyone with an atlas and a reasonable knowledge of the sudden striking force of modern war knows that it is stupid to wait until a probable enemy has gained a foothold from which to attack. Old-fashioned common sense calls for the use of a strategy which will prevent such an enemy from gaining a foothold in the first place.

We have, accordingly, extended our patrol in North and South Atlantic waters. We are steadily adding more and more ships and planes to that patrol. It is well known that the strength of the Atlantic fleet has been greatly increased during the past year, and is constantly being built up. . . .[6]

Approaching the troublesome word "attack" more boldly in July, 1941,[7] President Roosevelt attenuated the interpretation of it which he had given on May 27, 1941. As if recalling the language of the antiwar plank and yet without mentioning it by name, he spoke of the very idea as now obsolete. "There was a time," he said, "when we could afford to say that we would not fight unless attacked"; and he immediately added: "Modern techniques of warfare have changed all that." Here he seemed to be contending that the Democratic pledge

---

6. Arthur L. Funk, *Roosevelt's Foreign Policy, 1933–1941*, pp. 399 f. (Italics supplied.)

7. Introduction to *Public Papers,* 1940 Volume, dated July 17, 1941, p. xxxi.

against war "except in case of attack" was out of date when made in 1940 or had become untenable since that year or did not mean what it seemed to mean. The President's exegesis of July, 1941, read:

> Modern warfare has given us a new definition for that word "attack." There was a time when we could afford to say that we would not fight unless attacked, and then wait until the physical attack came upon us before starting to shoot. Modern techniques of warfare have changed all that. An attack today is a very different thing. An attack today begins as soon as any base has been occupied from which our security is threatened. That base may be thousands of miles away from our own shores. The American Government must, of necessity, decide at which point any threat of attack against this hemisphere has begun; and to make their stand when that point has been reached.

Evidently, President Roosevelt did not, in July, 1941, regard the word "attack" as necessarily implying an act of war at all against the United States—a physical assault in the form of shooting at or bombing the territory, shipping, or other possessions of the United States; for he said: "An attack *begins* as soon as *any base* has been occupied from which *our security* is *threatened*." (Italics supplied.) Since he added that this base might be thousands of miles away from our shores, he evidently meant that he could regard an attack on the United States as *beginning,* that is, as constituting an attack, if made on the territory of some foreign country thousands of miles away from the United States, not on any possessions of the United States. If this is what the word "attack," as used in the conditional clause of the Democratic antiwar plank, was actually intended to convey by its authors—representatives of President Roosevelt at Chicago—then it is noteworthy that no such explanation of the term was offered to the public by the President during his campaign of 1940 for the votes of the American people.

Although the interpretation of the word "attack," announced publicly by the President in July, 1941, seemed explicit in itself, the last sentence of his statement, bearing on action to be taken by the United States "in case of attack," was really open to a diversity of constructions. There, he said, *the American Government* must, of necessity, decide at which point *any threat* of attack against this hemisphere has *begun,* and to *make "their" stand* when that point has been reached. In ordinary usage the words "the American Government" mean the Legislative, Executive, and Judicial Departments of the federal system. Under the Constitution this is the proper usage; for the Constitution, Article I, Section 8, so indicates in speaking of the "powers vested by this Constitution in the Government of the United States, or in any Department or Officer thereof."

Did President Roosevelt intend to include Congress in his conception when he thus spoke of "the American Government"? Or was he referring to the Executive alone? Did he intend to imply that a mere *threat* of an attack on *this hemisphere,* as distinguished from an attack, would, of necessity, bring about American armed action against the authors of the threat? The text of his statement afforded no answers to these pertinent questions. Not until some of his "complicated moves" in the autumn of 1941 had produced results did President Roosevelt give intimations of the realities covered by his conception of the word "attack."

Appearances and Realities of the Attack on the *U.S.S.* Greer *(September)*

The hopes of those who were working to speed up American participation in the war by aiding the Allies were raised to a high pitch in September, 1941, not by an Executive appeal to Congress for a declaration of war on Hitler, but by events at sea. On September 4, the Navy Department announced that a submarine of undetermined nationality had attacked the American destroyer *Greer* that morning in the Atlantic on its way to Iceland; that torpedoes had been fired at the vessel; that the *Greer* had counterattacked by dropping depth charges, with unknown results. The destroyer, the department explained, was operating as a part of the Atlantic patrol established during the summer by President Roosevelt and was carrying mail. Was this the "attack" [8] that would emancipate President Roosevelt from his commitment to the Democratic plank of 1940 against participating in foreign wars "except in case of attack"?

On September 5, cables from Iceland reported that the *Greer* had arrived safely, that the incident was described as a German attack, and that the destroyer had been aided in repelling the attack by British aircraft, cooperating in the reconnaissance. It was also announced in the press that President Roosevelt had issued orders to the Navy to search out and "eliminate" the submarine which attacked the *Greer,* and that he considered the attack as deliberate. The President hinted that it might have been the work of a German submarine.

From Berlin came a German official version of the affair. The German version asserted that the attack had not been initiated by the German submarine; on the contrary, it contended, the submarine had

8. See *President Roosevelt and the Coming of the War,* p. 3. The evidence on which this narration of events is based appeared in the *New York Times,* September 5, 6, 7, 9, 12, 13, 14, 1941.

been attacked with depth bombs, pursued continuously in the German blockade zone, and assailed by depth bombs until midnight. The German statement concluded: "Roosevelt thereby is endeavoring with all the means at his disposal to provoke incidents for the purpose of baiting the American people into the war." The Navy Department quickly denied the German allegations and stated that the initial attack in the engagement had been made by the German submarine.

For days the war of words went on in the press, American and Axis, while anxious observers in the United States waited for an official statement by President Roosevelt. The statement came on September 11 in the form of a radio broadcast.

The *Greer*, the President said, "was carrying American mail to Iceland. She was flying the American flag. Her identity as an American ship was unmistakable. She was then and there attacked by a submarine. Germany admits that it was a German submarine. . . . I tell you the blunt fact that the German submarine fired first upon this American destroyer without warning, and with deliberate design to sink her"—at a point southeast of Greenland.

"We have sought no shooting war with Hitler," the President continued.

> We do not seek it now. . . . In the waters which we deem necessary for our defense, American naval vessels and American planes will no longer wait until Axis submarines lurking under water, or Axis raiders on the surface of the sea, strike their deadly blow—first. . . . The aggression is not ours. Ours is solely defense. But let this warning be clear. From now on, if German or Italian vessels of war enter the waters, the protection of which is necessary for American defense, they do so at their own peril. The orders which I have given as Commander in Chief to the United States Army and Navy are to carry out that policy—at once. . . . There will be no shooting unless Germany continues to seek it. . . . I have no illusions about the gravity of this step. . . . It is the result of months and months of constant thought and anxiety and prayer. . . .[9]

But, while the President stated that the Navy would not wait for Axis vessels to strike first, he did not invoke the escape clause of the Democratic antiwar plank and call upon Congress to authorize war; he announced, in effect, that as Commander in Chief, he was directing affairs relative to shooting in the Atlantic. Nor, indeed, were signs in Washington propitious for an invocation of the clause; for alert

9. Funk, *op. cit.*, pp. 470 ff.

journalists and members of Congress in the City of Rumors thought they had ground for believing that the President's account of the attack on the *Greer,* if not false, was lacking in exactitude and comprehensiveness. Stirred by the allegations and counter-allegations, the Senate Committee on Naval Affairs prepared to hold a hearing on the attack and sent a list of pointed questions to Admiral Harold R. Stark, Chief of Naval Operations, designed to secure a full official record of the *Greer* case.

In a letter to Senator David I. Walsh, chairman of the Senate Committee on Naval Affairs, dated September 20, 1941, Admiral Stark enclosed a statement giving what he believed to be "a good picture of what happened" and answers to the questions. Although Admiral Stark's letter, statement, and answers were not made public until late in October, 1941, the tenor of his reply was immediately disclosed to some members of Congress and it added fuel to the fire of opposition to President Roosevelt's methods and policies. Had the President made use of the *Greer* case in an appeal to Congress after September 11 for a declaration of war to implement the escalator clause, these documents, it was known in congressional circles, would be used as ammunition by his critics. Indeed, after the President, on October 9, 1941, called upon Congress for another step in legislation—an act to permit the arming of American merchant ships—Admiral Stark's papers on the *Greer* were inserted in the *Congressional Record* and thus made public before the next "case of attack." [10]

Admiral Stark's report to the Senate Committee, which filled several typewritten pages, presented an account of the *Greer* affair which made the President's statement of the case to the nation on September 11 appear in some respects inadequate, and, in others, incorrect. The following summary gives the essential facts of the *Greer* incident as supplied by Admiral Stark to the Senate Committee:

While en route to Iceland with mail, passengers, and some freight, the *Greer* was informed by a British plane of the presence of a submerged submarine about ten miles directly ahead.

Acting on this information from the British plane, the *Greer* proceeded to trail the submarine, broadcasting its position.

This chase of the submarine went on for over three hours; the British plane dropped four depth charges in the vicinity of the submarine and departed, leaving the *Greer* to continue the hunt, zigzagging and searching.

---

10. *Congressional Record,* 77th Congress, First Session, Vol. 87, Part 8, p. 8314. On September 22, Admiral Stark had written secretly to Admiral Hart: "We are now escorting convoys." See *President Roosevelt and the Coming of the War,* Chapter XIV.

The *Greer* thus had held contact with the submarine for three hours and twenty-eight minutes; the submarine fired a torpedo which crossed the *Greer* about 100 yards astern.

Then the *Greer* "attacked the submarine with a pattern of eight depth charges"; to which the submarine replied with another torpedo that missed the *Greer*.

After losing sound contact at this time with the submarine, the *Greer* started searching for it, made contact again about two hours later, and "attacked immediately with depth charges," without discoverable results.

The *Greer* thereupon continued its search for about three hours more and proceeded to its destination, Iceland.

Appearances and Realities of the Attack on the U.S.S. Kearny (October–November)

About six weeks after the attack on the *Greer*, while Congress had before it a measure to authorize the arming of American merchant ships on recommendation of President Roosevelt,[11] another serious attack on an American war vessel was reported in the news—an attack far more distressing in terms of death and suffering than the attack on the *Greer*. On October 17, 1941, the Navy Department announced that the U.S.S. *Kearny* "was torpedoed this morning while on patrol duty about 350 miles south and west of Iceland." Although the President declined to issue any statement on this new case until all the facts were in, he said that the *Kearny* was within the American defense zone when torpedoed and that orders to shoot on sight German and Italian raiders in waters vital to American defense were still unchanged. At a press conference, Secretary Hull described German attacks as acts of piracy and attempted frightfulness as a part of a general world movement of conquest.[12]

After a brief period of silence in Berlin, a German radio broadcast denied responsibility and declared that there was not a word of truth in the story that a German submarine had torpedoed the *Kearny*. October 19, the Navy Department announced that the *Kearny*, attacked by a submarine, undoubtedly German, had reached port, with eleven members of the crew missing and several men injured. When asked the next day about any plans for making an official protest to the German Government, Secretary Hull "remarked acidly that one did not very often send diplomatic notes to an international highwayman." [13]

On October 27, 1941, President Roosevelt delivered a long and

11. See *President Roosevelt and the Coming of the War,* Chapter VI.
12. *New York Times,* October 18, 1941, pp. 1–3.
13. *Ibid.,* October 20, 1941.

vehement address [14] to the nation on the subject of Axis attacks on American ships, dwelling at length on the *Kearny* case, and defied the Axis Powers: "All we Americans have cleared our decks and taken our battle stations." After opening briefly with references to previous attacks, the President took up the new case:

Five months ago tonight I proclaimed to the American people the existence of a state of unlimited emergency.

Since then much has happened. Our Army and Navy are temporarily in Iceland in the defense of the Western Hemisphere.

Hitler has attacked shipping in areas close to the Americas in the North and South Atlantic.

Many American-owned merchant ships have been sunk on the high seas. One American destroyer was attacked on September 4. Another destroyer was attacked and hit on October 17. Eleven brave and loyal men of our Navy were killed by the Nazis.

We have wished to avoid shooting. But the shooting has started. And history has recorded who fired the first shot.[15] In the long run, however, all that will matter is who fired the last shot.

America has been attacked. The U.S.S. *Kearny* is not just a Navy ship. She belongs to every man, woman, and child in this Nation.

Illinois, Alabama, California, North Carolina, Ohio, Louisiana, Texas, Pennsylvania, Georgia, Arkansas, New York, Virginia—those are the home States of the honored dead and wounded of the *Kearny*. Hitler's torpedo was directed at every American, whether he lives on our seacoasts or in the innermost part of the Nation far from the sea and far from the guns and tanks of the marching hordes of would-be conquerors of the world.

The purpose of Hitler's attack was to frighten the American people off the high seas—to force us to make a trembling retreat. This is not the first time he has misjudged the American spirit. That spirit is now aroused.

If our national policy were to be dominated by the fear of shooting, then all of our ships and those of our sister republics would have to be tied up in home harbors. Our Navy would have to remain respectfully—abjectly—behind any line which Hitler might decree on any ocean as his own dictated version of his own war zone.

Naturally, we reject that absurd and insulting suggestion. We reject it because of our own self-interest, because of our own

14. Funk, *op. cit.,* pp. 512 ff.
15. See below, p. 110.

self-respect, because, most of all, of our own good faith. Freedom of the seas is now, as it has always been, a fundamental policy of your Government and mine. . . .

After giving his version of the *Kearny* case and declaring that America had been attacked, President Roosevelt announced measures of retaliation:

Our determination not to take it lying down has been expressed in the orders to the American Navy to shoot on sight. Those orders stand. Furthermore, the House of Representatives has already voted to amend part of the Neutrality Act of 1937, today outmoded by force of violent circumstances. The Senate Committee on Foreign Relations has also recommended elimination of other hamstringing provisions in that Act. That is the course of honesty and of realism. . . . It can never be doubted that the goods *will* be delivered by this nation, whose Navy believes in the tradition of "Damn the torpedoes; full speed ahead!"

There was great rejoicing in the White House on the day after President Roosevelt's address on October 27. His secretary, Stephen Early, stated that a flood of messages was coming in and that they were favorable in a ratio of about eight to one. Evidently advocates of war for the United States were under the impression that the great day for which they had so longed had come at last.

"America has been attacked" were, indeed, electric words. They were immediately taken by journalists in Washington and other close observers to mean that President Roosevelt had cast off the shackles of the antiwar and pro-neutrality pledges he had made to the nation. Arthur Krock, one of the best informed journalists in the Capital and a shrewd inquirer into the significance of White House announcements, said in his column headed "America Attacked," under the dateline of October 28: "Four words in the President's Navy Day speech last night are being accepted here today as his own evidence in rebuttal of the charge that his present foreign policy violates the Democratic platform of 1940 and his antiwar campaign pledges in that same year. The words were: 'America has been attacked.' "

After referring to the President's radio address of September 11, 1941, and his assignment of the "first shot" to invaders of the American defense waters, Mr. Krock went on to say:

But not until his Navy Day speech [of October 27] did the President make use of phraseology which leads back to the 1940 Democratic platform plank and those campaign utterances his general conclusion is that last night the President made his official critics have since charged him with violating. Therefore the

defense for the present generation and for the judgment of history.
. . . The key to the historical importance of the utterance is identified here as the word "attacked."

Thereupon, Mr. Krock gave an inside history of the way in which
Senator James F. Byrnes, "who was representing the President" in
the drafting of the platform at the Democratic convention of 1940,
held up the antiwar plank and procured the addition of the words
"except in case of attack." [16] Mr. Krock added: "Now the President
has officially declared that 'America has been attacked.' Therefore, by
the very text of the platform pledge, the promise against dispatch of
our armed forces 'outside the Americas' as well as the rest of the
promise can be held to be automatically canceled. In this view any
further steps away from the remainder of the platform plank are
consistent with the full text."

But there remained the President's pledge against participation in
"foreign" wars. Mr. Krock took note of it and reported that this
word was no longer deemed an obstacle: "As for the word 'foreign,'
Mrs. Roosevelt and others close to the President have already said
that, since the European war is no longer 'foreign' to our interest,
our activity in it would not be activity in a 'foreign' war."

Notwithstanding this authoritative explication by Mrs. Roosevelt and
others close to President Roosevelt, there remained also for consideration certain outstanding and categorical peace pledges made by the
President personally during the campaign. Mr. Krock cited two of them
—the Boston pledge of October 30, 1940: "Your boys are not going to
be sent into any foreign war"; and the fireside chat of December
1940: "You can therefore nail any talk of sending armies to Europe
as a deliberate untruth."

These statements, too, Mr. Krock declared, "can, on the basis of this
reasoning [about attack and foreign war] and the complete platform
text, be held equally consistent with steps since taken or any of their
logical consequences."

In this presentation of the case, on October 28, Mr. Krock seemed
to be supporting the President's "official defense for the present generation and for the judgment of history." He seemed to be saying likewise
that the steps taken by the President in the direction of war since
1940 or "any of their logical consequences" (which certainly included
a call upon Congress for a declaration of war) could be held "consistent"
with the pledges and declarations of 1940.

Having applied his line of interpretation to other antiwar statements
by the President, Mr. Krock said: "This reasoning can be disputed during

16. See Beard, *American Foreign Policy in the Making*, pp. 288 ff., for
the proceedings at the Democratic convention in Chicago in 1940.

the development of our anti-aggressor policy, just as it has been disputed up to now. The factual argument over what constitutes initiating 'attack,' as in the instance of the U.S.S. *Greer*, may continue over the U.S.S. *Kearny's* experience if the full report shall show a similar set of preliminaries"; that is, shall show that the American destroyer had chased or attacked the German submarine first.[17]

Mr. Krock closed his elaborate argument for President Roosevelt's strategy, as presented to his generation and the bar of history to come, with the words: "But it now appears that, when 'attack' is conceded in any episode, the challenge of the critics will be met by the five immensely important words ["except in case of attack"] Mr. Byrnes caused to be added to the 1940 platform."

The next day, October 29, while the words, "America has been attacked," were still reverberating in the country, Secretary Knox made public a formal report on the way in which the *Kearny* had been attacked. In his address of October 27 on the *Kearny* case, President Roosevelt had said: "We have wished to avoid shooting. But the shooting has started. And history has recorded who fired the first shot." The report by Secretary Knox two days later read:

> On the night of October 16–17 the U.S.S. *Kearny* while escorting a convoy of merchant ships received distress signals from another convoy which was under attack from several submarines. The U.S.S. *Kearny* proceeded to the aid of the attacked convoy. On arriving at the scene of the attack the U.S.S. *Kearny* dropped depth bombs when she sighted a merchant ship under attack by a submarine. Some time afterward three torpedo tracks were observed approaching the U.S.S. *Kearny*. One passed ahead of the ship, one astern, and the third struck the U.S.S. *Kearny* on the starboard side in the vicinity of the forward fire room. . . . The U.S.S. *Kearny* was forced out of action by the explosion.[18]

The rejoicing of President Roosevelt's supporters over what seemed to be a sure case of an attack that meant war for the United States, at long last, proved to be premature; for the Senate Committee on Naval Affairs, remembering its experiences in the *Greer* case, immediately gave attention to the case of the *Kearny* and managed to get some of the facts in that affair from Admiral Stark, Chief of Naval Operations. Although the committee made no public report on these facts at once, news of its findings "leaked" out and spread among members

17. *New York Times,* October 29, 1941, p. 4. Perhaps Mr. Krock was not at the moment conversant with the "factual" phase of the incident, but he learned about it later and spoke bitterly about it.

18. Article by Charles Hurd in *New York Times,* October 30, 1941, pp. 1–5.

of Congress and their friends.[19] The leaks indicated that the *Kearny* was actually on convoy duty [20] at the time of the shooting and had been engaged at length in fighting a pack of German submarines before she was hit by a torpedo. Such facts were not released to the press by the committee until early in December,[21] but leaks and rumors in Washington completely dashed interventionist hopes that the *Kearny* attack would now bring full-fledged war in the Atlantic.

Other shootings and sinkings occurred in the Atlantic. Two of the most flagrant cases were those of the tanker *Salinas* on October 30, 1941, and the *Reuben James* on the night of October 30–31. But President Roosevelt did not make so much of these two cases as he had made of the *Greer* and *Kearny* cases. When asked on October 31, 1941, whether the sinking of the *Reuben James* would lead to the breaking of diplomatic relations with Germany, he "indicated surprise." The reporter inquired: "Will this first actual sinking make any difference in the international relations of the United States?" The President replied that he "did not think so—the destroyer was merely carrying out its

19. See Arthur Krock's statement.

20. Asked at a secret hearing of a Senate Committee, October 27, 1941, whether American vessels were convoying ships, Secretary Hull replied: "That is my guess." When Senator Wheeler made the charge that the Navy was convoying ships across the Atlantic to Great Britain, Secretary Knox declared: "That statement is not true." *Ibid.,* October 28 and November 20, 1941.

21. The following account of the Senate Committee's report to Congress was published in the *New York Times,* December 4, 1941:

"The destroyer *Kearny* fought nearly three hours against a pack of German submarines before she was hit by a torpedo, an official Navy report to Congress revealed today. . . .

"The Navy report—a letter from Admiral Harold R. Stark, Chief of Naval Operations, to Chairman David I. Walsh, Democrat, of Massachusetts, of the Senate Naval Affairs Committee—said the *Kearny* was on convoy duty, and 'a number' of merchant ships were damaged 'and some of them sunk during the battle.'

"Admiral Stark said that although United States vessels were in the convoy 'it may be stated . . . that no United States flag merchant ship was sunk at this time.'

"Senator Walsh, who had asked for answers to a series of questions on the *Kearny* incident, released Admiral Stark's report without comment, except to say that so far as the Senate's efforts to obtain information were concerned 'the *Kearny* incident is closed.'

"He said, however, that he had written Admiral Stark asking for similar information about the sinking of the destroyer *Reuben James,* which went down off Iceland with a loss of 100 officers and men.

"Senator Walsh had told Admiral Stark that information on the *Kearny* should be made public 'since it has become impossible to keep secret from the press the proceedings of committees of the Senate.' He waived replies that would reveal military or naval secrets. . . ."

assigned task." Asked whether Berlin had cause to worry about some
of its submarines that had encountered our Navy, "The President suggested that the reporter go to a good psychiatrist." [22] Thus the electric
words "America has been attacked," instead of setting off the real war
in the Atlantic, fizzled out in an anticlimax. If President Roosevelt had
actually been seeking war in the Atlantic by exploiting German "attacks,"
he had apparently exhausted the possibilities of that expedient by
November 1, 1941.

22. *Ibid.,* November 1, 1941. Later reports indicated: the *Salinas* and three
American freighters were in a convoy accompanied by five American
destroyers, joined on the voyage by thirty-eight British ships, most of them
tankers; American naval vessels took up the task of escorting the convoy
at a given point after British war vessels turned back; German submarines
attacked the convoy and a general engagement ensued; the *Reuben James*
came to the aid of the *Salinas;* later the *Reuben James* was sunk in an
engagement. *New York Times,* November 1, 5, 6, 8, 1941.

HERBERT FEIS

War Came at Pearl Harbor:
Suspicions Considered

The debate between revisionist and orthodox historians becomes most heated over Roosevelt's Far Eastern policy. The charge by Charles Beard, Charles Tansill, and other revisionists that FDR deliberately exposed Pearl Harbor to Japanese attack to force American entry into the war has led to a vigorous defense of the President's diplomacy. Herbert Feis presents a clear statement of the orthodox position in this article, and, in greater detail, in his book The Road to Pearl Harbor *(Princeton, 1950). The controversy can be traced in the many partisan books written on Pearl Harbor, notably Walter Millis,* This Is Pearl! *(New York, 1947), which defends the administration, and in Robert A. Theobald,* The Final Secret of Pearl Harbor *(New York, 1954), a severe indictment of FDR, and in an extensive article literature which includes Robert H. Ferrell, "Pearl Harbor and the Revisionists,"* Historian, *XVII (Spring 1955), 215–233, an orthodox account, and Percy Greaves, Frank Beatty, and Harry Elmer Barnes, "The Mystery of Pearl Harbor,"* National Review, *XXIII (December 13, 1966), 1260–1272, the most recent statement of the revisionist position. Paul W. Schroeder,* The Axis Alliance and Japanese-American Relations, 1941 *(Ithaca, 1958), is the most objective critique of administration policy.*

TEN YEARS after victory, we look ruefully at the way the world has gone. It is right and natural to search out any errors of judgment or faults of character that have led us to our present pass. But such self-scrutiny can go awry if governed by a wish to revile rather than a wish to understand. Unless we are alert, that could happen as a result of the suspicions that have come to cluster around the way in which the United States became engaged in the Second World War—torch-lit by the Pearl Harbor disaster.

The more recently available sources have added but little to our knowledge of the events that led to our entry into the war. The books of memoirs written by Japanese witnesses have told us something more, especially about the struggle within the Japanese Government. But in my reading, while they may improve our knowledge of details,

Reprinted by permission from the *Yale Review*, XLV (Spring 1956), 378–390.

they do not change the fundamental view of this experience or its main features. In American and British records still kept secret there may be information or explanations that would do so. But even this I doubt. With no new great revealing facts to display, and no great new insights to impart, the most useful service would seem to be to act as caretaker of what is known, and in particular to deal with certain warped comments and inferences that seasonally must feel the straightening edge of evidence.

Of all the accusations made, the one most shocking to me is that Roosevelt and his chief advisers deliberately left the Pacific Fleet and base at Pearl Harbor exposed as a lure to bring about a direct Japanese attack upon us.

This has been diffused in the face of the fact that the Japanese High Military Command conference before the Imperial throne on September 6, 1941, resolved that "If by the early part of October there is no reasonable hope of having our demands agreed to in the diplomatic negotiations mentioned above, we will immediately make up our minds to get ready for war against America (and England and Holland)." This on September 6. The plan for the attack on Pearl Harbor was not approved and adopted until October; and Secret Operation Order #1, the execution of the plan, was not issued until November 5. The presence of the Pacific Fleet at Pearl Harbor was not a lure but an obstacle.

The literature of accusation ignores or rejects the real reasons why the Pacific Fleet was kept in Hawaii. It must do so, since one of the main reasons was the hope that its presence there would deter the Japanese from making so threatening a move south or north that American armed forces might have to join in the war. It scorns the fact that the American military plans—to be executed in the event that we became engaged in war—assigned vital tasks to this Pacific Fleet. A mind must indeed be distracted if it can believe that the American Government could, at one and the same time, use the Pacific Fleet as a target and count on having it as part of its defending force.

A variant of this accusation, which at least does not require such a willingness to believe the worst, might also be noted—that despite ample knowledge that Pearl Harbor was about to be attacked, the American Government purposefully left it exposed and allowed the event to happen.

Those who do not find such an idea at odds with their view of the sense of duty and regard for human life of President Roosevelt and his chief advisers can find striking points about the occurrence that may be construed to correspond with this conception. How they glare out of the record in hindsight: Ambassador Grew's warnings; Secretary Hull's acute gleam put into words at least three times in Cabinet councils in November that the Japanese attack might come "at any moment, anywhere"; the intercepted Japanese messages telling of the Japanese effort to secure minute information as to the location of the ships of our Pacific Fleet in the Harbor; carelessness in checking up on the protective measures taken by the local commanders; failure to use the chance to give an effective last-minute warning to Hawaii. How else, it is asked, can these be explained except in terms of secret and conscious purpose?

However, just as hindsight makes the failure of perception plain, so it also makes it understandable—but only by bringing back to mind the total circumstances. That can be done here only in the barest way. Up to then, Japanese strategy had been wary, one small creeping step after another, from Manchuria to North China into China and down into Indo-China. American military circles came to take it for granted that it would go on that way. Then there was the fact that Japan's basic objectives lay to the south and southeast; there and there only it could get what it needed—raw materials, oil, and island bases to withstand the attack from the West. Expectation already set in that direction was kept there by impressive and accurate intelligence reports of movements under way. Against this flow of preconception, the signs pointing to Pearl Harbor were not heeded.

Such features of contemporary thinking within the American Government explain, though they do not excuse, the failure to discern that Pearl Harbor was going to be attacked. To think the contrary is to believe that the President and the heads of the American Army, Navy, and Air Force were given to deep deception, and in order to have us enter the war were ready to sacrifice not only the Pacific Fleet but the whole war plan for the Pacific. This, I think, is the difference between history and police-court history.

I have taken note of these accusations that have been built about the disaster at Pearl Harbor because they appeal to the sense of the sinister which is so lively in our times. But I am glad to turn to ideas and interpretations of broader historical import.

The first of these is that Roosevelt and the Joint Chiefs of Staff were obligated by secret agreements with Churchill and their British colleagues to enter the war at some time or other, in one way or other. Therefore, it is further supposed, the American authors of this agreement had to cause either Germany or Japan, or both, to attack us.

This view derives encouragement from the fact that the American Government *did* enter into a secret agreement about strategy with the British. The accord, known as ABC-I Staff Agreement, adopted at Washington in March 1941, set down the respective missions of the British and American elements in the event that the United States should be at war with Germany or Japan, or both; and subsequently the American basic joint war plan, Rainbow-5, was adjusted to fit this combined plan of operations. An attempt was made at a similar conference in Singapore soon after to work out a more detailed United States–British-Dutch operating plan for the Pacific. This attempt failed; but the discussion that took place there left a lasting mark on American official thinking, for the conferees defined the limits on land and sea beyond which Japanese forces could not be permitted to go without great risk to the defenders.

The ABC-I agreement did not place the Roosevelt Administration under *political* obligation to enter the war against either Germany or Japan, not even if Japan attacked British or Dutch areas in the Far East. Nor did Roosevelt give a promise to this effect to Churchill when they met at Newfoundland in August 1941. Up to the very eve of the Japanese assault, the President refused to tell the British or Dutch what we would do. In short, the Government kept itself officially free from any obligation to enter the war, certainly free of any obligation to thrust itself into the war.

But I do think this accord conveyed responsibilities of a moral sort. After ABC-I was adopted, production of weapons in the United States and the British Commonwealth took it into account; and the allocation of weapons, troops, ships, and planes as between threatened areas was based on the expectation that the United States would carry out the assignments set down in the plan.

Thus, it may be fairly thought, Roosevelt and his administration were obligated to try to gain the consent of Congress and the American people to play the part designated in the joint plans if Japanese assaults crossed the land and sea boundaries of resistance that were defined at these joint staff conferences. In the last November weeks, when the end of the diplomatic talks with Japan came into sight, and General Marshall and Admiral Stark were asked what measures should be taken in face of the threatened Japanese advances, they advised the President to declare the limits defined at Singapore, and to warn the Japanese that we would fight if these were crossed. There is much reason to think this would have been done even had the Japanese not struck at Pearl Harbor and the Philippines, and this boundary would have been the line between peace and war. But this reaffirmation was made not as a measure required to carry out a secret accord, but because it was believed to be the best course.

A variant explanation of the way we dealt with Japan runs somewhat as follows: that Roosevelt was determined to get into the war against Germany; that he had to find a release from his public promises that the United States would not enter "foreign wars" unless attacked; that his efforts to do so by unneutral aid to Britain and the Soviet Union had failed because Hitler had refused to accept the challenge; and so he sought another door into war, a back door, by inviting or compelling the Japanese attack.

This interpretation, with its kick at the end, twists the record around its own preconception. The actions taken did not flow from a settled wish to get us into war. They trailed along the rim of necessity of the true purpose—which was to sustain resistance against the Axis. How many times the American Government refused to do what the British, French, Chinese, Russians, Dutch asked it to do, because it might involve us in actual combat!

This slant of reasoning about American action passes by the course of Japanese conduct which aroused our fears and stimulated our opposition: the way in which, despite all our pleas and warnings, Japan pressed on. By not recognizing that these Japanese actions called for American counteraction, it excuses them. Thus our resistance is made to appear as nothing else but a deceitful plot to plunge us into war. Furthermore, it dismisses as insincere the patient attempt to calm Japan by diplomatic talks, by offers to join in safeguarding its security.

There were influential individuals in the Roosevelt Administration who wanted to get into the war and were indifferent as to how we got into it. Of these, Secretary of the Interior Ickes was, I believe, the most candid, at any rate in his diary entries. Secretary of the Treasury Morgenthau and his staff also had a positive wish that we should engage in war—but against Germany, not against Japan, for that might have brought a diversion of forces to the Pacific. Secretary of War Stimson thought that it would not be possible for Great Britain to sustain the fight unless we entered it; but toward the very end, particularly as it was becoming plain that the Soviet Union was going to survive the Nazi assault, he began to wish for delay. However, time and time again the memoirs and diaries record the impatience of these officials, and those who thought like them, with Hull's caution and Roosevelt's watchful indirection.

The most genuine point made by those who dissent, one that merits thorough analysis, is that the American Government, in conjunction with the British and Dutch, refused to continue to supply Japan with machines and materials vital to it—especially oil. It is contended that they thereby compelled Japan to resort to war, or at least fixed a time period in which Japan was faced with the need of deciding to yield to our terms or go to war.

In reflecting upon this action, one must not confuse the reasons for it with the Japanese response to it. Japan showed no signs of curbing its aggressive course. It paid no heed to repeated and friendly warnings that unless it did, the threatened countries would have to take counter-measures. As when on February 14, 1941, while the Lend-Lease Act

was being argued in Congress, Dooman, Counselor of the American
Embassy in Japan and known to be a firm and straightforward friend
of that country, carried back from Washington the message for the
Vice-Minister for Foreign Affairs: that the American people were
determined to support Britain even at the risk of war; that if Japan
or any other country menaced that effort "it would have to expect to
come in conflict with the United States"; and that the United States
had abstained from an oil embargo in order not to impel Japan to
create a situation that could only lead to the most serious outcome.
Japan's answer over the following months had been to force its way
further into Indo-China and threaten the Dutch East Indies.

This sustained proof that Japan was going on with its effort to
dominate Asia, and the alliance pledging it to stand by Germany if that
country got into war with the United States, made a continuation of
trade with Japan an act of meekness on our part. Japan was concentrating its foreign purchases on products needed for war, while reducing
civilian use by every means, and was thus accumulating great reserve
stocks. These were enabling it to maintain its invasion of China without
much strain, while continuing to expand its war-making power. Had
effective restraints—note that I do not say *total* restraints—not been
imposed, the American Government would have been in the strange
position of having declared an unlimited national emergency, of calling
upon the American people to strengthen their army, navy, and air force
in great urgency, while at the same time nourishing the opponent that
might have to be met in battle. This was a grave, if not intolerable,
responsibility.

It is hard to tell how squarely the American and British Governments faced the possible consequence of their restrictive measures.
My impression is that they knew the danger of war with Japan was
being increased; that Japan might try to get by force the means denied
it. The Japanese Government served plain warnings that this game
of thrust and counterthrust might so end. These were soberly regarded,
but did not weaken the will that Japan was not to have its way by
threat.

Mingled with the anxiety lest these restrictive measures make war
more likely, there was a real hope that they might be a deterrent to
war. Conceivably they would bring home to the Japanese people that
if it came to war, they might soon run out of the means for combat,
while the rapid growth of American military strength would make it
clear that they could not in the end win. And, as evidence of these
probabilities became plain, the conciliatory elements in the Japanese
Government would prevail over the more militant ones.

This almost happened. But the reckless ones, those who would rather
court fatality than accept frustration, managed to retain control of

Japanese decision. The pressure applied by us did not prevent war, and may have brought the time of decision for war closer. The valid question, however, is not whether the American Government resorted to these restrictions *in order* to drive Japan to attack; it is whether the American Government failed to grasp a real chance, after the restraints had begun to leave their mark in Japanese official circles, to arrive at a satisfactory understanding that would have averted war. Twice, in the opinion of some qualified students of the subject, such a chance emerged, or at least appeared on the horizon of diplomacy. Were they real opportunities or merely mirages or decoys?

The first of these was the occasion when, in the autumn of 1941, the Japanese Prime Minister, Prince Konoye, sought a personal meeting with the President. It is averred that the President's failure to respond lost a chance to avert the war without yielding any American principle or purpose. Some think the reason was that American diplomacy was inflexible, dull in its insight, and too soaked in mistrust. Others, more accusatory, explain the decision by a lack of desire for an agreement that would have thwarted the design for war.

Since there is no conclusive evidence of what Konoye intended to propose or could have achieved, comment on this subject must enter into "the boggy ground of what-might-have-been." Some observers, including Ambassador Grew, believe that Konoye could have made a real, and an irreversible, start toward meeting American terms. It will always be possible to think that this is so. But to the Americans in authority, the chance seemed small. Konoye was a man who in every past crisis had allowed himself to flounder between crisscrossed promises; hence there was good reason to fear an attempt at deception. Such glimpses as we have of what he might have proposed do not support the view that he could have offered a suspension or end to the fight against China. His freedom to negotiate would have been subject to the conditions stated by those who had controlled Japan's course up to then —their price for allowing him to go to meet the President.

Even so, to repeat, it is possible that skilled and more daring American diplomacy might have handled the meeting so as to get a satisfactory accord; or, failing that—and this is the more likely chance—to bring about so deep a division within the Japanese circle of decision as to have prevented warlike action. These alluring historical queries will continue to roam in the land of might-have-been.

But the risks were great. The echoes of Munich and its aftermath were still loud. The American Government might have found itself forced to make a miserable choice; either to accept an accord which would have left Japan free to complete its conquest of China and menace the rest of Asia, or to face a deep division among the American people. Any understanding with Japan that was not clear and decisive would have had unpredictable consequences. The Chinese Government might have felt justified in making a deal following our own. The Soviet Union, at this time just managing with the greatest effort and agony to prevent German victory, might also have chosen to compromise with Hitler rather than to fight it out. Speculations such as these must leave the subject unsettled. But in any case, I think it clear that the American decision was one of judgment, not of secret intent. Konoye was not told that the President would not meet with him; he was told that he would not do so until more progress had been made toward defining what the Japanese Government was prepared to propose.

The same basic question had to be faced in the final crisis of negotiation in November 1941: whether to relax restraints on Japan and leave it in a position to keep on trying to control much of Asia in return for a promise not to press on farther for the time being.

The opinion that the Japanese truce offer made at this last juncture accepted the main purposes and principles for which the American Government had been standing may be summarily dismissed. It was ambiguously worded, it was silent about the alliance with Germany, and it would have required the American Government to end its support of China—for the last of its numbered five points read: "The Government of the United States undertakes to refrain from such measures and actions as will be prejudicial to the endeavors for the restoration of general peace between Japan and China." This scant and unclear proposal was at once deemed "entirely unacceptable." Furthermore, there seemed little use and much possible damage in making a counter truce-offer of the same variety. The intercepted Japanese messages stated flatly that this was Japan's last and best offer. They told of the swift dismissal of a much more nearly acceptable one that Nomura and Kurusu asked their superiors in Tokyo to consider. A deadline had been set. Thus it was all but sure that the reduced counter-offer which had been patched together in Washington would be unheeded. But it might shake the coalition to which by then the opponents of the Axis had pledged their lives and national destinies.

This seems to have been the thought uppermost in Hull's mind in recommending to the President that the counter truce-offer be withheld. As set down in his historic memo of November 26, he had been led to this conclusion by the opposition of the Chinese, the half-hearted support or actual opposition of the British, Dutch, and Australian governments, and the further excited opposition to be expected because of lack of appreciation of the importance and value of a truce. This I believe to have been the true determining reason for a decision reluctantly taken. Even if by then Japan was genuinely ready for reform, the repentance had come too late. The situation had grown too entangled by then for minor measures, its momentum too great. Germany-Italy-

Japan had forced the creation of a defensive coalition more vast than the empire of the Pacific for which Japan plotted. This was not now to be quieted or endangered by a temporary halt along the fringe of the Japanese advance.

Even though these reasons for dropping the idea of a truce may seem sufficient, they leave the question why the American Government could not have given a softer and less declaratory answer. Why had it to give one so "bleakly uncompromising"? It could have said simply that the Japanese offer did not convey the assurances that would warrant us and the alliance for which we spoke to resume the shipment of war materials to Japan and end our aid to China. Why was it deemed advisable or essential at this juncture to state fully and forcibly our maximum terms for a settlement in the Pacific? Was it foreseen that, scanned with mistrust as it would almost surely be, this would be construed as a demand for the swift abandonment of Japan's whole program? Was it done, as the accusation runs, with the deliberate intent of banning any last chance for an accord? Of propelling the Japanese attack?

That this was not the reason I am as sure as anyone can be on a matter of this sort; but I can offer only conjecture as to what the inspiring purposes were. Perhaps to vindicate past actions and decisions. Perhaps a wish to use the dramatic chance to put in the record a statement of the aims for which the risk of war was being accepted, and of the basis on which the Americans would found the peace when the time came. Such an idea was in accord with the usual mode of thought of the men in charge of the Executive Branch of the Government and of most of the American people. It gave vent to the propensity exemplified in Hull to find a base in general principles meant to be at once political standards and moral ideals. After long caution, it appealed as a defiant contradiction of the Axis program. All this, however, is surmise rather than evidenced history.

But I think it is well within the realm of evidenced history that the memo of November 26 was not in any usual sense of the word an ultimatum. It did not threaten the Japanese with war or any other form of forceful punishment if our terms were not accepted. It simply left them in the state of distress in which they were, with the prospect that they might later have to submit to our requirements. The Japanese Government could have, as Konoye and Nomura pleaded with it to do, allowed the situation to drag along, with or without resuming talks with the American Government. Its power to make war would have been depleted, but neither quickly nor crucially. The armed forces and even the position in China could have been maintained.

Notably, the final Japanese answer which ended negotiations on December 7, 1941, does not accuse the American Government of confronting it with an ultimatum, but only of thwarting the larger Japanese aims. Part 14—the clinching part of this note—reads: "Obviously it is the intention of the American Government to conspire with Great Britain and other countries to obstruct Japan's efforts toward the establishment of peace through the creation of a New Order in East Asia, and especially to preserve Anglo-American rights and interests by keeping Japan and China at war. This intention has been revealed clearly during the course of the present negotiations. Thus, the earnest hope of the Japanese Government to adjust Japanese-American relations and to preserve and promote the peace of the Pacific through cooperation with the American Government has finally been lost."

This is a more nearly accurate description of the purposes of the American Government under Roosevelt than those attributed to it by hostile and suspicious American critics. Our Government did obstruct Japanese efforts, believing them to be unjust, cruel, and a threat to our national security, especially after Japan became a partner with Hitler's Germany and Mussolini's Italy and bent its efforts toward bringing the world under their combined control.

This determination stood on the proposition that it was better to take the risks of having to share in the suffering of the war than of finding ourselves moved or compelled to fight a more desperate battle against the Axis later on. The American Government, I believe, knew how serious a risk of war was being taken. But in its address to the American people it chose to put in the forefront the perils we would face if the Axis won, and to leave in the background, even to camouflage, the risks of finding ourselves plunged into wars which during the election campaign it had promised would not occur. Whether any large number of Americans were fooled by this, or whether most of them, in reality, were content to have the prospect presented that way rather than in a more blunt and candid way, I do not know.

This essay in interpretation has compelled me to recall and stress the aggressive Japanese assault—though I should have been glad to let that slip into the past. The passage of time does not alter facts, but it can bring a fuller and calmer understanding of them. It frees the mind for fairer appreciation of the causes and circumstances which impelled Japan along its tragic course and which impelled us to resist it. For both countries there are many common lessons. One of them is that continued friendliness requires mutual effort to relieve the other, to the extent it can, of deep cause for anxiety—the Japanese people of their anxiety over the means of living decently, the American people of anxiety about their security and power to defend the free world. Another is that they must both feel, speak, and act so honestly and steadily that their view of each other will be cleared of mistrust, and brightened by trust.

HANS L. TREFOUSSE

Germany and Pearl Harbor

One of the most fascinating questions relating to American entry into World War II is why Hitler declared war on the United States four days after Pearl Harbor. The revisionists assume that Germany was certain to declare war when they argue that Roosevelt provoked the Japanese attack in order to enter the European war via the Pacific back door. Yet Hitler had followed a restrained policy toward the United States despite a series of highly provocative American acts, including the destroyers-for-bases deal, lend-lease, and American naval patrols in the Atlantic. Hitler was not committed to declare war by the Tripartite Pact, and in many ways it would have been wiser for him to have let the Japanese fight the United States alone while Germany concentrated on conquering Russia. Several of Roosevelt's advisers feared Hitler would do just this in the days immediately after the Japanese attack.

Hans Trefousse explores Hitler's decision for war, using the evidence presented at the Nuremberg and Tokyo war crimes trials and at the congressional hearings on Pearl Harbor. German-American relations in this period are treated extensively in a book by Trefousse, Germany and American Neutrality, 1939–1941 *(New York, 1951), and in James V. Compton,* The Swastika and the Eagle *(Boston, 1967); Saul Friedlander,* Prelude to Downfall *(New York, 1967); and Alton Frye,* Nazi Germany and the American Hemisphere, 1933–1941 *(New Haven, 1967).*

GERMANY'S ROLE in the events leading up to Pearl Harbor needs to be reexamined in the light of documents published since the end of the war. These sources help correct certain misconceptions about German policy which were held during the conflict. The Allied powers believed at that time that Hitler had long-range plans for conquest and that as a part of these plans had, in one way or another, pushed Japan into war with the United States.

The evidence, however, suggests a different picture. Germany's chief aim in the Western Hemisphere was to keep the United States at least temporarily neutral, and to that end she tried to use Japan as a counterpoise. She attempted to persuade Japan to attack the Dutch and British empires, and later to attack Siberia. The Japanese, however, refused

Reprinted by permission from the *Far Eastern Quarterly,* XI (November 1951), 35–50.

to go along, and even tried to come to some agreement with the United States. When the negotiations initiated for that purpose failed, Japan attacked America. Hitler then chose to reverse his policy and to join Japan because he valued that country as an ally.

The world first realized the increasing friendliness between Germany and Japan when the two countries concluded the Anti-Comintern Pact of 1936.[1] Ostensibly directed against the Communist International, it nevertheless served notice upon the world of a community of interest between the German and Japanese governments. The pact had been negotiated on behalf of the Nazis, not by the German Foreign Office, but by *Dienststelle Ribbentrop*, whose head, later Foreign Minister, was one of the chief advocates of close collaboration with Japan.[2] Since Hitler considered the Japanese a "kindred heroic people,"[3] von Ribbentrop found a receptive atmosphere for his treaty with Japan.

In the years following 1936, relations between the two countries became ever friendlier. After initial Nazi attempts to mediate the "China Incident" had failed, Hitler withdrew his military mission of advisers to Chiang Kai-shek, recognized Manchukuo, and concluded a pact of cultural amity with Japan.[4] By June 1938, von Ribbentrop was seriously considering the conclusion of a military alliance.[5]

One of the reasons for Germany's increased friendliness toward Japan was her desire to find a counterweight to the United States. Von Ribbentrop was convinced that America would not mix in European affairs so long as Japan's position remained uncertain.[6] When the Japanese balked at his proposals for a military alliance against all potential enemies on the grounds that they did not wish to bind themselves in respect

1. For the text, providing for collaboration against the Comintern, cf. Germany, Reichsministerium des Inneren, *Reichsgesetzblatt 1937* (Berlin, 1937), II, 28–29; for the secret protocol, providing for mutual neutrality in case of war with Russia, cf. International Military Tribunal for the Far East, "Record of Proceedings . . ." (Hereafter referred to as "IMTFE"), Document 1561-E, pp. 5936–5937.

2. "The United States of America Against Ernst von Weizsäcker, et al., Defendants," Erich Kordt's testimony, p. 7418. (Hereafter referred to as "Weizsäcker Case.") This was true despite the fact that Ribbentrop knew so little about the Far East that he thought "Shimonoseki" was a person.

3. *Ibid.*

4. James T. Liu, "German Mediation in the Sino-Japanese War, 1937–1938" in *Far Eastern Quarterly*, VIII (February 1949), 157–71; United States, Department of State, Documents on *German Foreign Policy, 1918–1945* (Washington, 1949), Series D, I, 826–864. For the recognition of Manchukuo and the Pact, cf. *Dokumente der deutschen Politik* (Berlin, 1935–1944), VI, 85, 102.

5. Interrogation of General Oshima and Stahmer's affidavit, "IMTFE," pp. 6050 *ff.*, 24398.

6. Galeazzo Ciano, *L'Europa verso la catastrofe* (Milan, 1948), pp. 374–78.

to the Western powers,[7] he instructed Ambassador Ott in Tokyo to meet such objections with the rejoinder that the proposed alliance would be the best way of keeping the Americans out of any conflict.[8] These discusisons, however, temporarily came to an end with the conclusion of the Nazi-Soviet Pact in August 1939, and the recall of the Nazis' staunch supporter, Ambassador Hiroshi Oshima. Never since 1933 had relations between the two countries been cooler.[9]

In spite of apparent failure, von Ribbentrop did not give up. Since war had broken out in September, the Nazis were especially anxious to keep the United States neutral and thereby isolate the Western powers. They toned down their press attacks on America,[10] exercised surprising restraint in their naval operations,[11] and refused to be ruffled by American measures to help the Allies. They also hoped to obtain Japanese cooperation with this policy. As von Ribbentrop told Mussolini in March, 1940, he believed that the island empire constituted a strong counterweight to the possibility of American intervention.[12] It was because of this opinion that he endeavored to effect a rapprochement between Japan and Russia.[13] Moreover, the German press continued to picture Japan in a most favorable light,[14] and the Germany Navy viewed her as a friendly nation.[15]

Then came Germany's great victories in western and northern Europe. As America provided more aid to Great Britain, von Ribbentrop turned again to the Nazis' Far Eastern partner. According to his own testimony, he entered into closer relations with Japan in the summer of 1940 in order to keep the United States out of war and to obtain a compromise peace, if possible.[16] The facts apparently bear him out. When the Japanese Ministers of War, Navy, and Foreign Affairs held a joint conference on July 12, 1940, to discuss the possibility of an alliance

7. General Oshima's interrogation, *loc. cit.*

8. "IMTFE," p. 6115.

9. Document 4034, "IMTFE," pp. 6127 *ff.;* Document 1714, p. 2404; Document 2862, p. 34016; Kordt's testimony, "Weizsäcker Case," p. 7419.

10. *Zietschriften-Dienst,* September 23, 1939; *Völkischer Beobachter,* July–November, 1939.

11. Kurt Assmann, "Why U-Boat Warfare Failed," in *Foreign Affairs,* XXVIII (July 1950), p. 659; *Fuehrer Conferences on Matters Dealing with the German Navy* (Washington, 1947), 1939, pp. 3–5. (Hereafter referred to as *Fuehrer Conferences.*)

12. Ciano, *L'Europa verso la catastrofe,* p. 357.

13. "IMTFE," Document 4034, pp. 6127 *ff.*

14. *Nationalsozialistische Monashefte,* XI (April 1940), 201–203; *Das Archiv,* LXXIII (September 8, 1939), 29.

15. *Fuehrer Conferences,* 1939, p. 21.

16. International Military Tribunal, *Trial of the Major War Criminals Before the International Tribunal* (Nuremberg, 1947–1949), X, 295. (Hereafter referred to as *IMT.*)

with the Reich, they were most impressed by von Ribbentrop's assertions to Naotake Sato that Germany wanted to use the proposed pact to keep the United States out of the war.[17] Only one obstacle still remained. Hitler, unlike his Foreign Minister, was not yet prepared for an alliance; he felt that Great Britain would shortly capitulate and now dubbed the Japanese mere "harvest helpers." It was only when England refused to surrender and was encouraged to continue resistance by the receipt of fifty overage destroyers from America that he changed his mind.[18] Thus, the negotiations were carried to a speedy conclusion.

Throughout these discussions between Germany and Japan, both apparently had the idea of utilizing the alliance to keep America neutral by frightening her. Negotiators on both sides emphasized this fact,[19] while von Ribbentrop made the most of it in his discussions with Mussolini and Ciano.[20] While the latter still had some doubts,[21] the former was evidently impressed, and the Tripartite Pact was signed with great pomp and ceremony in Berlin on September 27, 1940.

The text of the agreement proved enlightening. After a preliminary article in which they asserted that each nation of the world was to be given its "proper place," the three signatories agreed to recognize one another's supremacy in their respective regions of the world. Article III contained the gist of the alliance:

> Germany, Italy, and Japan . . . undertake to assist one another with all political, economic, and military means, if one of the three Contracting Parties is attacked by a Power at present not involved in the European War or in the Chinese-Japanese conflict.[22]

As the Soviet Union was specifically exempted under Article V,[23] the treaty was obviously directed against the United States. Secretary of State von Weizsäcker, next to von Ribbentrop the Wilhelmstrasse's highest ranking official, made a point of specifically informing the Russian Ambassador of this fact on the day following the signing of the protocol,[24]

17. "IMTFE," Document 1308, pp. 6191–212.

18. "Weizsäcker Case," Kordt's testimony, pp. 7417 ff.

19. Masuo Kato, The Lost War (New York, 1946), p. 44; "IMTFE," Document 1714, pp. 24438 ff.; Document 3000, p. 36191.

20. IMT, Document 1842-PS, XXVIII, 573–74.

21. Hugh Gibson (ed.), The Ciano Diaries (Garden City, 1946), p. 291. (Hereafter referred to as Ciano Diaries.)

22. Reichsgesetzblatt, 1940, II, 280–81. According to Erich Kordt of the German Foreign Office, Special Emissary Stahmer entered into a secret oral understanding which gave Japan the right to decide whether the casus foederis existed in any given situation or not. "Weizsäcker Case," pp. 7426–427.

23. "Japan, Germany, and Italy affirm that the aforesaid terms do not in any way affect the political status which exists at present between each of the three Contracting Parties and the Soviet Union."

24. Document NG-3074, "Weizsäcker Case."

and the Nazi press advertised it to the whole world.[25] Nevertheless, it seems fairly clear that the pact was not intended to draw America into the war, but to keep her out, as the Germans had contended during the negotiations. Hitler explained this in great detail to Franco at Hendaye,[26] while von Ribbentrop repeated similar arguments to Count Ciano in November.[27] Upon interrogation after the war, all participants agreed on the restraining purpose of the alliance,[28] and the International Military Tribunal in Tokyo came to the same conclusion.[29] The most convincing proof of the matter, however, lies in the history of subsequent German-Japanese relations. Had the Nazis wanted war with America, they conceivably could have asked for Japanese assistance at various times under the terms of the alliance. They might simply have found an incident of "American aggression" to make it operative, especially after the first naval encounters in 1941 and Roosevelt's orders to shoot on sight. But the fact remains that they did not do so.[30] The Tripartite Pact fitted neatly into their scheme of keeping the United States out of war for the time being.

In many respects, Germany's Far Eastern policies in 1941 offer additional proof of the essentially restraining nature of the Tripartite Pact in reference to the United States. Far from inveigling the Japanese to strike against America, the Germans attempted to induce them to cooperate in an attack against the British and Dutch empires. By attacking Singapore and the Dutch East Indies, but bypassing American territories, Japan, it was suggested, might seize valuable areas with little trouble and at the same time shift attention from European to Asiatic waters. This was the plan that dominated the Germans' thoughts about the Far East.

In December 1940, Admiral Raeder, the Commander-in-Chief of the German navy, pointing out the evident weakness of Great Britain's position in Asia, suggested that Hitler incite Japan to attack Singapore. He

25. *Frankfurter Zeitung,* September 28, 1940.

26. James W. Gantenbein, *Documentary Background of World War II, 1931–1941* (New York, 1948), pp. 727–29.

27. Ciano, *L'Europa verso la catastrofe,* pp. 608–12.

28. Ribbentrop's testimony, *IMT,* X, 188, 294; von Weizsäcker's testimony, "Weizsäcker Case," p. 7898; Ott's affidavit, Document 2477, "IMTFE," pp. 28019–28022; for Toyoda's views, cf. United States, Congress, *Pearl Harbor Attack, Hearings Before the Joint Committee on the Investigation of the Pearl Harbor Attack* (hereafter referred to as *Pearl Harbor Attack*) (Washington, 1946), XII, 56–57; for Matsuoka's concurrence, cf. Kato, *op. cit.,* p. 20. Cf. also Ulrich von Hassel, *The Von Hassel Diaries, 1398–1944* (New York, 1947), p. 152.

29. "IMTFE," p. 48994.

30. It may be argued that the secret clause of the treaty left the decision of entry up to Japan and prevented the Nazis from invoking the alliance, but they never even approached the Japanese to inquire about the implementation of the pact, as far as the writer has been able to discover.

hoped that such an offensive would result in the withdrawal of some British naval units from the Atlantic. Well aware of the Fuehrer's aversion to provoking the United States, he emphasized that it was unlikely that America would take belligerent action in such a case. Hitler was not yet enthusiastic about the venture; he feared that Japan would not do anything decisive.[31] Less than two weeks later, however, he had changed his mind. The Japanese had evinced some interest in the British naval base themselves, and he decided that they should be given a free hand even at the risk of American intervention.[32] His desire to obtain Japanese help was beginning to blur his original resolve to keep the United States out of the war, but his alleged unconcern with eventual American steps, though repeated to the Duce shortly afterward,[33] appears to have been mainly braggadocio. In his subsequent dealings with Japan, Hitler continued to stress his interest in American neutrality. He consistently called for his Eastern partner to attack powers already at war with Germany and maintained that such a course would be most likely to keep America neutral by frightening her.[34]

Two excellent opportunities for pressing for this plan presented themselves to the Germans. Early in 1941, their supporter, General Oshima, returned to Berlin as Japanese Ambassador. Shortly afterward, Foreign Minister Matsuoka arrived in person for a series of talks with the Nazi leaders. Though the Nazis tried their best, they were unable to obtain any definite commitments.[35] Matsuoka, moreover, surprised the Germans by signing a neutrality pact with the Soviets, a development which caused Ambassador Ott in Tokyo to inquire anxiously what would happen in case of war between Russia and the Reich. Although the Japanese assured him that in such a case the pact would become inoperative, they still refused to follow his persistent suggestions to attack Singapore.[36]

Until the German attack on the Soviet Union, the Nazis had gen-

---

31. *Fuehrer Conferences*, 1940, II, 68–72. Cf. Samuel Eliot Morison, *History of United States Naval Operations in World War II*, Vol. III, *The Rising Sun in the Pacific* (Boston, 1948), 48, for earlier references to the plan.

32. *Fuehrer Conferences*, 1941, I, 1–4.

33. Document 134-C, *IMT*, XXXIV, 469.

34. Document 075-C, *IMT*, XXXIV, 302–305. This "Basic Order No. 24 Regarding Collaboration with Japan," issued to Hitler's armed forces, stated in part: "It must be the aim of the collaboration based on the Three Power Pact to induce Japan as soon as possible to take active measures in the Far East. . . . The common aim of the conduct of war is to be stressed as forcing England to the ground quickly and thereby keeping the United States out of war."

35. Document 1834-PS, *IMT*, XXVIII, 554–64; United States, Department of State, *Nazi-Soviet Relations, 1939–1941*, 2181–316; Paul Schmidt, *Statist auf diplomatischer Bühne, 1932–1945* (Bonn, 1949), 531.

36. Document NG-4422-C, "Weizsäcker Case."

erally advocated Japanese entry into war against the British and Dutch empires alone. After Hitler's break with Stalin, such objectives became inadequate. The Germans now desired that Japan attack not only Singapore but also Siberia. America's position in this new scheme of things remained the same: continued nonbelligerency, if at all possible. Von Ribbentrop believed that a Japanese offensive against Vladivostok would "prove the best argument to convince the United States of the utter futility of entering the war on the side of a Great Britain entirely isolated and confronted with the most powerful alliance in the world." [37] Ambassador Ott made repeated representations to this effect in Tokyo,[38] but the Japanese refused to commit themselves.

In other ways, too, a certain lack of harmony between the two ends of the Axis had become discernible even before the outbreak of the Russo-German war. Not only had the Japanese Government disregarded Hitler's strategic suggestions, but it had also initiated conversations with Secretary of State Cordell Hull for the purpose of coming to an understanding with the United States.[39] This development understandably did not please the Nazis. Should Japan and America reach an agreement, the purpose of the Tripartite Pact, to frighten the United States, would be defeated, and increased American attention to Europe might well be expected. The Germans were faced with a dilemma: unless they were prepared to give up their plans to utilize Japan as a diversionary force, they would have to attempt by some means to wreck the Washington conversations. In doing so, however, they might well be drawn into the very war they desired to avoid. In spite of this complication, they strained every effort to prevent any rapprochement between the two Pacific powers, lest the United States obtain a free hand in the Atlantic.[40]

Matsuoka, generally in sympathy with German views and ill-disposed toward the discussions,[41] tried to dispel Hitler's apprehensions by keeping the Nazis partially informed of the progress of the negotiations.[42] He assured the Germans that he would object to any provision not in accord with the Tripartite Pact and said that he would attempt to handle matters in such a way as to forestall participation by the United

---

37. Document NG-3437, "Weizsäcker Case." He thought Great Britain would shortly be completely isolated, as he considered Russia's collapse imminent; cf. Document 2896-PS, *IMT,* XXXI 258–62.

38. Document NG-3437, "Weizsäcker Case"; Document 2897-PS, *IMT,* XXXI, 258–62. Japan was to benefit by getting Eastern Siberia.

39. Herbert Feis, *The Road to Pearl Harbor* (Princeton, 1950), 192 *ff.*

40. United States, Office of United States Chief Counsel for Prosecution of Axis Criminality, *Nazi Conspiracy and Aggression* (Washington, 1946–1948), Supplement B, pp. 1200–1201; Document 4422-B, "Weizsäcker Case."

41. Feis, *op. cit.,* 193 *ff.*

42. Kato, *op. cit.,* 45.

States in the European war. He even promised to conduct the talks in a manner designed to prevent President Roosevelt from using convoys.[43] These may have been soothing assurances, but the Germans remained apprehensive and tried to induce the Japanese at least to make the abandonment of unneutral policies on the part of the United States a *sine qua non* in the discussions.[44]

In July, 1941, the Germanophile Matsuoka resigned. In spite of this evident setback, the Germans continued to attempt to wreck the discussions and press the Japanese to attack Vladivostok. Von Ribbentrop maintained that Japan must move quickly before the United States gained enough strength to become active.[45] The Japanese, however, were not impressed by this argument and even made plans for a personal meeting between Prince Konoye and President Roosevelt. When the German Ambassador expressed his concern about this unexpected development, Vice-Foreign Minister Amau reassured him that Japan only desired to carry out the old Axis policy of keeping America neutral,[46] a sentiment to which Foreign Minister Toyoda also subscribed.[47]

On October 16, 1941, the Konoye Cabinet fell, to be replaced by one headed by the militarist, General Hideki Tojo.[48] Oshima explained to the Wilhelmstrasse that this change represented a great gain for Axis solidarity; he had hopes for the rupture of the Washington conversations, but was unable to offer any assurance of a Japanese war against Russia.[49]

Either by accident or by design, Oshima failed to emphasize the real significance of the cabinet reorganization. The appointment of an extremist as prime minister was the logical consequence of Japan's determination to attack the United States should negotiations fail,[50] a possibility the Germans had scarcely ever discussed with their allies. If Hitler wanted to collaborate closely with Japan and possibly persuade her

43. Documents NG-4422-D and 4454, "Weizsäcker Case."
44. *Ibid.* For later efforts by the Germans to utilize the discussions to induce the United States to stop further participation in anti-German policies in the Atlantic, cf. Cordell Hull, *The Memoirs of Cordell Hull* (New York, 1948), 1034; United States, Department of State, *Papers Relating to the Foreign Relations of the United States, Japan, 1931–1941* (Washington, 1943), II, 686; Joseph C. Grew, *Ten Years in Japan* (New York, 1944), 464; *Pearl Harbor Attack*, XII, 71–72.
45. Document NG-3459, "Weizsäcker Case."
46. Document 3733-PS, *Nazi Conspiracy and Aggression*, VI, 545–46.
47. *Ibid.*
48. According to Konoye, Tojo was chosen as he was not so uncompromising as some of his army colleagues. Konoye Diary, *Pearl Harbor Attack*, XX, 4011.
49. Documents NG-4418, 4452, 4453, "Weizsäcker Case."
50. On July 2, 1941, an Imperial Conference had arrived at the decision to prepare for war with Great Britain and America should negotiations break down. *Pearl Harbor Attack*, XX, 4018–4019. Cf. Feis, *op. cit.*, pp. 209 *ff.*, 282.

to help him against Russia, he might have to follow that country's lead into policies quite different from those for which had long been working. He might find himself at war with America.

At first, the Nazis tried to meet this situation by virtually ignoring it and merely continued their original maneuvers.[51] Von Ribbentrop still urged his allies to act by bypassing American territories.[52] As for the Washington conversations, he persisted in his attempts to induce the Japanese to be firm in resisting American demands, presumably to counteract incessant American pressure upon Nomura to scrap the Tripartite Pact.[53] Otto von Erdmannsdorff, his special representative at the Japanese Embassy, followed instructions by continually urging on Ambassador Oshima offensives against Singapore and Vladivostok. Von Erdmannsdorff reported to the Foreign Minister that the long-expected advance might be directed against the Dutch East Indies alone, accompanied by a definite guaranty to the United States concerning the Philippines, although that archipelago would of course be taken should America enter the war.[54] The possibility of an attack on American possessions in the first place apparently did not even occur to von Erdmannsdorff.[55]

Nevertheless, indications of increased strain between the two Pacific powers mounted steadily. Foreign Minister Togo's notes to Nomura assumed a tone of ever greater urgency. Cordell Hull, informed of their contents by the "magic" code, correctly interpreted them as assuming the form of ultimata.[56] On November 19, American intelligence decoded the fateful "winds" message.[57]

Events were moving so quickly that in spite of all wishful thinking von Ribbentrop had to face the realities of the situation. As the negotiations in Washington showed little promise of success, Japan moved toward war with America. This involved, among other things, getting a German pledge of support. On November 18, the Japanese Government requested the Foreign Minister's assent to a treaty affirming Germany's intention never to conclude a separate peace treaty with common enemies. Who these were was not clear, but von Ribbentrop agreed in principle to the proposal.[58] Two days later, he received ominous news from Ambassa-

---

51. This incredible reaction may be accounted for by von Ribbentrop's illogical approach to problems of foreign policy.

52. Document 4421-NG, "Weizsäcker Case."

53. *Pearl Harbor Attack*, XII, 112, 143, 146, 147.

54. Document NG-4423, "Weizsäcker Case."

55. This blindness may have been conditioned by the Nazis' conviction of long standing that America ought not to be provoked prematurely.

56. Hull, *op. cit.,* p. 1055.

57. Should the Japanese newscaster insert the words, "East wind rain," in his daily broadcasts, war would break out with the United States. *Pearl Harbor Attack*, XII, 154–55.

58. Document 4070-B, "IMTFE," pp. 6637–638.

dor Ott. General Okamoto, a former military attaché in Berlin, had
asked if the Reich would join her partner even if Japan were to start
a war. The Ambassador had referred the General to von Ribbentrop's
promise to sign the no-separate-peace agreement, whereupon Okamoto
indicated that a decision on an advance toward the south was imminent.
Ott, adhering to the original German policy of keeping America on the
sidelines, explained that it might be wise to leave the initial decision up
to America, and believed the attack would be directed against Malaya,
Thailand, and Borneo.[59] The Germans evidently still hoped that actual
American entry might be postponed a little longer. They refused to be
provoked by the arming of American merchant ships and the occupation
of Surinam. The *Völkischer Beobachter* denounced these steps,[60] but the
Wilhelmstrasse failed to lodge a protest with the State Department, much
less make the occupation a *casus belli.*

The last two weeks of November were perhaps the most crucial
in the history of Axis-American relations. On the 20th, the Japanese
submitted their final proposals to Secretary Hull; on the 22nd, word
came to Nomura from Tokyo that a settlement must be reached by
the 29th at the very latest, and on the 26th, Secretary Hull delivered
what proved to be his final counter-offer to Nomura and Kurusu.
On the 25th, the Japanese task force set sail for Pearl Harbor—for
all practical purposes negotiations were coming to an end.[61]

Von Ribbentrop, too, was negotiating with the Japanese. Amid great
festivities, the Anti-Comintern Pact was renewed in Berlin on November
23,[62] and it was during these celebrations that he seems to have felt
called upon to make a decision concerning his American policy. Anxious
to cooperate with Japan as fully as possible, he was unwilling to let
that country reach any sort of understanding with the United States.
It had dawned upon him at last that the alternative might well involve
a development diametrically opposed to his two-year-old efforts to
neutralize the United States. Hence, he would either have to abandon his
neutrality policy or refuse to support Japan in her overall strategy.
Since the latter alternative did not fit in with his concept of Japan's
role as an allied power, he had to take the consequences and abandon
the idea of American nonbelligerency. It was characteristic of the erratic
nature of the Nazi regime that this weighty decision was made in a most
haphazard manner. Although he did not know that virtually the last
word had been spoken at Washington, he had a hunch and summoned

59. Document 4070, "IMTFE," pp. 6640–641.

60. *Völkischer Beobachter,* November 27, 1941.

61. Hull, *op. cit.,* 1074–1084; Robert E. Sherwood, *Roosevelt and Hopkins*
(New York, 1948), 421; Feis, *op. cit.,* 307 *ff.;* Walter P. Millis, *This Is Pearl*
(New York, 1947), 220 *ff.*

62. *Frankfurter Zeitung,* November 26 and 27, 1941.

Ambassador Oshima on November 28, 1941. After inquiring about the progress of the Hull-Nomura conversations, he said,

> We have received advice to the effect that there is practically no hope of the Japanese-U.S. negotiations being completed successfully, because of the fact that the United States is putting up a stiff front. If this is indeed the fact of the case, and if Japan reaches a decision to fight Britain and the United States, I am confident that that will not only be in the interest of Germany and Japan jointly, but would bring about favorable results for Japan herself.

This constituted a complete reversal. For years the Nazis had urged that Japan attack various nations but keep America neutral. Again and again Hitler had indicated that he wanted to finish other business, especially Russia, before dealing with the United States. Though the Soviets were far from defeated, the Foreign Minister was still willing to take on a new adversary. Oshima was taken aback by the sudden reversal. Just to make sure, he asked whether an actual state of war was to be established between Germany and the United States. At that moment, von Ribbentrop apparently realized that he had permitted his enthusiasm to carry him further than Hitler desired. All he said in reply was, "Roosevelt is a fanatic, so it is impossible to tell what he would do."

Oshima was considerably impressed by these statements. Emphasizing the change that had come over von Ribbentrop's thinking, he wrote to Tokyo on November 29,

> In view of the fact that Ribbentrop has said in the past that the United States would undoubtedly try to avoid war, and from the tenor of Hitler's recent speech and that of Ribbentrop, I feel that the German attitude toward the United States is considerably stiffened. There are indications at present that Germany would not refuse to fight the United States if necessary.[63]

In view of the Reich's past insistence on American "neutrality," Japan wanted to make sure to tie its partner closely to itself in its forthcoming war. Accordingly, on November 20, Oshima received instructions informing him that the Washington conversations stood "ruptured—broken." The directive continued,

> Will Your Honor, therefore, immediately interview Chancellor Hitler and Foreign Minister Ribbentrop and confidentially communicate to them a summary of the developments. . . . Say very secretly to them that there is extreme danger that war may suddenly break out between Japan and the Anglo-Saxon nations

63. *Pearl Harbor Attack*, XII, 200–202.

through some clash of arms and add that the time of the breaking out of that war may come quicker than anyone dreams.[64]

In Tokyo, Foreign Minister Togo went even further. After explaining in great detail to the German Ambassador that Japan's unwillingness to give up the Tripartite Pact had constituted the main reason for the failure of the Washington talks, he indicated that America was definitely preparing for a conflict. He emphasized again that his country had been firm with the Americans in order to keep them out of the European war as Germany had desired, but should worse come to worst, he wanted to be sure of German help. Ambassador Ott without hesitation promised all possible assistance.[65]

At first sight, these German assurances to the Japanese would indicate that the Nazis had made their choice and decided in favor of war-like support of Japan rather than continued attempts to keep the United States out. Apparently, however, they still were not sure of themselves. Von Ribbentrop himself evidently never realized his dilemma at all; after the end of the war, neither he nor Oshima was able to remember the interview of November 28. The Japanese managed to recall that "Germany tried to appease America in spite of the dangerous situation in the Atlantic." When confronted with the recorded transcript of the interview, he maintained that if von Ribbentrop had really voiced such sentiments, it was only to get some information from the Japanese or to keep them on his side.[66] Von Ribbentrop's memory also failed when he was questioned about his remarks to Oshima. Despite the fact that he was not clear about the circumstances of the conversation, he charged that the document contained an incorrect interpretation of the conference and insisted that he could not believe it to be true. Although his statements at Nuremberg must not be taken at face value, it is possible that the interview did not seem so important to him at the time as it actually turned out to be.[67] At any rate, he was not fully prepared to accept the consequences of his decisions. When the Japanese attempted to have the Germans sign a definite treaty of assistance, they encountered difficulties in spite of von Ribbentrop's promises.[68]

On December 1, Oshima received instructions to obtain specific pledges from the Germans.[69] When he approached von Ribbentrop concerning this matter, the Foreign Minister proved evasive and excused himself on the grounds that Hitler, temporarily absent from headquarters, would

64. *Ibid.,* 204.
65. Document 2889-PS, *IMT, XXXI,* 265–68.
66. "IMTFE," 34030.
67. *IMT,* X, 379–81.
68. *Infra,* 15–16.
69. Document 2157-D, "IMTFE," 6651; also 34033.

first have to be consulted.[70] On December 3, Oshima tried again. He averred that the situation was more critical than had been expected, but von Ribbentrop put him off once more, although he asserted his personal agreement with the proposed treaty of assistance.[71] The Nazis, in line with their previous policy, were stalling.

The Japanese found Mussolini more willing to comply with their wishes. He agreed to anything Japan might choose to undertake, including war against America.[72] The German Ambassador at Rome cabled Berlin that such a conflict was imminent and that the Japanese demanded an immediate declaration of war after its outbreak.[73]

Nevertheless, the Wilhelmstrasse still hesitated. In Ciano's words, Berlin's reaction to the Japanese move was extremely cautious. "Perhaps they will accept because they cannot get out of it," he wrote, "but the idea of provoking America's intervention pleases the Germans less and less." [74] As late as December 4, three days prior to the contemplated attack, they had not yet given a definite reply.[75]

All their stalling and hesitation could not obscure the fact that the Nazis had to come to an immediate decision. Japan was no longer willing to wait; Germany was unwilling to endanger its alliance with Japan. During the night of December 4–5, von Ribbentrop finally appears to have received Hitler's permission to comply with Japan's wishes. At 3 A.M., December 5, 1941, he gave Oshima a draft treaty embodying the Japanese demands for assistance against the United States and a pledge not to conclude a separate peace.[76] Simultaneously, he sent the German Ambassador at Rome to Ciano to submit the proposed treaties, a procedure which caused the latter to write, "After delaying two days, he [von Ribbentrop] cannot wait a minute longer to answer the Japanese." [77] Of course the vexatious Russian situation still remained to be disposed of; the Japanese had made up their minds to keep the Soviets neutral, an arrangement which their ambassadors were to attempt to explain as best they were able.[78] But when they dropped their bombs on Pearl Harbor, they could be fairly certain of German intervention, having a draft of an agreement to that effect virtually in their pocket.

Just how soon and under what circumstances they would be called

70. Document 1532-A, "IMTFE," 6654; *ibid.*, 34034.

71. *Pearl Harbor Attack,* IX, 4200.

72. *Ibid.,* XII, 228–29; Ciano, *L'Europa verso la catastrofe,* 684–87.

73. Document NG-4395, "Weizsäcker Case."

74. *Ciano Diaries,* 414 *ff.*

75. Leonardo Simoni, *Berlino Ambasciata d'Italia, 1939–1941* (Rome, 1946), 263.

76. *Pearl Harbor Attack,* XXXV, 684–85.

77. *Ciano Diaries,* 414–16.

78. *Pearl Harbor Attack,* XII, 245–46.

upon to honor their new pledges was not apparent to the Nazis until after the Pearl Harbor raid. While the German Naval Attaché in Tokyo heard on December 3 that action toward the south might be expected in the very near future, he was left in the dark concerning both date and place of such an offensive. On December 6, he was told that within three weeks simultaneous attacks upon Thailand, Borneo, and the Philippines might surprise the world,[79] while the German Ambassador heard from the Foreign Minister that a break of relations with America was expected. An official of the Japanese Foreign Office told Ott that Japan considered the Tripartite Pact to be applicable to any conflict between one of the signatories and the United States with the exception of a direct attack on the American continent, but he still maintained that it might be wiser to leave the first move up to the United States.[80] The Germans knew something was going to happen; von Ribbentrop declined a hunting invitation from the Hungarian Regent on December 6 because of the Far Eastern Crisis,[81] but what that something involved they never knew until after the surprise raid.

Pearl Harbor day must have been an unforgettable experience in Berlin as well as in Washington. When a member of the press department told the news to von Ribbentrop, the Foreign Minister's first reaction was one of skepticism. He felt that the story was merely an Allied propaganda trick by which the department had been taken in.[82] Hitler, too, refused to believe the first sensational reports.[83] When the news was confirmed, however, von Ribbentrop expressed great satisfaction with the acquisition of a new ally, forgetful for the moment of his former efforts to neutralize America and the implications of the failure of the endeavor.[84]

When the nature of the attack is kept in mind, it is not surprising that the raid caught the Germans, like so many others, completely unaware. Even in Japan, very few people knew about the preparations for the stroke. Neither Ambassador Nomura nor Kurusu knew exactly what was in store for their hosts.[85] Nor did the American Government, well informed as it was through the "magic" code, have any specific knowledge of what was coming.[86] The Germans knew even less. Von Weizsäcker recalled that it had generally been believed that Japan would attack Singapore, but no one had thought of Hawaii, nor con-

79. Document 872-D, *IMT*, XXXV, 619–23.

80. Document NG-4367, "Weizsäcker Case"; Erich Kordt, *Wahn und Wirklichkeit* (Stuttgart, 1948), 331.

81. Document NG-2705, "Weizsäcker Case."

82. *IMT*, X, 201; Schmidt, *op. cit.*, 541.

83. "Weizsäcker Case," 7807.

84. *Ciano Diaries*, 416.

85. *Pearl Harbor Attack*, XIII, 401.

86. Hull, *op. cit.*, 1093; Sherwood, *op. cit.*, 430.

sidered an outright attack on the United States possible.[87] Other officials substantially agreed with him.[88] Even the German Embassy in Tokyo was taken by surprise. According to Heinrich Stahmer, the impression had prevailed that Japan still wished to avoid war with the United States. "I, as an officer," he said, "could have no understanding [sic] at this time for creating a new enemy." [89] Prime Minister Tojo's deposition corroborated these statements. The General affirmed, "No close cooperation existed between Japan and Germany and Italy prior to the outbreak of war, and Japan's decision to go to war was made without regard to the attitude of Germany and Italy, and was dictated purely by the needs of self-defense." [90]

No matter how astonished the Nazis may have been, the opening of hostilities in the Pacific confronted them with the necessity of action. On Pearl Harbor day, Oshima formally called on the Foreign Minister and demanded that Germany declare war on the United States without fail. Von Ribbentrop assured him that he would do everything in his power to comply with Japan's wishes; Hitler was at that very moment at headquarters discussing the formalities of Germany's entry.[91] Simultaneously, the Japanese Foreign Minister submitted identical demands to the German Ambassador.[92]

Germany did what she had promised. On December 8, Hitler authorized the navy to attack all American ships on sight,[93] although he waited three days longer to address the Reichstag and formally declare war on the United States.[94] To emphasize the brotherhood of arms between Germany and Japan, he bestowed the Order of Merit of the German Eagle on Ambassador Oshima, cordially acknowledging services rendered in the achievement of German-Japanese cooperation.[95]

One question especially remains to be answered. Why did the Germans comply with Japan's request to declare war on the United States after having attempted to keep that country out of war for over two years? The Tripartite Pact did not obligate Hitler to join an offensive venture, for the draft treaty of December 5 had not yet been signed. Yet he

87. "Weizsäcker Case," 7907.

88. *IMT*, X, 296–97; XIII, 477; XIV, 120, 323.

89. Documents 2477, 2744-A, 29021, 2411; "IMTFE," 24643.

90. Document 3000, "IMTFE," 36396.

91. *Pearl Harbor Attack*, XII, 253.

92. Document NG-4424, "Weizsäcker Case."

93. *Pearl Harbor Attack*, XII, 253.

94. According to Louis P. Lochner, most Berliners believed their Fuehrer was too smart to declare war, and Hitler himself was not too sure. He had called the Reichstag to meet on December 9 at first, but did not convoke it until December 11. Louis P. Lochner, *What About Germany* (New York, 1943), 199–200.

95. Document 2932-PS, *IMT*, XXXI, 316–21.

interpreted both as binding. As a matter of fact, he took this decision at the very moment when his attempts to exert pressure on the Roosevelt Administration had met with partial success. The President and his advisers, expecting a Japanese attack on British outposts in the Far East, were faced with a serious dilemma. They knew how perilous such a move would be for their country but had no sure way of counteracting it because of isolationist sentiment.[96]

The following hypothesis may help to explain Hitler's actions under these circumstances. It must be remembered that he had long looked upon the Japanese alliance as one of the cornerstones of his global plans. As American aid to his enemies steadily increased, he became seriously worried lest the two Pacific powers compose their differences in the course of the Hull-Nomura conversations.[97] Under no circumstances was he willing to lose Japan as an ally. He would have preferred her to have attacked British, Russian, and Dutch territories, but since she would not do his bidding and was even negotiating with the Americans, he apparently felt he had to make concessions to her to keep her good will. Hence, in the later stages of the discussions, he was unable to press too much his determination to keep the United States out. If the Americans were to come into the conflict as a result, it would be the lesser of two evils, especially as the Foreign Office expected them to come in eventually.[98] It may be argued that he still could have refused to declare war on the United States after Pearl Harbor, but he could ill afford to break his promise to Japan two days after he had made them. Moreover, he felt he had to cooperate, since he still hoped that Japan might reciprocate and attack Russia from the rear. That he never abandoned this hope is shown by subsequent attempts to realize it.[99]

Hitler's decision violated his own principle of never striking until ready, but he had long fallen victim to his own propaganda concerning the weakness of the United States. He had refused to be impressed by warnings from the traveler and author, Colin Ross, against underestimating American war potential, although they had been delivered as early as October 1939.[100] He had maintained an equally supercilious attitude in his correspondence with Mussolini,[101] and in April 1941, he had boasted to Matsuoka of the superiority of the German soldier over his

96. Sherwood, *op. cit.*, 427.

97. Kordt, *op. cit.*, 332.

98. "Weizsäcker Case," 7904 *ff.*

99. Document 2911-PS and 2929-PS, *IMT*, XXXI, 273–80; 305–15.

100. *IMT*, XIV, 548–49.

101. *Les Lettres Secrètes échangées par Hitler et Mussolini* (Paris, 1946), 121–31.

American counterpart.[102] The Foreign Office in general and von Ribbentrop in particular had also become affected by this self-delusion.[103] The latter even justified the declaration of war on the ground that "a great power does not let others declare war on it, it declares it itself." [104] Last but not least, the German navy had made Hitler's decision easier for him, as his admirals had implored him for months to ease the restrictions imposed upon them to keep America neutral.[105] Some had even become convinced that Japan's active aid was preferable to continued American neutrality.[106] Consequently, he let himself be carried along by the ill-advised acts of his allies, instantaneously solving Roosevelt's dilemma. The isolationists, angered by the attack on the great Hawaiian naval base, ceased their opposition and rallied to their country's defense. Hitler had not only blundered, but had committed a folly which proved well-nigh irrevocable. He had ruined his own cause.

In conclusion, it would appear that Hitler's role in the Pearl Harbor attack was a very subordinate one. He had attempted for years to keep America out of war and had desired Japanese help against his other enemies. Only when Japan refused to heed his advice did he consent rather reluctantly to a different course of action, although he never had a clear idea of what his allies had in mind. This involved him in the very conflict he had desired to avoid, thus making certain the defeat of the Axis and the survival of the democratic powers.

102. *Nazi-Soviet Relations,* 314. On this occasion, he also promised assistance to Japan should she become involved in war with the United States, although his main theme remained the attack on Singapore and American non-belligerency. *Ibid.,* 311–16.

103. *Ibid.,* 303; Document NG-4371, "Weizsäcker Case."

104. Ernst von Weizsäcker, *Erinnerrungen* (Munich, Leipzig, Freiburg, 1950), 328.

105. *Fuehrer Conferences,* 1940, I, 12–19, II, 37–58, 1941, I, 12–19, 50–60, 62–76, 77–78, II, 1–2, 3–12, 13–22, 49; Dorothy E. Richard, "Hitler at Sea" (unpublished paper, Georgetown University, 1949).

106. "Weizsäcker Case," pp. 1904–920.

III

Wartime Diplomacy

SUMNER WELLES

Two Roosevelt Decisions:
One Debit, One Credit

The two most far-reaching issues of the Second World War were the territorial settlements in Eastern and Central Europe and the creation of a new world security organization. The Soviet Union stressed the territorial issue throughout the war, insisting that Russian security rather than the Wilsonian formula of self-determination be the basis for the postwar settlement in Europe. The United States concentrated on the concept of collective security in the belief that world peace rested on the formation of a new and stronger League of Nations. The clash between these pragmatic and idealistic goals reached a climax in the wartime conferences between the Big Three at Teheran and Yalta.

Sumner Welles, Under Secretary of State until mid-1943 and a lifelong Wilsonian, focuses on these incompatible political objectives in this article, which was later incorporated into his book Seven Decisions That Shaped History *(New York, 1951). Welles has also written on wartime diplomacy in* The Time for Decision *(New York, 1944) and in* Where Are We Heading? *(New York, 1946). The fullest accounts of the American role in the founding of the United Nations are Ruth B. Russell,* A History of the United Nations Charter *(Washington, D.C., 1958), and Robert A. Divine,* Second Chance *(New York, 1967).*

I

WHY DID THE United States not try to reach agreements with other members of the United Nations on political and territorial problems while the war was still in progress? Perhaps no one question about the conduct of wartime diplomacy is asked more frequently than this, and in no field of policy are critics—writing in the perspective of 1950—more sharp in their comments on the shortsightedness of Allied leaders. It is true that the President and his Secretary of State were officially committed to a policy of no agreements on territorial adjustments or political settlements until the war was over, at which time these could be taken up for consideration and decision at a peace conference

Reprinted by permission from *Foreign Affairs*, XIX (January 1951), 182–204.

of the United Nations. This very definitely was also the policy favored by the Foreign Relations Committee of the Senate. Perhaps it may be helpful at this crucial juncture of our affairs to review the background of this decision. Another fateful wartime decision, to create the United Nations organization while the war was still in progress, had a happier outcome. How and why that decision was reached I shall also attempt to relate in the pages which follow.

If the great peace conferences of Vienna in 1915 and of Paris in 1919 had taught any one lesson clearly, surely it was that victorious allies invariably quarrel among themselves over the division of the spoils. At Paris in 1919 we saw in particular how appallingly difficult it was to overcome the exaggerated forms of selfish nationalism to which a victorious war gives rise. This was so even though we then were negotiating primarily with Great Britain, France, and Italy, Western nations with ideals and practices similar to our own. This time we would be dealing with the Soviet Union. The Stalin-Hitler deal of August 1939 and the Kremlin's subsequent course hardly gave ground for confidence in the inherent altruism of the Bolshevik Politburo's foreign policy. What reason was there to think that, after the defeat of our common enemies, Russia triumphant would be disposed to give the claims of humanity to peace, freedom, happiness, and prosperity priority over her own demands for what Stalin would term "security"?

All the "spoils" that the United States wanted for itself at the end of the Second World War were a peace founded on justice and practical common sense so that future wars might be avoided. We would hardly be likely to secure this single end if we postponed taking action until once again the victors were quarreling around the peace conference table. Yet at the very outset the possibility that we would be able to take any steps in that direction seemed to be precluded.

Early in December 1941, Anthony Eden, then British Foreign Secretary, was about to go to Moscow. The United States was not yet at war, but he had let us know that the future status of the Baltic Republics would undoubtedly come up in his talks with Stalin and Molotov. I myself expressed the strong hope in talking with both the President and Secretary Hull that we would urge the British Government not to make any final agreement which would commit Great Britain to support the permanent obliteration of the three states in question— Lithuania, Latvia, and Estonia. A message in that sense was sent to Foreign Secretary Eden on December 5, 1941, through Ambassador Winant in London.

But the message sent by Secretary Hull went much farther indeed than a mere note of caution on this specific issue. The position he took was that, inasmuch as the Soviet, British, and United States Governments were bound by their acceptance of the Atlantic Charter to be guided by its principles in all postwar settlements, no specific terms of settlement should be agreed upon before the final peace conference. The Secretary of State very properly concluded by also urging that in any event no secret commitments should be made. At the moment when the message was sent (only two days before Pearl Harbor), the terms in which it was couched seemed innocuous enough. The principles for postwar policy laid down by the Atlantic Charter provided an altogether desirable pattern.

Yet they constituted a pattern, and nothing more. They gave no slightest indication, for example, as to the justice or injustice of a given settlement covering eastern Poland. The Soviet Government might claim quite plausibly that its retention of eastern Poland would not be territorial aggrandizement of the sort prohibited by the first article of the Atlantic Charter, but, on the contrary, a "territorial change" that fully accorded "with the freely expressed wishes of the peoples concerned," as authorized by the second article. Yet the Polish Government-in-Exile would inevitably maintain that such a "territorial change" was aggrandizement at its worst and that the wishes of "the peoples concerned" could not be "freely expressed." Agreement upon the broad principles of the Atlantic Charter would never in itself prevent future controversies over frontiers and zones of influence.

In any event, the message to Anthony Eden created a precedent upon which a policy was soon erected. When the British Foreign Secretary left for Moscow, he took instructions from his Cabinet which were similar in intent to the request made by the United States Government. In Moscow, however, he was met with an insistent demand that Great Britain without further ado formally commit herself to the recognition of Russia's 1941 frontiers as they had been established by Stalin's deal with Hitler in 1939. Stalin also proposed the restoration of Austria as an independent state, the detachment of the Rhineland from Prussia as an independent state or protectorate, and possibly the constitution of an independent state of Bavaria. Other suggested territorial changes included the transfer of East Prussia to Poland and of Sudetenland to Czechoslovakia, as well as certain adjustments in the Balkans. "As regards the special interests of the Soviet Union," according to Mr. Eden, "Stalin desired the restoration of the position in 1941, prior to the German attack, in respect of the Baltic States, Finland and Bessarabia. The 'Curzon Line' should form the basis for the future Soviet-Polish frontier, and Rumania should give special facilities for bases, etc., to the Soviet Union, receiving compensation from territory now occupied by Hungary." [1] British recognition of the Soviet demands was to be a preliminary to any Anglo-Soviet treaty of alliance.

1. Winston S. Churchill, *The Grand Alliance* (Boston: Houghton Mifflin, 1950), p. 628.

In accordance with his instructions, Mr. Eden limited himself while in Moscow to the promise that the Russian claims would at some future time be considered by the British Commonwealth as well as by the United States. But upon his return to London he was further pressed by Mr. Molotov, and from Mr. Eden's messages it appeared that he felt the need to comply unless the English-speaking powers were willing to run the risk of an early break with their Soviet ally and of a separate peace treaty between the Soviet Union and Germany.

The issue was, of course, clear-cut. It was evident that even at the climax of the furious German assault upon the Soviet armies Stalin wished to be sure that he would retain the fruits of his earlier collusion with Hitler. The Soviet Government had just subscribed to the United Nations declaration and, consequently, to the provisions of the Atlantic Charter. Yet it was now pressing for a commitment which would violate the spirit as well as the letter of the Charter.

From our standpoint in Washington such an agreement was unthinkable. Our acquiescence in it would have been interpreted in every quarter of the globe as meaning that the Atlantic Charter, in which the British and American Governments had solemnly announced their intention of securing a future peace which would assure "the right of all peoples to choose the form of government under which they will live," was, in fact, no more than a hollow sham, a collection of high-sounding phrases designed merely to impress the ingenuous. It would have lost the United States that invaluable measure of moral support which was forthcoming in all the countries where people were still able to think and speak freely, and which eventually proved to be of such great avail in the winning of the war.

We found that Mr. Churchill stood four-square with us on this issue. He stated categorically during his first visit to Washington as Prime Minister what he has frequently since reiterated, that "the Baltic States should be sovereign independent peoples." In a message to Mr. Eden of January 8, 1942, he said: "The transfer of the peoples of the Baltic States to Soviet Russia against their will would be contrary to all the principles for which we are fighting this war and would dishonor our cause. This also applies to Bessarabia and to Northern Bukovina and in a lesser degree to Finland, which I gather it is not intended wholly to subjugate and absorb. . . . In any case there can be no question of settling frontiers until the peace conference. I know President Roosevelt holds this view as strongly as I do, and he has several times expressed his pleasure to me at the firm line we took at Moscow. . . . There must be no mistake about the opinion of any British Government of which I am the head, namely, that it adheres to those principles of freedom and democracy set forth in the Atlantic Charter, and that these principles must become especially active whenever any question of transferring territory is raised." [2]

It was thus, barely a month after the United States entered the war, that a firm agreement was reached between the American and British Governments that no commitments upon postwar political and territorial settlements should be made until the peace conference. For the time being, the Soviet Government acquiesced. When Molotov visited Washington six months later, in June 1942, he proffered no demand for a reconsideration of the American and British refusal to recognize Russia's frontiers prior to June 1941.

Yet it was inconceivable, of course, that the lesser powers which had territorial or political disputes with the Soviet Union, or with their smaller neighbors, should not seek during the war, while they were bound together in the common cause against Hitler, to get by direct negotiation a settlement that would be confirmed after the victory. If any demonstration of this had been needed, it was soon afforded, first by the several visits to Washington of General Sikorski, the Prime Minister of the Polish Government-in-Exile, and later by the visits of President Beneš of Czechoslovakia.

Sikorski recognized, of course, that no final commitments as to the future status of Poland or the future extension of Polish territory could be made by any Polish Government-in-Exile, but that these matters must await the freely expressed decision of the Polish people themselves. Nevertheless, he told me that it would be criminally shortsighted on his part not to seek an opportunity during the war of reaching an agreement with the Soviet Union and with Czechoslovakia on political and territorial isues, so that the entire problem could be successfully clarified before any peace conference was held.

He felt—correctly, I think—that there would be no difficulty in finding an agreement with Czechoslovakia. Whether he was equally justified in speaking so confidently, on the basis of his conversations with Stalin in Moscow in 1941, of his ability to negotiate a fair settlement with the Soviet Union, is another matter. I remember clearly how he told me that Stalin had quoted to him, with apparent approval, Lenin's remark to the effect that the Soviet Government must realize that the Poles had reason to hate Russia and must treat them in a friendly way and give Polish nationalism full recognition. In any event, after Sikorski had succeeded, with British help, in restoring diplomatic relations with Moscow, and had arranged for the formation of a Polish Army to fight against Germany on Russian soil, he felt that he had made concrete progress and that he was not unduly optimistic in

---

2. Churchill, *op. cit.*, p. 695.

believing that fair political and territorial adjustments might be negotiated with Stalin.

President Beneš had had greater experience in the international arena and so was less sanguine. He recognized realistically, as he told me, that the future independence and security of Czechoslovakia lay solely in her ability to walk the tightrope over the abyss between the East and the West. For that reason he undertook his wartime visits to Moscow in the belief that only through understandings reached directly with Stalin could there be any hope that his country would be saved from Russian hegemony in the years to come.

In the same way, the representatives of almost all the smaller European members of the United Nations spoke to me of this, that, or the other territorial rectification or reparation which they were determined to seek and which they hoped to consolidate by prior agreement before the end of the war.

In fact, one of the questions uppermost in my mind during the two years after Pearl Harbor was whether the United States Government was not losing an unparalleled opportunity to further the achievement of the kind of peace desired by the American people. By the spring of 1942 we had already commenced within the State Department our intensive study of the kind of world organization and of the kind of political and territorial settlements that we wanted to see made. The work was undertaken by the Advisory Committee on Post-War Foreign Policy, set up in the State Department under my chairmanship, on the authority of President Roosevelt, exactly three weeks after Pearl Harbor. The Committee at first was small, consisting of a few Department officials, a handful of private citizens called in because of their special knowledge, and several Congressional leaders of both parties whom the President had authorized me to invite. Later it became unwieldy and was the subject of endless bickering and internecine feuds.

But even in the period when the Advisory Committee could function effectively, the results of its studies necessarily represented merely the formulation of what we Americans believed to be wise, right, and just. We might assume that our views would be found to coincide very largely with those of the British Commonwealth, of our neighbors of the Western Hemisphere, and of the lesser powers of Western Europe. But in the light of our experience to date with the Soviet Union, what possible assurance could we have that when the peace conference arrived Moscow would be willing to accept even a small percentage of our recommendations? Was it not the part of wisdom, as soon as our views had been formulated, and as soon as we had ascertained what the views of our American neighbors and of some of the smaller countries of Europe might be, to try to do what Mrs. Roosevelt had suggested three years before, namely, set up officially an international group "continuously to plan for future peace"? Should we not create a body, similar in its composition to what later became the Security Council of the United Nations, and representing all of the United Nations, so that this organism might commence without delay to study the future structure of the world, iron out so far as might be possible difficulties among the several members of the United Nations, and be prepared at the end of the war to present for the final approval of the peace conference a series of settlements and of postwar policies already agreed upon in principle? I naturally discussed this possibility with the other members of the Advisory Committee. There the suggestion met with general approval, enthusiastic on the part of some and tepid on the part of others. Yet at the highest level it was summarily turned down.

I think it is wholly accurate to say that, while the President decided to reject the proposal, the intrinsic idea commended itself to him. In judging his decision we must remember the several influences which were being brought to bear upon him and the considerations by which a Commander-in-Chief must necessarily be guided. Winning the war was and had to remain the foremost objective. No step in the political realm, however beneficial it might promise to be later on, could properly be taken if it jeopardized or threatened to postpone the victory.

The first ten months of 1942 were for us the darkest period of the war. We had to face not only the succession of disasters which had struck us in the Pacific but also the series of calamities which had overtaken the British war effort since Pearl Harbor—the setbacks in Libya, the Nazi occupation of Greece, the fall of Crete, and the growing threat to the security of Egypt. The Russian armies were resisting the German onslaught magnificently, but how long could they hold?

It was altogether natural that the Joint Chiefs of Staff should constantly warn the President that, whatever advantages might theoretically be gained by trying to settle political and territorial problems during the war, these future assets must be regarded as offset by the immediate dangers of awakening controversies with Russia. If we joined with the British in such an attempt we would at once run headlong into a renewed demand that we recognize the 1941 frontiers of Soviet Russia. How could we do so in view of the position which we had already taken? And would we not inevitably find it impossible to concede other claims that Russia might advance later—for control of the Straits, for a predominant position in Iran, and for strategic and territorial concessions in the Far East—without incurring the legitimate resentment of the peoples of Turkey, the Middle East, and China?

On the other hand, suppose we continued firm in rejecting the Russian claims. Would we not, at best, bring about a breakdown in Russian cooperation with us in the war against Germany, or, at the worst (and this possibility was in the minds of the Joint Chiefs of Staff throughout the war), encourage the Kremlin to negotiate a separate peace with Hitler? The Joint Chiefs of Staff frequently emphasized the significance of the British Cabinet's belief that a message received from Moscow as early as September 5, 1941, conveyed the impression that Stalin was already then thinking of coming to terms with Germany separately. Representations like these would have been persuasive at any time. During the dark year of 1942 they were necessarily decisive.

There were other considerations as well. The Secretary of State was temperamentally disposed to put off dealing with controversial isues as long as possible. He preferred not to cross the proverbial bridge until he came to it. A remedial policy was to him preferable to a preventive policy. If the discussion of such exceedingly thorny problems as the Baltic States or Poland's eastern frontiers could be postponed until a peace conference, that was infinitely better than grasping the nettle now with decision and dispatch. And this was a moment, it is to be remembered, when as a consequence of the extreme friction that had arisen between President Roosevelt and Mr. Hull in January 1942 the President was making every effort to avoid running counter to Mr. Hull's recommendations.

Nor must we lose sight of the President's never-failing preoccupation with his role as wartime leader of the American people. He was determined to preserve national unity. If it became known that the Government was engaged in discussions about the future frontiers of Poland, the future status of the Baltic States, and other East European postwar settlements, there could be little doubt that large racial minorities in this country would at once be greatly exercised and become divided into quarreling and antagonistic groups.

Last, but by no means least, was the fact that while the President saw clearly the advantages of going to the peace conference with prior agreements on political and territorial problems, he by no means felt that our hope of securing a good peace would necessarily be prejudiced by postponing the discussion of these issues. For he had—and justly— great confidence in his own ability as a negotiator.

It is perhaps only fair to add that President Roosevelt was apt occasionally to place too much reliance upon a few favorite panaceas in his approach to problems which actually were too basic and far-reaching in their origins and nature to admit of easy solutions. For example, he had a faith in the efficacy of plebiscites as a cure-all for most of Europe's territorial controversies. He was even more wedded than Woodrow Wilson had been to the idea that plebiscites are a universal remedy. It was at about this time that he talked to me one evening for well over an hour about the desirability of employing this method to settle once and for all the friction among the Serbs, Croats, and Slovenes which had so beclouded the history of Jugoslavia as an independent state. He apparently did not attribute much importance to the harm that would be done to the national economies of all three peoples should they decide to become independent entities. It was also his original intention to recommend this same plebiscite principle if and when the time came to discuss the future of the Baltic States with Stalin. He said that he was certain that he could get Stalin to agree that a freely-conducted plebiscite should be held in all three of the republics, under international auspices. As is now well known, the President found out at Yalta how vain this illusion had been. Stalin told him that the subject was one which he refused to discuss, inasmuch as the Baltic peoples had already voted to join the Soviet Union.

As the months passed, however, it became plain that while it might be much easier and in some ways perhaps more expedient to postpone discussions of such problems as these until the peace conference, the morale of certain countries—China, for example—would be seriously impaired if their governments could not be given a firm assurance as to their future status. It was also becoming more and more apparent that the appetite of a victorious Soviet Union might well become inordinate if no effort was made to check it before the end of the war. The recognition of these imperious necessities resulted in several purely political actions. Declarations covering the restoration of Austrian independence and the future status of Italy were issued when the Foreign Ministers of the four major allies met in Moscow in October 1943; and a declaration covering Korean independence and the restoration to China of Manchuria, Formosa, and the Pescadores was made when the President met with Chiang Kai-shek and Churchill at Cairo in December of the same year.

At Teheran and at Yalta, new and significant political agreements were reached. It was at Teheran that the President first brought up the suggestion that Russia should have access to the Manchurian port of Dairen. At Teheran, too, Stalin temporarily reversed the position which he had taken in his conferences with Eden the year before; he stated that there was no need at that moment for him to speak of Russia's future territorial interests, but added, not without grim significance, that "when the time comes we will speak." It was at Yalta that Roosevelt and Churchill conceded Stalin's demands in the Far East, including the recovery of Southern Sakhalin and the Kurile Islands and the acquisition of a position in Manchuria that was tantamount to full control of that ancient Chinese province. At Yalta, also, Poland's future limits and the political composition of her future government were taken up.

What this brief record shows is that the position so confidently and firmly taken by the British and American Governments in January 1942 was wholly at variance with the course which they later actually pursued, and that this change of policy in a matter of vital significance apparently was not due to a conscious decision by either of them. They seem to have been drifting into a fundamental modification of policy without any realistic apprehension of all its implications.

It must be ruefully admitted, also, that many of the American discussions of postwar territorial and political problems with the Soviet Union were undertaken in a singularly haphazard fashion and without full consideration or preparation. In January 1942, there were two clear-cut alternatives before the United States. One was to create an official international commission, "continuously to plan for future peace." The other was to refuse resolutely to discuss any political or territorial question until a peace conference assembled. Each course had its advantages and disadvantages. My own judgment now, as it was then, is that the advantages of the former far outweighed its disadvantages. By sticking neither to one nor the other, we fell between two stools. The immense influence which the United States possessed immediately after Pearl Harbor was not exercised. When the United States did attempt to negotiate political settlements, its influence was no longer decisive.

Further, it would be hard to deny that before 1943 the influence of the United States would probably have been conclusive if it had been utilized to support postwar settlements which, although insuring legitimate security to the Russian people, would at the same time have seemed just and wise to the remaining peoples of Europe, the New World, and the Far East. At that stage its moral influence was incomparably greater than that of either of its major allies. Mr. Churchill had aroused the hearts and souls of the English-speaking world by his resplendent war leadership. Nevertheless, the part played by his predecessors in European affairs during the decades between the two world wars, his own more recent quarrel with the French, and Britain's role as a colonial power in Asia, Africa, and the Near East, diminished popular confidence in the British Government. As for the Soviet Government, the suspicion and mistrust aroused by its policy after 1917, and the long war waged by the Kremlin upon organized religion, had deprived Soviet Russia of the moral support of a large part of the world outside of the Communist party membership. Her struggle against Hitlerism had brought her admiration and a measure of popular backing. Nevertheless, it was to the United States, and in particular to Roosevelt himself, that countless millions of men and women in every part of the globe were turning more and more for leadership in winning freedom and security.

The political influence of the United States was at its peak. Its military strength was already far greater, in proportion to the strength of its allies, than it ever had been during the First World War. The success of the North African operation had revealed its military potentialities. In the production field it was plainly supreme. Two years later, it is true, the Navy, the Army, and the Air Force were to be immeasurably greater in striking power. Yet by then the Soviet armies had demonstrably defeated the Nazi invaders.

Stalin himself, at the Teheran Conference at the end of 1942, declared that, except for American production, "the war would have been lost." The armament production which he wrested from the hardly beset Russian people after the German invasion was nothing short of miraculous. But the arms and airplanes which he received from the then limited resources of the United States, in those first dire months when the Russian armies were so sorely pressed that he begged both the British and American Governments to send divisions under their own command to fight on Russian soil, helped greatly to make possible the victory at Moscow.

Should not the United States, at the moment of which I speak, have explored the postwar political and territorial settlements? Is it not probable that if it had done so its influence would have been sufficiently potent to have kept those settlements within the bounds which a subsequent peace conference of all the United Nations would have been disposed to accept as legitimate and equitable?

To answer these questions we must try to estimate what Stalin would have regarded as the irreducible minimum of his demands. We know what those demands were in December 1941, when he presented them to Mr. Eden. At that very moment the German armies had reached a point only a few miles from Moscow. It would be logical to assume that when Russia's fortunes seemed to be at their lowest ebb Stalin was not resorting to sheer bargaining, and that he was sincere in maintaining that if Russia were victorious she could not accept less than the territorial security that his demands represented.

Of the commitments for which Stalin then asked, one, the Curzon Line, had long been regarded in the West as a legitimate boundary between Poland and Russia, for ethnic as well as strategic reasons. It was, in fact, accepted by Churchill and Roosevelt at the Teheran Conference later that year. The adjustments involving Bessarabia and Bukovina were not a major difficulty. From the American standpoint, the only one of the commitments sought by Stalin that could not have been accepted was that for the permanent incorporation of the three Baltic Republics into the Soviet Union.

Yet even here it is doubtful whether Stalin in the winter of 1943 would have proved altogether obdurate. Up to the time of the deal with Hitler, his own record had been one of consistent opposition to all projects for the increase of Russian territory. It is not often remarked nowadays that it was Stalin himself who went to Helsinki in 1917 to declare the independence of Finland from Russia. Time and again he had anounced as his immutable policy, "Not one foot of foreign soil." In this he was, of course, repeating one of Lenin's most cherished tenets. And we find him in 1925 announcing that any effort on the part of the Soviet Union to acquire spheres of influence abroad would be "the road to nationalism and degeneration, the road of full liquidation of the international policy of the proletariat." Until the eve of the Second World War, so far as we can tell from the documents so far made public, as well as by Stalin's support of Litvinov's efforts on behalf of collective security, he had never wavered from that position. It seems by no means unreasonable to assume that some fair solution of this one basic difficulty might have been found if the matter had been broached in the early days of the joint war effort. Such a settlement would, of course, have had to include an assurance to Stalin that the solution would provide security against a new attack from a rearmed Germany in the years to come. This danger was an obsession with him which governed all his thinking in his dealings with his major allies.

But if Stalin had proved impervious to all American suggestions, what course could he have pursued in the winter of 1943? He could not have risked a withdrawal of lend-lease assistance or a diminution of Anglo-American cooperation without inviting a Russian defeat. The consensus of opinion in Washington and London was that he might sue for a separate peace with Germany. We now know that he was equally fearful that his Western allies might make such a peace. Yet Stalin at that time had by no means attained the measure of popularity that was to be his during the last years of the war; and to sue for a separate peace would have been most unpopular with the Russian people, then in a state of savage fury over the devastation of their homeland and the atrocities perpetrated by the Nazis. Finally, what prospect was there at that moment that he could secure even as good peace terms from an enraged Hitler as had been granted to Russia in the shameful Brest-Litovsk Treaty 25 years before?

From that time on the situation altered rapidly. The victory at Stalingrad was followed by the ultimate German retreat. The Red armies occupied the territory to which Stalin had laid claim. The moment for negotiation was gone. Simultaneously, as Russia's military strength increased, the leverage which American political, military, and industrial strength could exert upon the Kremlin correspondingly diminished. Soviet Russia had become the principal power in Europe and in Asia, and her ambitions grew proportionately.

As I see it, the critics of the agreements reached at Teheran, Yalta, and Potsdam confuse cause and effect. The agreements so bitterly assailed would have been far different in their nature had the President decided in 1942 to insist upon the creation of a United Nations Council charged with the duty of finding solutions for political and territorial problems before the end of the war. His refusal to do so was in accord with the advice given him by the Joint Chiefs of Staff, by his Secretary of State, and by most of his White House advisers, as well as with the views then held by the Prime Minister of Great Britain. He made his decision in the conviction that as Commander-in-Chief he possessed the paramount obligation to permit nothing to jeopardize the winning of the war. Yet with the advantage that hindsight gives us, is it not fair to say that it was that decision which was largely responsible for the division of the world today into two hostile camps?

II

In another field where the Advisory Committee on Post-War Problems did long and careful work, the accomplishment was more satisfactory. The planning for future international organization which was undertaken in the Department of State during the war did not at first appeal to the President. But in 1942, counter to his early inclinations, he approved it as the basis for the Moscow Declaration which opened the way for the subsequent Dumbarton Oaks Conference. In the early stages of the war he had not believed that the time was propitious to create a world organization. Yet at Teheran in 1943 he initiated the discussions with Churchill and Stalin which later made possible the negotiation of the U.N. Charter at San Francisco. To him, indeed, and to him alone, we owe the fact that a preliminary United Nations organization came into existence before the end of the war; and without that there would have been no United Nations today.

Why did Roosevelt believe, as late as 1941, that the United States should make no commitment to help rebuild an "effective international organization"? As a vice-presidential nominee in the campaign of 1920, he had made more than 800 speeches in support of the League of Nations. Yet all of his intimates knew that during the following two decades his enthusiasm for the League had cooled to a point where it might fairly be described as glacial.

This was due in part, I think, to his disgust, after the first few years of the League's existence, with the way the British and the French, particularly the former, so frequently prevented the League from facing any major issue squarely. He said to me once, in 1935: "The League of Nations has become nothing more than a debating society, and a poor one at that!"

But it must also be remembered that the President himself, consummate politician that he was, was never blind to what was politically inexpedient. In the early thirties he felt that the American people were firmly wedded to a policy of isolation, and that the question of American participation in the League—as distinguished from the World Court—had become altogether academic. Had he raised the League issue in the campaigns of 1932 or 1936, he knew his Republican opponents would have secured great political advantage from playing again on all of those jealousies, fears, and suspicions that had so fatally confused the voters in the 1920 campaign.

It is also, perhaps, a characteristic of many of the members of the Roosevelt clan to overestimate the value of success in itself and to appraise unsuccessful causes and endeavors too cheaply merely because of their failure. And no one could deny that the League of Nations had been an abject failure.

Another compelling motive for the President's failure to devote much thought to the details of international organization immediately before and after Pearl Harbor was his preoccupation with his role as Commander-in-Chief of America's armed forces. He felt that his first obligation was to persuade the American people to subordinate every other consideration to winning the war. As early as September 11, 1939, Mrs. Roosevelt had publicly stated: "Let us pray that this time we will have strength and foresight enough to plan a more permanent way of peace. . . . I should like to see an international group meeting now continuously to plan for future peace." But I know that her view was not shared by most of the President's White House advisers. Some of them, like Harry Hopkins, were inclined toward isolationism because of early environment and individual preference. Others whose duties were largely confined to the field of practical politics strongly felt that anything resembling an appeal for American participation in a postwar international organization would resurrect the old League of Nations controversy and would be filled with political dynamite. They insisted that it was a dangerous and unnecessary risk.

These influences were all the stronger because they coincided with certain of the President's own inclinations and prejudices. Yet the factors which brought about a complete change in his viewpoint proved in the long run more powerful still.

There were, first of all, the spectacular results of his own initiative in summoning the Inter-American Conference for the Maintenance of Peace at Buenos Aires in 1936. During the next five years the President had seen the rapid and steady growth of a regional organization composed of the 21 American republics. He had seen this organization bring hemispheric solidarity against the Axis powers. He had also been profoundly impressed, and somewhat surprised, by the enthusiastic reception which American public opinion had given the Atlantic Charter. The Charter represented a total break with the narrowly isolationist policies of the Harding, Coolidge, and Hoover administrations. It declared that the United States, a nation still nominally neutral, would cooperate after the war in laying the foundations for a decent and peaceful world. He had seen the American people respond with almost universal approval.

The mounting list of casualties within the family of nations also affected his thinking. He had been revolted to the very depths of his soul in 1939 and 1940 by the prospect of the kind of world that Hitler, Mussolini, and Stalin were so rapidly creating. His original reaction had been the concept of an Anglo-American policing job. But as time went on he saw that, appealing as the idea might be, it could not work. Britain, even though victorious, would be ruined at the end of the war. New and mighty revolutionary forces were arising throughout the world, and even the unparalleled power and resources of the United States could not successfully cope with them alone. Some other answer had to be found.

But I am convinced that the determining factor was the immense impact of Pearl Harbor itself. The disaster brought home to him the full realization that today Great Power aggression can be forestalled only by effective collective security. In any event, the definitive change in Roosevelt's beliefs took place between the Atlantic Charter meeting and the spring of 1942.

The reason I feel that I can speak with authority on this is that, in the very many talks which I had with the President between 1936 and the summer of 1941 on the subject of international organization he never once was willing to agree that an organization composed of all non-totalitarian countries was as yet feasible. Much less did he agree that the United States should attempt to participate in the construction of a new international organization. After Pearl Harbor, however, he not only became steadily more engrossed in the possibility of international organization; he made plain that I might take it for granted that, when and if, in his judgment, the moment became ripe, he would assert American leadership in an attempt to create the kind of new world envisaged in the Atlantic Charter.

During the first part of 1942 it is quite true the President frequently used to say that he did not want to become drawn into the intensive studies of postwar settlements already under way in the Department of State. This was primarily because he feared that if he did really get into them he would become so interested that he might be tempted to devote less of his time and thought to the war effort itself. It was also probably due to his wish to keep an open mind regarding frontiers and other postwar problems, knowing that some compromises would be inevitable and that it would be inexpedient for him to become too fixed in advance in his own convictions about particular solutions.

At the beginning of 1943, after I had been urging him to let me have the needed time, the President finally gave me an uninterrupted two hours at the White House in which I might show him in written form the tentative conclusions reached by our Advisory Committee regarding a future international organization. He saw me in his office late one afternoon after the day's appointments were finished and after he had signed the urgent papers in the wire baskets which flowed so endlessly across his desk. For once he was not in a digressive mood. He read very carefully the memoranda and charts that I placed before him.

At that stage the members of the Departmental committee were almost unanimously of the opinion that any new world structure should be built upon regional organizations similar to the Organization of American States. Each of these regional organizations would periodically elect representatives to sit in a superior executive council to which supreme authority would be delegated by all of the members of the United Nations. This executive council was to be composed of 11 members, seven of them to be elected by the regional organizations and the remaining four to be delegates of the United States, the Soviet Union, Great Britain, and China. These four were to have permanent seats, with a veto to the extent that the employment of military force could be ordered by the supreme executive council only if nine of its members voted affirmatively. However, if any one of the major powers was found guilty of aggression, that country should not be permitted to veto the use of military sanctions upon it.

In general, the President thought well of the project. He expressed considerable doubt, however, whether regional organizations of the Near East and, for that matter, of Asia, could be expected to function efficiently, in view of the lack of experience in self-government of most of the peoples in those areas.

The President held some exceedingly decided views as to the nations that should be given the ultimate authority to run the world during the first years after the war. There was naturally no question about the Soviet Union, Great Britain, and the United States. But he could not persuade himself that France was entitled at that juncture to be regarded as a major power. He felt that her recovery would be impossible if she continued to spend the major part of her national revenues upon armaments and a standing army, and that, since Germany must be dismembered, disarmed, and placed under international control, there was no reason why France should continue to maintain a great military establishment.

On the other hand, he was equally positive that China from the outset should be regarded as a major power, with a permanent seat on the supreme executive committee of the United Nations. He felt, he said, that recognition of China's status as one of the four major powers would prevent any charge that the white races were undertaking to dominate the world; that it would do much to stimulate patriotism and national pride in China, and to pull the various contending factions together; and that a stable China, recognized as one of the Great Powers, would be a barrier to Soviet ambitions in the Far East and serve as a centripetal force in Asia. This would be of the utmost value in limiting the effects of the revolutionary tidal wave already looming in the Far East.

I fully agreed with the President's conclusions concerning China. But I believed that only harm would result if he persisted in his views about France. In fact, I argued with him for some time, pointing out that if, as I hoped, Germany was going to be disarmed and divided into a number of autonomous sovereign states, Great Britain alone could not be expected—especially in view of her losses during the Second World War —to balance in Western Europe the weight of the Soviet Union in Eastern Europe. I doubt that my arguments had much effect at that time. Two years later, however, the President himself was to urge the Soviet Union to agree to French participation in the military control of Germany. He also subsequently dropped all ideas of French disarmament, probably as a result of the representation made to him by Mr. Churchill. At all events I never heard him refer to it again.

The State Department's projects had been thoroughly digested by the President and were very much in his mind when Anthony Eden, then British Secretary of State for Foreign Affairs, came to Washington in March 1943 to canvass our Government's views on postwar problems. Shortly before his arrival, Mr. Churchill had delivered a speech on postwar problems which gave the impression that he was interested solely in the creation after the war of a regional European organization which the United States should be invited to join, and that he had abandoned his earlier support for a more general international organization. Mr. Eden made it plain that he himself staunchly favored the construction of a new, universal, international organization, though he deprecated the idea that the Prime Minister really differed with him in that regard.

Mr. Eden came to the White House one day late in March for a full discussion with the President, the British Ambassador, Secretary Hull, and myself. The President outlined the kind of international organization which he had been thinking over since my talk with him in January. He emphasized, rather more strongly than I hoped he would, his belief that Great Britain, the Soviet Union, and the United States, together with China, must for a long time to come assert the right to make all the basic decisions affecting the maintenance of world order. As I remember the conversation—which was comprehensive, although at times it ran off on side issues—there was already a very remarkable meeting of minds between the British and ourselves, even on the subject of trusteeships.

In June of that year I gave the President the final blueprint of the United Nations as we had formulated it in the Department, and when

3. Robert E. Sherwood, *Roosevelt and Hopkins* (New York: Harper, 1948), p. 789.

I went to see him the day before he left for the Teheran Conference this draft, with his own notes and suggested amendments, was lying on his bed. The sketch drawn by the President at the Teheran meeting, reproduced in Sherwood's *Roosevelt and Hopkins,*[3] conveys simply but graphically all of the essential features of the project we had so often discussed. In the meantime, the major members of the United Nations, including China and so far excluding France, had issued at Moscow the joint declaration announcing their intention of establishing a universal organization. But it was at Teheran that Roosevelt and Stalin first discussed, around the table, the form which that organization should assume.

In view of Russian policy since the war, it is worth noting that at Teheran Stalin opposed the inclusion of China as a major power. China would never have been so accepted had not Roosevelt overridden the joint British and Russian objections. Moreover, by then Stalin had come to favor the creation of regional councils entrusted with responsibility for maintaining peace, and he advocated that the United States be included in such a regional council for Europe. What is equally worthy of note is the President's blunt statement at the conference that the chief threat to the future peace of the world would be aggression on the part of a major power. He insisted that in this case such a power must automatically be subject to bombardment, or invasion, or both, by the police force of the world organization.

During the months between the Teheran Conference and the meeting of the four major powers at Dumbarton Oaks in the late summer of 1944, much was accomplished in ironing out the differences regarding world organization which had begun to show at Teheran. The President had long since reached the conclusion that these differences must be solved before the end of the war if there was to be an international organization in which all the major Allies could take part. He had not failed to recognize the sinister significance of the insulting message sent by Stalin to Churchill in the spring of 1944, containing the threat that unless the Soviet Union could have her own way with regard to the Polish settlement, Russian "cooperation in other spheres" would not be forthcoming. President Roosevelt's final correspondence with Stalin shows plainly how well he realized not only that the Kremlin's suspicions of United States motives had by no means been dispelled, but also that the Soviet Union would probably refuse to live up to the spirit of her political agreements with the West if her strategic position enabled her to evade them with impunity. He was not blind to the signs that the Russian defeat of Hitler's armies had rapidly stimulated the Russian ego, nor to the fact that after Germany's defeat the Soviet state would be by far the most powerful entity in Europe and in Asia.

Yet for these very reasons he was more than ever convinced that the only form of insurance which could be devised at that stage was to secure the active participation of the Soviet Union in the United Nations organization, with all of the restrictions and limitations upon her that this would provide. What is surprising is that at this very juncture the President succeeded so well in dealing with Stalin that there was little difficulty at Dumbarton Oaks in securing a joint agreement upon most of the principles which we regarded as basic in any new international organization.

The serious difficulties, in fact, were only two. One was whether the Soviet Union should be given what amounted to three votes in the Assembly instead of the one vote to which it was legitimately entitled. The other, far more important, was whether the right of the veto granted the permanent members of the Security Council should be unlimited or whether, as the British and Americans desired, the veto should be restricted to proposals to use sanctions in disputes in which the major powers were not themselves participants.

The Soviet Union was adamant at Dumbarton Oaks that every Great Power should have not only the right to veto the imposition of sanctions by the Security Council against itself but also to veto the mere consideration by the Security Council of any international dispute in which that Great Power might claim it was a participant. The Soviet Government at first threatened that it would never join an international organization which did not guarantee it an unlimited veto power. Yet here again by direct negotiations with Moscow—undertaken, it may be remembered, during an exhausting presidential campaign—the President secured agreement on a compromise formula which was later officially approved at the Yalta Conference.

This compromise admitted the Soviet contention that the veto might legitimately be employed by a major power to prevent sanctions against itself. But the Soviet Union conceded the American contention that the veto should not include the right to prevent consideration of any dispute by the Security Council, even if a major power was a participant in the dispute. The compromise formula, therefore, made it possible for the Security Council to ventilate publicly all controversies in which Russia or any other Great Power was involved.

From our standpoint the formula is, of course, imperfect, since it admits the right of the Soviet Union to prevent the Security Council from imposing sanctions upon her if she commits an act of aggression. Resort to collective action to check the aggression must, therefore, be undertaken by recourse to other instrumentalities. Yet after all, the fact is that the world organization does exist and action has been possible. As we saw when Russia threatened aggression against Iran in 1946, the ventilation of such a dispute by the Security Council and the consequent impact on public opinion throughout the world can be extremely effective. And in the recent case of aggression against South Korea, 53 members of the United Nations were able to join in armed resistance to the aggression, notwithstanding the Soviet resort to blackmail, intimidation, and parliamentary filibuster.

In the light of conditions as they existed in 1945, could any objective observer who believed in a universal international organization as the only efficient means of securing peace have seriously maintained that it was not far better to obtain a United Nations of which Russia would be a member from the outset than to risk having no United Nations at all by refusing to compromise? It is possible to amend the Charter, moreover, whenever world experience shows such amendment to be necessary.

The President's concession that the Soviet republics of the Ukraine and Byelorussia should be invited to become members of the Assembly, whereby the Soviet Union secured three votes in that body, was made reluctantly. At the outset he was determined to refuse. He felt that he could persuade Stalin not to press this demand by telling him that he would agree provided Stalin also agreed that the United States should be given 48 votes in the General Assembly, one for each of the sovereign states in the American Union. I can only assume that the President finally gave in because he believed that the question was not in itself of practical importance—as, in fact, it was not—and because the British felt strongly that the concession might prevent Soviet opposition to the voting rights of the members of the British Commonwealth—as, in fact, it did.

I have known no man in American public life who believed more implicitly than President Roosevelt that the hope of the world lay in the renewal of the people's faith in democracy. He saw more clearly than most of his contemporaries that the power and menace of Communism lay in the fanatical faith of its prophets and of its addicts, even more than in the military force and vast potential resources of the Soviet Union. To him, Communism was bloody, stifling, and intolerable. It was revolting to the passion for individual freedom which he had inherited from his Dutch and New England forebears. He frankly recognized the appeal which Communism's promise of economic security held for millions of starving and downtrodden men and women in many parts of the world. But he believed Communism would never prevail provided democracy became a living reality here in the United States and in the other free nations, and provided those who cherished democracy were willing to strive for its fulfillment and eventual supremacy with the same self-sacrificing fervor shown by the Marxists in fighting for their ideology.

Beyond and above all else, he had reached the conclusion that Communism's stoutest ally was war, and that only in a world at peace could the basic tenets of democracy ultimately triumph. He was one of that rare and select number who "see visions and dream dreams."

HANSON W. BALDWIN

Our Worst Blunders in the War: Europe and the Russians

The relationship between military strategy and diplomacy has domi-nated the historiography of World War II. Historians critical of American policy argue that Roosevelt was so intent on defeating Hitler quickly and decisively that he ignored vital long-run political considerations. Defenders of the President accuse these critics of writing from hindsight, claiming that they fail to take into account the urgency and sense of crisis that prevailed during the war years. This controversy, which began immediately after the war and shows no sign of dying out, centers on the issues of unconditional surrender, the cross-channel invasion of Europe, and the American decision to stop at the Elbe in Germany in 1945.

Although this dispute has nationalistic overtones, with British writers critical of the wartime strategy and Americans defensive, the most sweeping charges have come from Hanson Baldwin, for many years the military affairs editor of the New York Times. This article is the first of two which Baldwin later published as a book, Great Mistakes of the War *(New York, 1950). For a differ-ing assessment of the issues Baldwin discusses, see William L. Langer, "Political Problems of a Coalition,"* Foreign Affairs, *XXVI (October 1947), 73–89, a much more sympathetic critique of FDR's diplomacy; Richard M. Leighton, "OVERLORD Revisited: An Interpretation of American Strategy in the European War, 1942–1944,"* American Historical Review, *LXVIII (July 1963), 919–937, which minimizes the wartime disagreement over strategy between American and British military leaders; and Forrest Pogue, "Why Eisenhower's Forces Stopped at the Elbe,"* World Politics, *IV (April 1952), 356–368, which defends on military grounds the decision not to drive toward Berlin.*

I

IN FEBRUARY, 1945, at Yalta and on June 6, 1944, the date of the Allied invasion of Normandy, it might be said that we lost the peace. American

Reprinted by permission from the *Atlantic Monthly,* CLXXXV (January 1950), 30–39.

political and strategic mistakes during the war possibly lengthened it, certainly made it more difficult, and are largely responsible for the difficulties and crises through which we have been passing since the war.

It is, of course, easy to be wise in retrospect and to look back with the benefit of hindsight at the greatest war in history and to point to errors and confusion. They were inevitable, for war is conducted by men and men are fallible. A historian's judgments, moreover, are something like those of a global Monday morning quarterback. Yet if we are ever to learn from our mistakes we must identify them.

The major American wartime errors were all part and parcel of our political immaturity. We fought to win, period. We did not remember that wars are merely an extension of politics by other means; that wars have objectives; that wars without objectives represent particularly senseless slaughters; that unless a nation is to engage in an unlimited holocaust those objectives must be attainable by the available strength and are limited by the victor's capacity to enforce them and by the willingness of the vanquished state to accept them; and that the general objective of war is a more stable peace. We forgot that, in the words of Colonel the Honorable E. H. Wyndham, "the unity of outlook between allies in war never extends to the subsequent discussion of peace terms." We forgot that "while the attainment of military objectives brings victory in war, it is the attainment of political objectives which wins the subsequent peace." The United States, in other words, had no peace aims; we had only the vaguest kind of idea, expressed in the vaguest kind of general principles (the Atlantic Charter; the United Nations), of the kind of postwar world we wanted.

Our judgments were emotionally clouded by the perennial American hope for the millennium, the Russian military accomplishments, the warm sense of comradeship with our allies which the common purpose of victory induced, and by the very single-mindedness of our military-industrial effort. Wartime propaganda added to illusion; all our enemies were knaves, all our allies friends and comrades—military victory our only purpose. We were, in other words, idealists but not pragmatists. We embarked upon total war with all the zeal and energy and courage for which Americans are famous, but we fought to win; in the broader sense of an objective, we did not know what we were fighting for.

The political mistakes we made sprang, therefore, from the receptive soil of this immaturity, but they were fertilized, too, by a lack of knowledge or a lack of adequate interpretation of that knowledge. This was particularly true of our wartime relationship with Russia. Our policy was founded basically on four great and *false* premises—certainly false in retrospect, and seen by some to be false at the time. These were:

1. That the Politburo had abandoned with the ostensible end of the

Communist International) its policy of a world Communist revolution and was honestly interested in the maintenance of friendly relations with capitalist governments.

2. That "Joe" Stalin was a good fellow and that we could "get along with him." This was primarily a personal Rooseveltian policy and was based in part upon the judgments formed by Roosevelt as a result of his direct and indirect contacts with Stalin during the war. This belief was shaken in the last months of Roosevelt's life, partly by the Soviet stand on Poland.

3. That Russia might make a separate peace with Germany. Fear of this dominated the waking thoughts of our politico-strategists throughout the early phase of the war, and some anticipated such an eventuality even after our landing in Normandy.

4. That Russian entry into the war against Japan was either (*a*) essential to victory, or (*b*) necessary to save thousands of American lives. Some of our military men clung to this concept even after the capture of the Marianas and Okinawa.

All these basic misconceptions except the second had one common denominator: lack of adequate knowledge about Russian strengths, purposes, and motivations, and inadequate evaluation and interpretation of the knowledge we did possess.

II

The second mistaken premise could not have been avoided by any amount of knowledge or by the best possible interpretation. The presidential office with its vast powers can, under an executive who is so inclined, formulate a personal foreign policy. This is particularly true in wartime. President Roosevelt liked to transact business—even international business—on a man-to-man basis; he depended heavily upon personal emissaries like Harry Hopkins and upon his own judgment, and was confident that his estimate of the other fellow was correct. "I just have a hunch," William C. Bullitt quotes Roosevelt as telling him, "that Stalin . . . doesn't want anything but security for his country, and I think that if I give him everything I possibly can and ask nothing from him in return, *noblesse oblige,* he won't try to annex anything and will work with me for a world of democracy and peace."

It was in the character of the President to administer and to govern and to bargain on a "first-name" basis; he relied heavily upon his great persuasive powers and charm, as well as upon his political ego.

A graphic instance of this tendency toward snap decisions and casual dependence upon Stalin's good intentions was provided at Teheran. At that conference, in late 1943, Roosevelt, in one of his tête-à-têtes with Stalin and Churchill, casually agreed, unknown to virtually all his advisers, that the Russians ought to have one-third of the surrendered Italian fleet. This agreement was put in the form of an oral promise and Stalin was not one to forget promises.

Our Navy and the British Navy, which were then trying to utilize the surrendered Italian ships—manned by their own crews—to best advantage in Mediterranean convoy and antisubmarine work, knew nothing of this agreement until Russian representatives in Washington asked early in 1944 when they could expect "their share of the Italian fleet." Navy, State Department, and Joint Chiefs of Staff were dumbfounded. All our efforts had been directed toward enlisting Italian support in the war against Germany; assignment of one-third of the Italian fleet to the Russians as spoils of war would have been a political bombshell which would have handicapped the war effort in the Mediterranean. Accordingly, and to repair the damages of a casual promise made cavalierly without benefit of advice, the Russians were persuaded to accept, in lieu of the Italian vessels, some American and British men-of-war.

This is but one example of Roosevelt's personalized foreign policy— a foreign policy marked more, perhaps, by idealism and altruism than by realism. This Rooseveltian tendency toward international altruism, too often unmoderated by practical politics, seems a strange manifestation in one who domestically was a pragmatic and consummate politician. But it must be remembered that the vision of a "brave new world" was strong in Roosevelt's mind, and his optimistic nature and the great inner wellspring of his faith in man sometimes affected his judgment.

As William L. Langer notes, Roosevelt regarded Russia as the lesser of two evils, and he "shared an idea common at the time that the cult of world revolution was already receding in the minds of the Soviet leaders and they were becoming more and more engrossed in purely national problems." As a result he turned away from the only practical policy that should have governed our actions, opposition to all dictatorships and reliance upon the time-tested balance-of-power policy, to the chimera of so many Americans—a brave, new world.

The presidential ego unavoidably became stronger in Roosevelt's closing years. His great wartime power, the record of victory, the high esteem in which he was held by the world, and the weakness of the State Department all combined to reinforce the President's tendency to depend upon himself.

One of our greatest weaknesses in the policy field during the war was the failure to equate, evaluate, and integrate military and political policy; there was then no adequate government mechanism, save in the person of the President himself, for such integration.

Former Secretary of War Stimson points out in his book *On Active Service* that the formal organization of the Joint Chiefs of Staff had "a most salutary effect [in the military field] on the President's weakness for snap decisions; it thus offset a characteristic which might otherwise have been a serious handicap to his basically sound strategic instincts." But there was no political counterpart of the Joint Chiefs of Staff; and even if there had been, it is difficult to conceive that such an organization could have tempered materially the personal views which Roosevelt formed about Stalin.

The other fallacious premises upon which our wartime Russian policy was based could, however, have been avoided. We became victims of our own propaganda: Russian aims were good and noble, Communism had changed its stripes. A study of Marxian literature and of the speeches and writings of its high apostles, Lenin and Stalin, coupled with the expert knowledge of numerous American specialists, should have convinced an unbiased mind that international Communism had not altered its ultimate aim; the wolf had merely donned a sheep's skin. Had we recognized this—and all past experience indicates we should have recognized it—our wartime alliance with Russia would have been understood for what it clearly was: a temporary marriage of expediency. In the same manner a careful study of strategical facts and available military information should have indicated clearly the impossibility, *from the Russian point of view,* of a separate peace with Germany. Such a peace could only have been bought in the opening years of the war by major territorial concessions on Russia's part—concessions which might well have imperiled the Stalin regime, and which, in any case, would have left the Russo-German conflict in the category of "unfinished business." In the closing years of the war, when Russia had everything to gain and nothing to lose by continuing the struggle to complete victory, a separate peace would have been politically ludicrous.

There is no doubt whatsoever that it would have been to the interest of Britain, the United States, and the world to have allowed—and indeed encouraged—the world's two great dictatorships to fight each other to a frazzle. Such a struggle, with its resultant weakening of both Communism and Nazism, could only have aided in the establishment of a more stable peace. It would have placed the democracies in supreme power in the world, instead of elevating one totalitarianism at the expense of another and *of the democracies.*

The great opportunity of the democracies for establishing a stable peace came on June 22, 1941, when Germany invaded Russia, but we muffed the chance. Instead of aiding Russia with supplies and munitions, but not too much; instead of bombing and blockading Germany, but not too much, Britain—joined after Pearl Harbor by the United States —went all out for "unconditional surrender." We should, in other words, have occupied the bargaining position during the war, vis-à-vis Russia. Russia was the invaded power; Russia, fighting a desperate battle on her own soil, was in a death grapple with Germany. We were not similarly threatened. Russia *had* to have our help; we did not, to the same extent, require hers. This misjudgment put us in the role—at times a disgraceful role—of fearful suppliant and propitiating ally, anxious at nearly any cost to keep Russia fighting. As William C. Bullitt put it, "This topsy-turvy world turned upside down, Alice Through the Looking Glass attitude toward the Soviet Union, which our government adopted in the latter part of 1941 was our first step down the road to our present danger."

In retrospect, how stupid we were! A man being strangled to death struggles with all that's in him; Russia could not quit.

In the same manner and for much the same reasons we reversed the policy we should have followed in the Pacific War. Instead of recognizing that Russia, at nearly all costs, would have to participate in that war if she was to serve her own interests, we "bribed" her to enter it. Port Arthur is written upon the Russian heart; Manchuria has been the locale of Russian expansionist ambitions for nearly a century. Russia had everything to gain and nothing to lose by entering the Pacific War, particularly in 1944 and 1945 when the power of Germany was broken and Japan was beleaguered and in a strategically hopeless position. Yet again we begged and induced, though we, not Russia, occupied the commanding position. We should have tried to keep Russia out of the war against Japan instead of inviting her entry.

Such were the mistakes of basic policy and principle—most of them stemming from a political immaturity and an international naïveté—which influenced most of our wartime decisions and dominated the nature of the peace. They form the psychological background for many of the mistakes of detail here recounted. But a cautionary and qualifying caveat must immediately be entered. Some of these itemized errors were purely fortuitous, the illegitimate offspring of peculiar personalities or specialized circumstance; others were powerfully influenced by American humanitarianism—a desire to save lives; still others were military mistakes, with political connotations—what Bullitt has called "military imagination functioning in political ignorance." But, regardless of their psychological origins, they have one thing in common: they were mistakes.

III

I am not presenting here a comprehensive catalogue of error, nor am I concerned with tactical mistakes or with those military decisions which had no political conseqence. I have selected a few of the broad and far-reaching errors which influenced the course of the war or affected the peace.

Unconditional Surrender—Casablanca. The insistence on unconditional surrender was perhaps the biggest political mistake of the war. In the First World War, Wilson took care to distinguish between the Kaiser and the militaristic Junker class, and the German people; in the Second Stalin drew a clear line between Hitler and the Nazis, and the German people and even the German Army. The opportunity of driving a wedge between rulers and ruled, so clearly seized by Wilson and by Stalin, was muffed by Roosevelt and Churchill. Unconditional surrender was an open invitation to unconditional resistance; it discouraged opposition to Hitler, probably lengthened the war, cost us lives, and helped to lead to the present abortive peace.

This policy grew in part out of the need for a psychological war cry; in part it was intended, as William L. Langer points out, as a reassurance to "the Bolshevik leaders that there would be no compromise with Hitler and that the Allies would fight on to total victory." The haunting fear that motivated so many of our actions during the war—the fear of a separate Russian peace with Germany—and Russia's growing suspicions of the Western Allies because of their inability until that time (January 1943) to open a "second front" on land in Western Europe, dictated the famous declaration of Casablanca. It is noteworthy that Stalin was never associated with formulating "unconditional surrender" as a doctrine; he refused the invitation to the Casablanca conference and later specifically criticized this doctrine. Some historians point to the Four-Power declaration at Moscow, in October 1943, as an indication of Soviet acceptance of the unconditional surrender policy.

Actually, however, this is an oversimplified and inaccurate assessment of the Russian reaction. Prior to and after the Casablanca-Moscow conferences, Stalin took peculiar care to differentiate between the unconditional surrender of Hitlerism and the unconditional surrender of Germany. Obviously the more complete the German defeat, the greater the extension of Russian power, but Stalin understood well the political advantages of strengthening the anti-Hitler opposition in Germany. In one pronouncement (November 6, 1942) he even promised that a German defeat would not mean the end of "all military force in Germany," and the Soviets took active measures through the Free Germany Committee, the Union of German Officers, and the high-ranking Germans captured at Stalingrad and elsewhere (Field Marshal von Paulus, Major General Seydlitz, and others) to back up words with deeds and to build up an active opposition to Hitler.

"This 'soft line' was developed to Germany [by Russia] all through the Summer and Autumn of 1943," Wallace Carroll, who did so much to form our psychological warfare policy during the war, comments. ". . . in November, Stalin challenged the use of the 'hard line' of unconditional surrender at the Teheran Conference." Even as late as May 1945, when Harry Hopkins was conferring with Stalin in Moscow, Stalin balked at unconditional surrender for Japan, since "if we stick to [it] . . . the Japs will not give up and we will have to destroy them as we did

Germany." President Roosevelt ignored these challenges to his "hard line" at Teheran, in December 1943, after the conference, when he was asked by the British in Washington what he was going to do to meet Stalin's objections, and again on later occasions.

Unconditional surrender was a policy of political bankruptcy which delayed our military objective—victory—and confirmed our lack of a reasoned program for peace. It cost us dearly in lives and time, and its essentially negative concept has handicapped the development of a positive peace program. By endorsing the policy, we abandoned any pragmatic political aims; victory, as defined in these terms, could not possibly mean a more stable peace, for "unconditional surrender" meant, as Liddell Hart has noted, the "complete disappearance of any European balance. War to the bitter end was bound to make Russia 'top dog' on the Continent, to leave the countries of Western Europe gravely weakened and to destroy any buffer."

IV

Invasion of Western Europe—Loss of Eastern Europe. The long wartime history of strategic differences between Britain and the United States started soon after Pearl Harbor. From then until just before the invasion of Southern France in August 1944—when the British finally failed in their last effort to persuade us to undertake a Balkan invasion—we steadily championed an invasion of Western Europe and the British consistently proposed an invasion of the "underbelly."

The two differing strategic concepts were separated not only by geography and terrain but by centuries of experience. We sought only military victory, the quickest possible victory. The British looked toward the peace; victory to them had little meaning if it resulted in political losses. We saw in the British insistence upon Southern European "adventures" all sorts of malevolent motives; some of our brash young strategists even claimed the British did not want to fight.

It is true that Churchill and his advisers were concerned about saving lives; the blood bath of World War I had weakened Britain dangerously. Churchill was determined to avoid the holocaust of great casualties and long stalemate. As Stimson put it, "the shadows of Passchendaele and Dunkerque still hang too heavily over the imagination of the British." It is also true that to Churchill, victim of the Dardanelles fiasco in World War I, the Balkans were a psychological magnet; victory there in World War II would justify the ill-executed plans of World War I. The great war leader believed in "eccentric" strategy: the utilization of the Allies' superior naval and air power to conduct attrition attacks against the enemy's coastlines. The pattern of England's strategy in the Napoleonic wars was in his mind.

These, perhaps, were contributory reasons behind the British strategy.

But fundamentally the British evaluation was politico-military; we ignored the first part of that compound word. The British wanted to invade Southern Europe because its lands abut upon the Mediterranean and are contiguous to the Near East, important to Britain's power position in the world. For centuries Britain had had major politico-economic interests in Greece, other Balkan states, and Turkey; for centuries her traditional policy had been to check the expansionism of Russia, to support Turkish control of the Dardanelles, to participate in Danubian riparian rights. In 1942 and 1943, with the Russians in deep retreat and the Germans almost at the Caspian, the British may not have foreseen 1944 and 1945, with the Russians entering the Balkans, but they perceived clearly the political importance of this area, and they saw that an invasion there would preserve it—in the best possible manner, by soldiers on the ground—against either Russian or German interests, and in so doing would safeguard the British "lifeline" through the Mediterranean. Thus the British believed Germany could be beaten and the peace won by a series of attritions in Northern Italy, in the Eastern Mediterranean, in Greece, in the Balkans, in Rumania, and in other satellite countries. They believed an invasion through the "soft underbelly" would catch the German Army in the rear, would find a recruitment of strength from the doughty Slavs of the occupied countries, and would provide via the Danube a broad highway into Germany.

These proposals were advanced not only by British generals, but chiefly and most vigorously by British statesmen—Churchill, Eden, and Smuts. Stimson noted their insistence, yet in his book *On Active Service*, after citing the factual history of our strategic divergences, he describes as "wholly erroneous" the view that "the British opposition to Overlord [invasion of Western France] was guided by a desire to block Soviet Russia by an invasion further east.

"Never in any of his [Stimson's] long and frank discussions with the British leaders was any such argument advanced, and he saw no need whatever to assume any such grounds for the British position. Not only did the British have many good grounds to fear a cross-Channel undertaking, but Mr. Churchill had been for nearly thirty years a believer in what he called the 'right hook.' In 1943 he retained all his long-held strategic convictions, combined with a natural British concern for the Mediterranean theatre," and in Stimson's view that was all there was to it.

But there was more behind the British position than military logic, Stimson notwithstanding. It is true that the British in general, and except in their most intimate conversations with lower-level Americans than Stimson, utilized military rather than political arguments to bolster their case. But this was natural; Mr. Roosevelt at some of the conferences sided with the Russians rather than with Churchill. Moreover, many of our strategic discussions were three-cornered; the British could not very well utilize political arguments—the hope of blocking Russia—in conferences which Russian representatives attended; an effort had to be made to maintain the stability of the unnatural "Big Three" alliance that had been created. It must be remembered that during the latter part of the war it was Britain that filled the role the United States now occupies, of chief protagonist vis-à-vis Russia, in the battle for Europe. Roosevelt was the "mediator," Stalin and Churchill the polite but definite antagonists of the conference tables.

Thus, soon after we entered the war, the British proposed Operation Gymnast (later called Super-Gymnast and finally Torch)—an invasion of North Africa, at Dakar, Casablanca, the Cape Verdes, or Oran. The original date mentioned was March, 1942! By January 2, 1942, when General Joseph W. Stilwell, then slated to command Gymnast, attended one of his early conferences in Washington, the lines had been drawn: "Gerow, Somervell, Arnold, Clark, Chief of Staff, and I. All against it. Limeys claim Spain would 'bitterly oppose' Germans. What rot."

The dispute roared on down the roads of time, exploding now and again at conferences—never settled, always recurrent. The British won the first round; they got the North African invasion, then Sicily and Italy. But they lost in the end; the growing military power of the United States and the self-assurance of our strategists—sound militarily but weak politically—overbalanced them.

V

From the time of our entry into the war, and even prior to it, our strategists—Eisenhower, Wedemeyer, Marshall, and Stimson particularly—advocated the defeat of Germany by an invasion of Western France. This proposal, as Stimson puts it, was the "brain child of the United States Army." This invasion was to be timed for 1943; if necessary, to save the Russian front from utter collapse, a small diversionary landing was to be made in France in 1942. The British were distinctly lukewarm about the plan; Churchill was particularly horrified at the thought of the projected 1942 "sacrifice" landing, and from the beginning championed the invasion of North Africa. The President initially lent tacit support to the 1943 invasion and, if necessary, to the 1942 diversionary landing, but he was never fully persuaded, and in June 1942, the whole subject was reopened.

Then, in a famous meeting at the White House, described by Martin Sommers in the *Saturday Evening Post* (February 8, 1947—"Why Russia Got the Drop on Us"), Churchill and the American strategists, with Wedemeyer as our spokesman, debated strategy. In this meeting Churchill was eloquent in favor of a "surge from the Mediterranean along the historic Belgrade-Warsaw axis"; Wedemeyer, without the benefit of the

Churchillian rhetoric, spoke logically in favor of the 1943 cross-Channel operation. According to Sommers, "Churchill, because of his influence on President Roosevelt, won his fight to avoid a cross-Channel operation in 1943. He lost on his determination to force an offensive via Belgrade to Warsaw—*to an extent because when the Russians heard about this plan, they raised shrill objections*" (italics mine).

The President, moved in part by his impatience for action, in part by domestic political considerations, insisted upon some American operation in the European–North African theater in 1942; and, as Stimson puts it, Gymnast, the North African invasion, was the "President's great secret baby." The President's insistence upon action, plus the course of events —the Russians, in July 1942, were fighting with their backs to the wall at Stalingrad and in the Caucasus—led to a conference in London in late July, 1942. At this conference, as Admiral Ernest J. King, wartime commander of the U.S. Fleet, puts it, "the British Chiefs of Staff were adamant in their view that the invasion of northern France [Sledge-hammer] could not be undertaken. This view was initially opposed by the United States Chiefs of Staff and the United States Government. The conference decided, however, that invasion of French Northwest Africa could and should be undertaken. . . ."

At Casablanca in January 1943, after the successful invasion of North Africa, the British—to the ill-concealed fury of our strategists—insisted that the cross-Channel operation tentatively scheduled for the spring of 1943 could not possibly be undertaken before the fall, if then.

In retrospect it is now obvious that our concept of invading Western Europe in 1942 was fantastic; our deficiencies in North Africa, which was a much needed training school for our troops, proved that. The British objection to a 1943 cross-Channel operation was also soundly taken militarily; we would have had in that year neither the trained divisions, the equipment, the planes, the experience, nor (particularly) the landing craft to have invaded the most strongly held part of the Continent against an enemy whose strength was far greater than it was a year later.

Sicily inevitably led to an invasion of Italy, an operation envisaged first as a limited one against the heel and toe of the boot of the Italian peninsula, then later aimed at the seizure of air bases at Foggia, the quick capture of Rome, and the consequent political-psychological advantage. Churchill saw Italy and Sicily as bases for a jump eastward into the Balkans and he continued, with the aid of his military leaders, to push this project.

Admiral King points out that, although the British specifically agreed to limit the Italian operations and the Mediterranean effort, "they nevertheless as time went on and succeeding conferences took place, continued to press more and more for operations in the Mediterranean and to oppose final and firm commitments for the cross-channel operation. Indeed at ANFA [Casablanca] a number of the British delegation were confident that Germany would accept defeat by January 1, 1944."

But American strength had now been mobilized; Roosevelt was firm for Overlord (formerly called Roundup), the invasion of Normandy, and the British were forced to agree at Quebec in August, 1943, that Overlord should have the "inside track." While planning and preparations for the cross-Channel operation in late spring of 1944 were being made, the indefatigable "P.M."—never one to surrender easily once he had sunk his teeth into an argument—tried in various ways to modify or postpone Overlord, or at least to parallel it by an invasion of the Balkans. He was persistent and insistent, and so were his advisers. Churchill returned to the charge at the Moscow Conference of Foreign Ministers in October, and at Cairo on November 24 he made a long and eloquent talk to the American and British staff and to Roosevelt about the advantages of operations in the Aegean Sea and against the island of Rhodes.

At Teheran in late 1943 the British again advocated the Balkan invasion, but Roosevelt, stressing the geographical advantages of the cross-Channel assault and the terrain difficulties of the Balkans, said that only an invasion of Western France could be considered, from the Russian point of view, a "second front." Stalin naturally sided with Roosevelt; indeed, the two "got along" not only at Teheran but at Yalta. The personality of each attracted the other; the language barrier helped rather than handicapped the process; Stalin's flattery, but not Stalin's subtle manipulations, reached the President. And so it was that on November 30, 1943, the invasion of Normandy was finally decided at Teheran, and *Stalin strongly supported the Southern France invasion*, rather than a trans-Adriatic operation into the Balkans, which was mentioned by Roosevelt and backed strongly by Churchill.

Major General John R. Deane in his book *The Strange Alliance* says of Teheran: "Stalin appeared to know exactly what he wanted at the Conference. This was also true of Churchill, but not so of Roosevelt. This is not said as a reflection on our President, but his apparent indecision was probably the *direct result of our obscure foreign policy*. President Roosevelt was thinking of *winning the war;* the others were thinking of their *relative positions when the war was won*. Stalin wanted the Anglo-American forces in Western, not Southern Europe; Churchill thought our postwar position would be improved and British interests best served if the Anglo-Americans as well as the Russians participated in the occupation of the Balkans" (*italics mine*).

VI

Even after the definitive decisions of Teheran, Churchill was not quite done; although the Normandy operation was now certain, a companion invasion of the Balkans might be possible.

In Italy the Allies had been halted in the tangled mountain country south of Rome; the Rapido ran red with blood. Churchill conceived, pushed, and all but executed an amphibious end run. Operation Shingle, the Anzio beachhead landing, was intended to expedite the taking of Rome. But Anzio, too, bogged down and major American energies were now concentrated on Overlord and Normandy.

Rome fell, and Normandy was invaded, and in the summer of 1944— a summer of Allied triumphs, with the Russian armies still in Russia— Churchill made his final efforts to influence the future fate of the world. The British tried repeatedly to have the forces that were to be used in the invasion of Southern France committed instead to a cross-Adriatic operation—the objective a landing in the Trieste-Fiume area to take the German armies in Italy on the flank, a push through the Ljubljana gap into Austria, and a fanning out into the Austro-Hungarian plain with its ideal sites for air bases.

By then Churchill, as he has revealed in private discussions since the war, had no illusions about saving the Balkans from Russian domination; he knew possession, in the Russian lexicon, was nine-tenths of the law, but he did hope that Central Europe could be liberated first by the Western Allies. At a meeting at the headquarters of Field Marshal Sir Henry Maitland Wilson, British supreme commander in the Mediterranean, General Marshall tried to sound out the British and American Mediterranean commanders about the project, which in view of strong British backing was assuming formidable dimensions. General Ira Eaker, then commanding the Mediterranean Air Forces, had not been briefed about General Marshall's antipathy for what he considered an unsound (militarily) diversion, and when asked his opinion in the meeting Eaker said that from the air point of view it would be easier to support a trans-Adriatic operation than the invasion of Southern France. The bases, he pointed out, already had been established in Italy and our planes could operate in support of the Trieste move from these bases. But the Southern France operation would have to be supported from new bases in Corsica.

After the meeting was over, General Marshall commented wryly and somewhat bitterly to General Eaker: "You've been too damned long with the British."

In furtherance of their final effort to put Allied troops into Central Europe before the Red Armies occupied those countries, the British "worked" on General Mark W. Clark, then commanding our army in Italy. The King of England, on a visit to the Italian front in July 1944, about a month before the Southern France invasion, is said to have suggested to Clark the advantages of such a Balkan operation and reportedly tried to enlist his support of the project with the Joint Chiefs of Staff.

General Clark, in a letter to me dated October 15, 1948, recalls the King's visit "when we were approaching the Apennines," but adds: "I do not recall that he discussed with me the advisability of pushing our principal effort into the Balkans. . . .

"It was common knowledge that the British were desirous of carrying the war into the Balkans. This subject was discussed with me on several occasions by various Britishers in high places, commencing early in 1944. I recall General Alexander [later Field Marshal Viscount Alexander, then in command of all land forces in Italy] presenting his views on this subject. . . . I must say that I agreed with the wisdom of pushing our main effort to the East rather than continue to buck straight ahead against the mountains and the overwhelming resistance of the Germans. To have taken advantage of Tito's situation with the opportunity of landing a part of our forces across the Adriatic, behind protected beachheads which Tito could have provided, with the bulk of our forces in Italy attacking through the Ljubljana Gap would, if successful, have placed the Western Allies in a much stronger position at the end of the war to meet the ever-increasing challenge of Soviet world domination."

In all these discussions of a trans-Adriatic operation, the Ljubljana gap and the Istrian peninsula were usually favored, but landings further south along the Dalmatian coast near Zara or Split were also mentioned. The British were persistent; the project was pushed even as late as September 1944, after the forces that invaded Southern France had formed a junction with Patton's rampaging army that had broken out of the Normandy beachhead.

Much has been made, since the war, of the strategic importance of the Southern France invasion; without it, it has been said, most of the German forces south of Brittany would have escaped. But we now know that most of the German forces did escape. The Southern France invasion was originally timed to coincide with the invasion of Normandy in June 1944, and simultaneous invasions in West and South would have divided the German forces in France. But lack of landing craft forced a postponement of the Southern France operation until August 15, and we now know from German records that a Nazi withdrawal from France already had started even before the Anvil-Dragoon (Southern France) landings. Many German troops were cut up and captured by the junction of Patton's forces with those that landed on the Côte d'Azur, but many of the enemy combat units completed successfully their withdrawal to the German frontier. Much of the strategic meaning of the Southern France invasion undoubtedly was lost when the two-month postponement became necessary; when this decision was reached, the arguments for the trans-Adriatic invasion became overwhelming.

Despite these arguments it was not to be; the British, notwithstanding the great eloquence of Churchill and the reasoned logic of his staff, had failed; the American strategy—heartily endorsed by the Russians—was the pattern of conquest.

It was, of course, a successful pattern, for it was a sound plan militarily and it led to unconditional surrender. But it also led to the domination of Eastern and Central Europe by Russia and to the postwar upset in the European balance of power which has been so obvious since the war.

American strategy was not, of course, the only factor in this political defeat. Churchill made his share of mistakes. His—and our—abandonment of Mikhailovitch in Yugoslavia and his endorsement of Tito (formalized at Teheran), whom he thought he could control with British gold; and the tacit acceptance of Russia's claims to Poland's eastern territories and the division of Europe into spheres of influence, with predominant control in the Balkans—except for Greece and Yugoslavia —allotted to Russia, also contributed to our loss of the peace. The latter was a particularly heinous mistake. Churchill was its principal architect. He recognized—apparently as early as 1942—Russia's "predominant interest" in Eastern Europe. Secretary Hull opposed this concept but the President, without Hull's knowledge, agreed to the initial arrangement. Further agreements between London and Moscow in 1944, *coupled with the concentration of Western military strength in France instead of Southern Europe,* further fortified the Russian position.

But the dominant factor in the political complexion of Europe after the war was the presence of Red Army soldiers in all the countries east of the Trieste-Stettin line. The eruption of the Russians into the Danube basin gave them control over one of Europe's greatest waterways, access to Central Europe's granaries and great cities, and a strategical position of tremendous power at the center of Europe.

All of this Churchill and the British had clearly foreseen; none of this, so far as the record goes, did we foresee. Yet, so great was our physical strength, so impeccable our military logic, that rationalization triumphed over foresight. Today the principal architects of our policy understand their mistakes; many of the great military figures of the war admit freely that the British were right and we were wrong. For we forgot that all wars have objectives and all victories conditions; we forgot that winning the peace is fully as important as winning the war; we forgot that politico-military is a compound word.

VII

Loss of Central Europe. Our postwar difficulties and defeats in Central

Europe—notably in Berlin and Vienna and Czechoslovakia—are the fruit of mistakes made during the war in discussions in Washington and London, Quebec and Yalta.

The Soviet ground blockade of Berlin, which brought the United States so close to war with Russia in 1948, was possible only because the United States had no control over the communications to Berlin and no precise written definition of our communication rights. The postwar Communist coup in Czechoslovakia was aided by Russian propaganda which pointed out that Prague had been liberated by Russian arms. In Austria, too, the Russians made good postwar political capital of their wartime accomplishments. These difficulties stem directly from our lack of politico-military realism during the war.

Our failure to define properly our right of access to Berlin has been placed publicly almost exclusively on the shoulders of a dead man— the late John G. Winant, wartime Ambassador to Britain, and the chief U.S. representative on the European Advisory Commission. This commission, composed of representatives of the United States, Great Britain, and Russia, commenced after the Teheran conference in December, 1943 (where Roosevelt, Churchill, and Stalin briefly discussed the subject of postwar Germany), to consider the German problem, including the problems of occupation and government, and the geographical limitations of the zones to be occupied by the various Allies.

Winant was a sincere idealist, who hoped for the "brave new world." He was devoted to his country's interests and to the welfare of man, but as an Ambassador he was somewhat vague and his administration was more distinguished for its impulsive warmth than its precision.

I am convinced that the blame for Berlin cannot be laid—exclusively, or even to a major degree—upon the shoulders of Winant. One who knew his work well in the European Advisory Commission has written that "Mr. Winant's basic position was that our most difficult and dangerous post-war problem would be our relations [and Britain's] with Russia; that it was important to secure as wide a measure of written agreement as possible during hostilities since our direct bargaining power would decline rapidly after the end of hostilities; that America was in the strongest position to press for such agreements; that the agreements should be so detailed and precise that the Russians could not quibble out of them; and that we must deal frankly and fully with the Russians. . . . Mr. Winant was neither 'a trusting soul,' nor an 'appeaser.' "

The truth is that the old and dangerous dichotomy between foreign and military policies seems to have been, in large part, responsible for the lack of definition of a Berlin approach corridor. Winant and the U.S. delegation to the European Advisory Commission did not really make policy; they had a certain amount of freedom and initiative, but all major instructions were the product of Washington and emanated primarily from the President and the Secretaries of War and State.

When the European Advisory Commission was meeting in its first months of life, in December 1943 and January 1944, the State Department proposed in Washington that the three zones of postwar occupation in Germany (France had not then been included as an occupying power) be so drawn as to bring each into contact with Berlin. For some reason that defies logical understanding now, the War Department rejected this suggestion, which would have solved nearly all our postwar Berlin difficulties, so that it was never even broached in the EAC. In February 1944, the British informally suggested that a "corridor" to Berlin be established and defined, but the War Department again objected, stating that this was not a subject for the European Advisory Commission and that the entire question of access to Berlin was "a military matter" which should be settled at the proper time by military representatives.

This eventually was the solution, but the military representatives made a botch of it. In May 1945, our armies stood deep on German soil. The zonal occupation agreements for Germany, worked out by the EAC, approved at the Quebec conference, and modified at Yalta (to include France), placed Berlin in the Russian zone; the British and U.S. zonal boundaries—contrary to the original recommendation of the State Department—lay 100 miles to the west. In May 1945, EAC's work was done, and SHAEF was briefed as to its accomplishments.

The SHAEF representative inquired about access to Berlin and was told by the European Advisory Commission that this problem had been left to the military at the War Department's insistence, and that with U.S. troops already fighting in what eventually was scheduled to become part of the Russian zone of occupation of Germany, the whole question of withdrawal of our troops from the Russian zone and access to Berlin ought to be taken up together. In other words, even as late as May 1945, at the war's end, we still had a bargaining point; we were in possession—by conquest—of large parts of Germany, including areas slated to be in the Russian zone; we could have conditioned our withdrawal upon acceptance by the Russians of a secure access corridor to our zone in Berlin. The SHAEF representative, in fact, was told that such a corridor agreement ought to include the establishment of our own guard with U.S. troops along the access road and railroad, establishment of vehicle repair and supply points, military telegraph and telephone, right to repair and maintain the road and railroads, and provision for definite alternative routes in case the named routes were not usable for any reason.

This advice was not heeded. The military themselves, after the German collapse, in an agreement of June 1945, concluded an arrangement which was so general and imprecise as to be productive of future trouble. General Lucius D. Clay has assumed responsibility for the terms of this agreement, and he must bear part of this burden, but he alone is not responsible. The advice he received was none too good; the dangerous breach between State and War still existed, and Eisenhower, Clay, and their advisers negotiated against the background of the psychological delusion then so prevalent in our government—that the Russians were our political as well as military "buddies," and that we could "get along" with Stalin. But basically and fundamentally the responsibility for the Berlin corridor fiasco rests with the War Department in Washington. At the time the European Advisory Commission was conducting negotiations, the War Department—working with a weak State Department— had the bit in its teeth and assumed a mantle it had neither competence nor right to wear: the mantle of divine political wisdom.

In retrospect, it seems probable that the War Department's triumph in this interdepartment struggle for power in Washington was foreordained. The War Department's senior personnel were stronger and more able men; they had behind them, in war, the great force of public backing.

It was thus largely on the basis of "faith"—faith not alone in the Russians but military faith in the military interpretation of political problems—that the Berlin corridor agreement was drawn up.

VIII

In March and April, 1945, as the war against Germany was drawing to an end, Eastern Europe had gone irretrievably; our earlier failure to invade the Balkans had cost us dearly. But important parts of Central Europe—Berlin, the Bohemian bastion and Prague, and possibly Vienna —were still at stake.

As early as March 28, with the Allied armies on the Rhine 300 miles from Berlin and the Russians on the Oder 30 miles from Berlin, General Eisenhower sent a personal message to Stalin via the U.S. Military Mission in Moscow. This message outlined his plans for a strong push in the center by General Omar Bradley's American forces to a junction with the Russians on the Elbe, to be followed by flank drives by the British in the north to cut off the Danish peninsula and seize the North German ports, and by the Americans and French in the south into Austria to eliminate the possibility of a last-ditch stand by the Nazis in the so-called "National Redoubt." Churchill protested this communication by Eisenhower to Stalin as an intrusion by the military into political matters, and was vehemently critical of the plan; in Eisenhower's words, "he was greatly disappointed and disturbed because my plan did not first throw Montgomery forward with all the strength I could give him from the American forces in the desperate attempt to capture Berlin before the Russians could do so." But Churchill's protest to Washington was overruled.

Eisenhower's defense against this protest has some merits. There is no doubt that he was perfectly within his rights in communicating his plans to Stalin; he had been previously authorized to do so. But his dismissal of the Berlin plan as militarily unwise, and his fear that an attempt to take the city would force diversion of forces from other parts of the front to that sole task—a "stupid" diversion—and his overemphasis upon the "National Redoubt" were, it is now clear, mistaken. Intelligence failures again played a part in this mistake. The "National Redoubt" (fortifications and supplies supposed to have been prepared by the Nazi SS formations in the German-Austrian Alps for a last stand) was grossly overrated in our estimates; we learned later that relatively little work on the "Redoubt" had been done; the scheme was more an idea than an accomplishment. Churchill, in other words, again emerges in the Berlin matter a wily old fox of international politics; his vision was not obscured by the needs of the moment.

Our troops, after crossing the Rhine, swept eastward with relatively little opposition. Agreements had been reached with the Russians that when contact between the two armies seemed imminent, a line of demarcation should be arranged beyond which each army should not move. This boundary was "temporarily fixed"—in the words of General Eisenhower's final report—"in the central sector" along the easily identified line of the Elbe and Mulde rivers; the Russians were so notified in Eisenhower's message to Stalin of March 28 (which evoked the Churchill protest). By April 12, the first American bridgehead across the Elbe had been established; we were 100 miles from Berlin and the Russians, 30 miles from that city on the Oder, were just starting their final offensive. It was not until April 25 that the Russians reached the Elbe; in other words, for about three weeks our forces remained virtually static on that line of demarcation, and not until early May was the Russian battle for Berlin finally won.

Further south our troops moved into Czechoslovakia on April 18, and then on to Pilsen. Prague lay virtually defenseless near at hand; reconnaissance elements of the Third Army were in its outskirts. The Soviet High Command, when informed by General Eisenhower that our troops would move on toward Prague if (in former Secretary of State Byrnes's words) "the situation required it," requested that our forces "should not advance beyond the Budejovice-Pilsen-Karlsbad line." So again our troops marked time, and the political prestige of taking Prague went to the Russians.

So, too, in the south, where the agreed demarcation line ran down the Budejovice-Linz railroad and along the valley of the Enns. Vienna, a possible prize, was voluntarily relinquished.

There was some military reason for this restraint. Two armies surging forward toward each other—a desperate enemy in between—are difficult to control; Eisenhower was concerned about accidental collisions. Moreover, it would not have been easy for us to take Berlin first. The Russians were only 30 miles from that city when we were 100 miles away on the Elbe. Furthermore, General Omar N. Bradley had estimated that though we could take the city, it would be at the cost of perhaps 100,000 casualties. Our troops had been moving fast and hard; the supply problem was difficult—and in any case the Western Allies had advanced far beyond the zonal boundaries agreed upon by the Allied governments, and further advance would only have meant eventual evacuation of additional territory east of the Elbe.

Eisenhower felt, moreover (in his own words in his final report), that "Berlin no longer represented a military objective of major importance" and that "military factors, when the enemy was on the brink of final defeat, were more important . . . than the political considerations involved in an Allied capture of the capital."

Both political and military decisions, therefore, halted our armies along the Elbe, the Mulde, and the Enns in the closing days of the Third Reich. There *were* military reasons, which seemed good at the time, for not pressing the advance to the utmost, but they were not decisive. The boundaries marked out by the European Advisory Commission and approved at Quebec and Yalta colored the thinking of our commanders. We *could* have moved further eastward. But the political die had been cast; there was not much point in military sacrifice for a political lost cause.

The effect of all these decisions was to make Berlin an island in a Russian sea and to give Soviet troops firm control of Central Europe.

JOHN L. CHASE

Unconditional Surrender Reconsidered

Hanson Baldwin's charge that unconditional surrender was "a policy of political bankruptcy" has led to a lively debate. The major issues are speculative in nature—would a more flexible formula have permitted a negotiated peace with Germany that would have shortened the war and blocked subsequent Soviet domination of Eastern and Central Europe? Critics of American policy, notably Ann Armstrong in her book Unconditional Surrender *(New Brunswick, N.J., 1961), give an affirmative answer on both points.*

In this article John Chase, a political scientist, presents the case for the policy of unconditional surrender. For an authoritative account of American undercover contacts with the anti-Nazi movement in Germany, see Allen W. Dulles, Germany's Underground *(New York, 1947).*

OF ALL AMERICAN policies during the period of World War II, that of unconditional surrender toward the Axis powers appears to have given rise to the most controversy and adverse comment. Secretary Hull has revealed that he opposed it, the psychological warfare specialists obviously had difficulties with it, and even Mr. Churchill has commented on it at least twice—and with somewhat confusing effect.[1] In the United States the prominent military analyst Hanson Baldwin took exception to the policy some time ago in a book,[2] and more recently he has returned to the attack in an article aimed at a wider audience.[3] Plainly, the issues involved are by no means dead, and perhaps cannot even be laid to rest easily.

In spite of the frequency of previous discussions of the subject, there

Reprinted by permission from the *Political Science Quarterly*, LXX (June 1955), 258–279.

1. Secretary Hull's comments may be found in his *Memoirs* (New York, 1948), pp. 1570 *et seq.*; James Warburg's views seem to represent those of some of the psychological warfare specialists, as in his *Germany—Bridge or Battleground* (New York, 1946), Appendix II, pp. 259–65; Mr. Churchill's statements will be cited in detail later.

2. *Great Mistakes of the War* (New York, 1949), pp. 14–25.

3. "Churchill Was Right," *The Atlantic*, 194, No. 1 (July 1954).

is in them something not entirely satisfactory from the scholarly point of view. In the first place, much of the adverse comment has been made in the heat of the immediate postwar period, and seems to be related directly to the author's satisfaction or indignation with postwar American policy in Germany.[4] Secondly, the dispute over the consequences has left one really important aspect of the problem untouched—namely, the way in which it grew out of the actual historical context of the times, and especially President Roosevelt's reasons for endorsing it. Thus little attention has been given to the problem of understanding a major problem in American foreign policy as an American decision. Finally, a good deal has been published recently on the war period, and some of this new material is relevant to the problem involved. For all of these reasons, it is thought worth while to reconsider the policy.

I. The Origins of "Unconditional Surrender"

In his *Atlantic* article Mr. Baldwin repeats, with some new material, the earliest recollection of Mr. Churchill that he first heard the term "unconditional surrender" from the lips of the President at the joint press conference held by the two leaders at Casablanca. Relying also on the study by Matloff and Snell,[5] Mr. Baldwin declares that "unconditional surrender was laid down as a *diktat*—a one-man decision—without any study of its political or military implications and was announced publicly and unilaterally at a press conference to the surprise of the nation's chief ally, Great Britain." [6]

As Mr. Churchill subsequently acknowledged, his first recollection of the episode proved somewhat inaccurate. Elliott Roosevelt, who was present at the conference as an aide to his father, first challenged the "surprise" nature of the announcement when he wrote that at a luncheon *prior* to the press conference, the President tried out the slogan on the Prime Minister. He stated that

> . . . it was at that lunch table that the phrase "unconditional surrender" was born. For what it was worth, it can be recorded that it was Father's phrase, that Harry Hopkins took an immediate and strong liking to it, and that Churchill, while he slowly munched a mouthful of food, thought, frowned, thought, finally grinned, and at length announced, "Perfect! And I can just see how Goebbels and the rest of 'em 'll squeal." [7]

4. This view is naturally strongest among the Germans themselves. See Baldwin, *Great Mistakes*, pp. 22–23.

5. Maurice Matloff and Edwin M. Snell, *United States Army in World War II. The War Department: Strategic Planning for Coalition Warfare, 1941–1942* (Washington, 1953).

6. Baldwin, "Churchill Was Right," p. 27.

7. Elliott Roosevelt, *As He Saw It* (New York, 1946), p. 117.

Mr. Churchill subsequently took note of this variant account, and stated that later research in his own files confirmed Elliott's impression that the whole matter had been discussed previously. Apparently it was even earlier than Elliott believed, however, for Mr. Churchill prints a report of his to the Deputy Prime Minister and War Cabinet, dated January 20, 1943, in which he stated:

> I would like to know what the War Cabinet would think of our including in this statement to the press a declaration of the firm intention of the United States and the British Empire to continue the war relentlessly until we have brought about the "unconditional surrender" of Germany and Japan. The omission of Italy would be to encourage a break-up there. The President liked this idea, and it would stimulate our friends in every country.[8]

Mr. Churchill adds that, in the Cabinet discussion which followed receipt of his message, it was not the principle itself which was questioned, but the possibility of making the exception in favor of Italy. The Cabinet definitely opposed any such exception. Mr. Churchill continues that he had neither record nor recollection of any conversation with the President on the matter subsequent to his receiving the views of the War Cabinet. He makes it clear that both he and the President approved the official communiqué, which had been prepared by the various staffs and which contained no reference to unconditional surrender, and that the War Cabinet had also approved this.[9]

Mr. Churchill confesses his surprise at hearing the President use the phrase at the press conference. He says that "It was natural to suppose that the agreed communiqué had superseded anything said in conversation," and that General Ismay, who was well acquainted with his thoughts, was also surprised.[10] But he quotes the President's own explanation, as given by Robert Sherwood, as finally disposing of the matter:

> Roosevelt himself absolved Churchill from all responsibility for the statement. Indeed, he suggested that it was an unpremeditated one on his own part. "We had so much trouble getting those two French generals [de Gaulle and Giraud] together that I thought to myself that this was as difficult as arranging the meeting of Grant and Lee—and then suddenly the press conference was on, and Winston and I had had no time to prepare for it, and the thought

---

8. Winston S. Churchill, *The Second World War: The Hinge of Fate* (Boston, 1950), p. 684.

9. *Ibid.*, pp. 685–86.

10. *Ibid.*, pp. 686–87.

popped into my mind that they had called Grant 'Old Unconditional Surrender' and the next thing I knew I had said it." [11]

Sherwood comments that for some reason or other the President liked to cultivate the impression of himself as "a rather frivolous fellow who did not give sufficient attention to the consequences of chance remarks." [12] As applied to this particular case, however, two well-known facts have to be weighed against the accuracy of any such characterization. One is the fact that the President spoke from notes, and these—which were not allowed to be quoted—contained the following statement:

> The President and the Prime Minister . . . are more than ever determined that peace can come to the world only by a total elimination of German and Japanese war power. This involves the simple formula of placing the objective of this war in terms of an unconditional surrender by Germany, Italy, and Japan. Unconditional surrender by them means a reasonable assurance of world peace, for generations. Unconditional surrender means not the destruction of the German populace, nor of the Italian or Japanese populace, but does mean the destruction of a philosophy in Germany, Italy and Japan which is based on the conquest and subjugation of other peoples. [13]

It might be suggested that the President's notes also may have been composed only a few minutes prior to the press conference, so that their existence does not disprove the unpremeditated nature of the phrase. As against this, however, we have the evidence of Churchill's own memorandum to the War Cabinet, dated January 20, and including the vital phrase, while the press conference did not occur until four days later. [14] The evidence seems incontrovertible, therefore, that the President had been thinking about the phrase for at least several days before the public announcement.

A second reason mentioned by Sherwood for believing the President's selection of the phrase to have been a carefully considered one is his determined resistance to any modification of it. Objection to it came from many sources: from Secretary Hull, from some of the American

11. Quoted in part by Churchill, *ibid.*, p. 687, and in Robert Sherwood, *Roosevelt and Hopkins: An Intimate History* (New York, 1948), p. 696. It is somewhat strange that in his book Hanson Baldwin recognizes the error in Churchill's first recollection and the correctness of Elliott Roosevelt's account, while in his article he does not. The point would seem to be important enough to emphasize, even in a popular account.

12. Sherwood, *op. cit.*, p. 696.

13. *Ibid.*, pp. 696–97.

14. Elliott Roosevelt, *op. cit.*, pp. 117–21.

psychological warfare specialists, from the War Department, from the British Foreign Office, and even, after the Teheran Conference, from the Soviet government.[15] Despite all the pressure, however, the President clung determinedly to his position, and would not consent to any modification of the principle. Plainly, then, as Sherwood says, the announcement was no casual slip of the tongue, but "very deeply deliberated," and "a true statement of Roosevelt's considered policy." [16] Further, "One thing about Roosevelt's statement is certain . . . —he had his eyes wide open when he made it." [17]

Since the President insisted on retention of the policy over so much opposition, it seems clear that in his own mind it must have served some very basic function or have entailed some very definite advantages. Careful analysis of the available records indicates that the slogan did, in fact, have such a basic function in the over-all development of American policy, and there were very considerable advantages in it from the President's point of view. The main function, briefly stated, was to impose a damper on premature discussion of the postwar settlement, and the advantages related to three areas: the existing German government and the German people, the policy of the Soviet government, and the attitude of the American people toward the winning of the war. In the following sections the relevance of the policy to each of these subjects is examined in greater detail.

II. Unconditional Surrender and the German Government

The most immediate and obvious bearing of the unconditional surrender policy was its relation to Germany and the ending of the war. Sherwood has stated the President's view on this point as follows:

> What Roosevelt was saying was that there would be no negotiated peace, no compromise with Nazism and Fascism, no "escape clauses" provided by another Fourteen Points which could lead to another Hitler. (The ghost of Woodrow Wilson was again at his shoulder.) Roosevelt wanted this uncompromising purpose brought home to the American people and the Russians and the Chinese, and to the people of France and other occupied nations, and he wanted it brought home to the Germans—that neither by continuance of force nor by contrivance of a new spirit of sweet reasonableness could their present leaders gain for them a soft peace.

15. Hull makes his own lack of agreement clear, and also mentions other examples of opposition to the phrase in his discussion, *op. cit.*, pp. 1570 *et seq.*
16. Sherwood, *op. cit.*, p. 696.
17. *Ibid.*, p. 697.

He wanted to ensure that when the war was won it would stay won.[18]

Sherwood goes on to explain that it was particularly important for the President to stress the uncompromising nature of American policy toward the Nazis at this time because of the "uproar over Darlan and Peyrouton," and the fears of the enemies of fascism everywhere that this might indicate an American willingness to compromise and to accept less than the total defeat of the enemy.[19] This interpretation of the policy stresses primarily its importance as a statement of the attitude: No negotiated peace with existing enemy governments!

An additional, complementary interpretation of the policy, also bearing on Germany, has been suggested by Wallace Carroll, formerly Deputy Director of the Overseas Branch of the Office of War Information. He quotes an anonymous source—a person present at the Casablanca Conference, as having been told by the President that

> he wanted to rule out any pledge or offer like the Fourteen Points and still convey to the enemy peoples the idea that they would be treated generously by the Allies. He thought that the story of Grant and Lee at Appomattox would convey this idea . . . what he especially wanted to bring out was Grant's gesture in letting the Confederates keep their horses. The President felt that this incident from American history would help the enemy peoples to realize that they were facing chivalrous foes who did not desire to impoverish them or humiliate them, but who would treat them with magnanimity. *That is, he meant to reassure the peoples of enemy countries about Allied intentions, not to terrorize them.*[20]

To those who have associated the President with the Morgenthau Plan, this hypothesis will seem both novel and improbable. Nevertheless, it is borne out by a number of the President's later statements, of which the following is typical: "In our uncompromising policy we mean no harm to the common people of the Axis nations. But we do mean to impose punishment and retribution in full upon their guilty, barbaric leaders." [21]

The foregoing statement was made in February 1943. Late in August

18. *Ibid.* Sherwood's interpretation is borne out by the President's remarks on two subsequent occasions. See Samuel I. Rosenman, *Public Papers and Addresses of Franklin D. Roosevelt* (New York, 1948), 1943 volume, Item 10, pp. 59–60; and 1944–45 volume, Item 55, p. 210.

19. Sherwood, *op. cit.,* p. 697.

20. Wallace Carroll, *Persuade or Perish* (Boston, 1948), p. 309. Italics mine.

21. Hull, *op. cit.,* p. 1571.

of the same year, in what seemed a clear reference to the Atlantic Charter, the President declared:

> Except for the responsible fascist leaders, the people of the Axis need not fear unconditional surrender to the United Nations. . . . The people of the Axis-controlled areas may be assured that when they agree to unconditional surrender they will not be trading Axis despotism for ruin under the United Nations. The goal of the United Nations is to permit liberated peoples to create a free political life of their own choosing and to attain economic security.[22]

That the policy did not exclude the probability of generous Allied action was also emphasized by the President in his exchanges with Hull. On two occasions the President said that the best definition of the policy was exemplified by Lee's surrender to Grant. Lee had relied upon Grant's fairness, and Grant had responded with a generous gesture. On one occasion the President added that "both the German people and Russia" should be told what this "best definition" meant.[23] On the other, the President added the apparently contradictory thought: "That is the spirit I should like to see abroad—but it does not apply to Germany. Germany understands only one kind of language." [24]

But, taken in its context, the latter statement makes clear that what the President meant was that the Germans would misconstrue as a sign of weakness any magnanimous gesture *in advance* of unconditional surrender. Is it possible to disagree with him in this?

The similarity between the President's view and that of the Prime Minister on this point should be clear from the following explanation by Mr. Churchill:

> The term "unconditional surrender" does not mean that the German people will be enslaved or destroyed. It means however that the Allies will not be bound to them at the moment of surrender by any pact or obligation. There will be, for instance, no question of the Atlantic Charter applying to Germany as a matter of right and barring territorial transferences or adjustments in enemy countries. . . . If we are bound, we are bound by our own consciences to civilization. We are not bound to the Germans as the result of a bargain struck. That is the meaning of "unconditional surrender." [25]

22. *Ibid.*

23. *Ibid.*, p. 1574. The President repeated the illustration at considerable length in a press conference late in July 1944. Cf. Rosenman, *op. cit.*, 1944–45 volume, Item 55, pp. 209–11.

24. Hull, *op. cit.*, p. 1576.

25. Churchill, *Hinge of Fate*, pp. 690–91.

It only remains to point out that, so far as the example of Lee's surrender to Grant was concerned, the example did nothing to clarify the President's intention. One reason is that the President's recollection was, unfortunately, somewhat erroneous. As Carroll has explained,

> The President bungled the announcement of the decision. The correspondents at Casablanca were not permitted to quote his words directly and it is therefore impossible to ascertain exactly what he said. From the newspaper accounts it appears that he may have mentioned Grant, but he forgot to mention Lee and the horses. Those American correspondents and newspapers which sought to explain what he had in mind assumed that he referred to Grant's letter to General Buckner. . . . Grant's demand for unconditional surrender at that time had not been tempered by an act of magnanimity. Consequently, Allied propagandists, who received all their news of the Conference from the press, never got the point of the generous gesture to the defeated foe.[26]

Carroll adds that when the President again used the example in his exchanges with Hull, "Secretary Hull forgot to pass it on to the Office of War Information." [27]

It seems clear, then, that so far as Germany was concerned the unconditional surrender policy was intended to inform the world—Germans, Americans, and everyone else—that the Allies would accept nothing less than the complete defeat of existing enemy governments, and would not bargain or compromise with them. Both the President and Mr. Churchill agreed on this, and both went out of their way to explain that this did *not* mean a policy of unnecessary harshness or vindictiveness toward the common people of the Axis nations.

So much, then, for the President's purpose where Germany was concerned. The question has often been raised as to the effect of the policy in Germany, and the allegation has been made that the policy unnecessarily prolonged the war.[28] This question is probably too large to be discussed in detail here, but a few pertinent considerations may be mentioned. The first and most obvious point is that there is no necessary connection between the unconditional surrender formula and the "Morgenthau Plan," which in point of time came almost two years later. Either one could have been adopted without the other, although

26. Carroll, *op. cit.*, pp. 310–11. A transcript of the press conference, corroborating Carroll's observation, is printed by Rosenman, *op. cit.*, 1943 volume, Item 6, pp. 37 *et seq.*

27. Carroll, *op. cit.*, p. 317.

28. This is Hanson Baldwin's view, in both his book and later article.

most of the critics treat them as identical.[29] But it seems evident that one could accept unconditional surrender without accepting Mr. Morgenthau's ideas—as in fact Secretary Stimson appears to have done.

A second point is also worth consideration. Many of the critics of the policy appear to place overly great emphasis on the effect of mere propaganda alone, divorcing stated aims of policy from the effects of actual wartime conditions. Allen Dulles, however, in commenting upon American policy in Germany, couples the two significantly when he says:

> Our propaganda consisted of the slogan "unconditional surrender," and was coupled with the bombing of German cities, high civilian casualties and the destruction of thousands of workers' dwellings. That this type of bombing came only from the west made a deep impression on the German masses who ascribed it to a deliberate difference in policy between East and West. They overlooked the fact that Russian aviation was not adapted to that type of bombing. . . .[30]

Dulles' point is, it seems to me, well taken. The critics decry unconditional surrender, but do not suggest that our strategy with respect to bombing should have been different. The implication is that a mere difference in words would have been greatly to the American advantage. It seems hard to believe that Goebbels would have had any greater difficulty countering such a policy than he had with the actually existing one. The argument strains credulity a bit too far.

It is interesting to note Churchill's response to this kind of criticism. "It is false to suggest," he wrote, "that it [i.e., unconditional surrender] prolonged the war. Negotiation with Hitler was impossible. He was a maniac with supreme power to play his hand out to the end, which he did; and so did we." [31]

Finally, admitting that the present discussion is not conclusive, Sherwood's comment is pertinent that

> It is a matter of record that the Italians and the Japanese were ready to accept unconditional surrender as soon as effective force was applied to their homelands. Whether they might have done so

29. Baldwin states that "The Casablanca policy came to logical fruition in the Morgenthau 'pastoral Germany' policy at Quebec. . . ." *Great Mistakes*, p. 24. For a fuller discussion of the Morgenthau Plan and the Quebec conference, see the author's "The Development of the Morgenthau Plan Through the Quebec Conference," *Journal of Politics*, 16, No. 2 (May 1954).

30. Allen W. Dulles, *Germany's Underground* (New York, 1947), p. 168.

31. Sherwood, *op. cit.*, p. 696.

sooner, or whether the Germans might ever have done so, under any circumstances whatsoever, are matters for eternal speculation.[32]

III. Unconditional Surrender and the Soviet Government

So important an aim as unconditional surrender must also, obviously, have been considered for its bearing on other Allies, and particularly the Soviet government. In this connection it should be recalled that only six months prior to the Casablanca Conference the United States had intervened forcibly in the Anglo-Soviet treaty negotiations. At the outset of these negotiations, Churchill had been willing to pledge British support for a guaranty of Soviet territorial acquisitions made during the period of the Nazi-Soviet pact. But the President, with Woodrow Wilson and the secret treaties of World War I clearly in mind, had intervened to prevent any discussion of commitments with regard to territorial issues in postwar Europe.[33] Nevertheless the question, so long as it was not finally disposed of, was bound to hang heavily over the future and to exert an unsettling effect on the policies of all the Allies. One of the major consequences of the unconditional surrender policy was to reinforce the ban on any such premature discussion, and to forestall any further demand to reach a territorial settlement, which the United States could not support, before the ending of the war.

The policy also had another important bearing on the relations of the two Western Powers to Russia. It may be recalled that in May of 1942 the United States and Britain had made a rather tenuous promise to the Soviets to open a second front in Western Europe in 1942.[34] Subsequently, some misunderstanding developed over the implementation of this commitment. In August 1942, Mr. Churchill felt it necessary to make a special trip to Moscow to explain to Stalin why the front could not be created that year.[35] Following his visit, and in part as the result of a curtailment of Western supplies to Russia made necessary by the planned invasion of Africa, the Soviets became very uncommunicative. In October there were indications, according to Mr. Churchill, that the Russians feared a British attempt to negotiate a separate peace with Germany. In November, a combination of rain and German reinforcements caused the Western campaign in North Africa to bog down.[36]

In the light of these developments and accompanying Russian suspicion, it was perhaps not surprising that Stalin found it impossible to leave

32. *Ibid.*, p. 697.

33. *Ibid.*, pp. 401 *et seq.*; Churchill, *The Second World War: The Grand Alliance* (Boston, 1950), pp. 528 *et seq.*; and Hull, *op. cit.*, pp. 1165 *et seq.*

34. See Sherwood, *op. cit.*, p. 577; and Churchill, *Hinge of Fate*, pp. 341–42.

35. Churchill, *Hinge of Fate*, pp. 472–502.

36. *Ibid.*, pp. 569, 575, 577, and 660–67.

Moscow to participate in the Casablanca Conference. His reply to the urgings of Roosevelt and Churchill made it clear that he still felt that the next Western move should be ". . . a second front in Europe . . . by the joint forces of Great Britain and the United States of America in the spring of the next year." [37]

At the Casablanca Conference itself, Western strategy for the rest of 1943 was agreed upon by the combined staffs and political leaders. General Marshall and Harry Hopkins wanted the main objective to be the invasion of northern France, but they were overruled.[38] Instead, it was agreed to advance on Sicily next, and to secure the Mediterranean lines of communication and air bases. It did not require a very careful reading between the lines of the Combined Chiefs' report on "The Conduct of the War in 1943" to perceive that the invasion of Western Europe had again come off second- or even third-best.[39]

In view of this background, one can better appreciate the force of Wallace Carroll's argument that the policy of unconditional surrender was designed to take the sting out of the further postponement of the European front. In his opinion,

> The Russians had been displeased by the failure of the British and Americans to open a "second front" in Western Europe in 1942, and it seemed likely at Casablanca that they would be still more displeased when they learned that the decision had been taken to invade Italy, ruling out the possibility of a western front in 1943. The announcement of a policy of no compromise and no bargaining by the western Allies would therefore help to counter Russian suspicions.[40]

Carroll goes on to argue that the Russians agreed to unconditional surrender as "basic policy" and wanted to modify it later only because they considered it "bad tactics" to insist on it "in public." [41] Without it, Soviet suspicions of treachery and double-dealing could not have been allayed; "with it, they [i.e., the Western Allies] exposed themselves to a few gentle complaints that they were being unnecessarily stern in their propaganda." [42]

Carroll's interpretation is borne out in all respects not only by the facts already cited, but also by two remarks of the President as reported

---

37. *Ibid.*, pp. 662 *et seq.* and 667.
38. Sherwood, *op. cit.*, pp. 674–75.
39. The official agreement of the Combined Chiefs is given by Churchill, *Hinge of Fate*, pp. 692–93.
40. Carroll, *op. cit.*, p. 312.
41. *Ibid.*, p. 333.
42. *Ibid.*, p. 334.

by his son Elliott, who was present at the time. The first occurred at the previously mentioned luncheon with Mr. Churchill:

> Father, once his phrase had been approved by the others, speculated about its effect in another direction.
>
> "Of course, it's just the thing for the Russians. Unconditional surrender," he repeated, . . . "Uncle Joe might have made it up himself." [43]

The second was a conversation between the President and his son, in which Mr. Roosevelt discoursed philosophically about the disagreements on invasion strategy between the American and British chiefs, and the nature of the agreement reached:

> Father was to tell me about the rocky path the Combined Chiefs had travelled to reach the plan for the invasion of Sicily; he was to complain, but philosophically, about the continuing British insistence on striking Europe from the south rather than from the west; he was to note his misgivings as to Stalin's attitude when the news arrived of a further postponement of the invasion cross-channel; he was to comment that "Wars are uncertain affairs. To win this one, we must maintain a difficult unity with one ally by apparently letting another down. To win this war, we have been forced into a strategic compromise which will most certainly offend the Russians, so that later we will be able in turn to force a compromise which will most certainly offend the British. The compelling needs of war dictate a difficult course." [44]

Finally, one might note that the official communiqué of the conference made a great point of Stalin's having been invited to join the other two leaders. It added that

> The President and Prime Minister realized up to the full the enormous weight of the war which Russia is successfully bearing along her whole land front, and their prime object has been to draw as much weight as possible off the Russian armies by engaging the enemy as heavily as possible at the best selected points.
>
> Premier Stalin has been fully informed of the military proposals. [45]

The evidence on this aspect of the policy now seems conclusive. Unconditional surrender served the important function not only of reinforcing the ban on premature discussion of postwar territorial issues, but also of reassuring the Russians that, in spite of necessary delays

43. Elliott Roosevelt, *op. cit.,* p. 117.
44. *Ibid.,* p. 109.
45. Rosenman, *Public Papers,* 1943 volume, Item 7, p. 50.

over the opening of the second front, it was still the Western determination to press on unremittingly to victory, in fulfillment of Allied commitments, as soon as the physical forces could be assembled to do the job.[46]

It only remains to point out that from the standpoint of satisfying the Russians the policy was not, and indeed could not be, completely satisfactory. Nothing short of the second front itself could have been. Stalin's reply to the conference message of Roosevelt and Churchill made this crystal-clear. He said: "It is my understanding that by the decisions you have taken you have set yourselves the task of crushing Germany by the opening of a Second Front in Europe in 1943 and I should be very obliged for information concerning the actual operations planned for this purpose. . . ."[47]

But it seems evident that the policy did convince the Russians of the Western determination to get on with the war as fast as possible, and in this respect the policy, as President Roosevelt hoped, averted a threat to Allied unity at a crucial moment.[48]

The subsequent record of Soviet pronouncements with regard to unconditional surrender bears out this interpretation. Stalin endorsed the policy in his Order of the Day of May 1, 1943.[49] Soviet objections to it were not voiced until the Teheran Conference. By that time, however, the Western Allies were fully committed to the opening of the western front, so that the Russians may well have figured that the policy had served its main immediate purpose. It is a notable fact that even at Teheran the Russian objections were based upon tactical considerations, and that their situation was in this respect less happy than that of the Western Allies, whose tactical problem was to convince the Germans of their deadly seriousness, not of their humaneness.[50] On the whole, it can

46. Professor William L. Langer has expressed essentially the same view as follows: "The Soviet leaders were quite as suspicious of their Allies as we were of them. Whether sincerely or otherwise, they took the line that refusal to open a second front was an indication of unwillingness to crush the Nazi power or permit Communist Russia an unqualified victory. It was this mutual suspicion and constant recrimination more than anything else that lay behind the demand for unconditional surrender. . . ." ("Turning Points of the War: Political Problems of a Coalition," *Foreign Affairs*, 26, No. 1 [October 1947], 84.)

47. Sherwood, *op. cit.*, p. 701.

48. Hans Speier takes the same view as Langer, but adds that the policy may also have served as a warning to the Russians to stop flirting with the National Committee "Free Germany" and the Union of German Officers. "War Aims in Political Warfare," *Social Research: An International Quarterly of Political and Social Science*, 12, No. 2 (May 1945), 157–80.

49. Embassy of the U.S.S.R., *Information Bulletin*, No. 47, May 4, 1943, p. 1.

50. Carroll, *op. cit.*, pp. 314–15.

be said that at the time it was announced, and until the tactical, propaganda argument could seem more important, the Soviets accepted unconditional surrender as the President apparently hoped and felt they would. In this respect the policy was clearly successful and achieved what it was designed to do.

IV. Unconditional Surrender and American Public Opinion

The final advantage of the policy in the President's mind undoubtedly lay in the fact that it helped to preserve American unity of feeling, both within itself and in relation to our major Allies. This emerges clearly, not only from the President's own remarks, but also from those of persons close to him. So far as the President's own thoughts are concerned, his clearest explanation of the policy was in his address to the White House Correspondents' Association, two and a half weeks after the Casablanca Conference.

In that speech the President referred to his talks with American servicemen abroad, and to their concern "about the state of the home front." Diplomatically the President suggested that the reports of grumbling over petty discomforts, the self-seeking, and the profiteering were "gross exaggerations," and that "the people as a whole in the United States are in this war to see it through with heart and body and soul." The President felt that the faultfinders and "pettifoggers" could not obscure the fact that "one of the major battles of the war" was impending in North Africa, and that this fact revealed "not merely cooperation but active collaboration between the United Nations." He mentioned the likelihood of heavy casualties and the necessity for facing this prospect with the same courage as that of the men on the battlefield.[51]

Turning to the Axis propagandists, the President ridiculed their efforts to divide the United Nations by trying "to create the idea that if we win the war, Russia, and England, and China, and the United States are going to get into a cat-and-dog fight." [52] This, said the President,

> is their final effort to turn one Nation against another, in the vain hope that they may settle with one or two at a time—that any of us may be so gullible and so forgetful as to be duped into making "deals" at the expense of the allies.
>
> To these panicky attempts . . . we say—all the United Nations say—that the only terms on which we shall deal with any Axis Government . . . are the terms proclaimed at Casablanca: "unconditional surrender." . . .
>
> The Nazis must be frantic . . . if they believe that they can

51. Rosenman, *Public Papers*, 1943 volume, Item 16, pp. 74–77.
52. *Ibid.*, p. 79.

devise any propaganda that would turn the British and the American and the Chinese Governments and peoples against Russia—or Russia against the rest of us.[53]

Finally, the President said that the "tragedy of the war has sharpened the vision and leadership" of all the United Nations, and from this there resulted the conviction of "the utter necessity of our standing together after the war to secure a peace based on principles of permanence." [54]

It would be difficult to find a clearer example of the crucial role played by unconditional surrender in the President's grand strategy of the war. In the President's mind, unquestionably, preservation of American unity of opinion was an indispensable condition both of victory and of success in the peace to follow. The two major threats to this unity, as the President saw it, were: domestic indifference, arising from a failure to grasp the nature of the issues in this total war; and international resentment and hostility arising from a conflict of aims between the United States and, above all other Allies, the Soviet Union. In his address the President tried to deal with both these threats, explicitly and directly. He emphasized "our determination to fight this war through to the finish." [55] and he stressed the preservation of unity between all the Allies as the indispensable condition of victory. Of course, the two objectives were intimately related. Any relaxation of effort short of victory, on the home front, would result in disunity between the Allies; and any evidence of disunity—such as might arise from putting forward conflicting postwar aims—might well produce a relaxation of effort short of victory.

In this connection, it seems somewhat strange to this writer that no mention has been made—by Sherwood, Churchill, or Baldwin—of the controversial role played by "unconditional surrender" in World War I, and especially in the anti-Wilson speeches of Theodore Roosevelt. But the President's own memory was apparently not so short and, as Sherwood observes, the ghost of Woodrow Wilson was often at his shoulder. Indeed, in retrospect it may well be asked, what better device could be imagined to serve the President's purpose than the very slogan popularized by the "bitter-enders" in the previous war? Surely the President's political genius never burned more brightly than when he rescued this phrase from oblivion and made it serve American purposes.[56]

Additional evidence of the President's views may be gathered from

53. *Ibid.*, pp. 79–80.
54. *Ibid.*, p. 80.
55. This was the thought which, the President said at the beginning of his speech, was "uppermost in our minds." *Ibid.*, p. 72.
56. For an excellent study of the earlier controversy, see Earl S. Pomeroy, "Sentiment for a Strong Peace, 1917–1919," *The South Atlantic Quarterly*, 43, No. 4 (October 1944), 325–37.

the remarks of some of the President's associates. Wallace Carroll mentions the President's well-known aversion to stating positively any war aims at all, and the fact that the President gave the war the uninspiring name, "The Survival War." According to Carroll, the President believed that "if he attempted to give the war a social purpose, he would arouse the hostility of the same groups which had opposed his domestic policies." [57]

Similarly, Sumner Welles has written that the President

> believed his primary obligation was to concentrate the attention of public opinion upon the winning of the war. He was convinced that if he spoke to the American people . . . of postwar problems, they might be distracted from the cardinal objective of victory, and controversies might develop which would jeopardize national unity.[58]

*   *   *

The relevance of unconditional surrender to these purposes should be evident. It was in fact the inescapable product both of the conflicting streams of American public opinion about the war and of the divergent aims and purposes of the principal members of the Great Coalition. In both cases it served to bridge important differences and to make concerted action possible.

Brief reference may be made here to the President's unrelenting opposition to any modification of the policy. At Teheran a joint declaration to the Germans on the basis of unconditional surrender was considered by the three leaders. According to a British account, "Marshal Stalin . . . informed President Roosevelt on November 29 that he thought this [i.e., unconditional surrender] would be bad tactics toward Germany and suggested instead that the Allied Governments concerned should work out terms together and make them generally known to the German people." [59]

The President, however, was so unalterably opposed to any modification that he later denied any knowledge of the occurrence. This prompted Carroll to remark that the President may have "followed the example of Lord Nelson, who raised a telescope to his blind eye when he did not want to see, and turned a selective ear to Stalin when he chose not to hear." [60]

Russian opposition to the policy did not stop at Teheran. In December 1943, Molotov inquired of Harriman whether the policy could be modified. The President's instruction to Hull stated that the three major

57. Carroll, *op. cit.*, p. 308.
58. Sumner Welles, *Where Are We Heading?* (New York, 1946), pp. 18–19.
59. Hull, *op. cit.*, p. 1572.
60. Carroll, *op. cit.*, p. 316.

powers had "agreed not to make any peace without consultation with each other," and that "each case should stand on its own merits in that way." [61] Again in February 1944, the Russians began negotiations with the Finns, but not on the basis of unconditional surrender. The British made this the occasion for a proposal to drop the formula, at least toward the satellites, and the Soviets stated their agreement with the British view. Still the President persisted, however, stating that "from time to time there will have to be exceptions not to the surrender principle but to the application of it in specific cases. That is a very different thing from changing the principle." [62]

The net result from this and further requests for modification was the final consent of the President to omit mention of the formula, for propaganda purposes only, to the satellite states alone.[63] It was never explicitly renounced, and in the case of Germany was not even implicitly qualified. According to Robert Sherwood, even at Yalta Roosevelt was "adhering to the basic formula of unconditional surrender; beyond that, he demanded only . . . 'freedom of action.' " [64]

The record of Soviet opposition to the policy indicates that from their point of view it had probably served its usefulness after the United States had become irrevocably committed to opening the second front in Western Europe. It has already been suggested that one of the President's purposes in adopting the policy was to take the sting out of the Allied postponement of the promised second front. The fact that the Russians suggested modifying the policy only after the West was so committed indicates, therefore, that the President's immediate tactical purpose was well served by the policy.

Had this been his only purpose, however, no reason would have existed for retaining the policy once the United States was fully committed to the Western European invasion. Hence the President's continued opposition, after this point had been reached, must be understood as indicating his belief that there were still advantages to be gained from it, in spite of its tactical disadvantages—whose existence, incidentally, the President never denied. The question then is, what were these continuing advantages?

Sherwood's observation that the President wanted "freedom of action" probably provides the best clue to the answer. How could the President enjoy such freedom with respect to Germany (or any other postwar

61. Hull, *op. cit.*, pp. 1573 *et seq.*

62. *Ibid.*, p. 1577.

63. No mention was made of unconditional surrender in the Joint Declaration to the Four Axis Satellites, May 12, 1944. See *Documents on American Foreign Relations,* edited by L. M. Goodrich and M. J. Carroll (Boston, 1944), V, 189.

64. Sherwood, *op. cit.*, p. 862.

problem) unless he was in fact free to commit the United States fully and completely, or only partially, to whatever degree he saw fit? The President was well aware, as Sherwood makes clear, of the danger that the United States might return to a policy of isolationism after the war. He was also well aware of the vital importance attached by the Soviet government to a solution of the German problem; and of the necessity for ending the threat to the United States of recurring European wars caused by Germany. The danger of a return to isolationism could be averted, and the basis for Allied cooperation in Germany could be laid, only if the United States were fully committed not only to immediate victory but also to whatever measures of intervention in Germany were necessary after the war to keep the peace.

The President's determined adherence to the policy may therefore be taken as evidence of his determination to win the larger objectives, and of his judgment that the policy of unconditional surrender furthered these ends. Any just assessment of the policy must take these points into consideration, along with the tactical propaganda arguments so frequently mentioned.[65]

One final aspect of the policy may be mentioned here. Secretary Hull objected to the policy not only on tactical grounds but also because he felt that it "logically required the victor nations to be ready to take over every phase of the national and local Governments of the conquered countries, and to operate all governmental activities and properties. We and our Allies were in no way prepared to undertake this vast obligation." [66]

In simpler terms, Hull's objection seems to be that unconditional surrender is an assertion of unlimited power, and therefore of an unlimited obligation. This would seem to be additional confirmation of the point that unconditional surrender preserved the President's freedom to commit the United States in Germany after the war to any degree he desired. At the same time it should be noted that the nature of the Allied commitment, lacking any other statement, had been given a specific form in the Atlantic Charter. It does seem, therefore, that although the President successfully avoided the Wilsonian error (as the President and Mr. Churchill considered it) of giving the Germans a semi-legal basis for asserting their rights, he nevertheless involved the Allies, and particularly the United States, in a moral obligation of a

65. James Warburg discusses these at length in *Germany—Bridge or Battleground,* pp. 259–65; for the German reaction see also Allen W. Dulles, *Germany's Underground,* pp. 132 *et seq.;* B. H. Liddell Hart, *The German Generals Talk* (New York, 1948), pp. 292 *et seq.;* Hans Rothfels, *The German Opposition to Hitler* (Hinsdale, 1948), *passim;* H. R. Trevor-Roper, *The Last Days of Hitler* (New York, 1947), pp. 237–38; and Churchill, *Hinge of Fate,* pp. 685 and 688–91.

66. Hull, *op. cit.,* p. 1570.

very far-reaching extent. This was, at any rate, the feeling of some, and was to be voiced later by some critics of the policy.[67]

In conclusion, it may be stated that the unconditional surrender policy served both tactical and strategic purposes. For the short run it prevented Russian recrimination in spite of the further postponement of the promised second front. At the same time it served notice on Germans, Russians, and Americans alike that there would be no compromises or deals with the Axis governments by any of the Allies. Its longer-term advantages lay in the fact that it reinforced the ban on discussion of postwar territorial issues, thus preserving a measure of international harmony necessary to the effective prosecution of the war, and laid the basis for postwar cooperation between the Allies by preserving American freedom of action with regard to postwar policy in Germany. One might note in passing that there is nothing in the record to show that Mr. Churchill proposed any feasible alternative policy which would have achieved the same objectives. On all counts, and contemporary criticisms of it notwithstanding, it was one of the most effective achievements of American statesmanship of the entire war period.

67. This criticism was made, for example, by Ernest Bevin of Great Britain in the Commons, as reported in the *New York Times*, July 22, 1949.

PAUL WILLEN

Who "Collaborated" with Russia?

The strange alliance with the Soviet Union is the most emotional of all the issues of wartime diplomacy. The outbreak of the Cold War provoked bitter denunciations of Franklin Roosevelt's policy of accommodation with Stalin's Russia, culminating in charges of treason and betrayal during the 1952 presidential election campaign. Although few responsible historians repeated these accusations, the belief that a naive Roosevelt was deceived by a wily Stalin gained widespread acceptance in the 1950's. In this article, written at the climax of the postwar Red Scare, Paul Willen reminded the American people of how differently they viewed the Soviet Union during the war. Warren B. Walsh treats the same theme in "American Attitudes Toward Russia," Antioch Review, VII (Summer 1947), 183–109. In "Roosevelt Through Stalin's Spectacles," International Journal, XVIII (Spring 1963), 194–206, Robert McNeal suggests that Russian conceptions of Roosevelt's diplomacy may have been equally unrealistic during World War II.

I

IN SEPTEMBER 1944, three months after the invasion of France and eight months before the final capitulation of the Third Reich, a nationwide poll was taken of the American people in which the following question was asked:

> Do you think the kind of government Russia has at the present time is about the same kind she had five years ago, or do you think it is different?

Thirty-six per cent of those polled thought Russia had "the same kind of government." Twenty-nine per cent did not know. Five per cent thought it had "changed for the worse." But thirty per cent believed that it had changed "for the better."

In other words, almost a third of the American people acknowledged that between 1939 and 1944 they had come to hold a more favorable

Reprinted by permission from the *Antioch Review*, XIV (September 1954), 259–283.

view of the Soviet system. This is to say nothing of those whose picture of the USSR had altered in the same period but were unconscious of the change. Another poll, taken at the same time, asked:

> From what you have heard, do you think the kind of government Russia has is as good as she could have for her people at the present time, or do you think a different kind would do better for the Russians?

Twenty-eight per cent thought a different type of government might be more beneficial. Twenty-six per cent did not know. But forty-six per cent thought that the type of government Russia then enjoyed was "as good as she could have for her people."

At the same time the people were also asked, "Do you think the kind of government Russia has will have any effect on other countries?" Only twenty-one per cent stated that Russia's governmental system would have an "effect on other countries," and of that twenty-one per cent two-thirds believed that the effect would be indirect and emulative. Only seven per cent of the American people, in other words, foresaw an aggressive Russia in the postwar period.

Recalling these facts in 1954, ten years later, may startle some Americans, especially those who have, to one degree or another, accepted the now-popular theory that the postwar expansion of Communism in Europe and Asia was largely the result of White House capitulation to Communist advisers. This theory, which portrays the American people as innocent victims of a vast international conspiracy, is one of the basic ingredients of the trend in American politics which we now label McCarthyism. Indeed, the basic justification for whatever suspension of civil liberties has occurred in the past five years is the assumption that China would not have fallen to the Communists had Hiss, Lattimore, and Harry Dexter White been removed from the government many years ago.

McCarthy's accusation of "twenty years of treason" is the most crude and exaggerated expression of this viewpoint. More sophisticated observers, unwilling to accuse Roosevelt and Truman of outright and conscious betrayal, attribute the loss of China to the "softness" of the New Deal toward Communism, as the result of which Hiss and Lattimore assumed positions of such great influence.

I cannot take up either the accuracy (in terms of fact) or the realism (in terms of world politics) of these charges; rather I aim *to question their very pertinence.* If it is true, as the above-cited polls suggest, that the American people themselves were "soft" on Communism in the wartime period, the question of the undoubted gullibility of the White House politicians loses much of its weight and seriousness. But it is not my purpose here to apologize for the diplomacy of the Roosevelt administration; nor is it to deny the influence of Communist agents and spies in the American government; nor is it, incidentally, to embarrass politicians like McCarthy, who accepted Communist support in his 1946 campaign for the Senate, or McCarthyites like Walter Winchell, who told millions in 1944 that the "fear of Russia" is a "bogey." (Both men have survived such embarrassing revelations.)

My purpose is to show that wartime pro-Soviet feeling was far more widespread, had much deeper roots, received encouragement from much more respectable quarters, than it is discreet to remember now in the year 1954. Once the American people realize that the "softness" allegedly responsible for the fall of China was not confined to the White House and not the result of a conspiracy, they may begin to look for the real and deep-rooted causes of the tragic absorption of China into the Communist Empire.

II

In 1942 the excellent *New York Times* journalist, James Reston, came out with a book, *Prelude to Victory,* in which he discussed, among other things, the responsibilities of a newspaper toward the war effort. He was disturbed by the *Washington Times-Herald* which, in an editorial sharply attacking Russia for its failure to join the struggle against Japan, had written that "we cannot expect too much of Russia. The bear that walks like a man does not always think like a man." Reston commented:

> Now I ask you, what is the point of that kind of scurrilous criticism. . . . It is not alone that editorials like this have a negative quality. They can do positive harm, as any reporter who has ever stepped inside a Russian embassy will tell you. . . .

He explained that while he was not in favor of a "moratorium on criticism of our allies" he was against anything but "constructive criticism." He urged journalists to consider the political and military effect of their correspondence. Objective reporting which was "negative" and did not contribute to the winning of the war was more than unnecessary, it was harmful, "as any reporter who has stepped inside a Russian embassy can tell you."

James Reston, who was acutely conscious of the problems of a newspaper editor, voiced the wartime philosophy of journalism consciously. But for others the new demands were incorporated into the daily copy unconsciously. In a totalitarian country such alterations of "line" are made overnight by governmental decree and there are no loose ends—such as the *Times-Herald*—sticking out. But in the United States the changes demanded by war occurred slowly, with a certain degree of spontaneity. For some, however, it was too slow. Bishop Manning thundered on August 24, 1942: "Anything in the nature of anti-British propaganda or anti-Russian propaganda . . . is a dangerous and peculiarly despicable form of sabotage." This was an exaggerated expression of a general feeling which gripped America as the war consumed more and more of its energies.

The problem was deeper than that of maintaining cordial relations between the Allies. The problem of the maintenance of public morale under increasingly difficult conditions was even more pressing. Our soldiers were soon to risk their lives; our citizens were paying enormously high taxes and submitting to an ever-tightening rationing. Would the American people have permitted the shipment of billions of dollars of goods and war matériel to the Soviet Union had they felt a measure of the hatred they now feel toward the Soviet Union, even with the menace of Hitler's legions before them? Clearly it was necessary to create and intensify feelings of good will toward our Allies and to sustain a mood of optimism generally toward the future. Henry Wallace's naïve platitudes on the "century of the common man" were front-page stories in this era because, among many sections of the population, these words represented "something worth fighting for." Under these slogans men would fight with a valor and heroism which more stodgy and realistic slogans could hardly hope to elicit. In those days, when the nation itself seemed at stake, nothing was spared, not even inherited misgivings about the unnatural offspring of the Bolshevik revolution.

In November 1941, *Collier's* magazine ran an editorial in which it asked: "Why all these efforts to pretend that Russia is something which we know it is not? Russia is not a democracy . . . why kid ourselves otherwise?" Two years later, in December, 1943, *Collier's* again posed the question: "What kind of country is Russia, anyway?" It is surely neither Socialistic nor Communist, *Collier's* replied, but rather it has a "modified capitalist set-up," with wide wage differentials, industrial piece-rates, savings' banks, and well-paid industrial managers living at standards "enjoyed by leaders of private industry in this country." Therefore, *Collier's* concluded, Russia was "evolving from a sort of Fascism . . . toward something resembling our own and Great Britain's democracy."

The astounding political metamorphosis revealed in these two editorials was also evident in *Collier's* feature articles. Quentin Reynolds' article, "A Russian Family," published August 7, 1943, is a good example of *Collier's* wartime output. The central point of his correspondence was that Russian families were quite like American families, "much like the Smiths or the Jones on your block." Many homey touches were introduced to reinforce his point:

Grandma Starotsin looks much like any other grandmother, whether you'd meet her in Sevenoaks, Kent; Londonderry, Ireland; or Middletown, Ohio.

Reynolds assured his readers that the only reason the Starotsins had to share a kitchen with another family was that the building program had been interrupted by the war—as if crowded living conditions were unusual in urban Russia! As it was, the "average" Russian family Reynolds visited occupied three rooms!

Reynolds' article was typical of hundreds. Harrison Salisbury wrote up Eric Johnston's trip to Russia and noted with approval Johnston's observation that there was "no reason why close, friendly and cooperative business relations" could not be established between the two nations. Salisbury's technique for ingratiating Russia to his audience was impressive:

Mike Kulagin . . . boss of the [Urals] section . . . built like a Golden Gloves champ . . . tough as one of Zane Grey's Texas gunmen . . . could stand up and slug it out toe to toe with such American pioneers as Jim Hill, Jay Gould or Jim Fisk.

Collier's also published Donald Nelson's account of his trip to Russia in which Nelson concluded "we are both interested in the same thing —raising the standard of living and prosperity of our countries. . . . You do it your way. We'll do it in our way." Another issue of Collier's contained an optimistic account of TWA's plans for an air-route across Alaska and Siberia by Fred R. Neely. Siberia was portrayed as a rugged frontier land, with great wealth, and unlimited opportunities for enterprising men. Neely made no mention of the slave labor camps in Siberia —about which much was already known.

For a magazine which had declared in 1941 that it was unnecessary "to pretend that Russia is something which we know it is not," this was an extraordinary journalistic performance.

But Collier's was by no means alone. The Saturday Evening Post competed with it in pro-Soviet effusions, despite the fact that its chief political writer, Demaree Bess, in an analysis published in March 1943, displayed a remarkable awareness of the impending struggle. The Post's correspondent in Russia was Edgar Snow, whose pro-Soviet sympathies were unmistakable. Between 1943 and 1945, the Post printed twenty-four of his articles and made him an associate editor.

On December 14, 1942, Snow described the "People of Russia," and quoted a collective farmer as saying that "compared to old Russia, it is heaven compared to hell." Another collective farmer, borrowing a phrase from Stalinist propaganda, told Snow that "we are beginning to have a wonderfully rich life." Another article dealt with Russian military men. The generals were "men of the people . . . an example for his men in every respect . . . clean minded . . . free from Freudian complexes"; in some ways a typical general "reminds you of a good YMCA secretary," but not, however, a "prude." Summing up the Soviet military caste, Snow wrote, ". . . all his training and experience have made this man democratic."

With the exception of an analysis by Peter F. Drucker, Snow's ecstatic correspondence was all the material the *Post* published on the Soviet Union during the last three years of the war.

The outstanding contribution of American journalism to the growing wartime pro-Soviet mood came from *Life* magazine, which devoted its entire March 29, 1943 issue to "Soviet-American cooperation." Without this cooperation, *Life's* editors explained, "there can be no stable, peaceful world."

Life's editors gave an account of the difficulties encountered in putting this special issue together, owing to Soviet restrictions and secrecy. "They live under a system of tight, state-controlled information." And then followed this extraordinary passage:

> But probably the attitude to take toward this is not to get too excited about it. When we take into account what the U.S.S.R. has accomplished in 20 years of its existence we can make allowances for certain shortcomings, however deplorable.

And furthermore:

> If the Soviet leaders tell us that the control of information was necessary to get this job done, we can afford to take their word for it.

Life acknowledged some difficulties in American-Soviet relations: "Though we both have the same aims . . . the methods we employ are in many cases diametrically opposed." Their conclusions: The Russians should be less suspicious of us, and we, in turn, should put more confidence in them.

This editorial was followed by a multi-colored photographic essay on the Soviet Union, describing the "vast achievements in the first two decades of the U.S.S.R.," picturing our ally as a robust and healthy nation. The collective farms shown looked neat and prosperous. The Russian farmer: "though he grumbles sometimes like farmers everywhere, for the most part he is content." Soviet collective farmers "elect their governing body," and "whatever the cost of collectivization . . the historic fact is that it worked . . . the system satisfies both socialism which abhors private ownership . . . and the peasant, who wants to own land."

Life's condensation of Russian history followed the well-known pattern set by Soviet historians, lauding the great and brutal Czars who welded together the Russian state. Their history is climaxed by Lenin, the "well-balanced" leader of the Bolsheviks who "made the Revolution make sense and saved it from much of the folly of the French Revolution."

Adhering to the popular wartime glorification of the Great Russians, *Life* described them as "one hell of a people" who "look like Americans, dress like Americans, and think like Americans." Stalin is recognized as a dictator, but *Life's* editors seemed not especially disturbed by the fact. On the contrary, a formalistic discussion of Soviet election procedures leaves the impression of a large degree of self-government in the Soviet Union. A chart is included of the Soviet government, with arrows, designating lines of power, leading from the masses to the higher organs of power.

In order to familiarize the American people with the work of the NKVD (the successor to the GPU), *Life* refers to it as "a national police similar to the FBI" whose job is "tracking down traitors." The popular theory that all the objects of the NKVD's widespread and interminable activities were "traitors" and German spies was given thorough respectability by Joseph Davies, the former American envoy to the Soviet Union, whose analysis of the Russian role in world affairs appeared in this issue of *Life*. Davies, who was introduced by *Life* as a foremost expert, answered a series of questions, among them the following:

> Can we assume that the rulers of Russia are men of good will toward other nations and that they desire a peaceful, stable world? . . .

"Yes," Davies replied, ". . . the Soviet Union is not a predatory power like Germany and Japan. . . ." Davies' postwar forecasts were without exception optimistic; he expected complete Russian cooperation in building a strong postwar China under Chiang Kai-shek's leadership. *Life* registered no complaints on any of these judgments.

Davies was much in demand throughout America at this time. Three weeks after *Life's* memorable Russian edition appeared, Warner Brothers released its cinematic version of Davies' book *Mission to Moscow*. Critics found the movie even more favorable to the Soviet Union than the book. *Life* itself remarked, in a somewhat critical vein, that the film made the Russians "look and act like residents of Kansas City, and the American standard of living appears to prevail throughout the Soviet Union." Bosley Crowther, the *New York Times* critic, was not impressed with the movie, but observed that "still it should be a valuable influence to more clear-eyed and searching thought."

Davies was so popular that the *Reader's Digest* published *Mission to Moscow* in condensed form in one of its issues. The condensation included Davies' unforgettable analysis of the great purges of 1936–38:

"What about the fifth columnists in Russia?"
I replied, right off the anvil, "There aren't any—they shot them."

In the same article Davies explained away the Nazi-Soviet pact, justified the Stalinist dictatorship, and lionized the dictator himself.

The *Digest's* coverage of wartime Russia was not, in fact, very much more restrained than *Life's*. Its correspondent in Moscow was Maurice Hindus, who reported enthusiastically on the vigor and resourcefulness of the people brought up under Soviet rule. Hindus' accounts were written with a great deal more knowledge and discretion than those by reporters of Reynolds' caliber, but with essentially the same purpose and result.

The *Digest* also published a condensation of Summer Welles' *Time for Decision,* in which Welles predicted that "Russia will act on the theory that her prosperity can be assured only through an international organization capable of maintaining peace." Welles maintained more-over that Russia was "entitled to take such steps as it may judge best to create a regional system of Eastern Europe." As for the Soviet system itself, Welles expressed the view that it was "superficially true . . . from the standpoint of our Western tradition" that it was a dictator-ship, but that "from the standpoint of the Russian people, it is a hope-lessly inadequate appraisal." Like *Life* in the case of Davies, the *Digest* printed these views without editorial objection or qualification.

Early in the war—1942—the *Digest* condensed a book called *The Problems of Lasting Peace* by Herbert Hoover and Hugh Gibson. Their extensive survey of postwar possibilities was in no way distin-guished, and is mentioned here only for one reason: the Soviet Union was not even considered by the authors as one of the "problems" involved in achieving a "lasting peace." Indeed, the Soviet Union is hardly considered at all, and one can assume that the authors entertained few fears about postwar Soviet designs on the rest of the world. Of course, the book was written early in the war, when only the most far-sighted observer could foresee the enormous power with which the Soviet Union would emerge from the war. But that fact merely underlines the hypothesis of this essay by indicating how unprepared the American people were for the postwar years, even an American who was one of three Republican Presidents who refused to extend diplomatic recognition to the Soviet Union during their terms of office.

In all fairness, it should be pointed out that in the middle of 1944 both the *Digest* and *Life* recovered a portion of their balance with regard to the Soviet Union. In the latter half of 1944, *Life* published

William Bullitt's sharply critical analysis of the emerging Soviet policies in Eastern Europe, and the *Digest* published William L. White's controversial *Report on the Russians*. But the recovery, even late in 1944, was not complete. In the very same issue—October 1944—in which the *Digest* offered its readers Alexander Barmine's warning of the nefarious designs of his former Kremlin employers, it also published Eric Johnston's glowing account of his recent trip to Russia.

In this same period Johnston himself was evidently regaining his own equilibrium. After praising the Soviet Union in traditional wartime fashion to a Seattle audience on August 24, 1944, he departed from the "text" to observe that the Soviet Union was a land where "civil liberties are only a vague promise" and where, "if there is any religion, it is the worship of Stalin." And then he added this curious remark:

> In my travels I have rediscovered America. Never before did I realize the importance of our freedom, our standard of living, our right of habeas corpus, our Bill of Rights. Don't sell America short.

Did Johnston realize that he himself had come close to "selling America short"? Apparently so; the "travels" had served as a healthy corrective to impressions received abroad, and he had, perhaps belatedly, "rediscovered . . . the importance of our freedom."

But Johnston was not alone in his temporary flirtation with Soviet apologetics. On the contrary, those who did not pass through such a stage were in the minority, isolated, and useless to America at war. The pro-Soviet mood pervaded almost all our publications. The *Rotarian*, for example, printed very sympathetic portrayals of the Soviet Union by Leland Stowe and Sir Bernard Pares. Pares explained that "unlike Trotsky, who thought in terms of communizing the world, Stalin has but one big yet simple idea. It is to develop his country. . . ." Leland Stowe concurred. Another *Rotarian* writer, Harland H. Allen, forecast a rapid expansion of Soviet-American trade in the postwar period, made possible by the "peace-loving character" of the Russian people. The *Rotarian's* book reviewer offered the following reading list on Russia: Davies' *Mission to Moscow*, Pope's *Maxim Litvinov*, Edelman's *How Russia Prepared*, and Lesueur's *Twelve Months That Changed the World*. These books, all pro-Soviet, were becoming part of the national reading list.

Even nonpolitical magazines such as the *National Geographic Magazine* were caught up in the pervasive pro-Soviet atmosphere. The November 1943 issue contained an informal tribute to the Russian people by Eddy Gilmore which stressed the common characteristics of the American and Russian people.

I don't mean the way we comb our hair or wear our clothes, but the way we work and play and fight. Our impulses. Our emotions. Our violences and our greatnesses.

The May 1943 issue featured an excellent description of Magnitogorsk by John Scott, who had participated in its construction. Scott's objectivity was not, however, apparent in the captions (selected presumably by the editors) under the photographs accompanying the article. Beneath a photograph of three Russian peasant girls standing with shovels the editors wrote: "Such stalwart, smiling girls taught the Nazis the meaning of total war . . . these girls lent a hand digging a canal." Another photograph showed a man and his son reverently gazing at the Kremlin from one of the Moscow River bridges. "There, son," the father is alleged to be telling his son, "lives Marshal Stalin, Head of the Government."

III

To understand what had happened to American public opinion during the war, one must reconstruct in one's mind the whole atmosphere of the period. America was engaged in "total war." The newspaper headlines daily described the ebb and flow of battles on a front stretched across several continents. By 1944 the nation was spending 100 billion dollars a year to maintain the military forces that pushed that front ever closer to the German and Japanese borders.

From the low point of 1942, when victory was an uncertain goal in a very hazy future, the Allies had slowly gathered sufficient force to narrow the war to the long-awaited invasion of France and the encirclement of Japan. The invasion of the continent was the subject of ceaseless speculation and considerable anxiety. Many thought that hundreds of thousands would be lost in the undertaking.

This was a time when the American people needed every kind of emotional reassurance which could be supplied to them. To sustain fighting morale, to justify huge sacrifices, men had to be infused with great hatred of their enemies and, at the same time, great confidence in their Allies. To have questioned the intentions of these Allies—upon whom so much of the war strategy depended—would have been to have jeopardized the entire national morale.

Hence it came to be that the war bred so many illusions; but this was nothing new. War inevitably encourages men to dream, to entertain vast and spectacular hopes. One of these dreams was that the war would be followed by a long period of world peace; this dream was based upon the assumption that all evil in the world had its roots in the demented personalities who directed the German and Japanese war machines. The very idea that evil lurked anywhere else had implicit within it the possibility of future battles. For this few men were prepared.

Hence the destruction of the German and Japanese armies became synonymous with the ushering in of a world of peace and plenty. Hence the popularity of the term "unconditional surrender" which, despite its diplomatic awkwardness, neatly captured the intense feelings of hatred generated by the war.

For the very same reason that our propagandists distorted German history so that it became nothing but a series of military adventures, our propagandists expunged from Russian and Soviet history everything that might cause apprehension. Foster Rhea Dulles' book *The Road to Teheran: The Story of Russia and America* 1944) was a labored effort to demonstrate the historical precedents for Russo-American friendship. Summarizing the book, one critic wrote, ". . . as international relationships go, those between the United States and Russia have been exemplary . . . there is only one Great Power against which the United States has never taken up arms: Russia."

This was indeed true: but was it relevant? The question was not asked. The success of an effort such as the Russian War Relief— to which many distinguished Americans lent their names—depended upon the ability of our scholars and journalists to sell the idea of the basic compatibility of Soviet and American policies and war aims. As we have seen, they set about this task with great zeal.

They were joined by politicians and statesmen too numerous to mention. It was impossible to overpraise the contribution of the Red Army to the common effort. For example, on the 24th anniversary of the Red Army, February 23, 1942, General Douglas McArthur issued this typical statement:

> The world situation at the present time indicates that the hopes of civilization rest on the worthy banners of the courageous Russian Army. During my lifetime I have participated in a number of wars, as well as studying in great detail the campaigns of outstanding leaders of the past. In none have I observed such effective resistance to the heaviest blows of a hitherto undefeated enemy, followed by a smashing counterattack which is driving the enemy back to his own land.

His modest conclusion:

> The scale and grandeur of this effort marks it as the greatest military achievement in all history.

Many of Eisenhower's tributes were no less restrained, and his personal expressions of confidence in the Russian military and political leaders were very much in keeping with the spirit of the times.

A very typical tribute was the one the Utah Senator Elbert Thomas delivered at a New York dinner on February 23, 1943, in which he compared the Red Army with the forces of George Washington. "Freed by the people's army, Russia today knows what she is fighting for. Men, women, and even children, have tasted freedom. They call it good." The very same day the New York State Senate passed a special resolution commending the Red Army.

On the second anniversary of the German invasion of Russia, the governors of twenty-five states took the trouble to issue a proclamation extolling "our heroic allies of the Soviet Union," declaring that it was "eminently appropriate, and in the American tradition, that the American people should pay public tribute to such gallant and effective allies." A mass rally in New York on the same day heard the former Mayor of New York, James J. Walker, describe the "heart-warming gallantry" of the Red Army as an inspiration to civilization.

As if in reply to these gestures, two weeks later the Fourth of July was celebrated in the Soviet Union with American music, jazz, and laudatory speeches. The Soviet tributes to Anglo-American military achievements—since wiped from Soviet history texts—almost equalled the fervor of the Anglo-American tributes to the Red Army. This partial reciprocity of compliments naturally stimulated further expressions of admiration from the West. On the 26th anniversary of the founding of the Red Army (1944), Churchill dispatched a message to Stalin which included the following:

> I send you . . . this expression of my profound admiration of [the Red Army's] glorious record. Inspired and guided by your leadership and by their love of the soil of Russia, trusting their skillful and resolute commanders, they will go forward to victory and through victory to peace with honor.

Poet Laureate John Masefield composed an "Ode to the Red Army" which was read at celebrations of the Red Army's memorable foundation throughout England.

Every device was used to deepen friendship with the Soviet allies. Russian music became enormously popular; Russian dances and folk songs were in great demand; symphony orchestras vied with each other to play Shostakovich's new works. The Philadelphia Orchestra was honored with the task of introducing the new Soviet national anthem, the "Hymn to the Soviet Union," to the American people at a special 1944 performance attended by Andrei Gromyko. The "Internationale" was also frequently heard.

The demand for increased cultural interchange provided an excellent arena for a variety of Communist-sponsored front organizations, such as the Congress of American-Soviet Friendship. American opinion was so sympathetic to the Soviet Union that it was impossible to detect direct Communist manipulation. Indeed, the *New York Times* officially "welcomed" the commemoration meetings held in 1943 on the anniversary of the October Revolution "under the auspices of the Congress of American-Soviet Friendship."

On this occasion the Congress organized a great demonstration at Madison Square Garden in New York at which thousands heard speeches by Paul Robeson, Claude Pepper, and Corliss Lamont, and applauded enthusiastic messages from politicians such as Sam Rayburn, Daniel Tobin, and Jan Masaryk. Donald Nelson told the crowd that "the Russians who I met understood the meaning of a square deal and a firm agreement." Joseph Davies spoke too, stressing the common idealism of the Soviet and American peoples. William Green, President of the AFL, also addressed the gathering, and though his remarks lacked the blind enthusiasm of the other speakers, he too lauded the recent Moscow Conference upon which so much of the diplomacy of Yalta and Teheran was to be based.

The middle of 1943 was a period which *Life* labeled, apparently with some justification, "the era of good feeling," because the camaraderie between the Allies reached its highest pitch during those months. *Life's* Russian edition appeared in March, followed shortly by the Warner Brothers' version of *Mission to Moscow*. In April Wendell Willkie's widely read account of his good-will tour of our Allies, *One World*, appeared. Walter Lippmann said at the time that *One World* contained one of the two finest analyses of the Soviet Union that had reached the public (*Mission to Moscow*, incidentally, was the other). Willkie was conscious of potential sources of friction between the United States and Russia, but he had great confidence in our ability to overcome them, because, as he put it,

> The Russians, like us, are a hardy, direct people and have a great admiration for everything in America, except the capitalist system. And frankly, there are many things in Russia that we can admire—its vigor, its vast dreams, its tenacity of purpose.

Willkie's confidence did not waver in the early months of 1944 when, with the growing dispute over Russian plans for Poland and the timing of the Second Front, Russo-American relations cooled a little. In an article in the *Times* published January 2, 1944, Willkie wrote that while "some persons have suggested that Mr. Roosevelt has gone too far" at Moscow, Cairo, and Teheran, "in my judgment he has not gone far enough." At the same time, Willkie confessed that Soviet activities in the newly liberated regions of Eastern Europe were not absolutely clear.

The wartime American infatuation with things Soviet took a variety of forms. One tack was well represented by the aviator-turned-airlines-executive Eddie Rickenbacker, who upon his return from a trip to the USSR told a *Times* reporter that he was "particularly impressed" with the "iron discipline in [Soviet]) industrial plants, the severe punishment for chronic absenteeism, incentive pay, compulsory overtime work and 'no labor difficulties.'" In other words, like many Americans, Rickenbacker was delighted to find that, contrary to his fears, the Soviet Union did not pamper its working class. Indeed, the Russian workers did not even enjoy the basic rights and privileges accorded to the American workers, and Rickenbacker was "impressed."

The absence of anything resembling workers' control and the existence of a well-paid and privileged managerial class in the Soviet Union were frequently cited during the war as factors favoring Russo-American friendship. Walter Duranty wrote a series of articles in the *Times* showing exactly how far the Soviet Union had come from the utopian hopes of Lenin's days. For many, of course, this progression was not altogether welcome. But for Rickenbacker, Davies, and many others the reactionary character of Russia's industrial relations was something of a relief.

Rickenbacker did not, however, confine his enthusiasm to Soviet industrial relations. He stated that Stalin's dissolution of the Comintern (1943) was, in his opinion, "sincere and permanent." And he added that

> Stalin's failure to respond to repeated invitations to meet with President Roosevelt and . . . Churchill should not be misunderstood, since the Soviet leader has been extremely busy. . . . Let us keep an open mind. Let our great leaders, if necessary . . . visit Russia and Mr. Stalin with the hope of a more complete and better understanding not only during the war but for the postwar period as well. . . .

Stalin's refusal to meet Roosevelt and Churchill abroad was not the only incident which brought forth apprehensions of the type decried by Rickenbacker. In 1943 our ambassador in Moscow, Admiral Standley, publicly expressed his irritation with the Soviet refusal to publicize the amount of American aid it was receiving. His sudden outburst caused something of a flurry, and brought forth considerable concern lest the incident offend the Kremlin. Senator Tom Connally, speaking on the Senate floor, deplored the possibility "that there should be any incident to provoke friction between the United Nations," and said he couldn't understand "why he [Standley] should make such a statement." Senator Alexander Wiley from Wisconsin was just as vigorous in his rebuke of Standley:

All this fuss and feathers is just a tempest in a teapot. Stalin appreciates what the United States has done for Russia; . . . we must recognize that there is not going to be any selling short by anyone. We must paddle together or the boat will go down.

Senator Vandenberg was equally alarmed by the "fuss and feathers" that threatened the quiet of Wiley's "teapot": "I am amazed," he said, "by Admiral Standley's remarks. . . ." The Texas Representative Luther Johnson remarked that "the Admiral probably got his facts mixed up a bit. I think it is unwise, when we are engaged in war, to make faces at our allies."

Admiral Standley was, as a matter of fact, replaced in Moscow not long after his outburst. This action evidently made him realize that the American public would not tolerate skepticism toward its Allies from its officialdom, for after his return he took a stand fully conforming to the wartime cast. Speaking in New York on September 15, 1944, when the Second Front had been established and another "era of good feeling" had set in, he told a group of business executives that

after victory, security is the Soviet Government's next consideration. I feel confident that we are on the threshold of a postwar period of collaboration in the fullest sense of the word.

The concern for postwar "collaboration in the fullest sense of the word" was so great that even authentic reports of Soviet atrocities could not break through the solid front of inter-Allied cooperation. In 1943 the German radio announced the uncovering of proof of Soviet responsibility for the slaughter of 10,000 Polish officers in Katyn Forest. The Polish Government-in-Exile broke off relations with Moscow, and there was considerable disturbance in Allied quarters. The concern, however, was not over the authenticity of the report, but over the possible harm its issuance might have on Allied unity. The *New York Times* called the termination of diplomatic relations between Poland and Russia a "victory for German propaganda," implying that the Katyn Forest massacre itself was only "German propaganda." *Newsweek* also scoffed at the German report: "The worst feature of the situation was that the immediate break was caused directly by German propaganda." *Newsweek* explained that the "violence of the Russian reaction" to the report was due to the "sensibility of [the] Soviets in dealing with foreigners"; and it referred to the "mistaken . . . unrealism" of the Polish-Exile Government's request that the International Red Cross be permitted to investigate Katyn Forest.[1]

1. A House Committee which investigated the Katyn Forest massacre in 1952 declared that the suppression of information about the massacre was a product of the "strange psychosis" of the Roosevelt administration, a "psychosis" which apparently extended to *Newsweek* magazine.

During the war our propagandists and politicians were on continual alert lest a piece of "German propaganda" turn the American people from its Allies. In March 1943, Gardner Cowles, Jr., publisher of *Look* magazine and director of the domestic service of the Office of War Information (the OWI), demanded that the people make an "unequivocal commitment" to postwar cooperation. Stalin, he reassured the people,

> wants just what the United States wants—security and peace . . . we need to get over the strange notion which too many Americans have that we will have to fight Russia in another twenty or twenty-five years.

In June 1943, James Farley said that it was the "obligation" of all of the Allies to band together in the postwar world, and it was therefore necessary to allay the fears of those who still suspected the "ultimate aims of our Russian ally." This general line of reasoning continued until very late in the war. Late in 1945 General Eisenhower told a House committee, after his trip to Moscow where he had reviewed a Red Square parade from atop Lenin's tomb, that "nothing guides Russian policy so much as a desire for friendship with the United States."

It was in the spirit of these times that the *New York Times* published a number of articles by the Soviet writer Ilya Ehrenburg, articles which stressed cooperation and community of aims. Also in this spirit was Cyrus Sulzberger's report on his trip to Russia. The report was objective by wartime measures, but contained nothing critical of the Soviet Union.

But the *Times's* concern for postwar collaboration was mild compared to that of the New York *Herald Tribune,* which wrote editorially in the following fashion as late as January 26, 1945:

> There are no greater enthusiasts for "Uncle Joe's boys" today than our troops in the Ruhr and in the Ardennes. . . . Here is one aspect of the international relations too often overlooked by the theorists. "Uncle Joe's boys" may inspire alarm in some sections of the armchair brigade, but to the man in the street they are "ours," and to the fighting soldier they are heroes. . . .

The *Tribune*—despite the obvious bias—made a very valid point, one which was very evident in the aftermath of the terrible "battle of the bulge"; the Soviet Army had borne the brunt of the ground struggle with Germany, and, without it, there would have been many more "battles of the bulge" for the American Army. As the two armies raced across Germany in the early months of 1945, it was indeed natural that some sense of mutual indebtedness was felt.

But what was surprising about the *Tribune's* editorial stand was that it exulted in that indebtedness and attempted to exploit it for political purposes. Still, the *Tribune* was only an exaggerated expression of a national trend. The bulwark of national thinking on international relations, the Foreign Policy Association, had little else to offer. At its annual luncheon in 1942 its members had listened to Vera Micheles Dean's statement that America and Russia had "two fundamental things in common . . . a boundless optimism . . . an inherent desire to improve human welfare." The FPA report in 1943 declared that there was "little evidence as yet to indicate that Russia would want to dominate Europe."

To the annual dinner in 1944, the FPA invited Sir Bernard Pares and Vera Micheles Dean, who delivered customary pro-Soviet addresses, and Alexander Kerensky, the man who had since 1917 symbolized the struggle against Bolshevism. But apparently not even Kerensky's fervent anti-Bolshevism could withstand the impact of American wartime enthusiasms. The main burden of his address was to justify Stalin's reabsorption of the Baltic States and eastern Poland. Though he could not support Stalin as the leader of "international communism," he did recognize him, he said, as the present leader of the Russian people, and as such, congratulated him upon his triumphs. He assured his audience, furthermore, that the annexation of eastern Poland was in no manner in conflict with Stalin's concern for "international security," but rather an expression of it.

Another veteran of the old struggle against Bolshevism who now believed in the sincerity of Stalin's professions was Winston Churchill, who in a House of Commons' address of May 24, 1944 offered this analysis:

> Profound changes have taken place in Soviet Russia. The Trotzkyite form of communism has been completely wiped out. The victory of the Russian armies has been attended by a great rise in the strength of the Russian state and a remarkable broadening of its views. The religious side of Russian life has had a wonderful rebirth.

And, in particular, so far as postwar aims were concerned, he told the Commons after the Yalta conference early in 1945:

> The impression I brought from Crimea . . . is that Marshal Stalin and the other Soviet leaders wish to live in honorable friendship and democracy with the Western democracies. I also feel that no government stands more on its obligations than the Russian Soviet Government.

Thus Churchill gave expression, in his eloquent prose, to the hopes of the peoples of the Western democracies. These same sentiments were expressed, in humbler language, by the American Gold Star Mothers when, on September 30, 1943, they presented a plaque entitled "What America Means to Me" to the Soviet Government in appreciation of the "magnificent" fight of the Red Army and in token of the "common aims of the youth of Russia and of this country." Juri S. Okov, secretary to the Soviet Consul in New York, accepted the gift in the name of his government in a solemn ceremony at Rockefeller Center.

IV

As I have already indicated, resistance to the wartime enthusiasm in America for the Soviet Union was neither extensive nor powerful. But throughout the war a steady undercurrent of resistance—isolated, confined, and subdued—did exist, and continued to produce sideline hecklers. The resistance came from two widely separated centers of political thought.

On the one hand, there was the anti-Communist left, and on the other, there was the isolationist and anti-Communist right. As might be expected, the immunity of these two groups was based upon distinct and mutually exclusive premises and experiences. The isolationist right had fought America's entrance into the war and even in war was not altogether resigned to many of its political implications, particularly the degree to which the war compromised America's sovereignty. The anti-Communist left, on the contrary, had led the fight for American involvement in the anti-fascist struggle, and supported the military struggle wholeheartedly. It had, however, great misgivings about the collaboration with the Soviet Union, an uneasiness which had its roots in the genuine knowledge and hatred of totalitarianism of the anti-Stalinist left.

"Begging nobody's pardon," the *New York Daily News* recently boasted in an editorial, "this newspaper never did get suckered into believing that Bloody Joe was fighting for anything but eventual Communist domination of the world." The boast is largely accurate, even though the *News* and other reactionary newspapers published their share of praise for the "gallant and mighty Red Army" as well as the correspondence of journalists sympathetic to the Soviet Union. They published few full-scale attacks on the Soviet Union, and respected, to some degree, James Reston's strictures. But neither did they glorify the Soviet social system or forecast everlasting cooperation and peace between the wartime Allies. The conservative *Reader's Digest,* as we noted before, published the optimistic analysis of Welles and Johnston; but at the same time, when friction between the Allies began to grow ominous, it published Barmine's and White's attacks.

The approach of the anti-Communist left was different in character, much more positive and forthright. It did not control any mass media and was therefore under no compulsion to muffle its suspicions. When Davies' book *Mission to Moscow* was issued as a movie in April 1943, Norman Thomas organized a protest memorandum which was signed by 52 people, most of whom were anti-Communist liberals, leftists, and New Dealers. The statement asserted that the film "falsifies and glorifies dictatorship . . . creates the impression that the methods of Stalin were not incompatible with genuine democracy."

Members of the same general grouping organized a meeting to protest the Kremlin execution of two prominent Polish Socialist Bundists early in the war. While the *Times* buried the report of the execution in a back page, the Social Democratic *New Leader* displayed it prominently. The protest meeting reached the front page of the *Times,* but Litvinov's lame explanation of the execution was again given an insignificant niche in the *Times.*

The same pattern was followed when the story of the Katyn Forest massacre was made public by the Germans. *Newsweek* ridiculed the German claims; but the *New Leader,* the *American Mercury,* and *Commonweal* took it seriously, and tried to warn others of its meaning for America. These groups were composed of both Socialists who had fought Communists at home and ex-Communists who had gained a first-hand knowledge of Communist techniques; the wartime excitement could not dull their memories, and they tried to give America the benefit of their unique experiences with Communism.

For this group, the wartime period was one of intense frustration. They saw their country engulfed by the slogans and rationale of Soviet apologetics which they had fought in the labor movement for so many years. They watched painfully as our major organs of expression absorbed the arguments and atmosphere of the Popular Front. They looked on in anxiety as Communists infiltrated agencies of propaganda and public opinion, unnoticed because their own "line" so nearly coincided at the time with that of *Life, Collier's,* and the Office of War Information.

Indeed, in this period in American life, the Communists were in a far better position to serve American interests, as they were visualized at the time, than the anti-Communist liberals. The Communists were ready, indeed eager, to provide America with that type of rationale for Soviet injustices which America required for emotional reassurance. The Communists supported the war effort with a vigor and certainty which was compelling, and urged only that more of America's resources be given to the pursuit of victory. In the labor movement they advanced and supported the "no strike pledge"; they tolerated no serious criticisms of the American system; and, indeed, they opposed the efforts of Negro leaders to organize a march on Washington to protest segregation in the armed forces.

So well indeed had the Communists harmonized themselves with the wartime political atmosphere that Earl Browder, then the American Communist leader, told a reporter that he saw "nothing strange" about the resemblance of the Communist program to that of the NAM! Browder's reply to the reporter's question reveals a great deal about both the Communists and the general milieu of American politics during the last war.

V

The causes of the extraordinary success of world communism in the postwar years lie in social and economic conditions which this essay cannot deal with in any comprehensive fashion. In some places the powerful and victorious Red Army was the direct agent of social change; in others spontaneous and indigenous forces fed the growing Communist parties; in still others it was a combination of the two which, in the chaos that followed the destruction of the Japanese and German empires, toppled already shattered kingdoms.

Overnight—so it seemed—600 million people vanished behind the Iron Curtain, and Communist parties of immense strength in Europe and Asia were clamoring for entrance. Most of America still awaits an explanation for this shattering experience.

A small minority examines political systems, standards of living, economic doctrines, fading classes and cultures; and seeks an answer. The vast majority are convinced that the terrible onslaught was due to the policies of the American government.

Yet this essay should make it clear that hardly anyone in America was prepared for the aftermath of World War II. Had we been prepared, it is doubtful that we could have, short of war, denied the Russians the "fruits" of their military victory. But were we?

A nationwide poll taken in 1942 asked the American people, "If you had to choose, which would you rather see in control of Europe— Germany or Russia?" Six per cent replied Germany; twenty-three per cent did not know; and seventy-one per cent answered Russia! This was early in the war, and the possibility of Russian control was then extremely remote. But the statistics nonetheless indicate the gulf between wartime attitudes and those which were necessary for a full-scale counter-offensive against the Russians. In January 1945 the people were asked, "Do you think that we shall get along better with Russia in the future than we did in the past, not so well, or about the same?" Ten per cent did not know; twenty per cent foresaw relations "about the same"; forty-eight per cent envisaged improved relations; and only twenty-two per cent believed relations would deteriorate. Twenty-two per cent was not a very large margin within which politicians could conduct a resolute and forceful foreign policy to counter the emerging Soviet designs. And among those twenty-two per cent—how many were ready to risk war in order to retrieve Yugoslavia or hold Prague?

There can be no doubt on this score: the overwhelming majority of the American people were favorably disposed toward the Soviet Union at the end of the war. It is clear too that this sentiment was not the product of conspiratorial left-wing manipulations. A *Fortune* magazine poll conducted by Elmo Roper in 1943 indicated that, of various segments of the American population, the group designated as "executives" had the greatest confidence in Soviet postwar intentions! Forty-eight per cent of the "executives" were convinced that "after the war . . . Russia . . . will not try to bring about Communist governments in other countries." On the other hand, according to Roper, only thirty-one per cent of the entire population was of the same belief. Roper's poll indicated a greater degree of uncertainty regarding Soviet postwar intentions than the polls taken in 1944, a discrepancy which is not altogether understandable. But for our purposes, the importance of his poll lies in the fact that it suggests that the most responsible citizens in America were the very ones most imbued with the wartime confidence in the Soviet Union.

Roper's breakdown only reinforces our conviction that the pro-Soviet feelings were not primarily the product of Communist manipulations. "Executives" are hardly a class traditionally vulnerable to Communist propaganda; on the contrary, they are most nearly immune to it. But they are the group most attentive to the complex demands of the American national interest, and during the war a degree of "sympathy" with the Soviet Union was apparently in the American national interest.

The first discernible shift in American attitudes toward the Soviet Union came in the first six months of 1945, when the war with Germany was brought to an end, and when the Soviet intention to absorb all of Eastern Europe into her orbit became clear. Pro-Sovietism was no longer in the American national interest; and to many it was already evident that Russia had replaced Germany as America's chief protagonist for mastery of Europe. Polls taken in September reflected this shift, but also indicated that the mass of American people were far from ready to commit themselves to the costly and difficult struggle with the Soviet Union which was later to consume so much of their energies. Indeed, as late as 1948 the residue of wartime illusions was so great that only the Communist *coup* in Czechoslovakia insured the passage through Congress of the Marshall Plan.

The wartime illusions affected all segments of the population. But the only group which continued to act upon these illusions after the war was that portion of the labor movement and radical intelligentsia which the Communist party could organize into the Wallace movement. Employing all the slogans and apologies which *Life* and other magazines had popularized during the war, this movement was a direct outgrowth of the wartime atmosphere. Its size should not be underestimated; it was calculated in the spring of 1948 that Wallace would have received close to five million votes. That he did not was only because of the impact of the *coup* in Czechoslovakia, the Berlin Blockade, and the extraordinary campaign Truman subsequently waged.

But in long-range terms, the failure of the Wallace movement may be attributed to the failure of his gloomy economic forecasts to stand up before the dynamic expansion of American business activity in the postwar period. In Italy and France, where no such boom had occurred, the Communist parties were able to consolidate the hold on the labor movement they gained during the war. As a result, the illusions born of the wartime alliance still flourish in France and Italy. Only America's amazing industrial machine prevented a similar development here.

VI

Yet, despite the rapidity with which America recovered from her wartime illusions, she paid dearly for them—not so dearly as many of our contemporary politicians would have us believe, but the price was high nevertheless. Could it have been otherwise? It is difficult to say; no glib and simple answers are possible. The design here has been to show how irrelevant is the very suggestion that the failure to respond more resolutely can be pinned on any particular group of ignorant or neglectful people.

Our extreme reactionaries today declare that there was an alternative to pro-Soviet wartime enthusiasm: We should never have been in the war in the first place, and should have, instead, either allied with Germany and Japan against Russia, or permitted Russia and Germany to have exhausted themselves in a long war of mutual attrition! That this is the most fanciful thinking is obvious: but it provides an insight into their line of reasoning and their present view—that America should either destroy Russia by sudden atomic attack or withdraw from all our foreign commitments and turn America into an isolated fortress like Gibraltar.

In both cases they oppose an alliance with democracies in a war against totalitarianism because they instinctively realize that such an alliance, and such a war, have an essentially democratic foundation and would have democratizing effects both upon America and the world. Such a price is so high they would rather risk losing Europe and Asia to fascism or communism than pay it.

The wartime alliance with Soviet Russia had a similar role in the general political layout. The Soviet Union is a reactionary and totalitarian power; but the world does not see her so. On the contrary, her entrance into the Second World War gave hope to millions that a better world would result from the war; and millions fought inspired by this hope. Therefore any power that participated in the Second World War had to compete with the Soviet Union in the struggle for a "better tomorrow," and this meant the slogans of social progress. The same is the case today with regard to American alliances with the semi-socialist powers of England, India, France, and Italy.

Certain analysts—George Kennan is foremost among them—have deplored the lack of political realism in the slogans with which America has fought its wars. And certainly the cynical manipulation of emotions which accompanies every war is deplorable. But perhaps it is even more cynical to expect the American people to go to war without great feelings and passions. Should we be so harsh with the American people because they dared to hope that a better world was going to emerge from the terrible holocaust of the last war? These hopes were based upon many illusions; but the hopes themselves should be treasured, for without them our civilization is surely doomed.

G. F. HUDSON

The Lesson of Yalta

The debate over Roosevelt's policy toward the Soviet Union centers on the Yalta Conference. The meeting of Roosevelt, Churchill, and Stalin in the Crimea came at the war's climax, and in the absence of an overall peace conference after the war, the decisions reached there have assumed much greater significance than was apparent at the time. The initial American reaction to Yalta was highly enthusiastic, but as details of secret agreements concerning membership in the United Nations and concessions to the Soviet Union in the Far East leaked out, the public became increasingly skeptical. After the onset of the Cold War, critics like Geoffrey Hudson, an English historian and political analyst, highlighted the short-comings of the Yalta agreements. Edward J. Rozek criticizes the handling of the Polish issue at Yalta in Allied Wartime Diplomacy: A Pattern in Poland *(New York, 1958). For an equally critical view, see Clarence Manning, "The Yalta Conference,"* Ukrainian Quarterly, *XI (Spring 1955), 145–153.*

ONLY NINE YEARS have passed since the Yalta conference, but already it seems an enormously long time ago. The photographs of the Big Three seated together appear today to belong to as remote a past as representations of Pharaohs on the walls of Egyptian temples or figures in the Bayeux Tapestry. It is difficult indeed now to recapture the atmosphere of those far-off days when, as Robert Sherwood tells us in *The White House Papers of Harry L. Hopkins:*

> The mood of the American delegates, including Roosevelt and Hopkins, could be described as one of supreme exultation as they left Yalta. They were confident that their British colleagues agreed with them that this had been the most encouraging conference of all, and the immediate response of the principal spokesmen for British and American public opinion added immeasurably to their sense of satisfaction with the job that had been done.

If in 1954 there are few people who can see cause for satisfaction, and still less for exultation, in what was done at Yalta, it has to be remembered that we have the advantage of hindsight and there is always

Reprinted by permission from *Commentary*, XVII (April 1954), 373–380.

force in the proverb that it is easy to be wise after the event. Certainly there are some politicians who today most loudly condemn the Yalta decisions, but were hardly conspicuous in protest at the time. On the other hand, account must also be taken of the fact that the American and British governments had at their disposal information which was not then available to the general public or even to Congressmen and Members of Parliament—information which pointed very definitely to the long-term aims of Soviet policy. The historian who would arrive at a fair estimate of the Yalta record must try to avoid being prejudiced by the experience of the years since February 1945, but he must at the same time ask how far the hopes set on Yalta were reasonable in the light of the evidence the Western statesmen then already had before their eyes.

The case on their behalf was recently made, though not without substantial concessions to the critics, in an editorial of the *New York Times* (January 24, 1954):

> Yalta was a wartime conference at which some good agreements, some bad agreements, and some indifferent agreements were made. It was a grievous error that the whole of these agreements was not public or at least communicated to the Senate. It was a grievous error to promise the Soviet Union rights that belonged to the Nationalist Government of China. But Yalta was also a prelude to the United Nations; at Yalta Russia agreed with the other conferees on free elections with secret ballot in Poland and other lands plundered by the Nazis. If Russia had honorably and honestly carried out its part of the agreements, Yalta might be remembered with reasonable satisfaction. In any case there is every reason to suppose that under the circumstances that existed in early 1945 the Senate would have ratified the Yalta understanding for what then seemed to be the supremely important purpose of getting Soviet Russia into the war against Japan.

Three points are made in this argument: first, that some of the agreements made at Yalta were harmless, or even beneficial; second, that the agreements about Poland and other East European countries were in themselves just and only went wrong because of violations by Russia; and third, that the agreement about China was justified—or would at least have been endorsed by the Senate—because of the imperative need for inducing Russia to join in the war against Japan. The first of these points cannot be taken very seriously. The charge against the Western statesmen is, to put it briefly, that they yielded to Russia the sovereign rights of two allied nations, Poland and China, without the consent of their recognized governments, thereby violating the principles on which the policy of the Western powers was supposed to be based and facilitating the expansion of Communist power which has been the great disaster of the postwar period. In relation to this charge it is irrelevant to plead that Russia was at the same time persuaded to join the United Nations or to permit France to participate in the military occupation of Germany, just as it would be unhelpful for a man accused of murder to try to extenuate his crime by saying that on the same day that he killed his victim he also contributed generously to the funds of his local church.

Even if the various Yalta agreements are regarded as a single whole in which concessions were traded each way, it would still remain a matter for condemnation that the leaders of the Western democracies treated the sovereignties of their Allies as diplomatic trading assets. If these acts are to be justified at all, it must be by showing either that the vital interests of Poland and China were somehow safeguarded, at any rate on paper, or else that their sacrifice was required by overwhelming military necessity in the struggle against Germany and Japan.

On Poland, Harry Hopkins has recorded, in notes of a conversation between Roosevelt, Eden, and himself as far back as March 1943, that "the President said that, after all, the big powers would have to decide what Poland should have, and that he, the President, did not intend to go to the Peace Conference and bargain with Poland or the other small states; as far as Poland is concerned, the important thing is to set it up in a way that will help maintain the peace of the world." This attitude was curiously similar to that advocated in the same month by the Soviet Ambassador, who told Hopkins that "he felt that Great Britain and the United States should decide what was to be done about Poland and 'tell them' rather than ask them."

This talk of Great Power dictation to Poland was less than two years after the promulgation of the Atlantic Charter, in which Roosevelt and Churchill had declared it to be their policy to restore sovereignty to countries that had been deprived of it by the war. Already, it seems, wartime habits had inclined the President toward a distinctly arrogant and peremptory attitude toward weaker Allied nations, which was in striking contrast to his desire to soothe and conciliate the Soviet Union. By November of 1944, three months before the Yalta conference, his views on the Polish question are thus recorded by Arthur Bliss Lane, who had an interview with him after being appointed American Ambassador to Poland:

> I observed that the Soviet view of an independent Poland was quite different from our conception. The President stated that he had entire confidence in Stalin's word and he felt sure that he would not go back on it. I said that I regretted I could not agree with him, as Stalin's previous actions had shown him not to be

dependable. . . . Mr. Roosevelt said that he thought Stalin's idea of having a *cordon sanitaire* in the shape of a Poland under Russian influence, as a bulwark to protect the Soviet Union . . . was understandable; Stalin himself had pointed out to the President that after World War I the Allies had formed a *cordon sanitaire* . . . to protect them from the threat of Bolshevism and now he claimed a corresponding right to protect himself from the West.

Roosevelt was apparently unable to see that there was no valid analogy between the so-called *cordon sanitaire* of the years after World War I and what Stalin was doing in Poland in the autumn of 1944. It is true that in the former period the states along the western border of the Soviet Union—Finland, the Baltic States, and Poland, which had been formed in whole or in part from the territory of the old Russian empire, together with Rumania, which had annexed Bessarabia—had an intense fear and distrust of the new Communist Russia and were regarded by conservative politicians in Western Europe as a convenient barrier against the westward expansion of Soviet power. But their governments were not imposed on them by French or British military occupation, and far from being obedient satellites, they often acted in a manner of which London and Paris strongly disapproved. Stalin, on the other hand, having invaded and seized half the territory of Poland in 1939 in alliance with Nazi Germany and deported some 10 per cent of its population to Arctic Russia, Siberia, and Central Asia, had now in 1944 placed Russian-occupied Poland under the rule of a group of Polish Communists and their stooges, while the NKVD imprisoned or executed supporters of the Polish Government-in-Exile which had been recognized by the United States and Britain as legally representing the Polish state ever since the joint German-Russian conquest of the country.

Roosevelt must have been well aware of this situation, but he preferred to indulge his private vision of a postwar world controlled by a benevolent directorate of Great Powers—a fancy in which he was encouraged by amateur and unofficial advisers. Warned of Stalin's ambitions of European domination, he replied: "I just have a hunch that Stalin isn't that kind of a man. Harry tells me he's not and that he doesn't want anything but security for his country. I think that if I give him everything I possibly can and ask for nothing in return, he won't try to annex anything and will work with me for a world of peace and democracy."

It is clear that if Roosevelt was thus convinced that Stalin wanted nothing but security for his country, and if he found it so "understandable" that Stalin claimed a Poland "under Russian influence" as his *cordon sanitaire,* he could have no strong objection to Soviet nomination of Polish cabinet ministers as a means of insuring this influence. Indeed, had it not been for the agitation carried on in the United States by the Polish-American Congress and a certain restiveness in Congress, it seems doubtful whether Roosevelt would have made any difficulty at all about transferring diplomatic recognition to the Lublin Committee in its original form. Certainly he did not feel himself restrained from so doing by any considerations of international law, for, during the Yalta conference, according to Stettinius, who is not a hostile witness, he declared that "he did not attach much importance to the continuity or legality of any Polish Government, since he felt that for some years there had been in reality no Polish Government." In comment on this astonishing statement, it is only necessary to point out that since September 1939 President Roosevelt's administration had concluded several formally signed treaties with the government which he claimed at Yalta had never really existed.

Churchill's attitude to Poland was widely different from Roosevelt's, and yet in practice it converged with his toward the same outcome of surrender to Russian demands. Where Roosevelt saw Stalin as a just and good man who only wanted security for his country, Churchill saw him as an irresistible conqueror of Eastern Europe and held that only by abject submission to his demands could the Poles expect to retain even a fraction of their independence. In Moscow, in October 1944, he told Romer, the Foreign Minister of the Polish Government-in-Exile, that "Poland is threatened with virtual extinction and would be effaced as a nation" unless the Polish government agreed forthwith to cede to the Soviet Union nearly a half of Poland's prewar territory and amalgamate with the Lublin Committee, the latter's terms for the coalition being that the Communists should have three-quarters of the Cabinet seats, including control of the army and police.

Churchill's attitude was a strictly "realist" one; the Poles were faced with overwhelming force, and nobody was in a position to help them, so they must submit in the hope of obtaining some mitigation of the conqueror's terms. But Churchill's pressure on the Polish government to capitulate to Russia was not inspired by any illusions about Communism; on the contrary, Churchill was very much aware of the Communist menace in Europe at a time when the American government was totally blind to it, and he did not hesitate to oppose it wherever he had military force available. In November 1944, British troops were used to turn back Communist armed bands marching on Brussels for a *coup d'état* (similar Communist plans in France having been forestalled by the action of General de Gaulle); in Athens in December, British opposition to seizure of power by the Greek Communists led to severe and prolonged fighting.

There was no support from Washington for these anti-Communist moves; the British intervention in Greece evoked a storm of criticism in the American press and the official attitude was adverse to it. In spite of the lack of American cooperation, Churchill succeeded in preventing Communist domination of Greece—which would have involved the encirclement and subjugation of Turkey as well—but he was only able to obtain a free hand in Greece as far as Russia was concerned by an agreement recognizing similar Russian rights of temporary administration in Rumania and Bulgaria. Although Poland was not specifically included in this demarcation of zones of influence, it was implied that the Russians could arrange matters as they pleased where they had actual military occupation, and thereafter it was difficult to reassert any general principles applicable to all European countries. In saving Greece, Churchill had in effect written off the rest of Eastern Europe.

The memoirs of Stettinius bear witness to the pessimism of Churchill just before the Yalta conference. Of his meeting with Churchill at Malta on the way to the Crimea, Stettinius writes:

> During the course of conversation Churchill expressed utter dismay at the outlook of the world. He said that there were probably more units of suffering among humanity as of this hour, while we were meeting, than ever before in history. As he looked out on the world, he added, it was one of sorrow and bloodshed. It was his opinion that future peace, stability, and progress depended on Great Britain and the United States remaining in close harmony at all times.

The pessimism of Churchill, however, worked against the cause of Polish independence no less than the optimism of Roosevelt did. The only difference was that, whereas Roosevelt could see no harm in a Soviet *cordon sanitaire* covering Eastern Europe, Churchill regarded it as an evil which could not be prevented. Moreover, his resolve not to get out of step with America if he could avoid it inclined him to give way on issues combining Roosevelt and Stalin against him.

Shortly before the Yalta meeting, and in spite of a personal appeal from Roosevelt not to take such action before the conference, Stalin had formally recognized the Communist-controlled Lublin Committee as the *de jure* government of Poland. As both the United States and Britain still recognized the Polish Government-in-Exile in London—which had the allegiance of all the Polish armed forces operating in Western Europe—the Soviet move was a provocative challenge to them and they could not simply transfer recognition to the puppet regime without appearing to submit to Soviet pressure. There was enough sympathy and support for Poland both in America and in Britain to make it politically risky for the American and British governments to accept the Russian *fait accompli* in Poland unless they could present to their own peoples some appearance of having reached a compromise on the subject. They must be able plausibly to claim that they had not recognized the Lublin Committee, but had got Russia to agree to a new coalition government.

This, however, was only a matter of show for domestic consumption in America and Britain. The deeper political issue was whether the American and British leaders could in fact do anything to alter the situation created by Russian policy and restore the national independence of Poland. They had one high card to play—their power to grant or withhold recognition. Since Poland was under Russian military occupation, they could not directly intervene there, but they could declare that they would not transfer diplomatic recognition from the Polish Government-in-Exile to any newly created Polish authority until free elections had been held in Poland to ascertain the wishes of the Polish people.

Such a stand would have put Stalin in a dilemma, for he would either have to allow free elections—which, as he well knew, would give his puppets only a small minority of the votes cast—or dispense indefinitely with Western recognition for the regime he had set up in Poland. That he attached importance to Western recognition, in spite of his own monopoly of force in Poland, was shown by the intensity of the diplomatic pressure he brought to bear on the Western statesmen to accord it.

His armies had overrun vast areas of Eastern Europe outside the prewar boundaries of the Soviet Union and were followed by the terrorist detachments of the NKVD; everywhere they had the aid of groups of local Communists with a miscellaneous following of dupes, opportunists, and adventurers. But they were faced with the massive hostility of popular feeling which relied on the moral support of the Western Allies against Russian domination and hoped for better times when the war was over. To break the passive resistance of the conquered peoples, to reduce them to apathy and despair, and to turn their sentiments against the West, Stalin needed Western recognition of his puppet governments, and particularly the abandonment of that unsubdued Polish national leadership which had directed the heroic resistance of Poland to Nazi conquest ever since the beginning of the war.

If Roosevelt and Churchill had seriously hoped or intended to restore the independence of Poland, they would have made the transfer of diplomatic recognition to a new Polish government conditional on the actual holding of free elections in Poland, not on a mere promise to hold them. Instead they agreed, in a document which made no mention of the Polish government with which they were still in diplomatic relations, that "the Provisional Government which is now functioning in Poland (i.e., the Lublin Committee) should be reorganized on a broader democratic basis with the inclusion of democratic leaders from Poland itself and from Poles abroad"; that this "reorganized" government "shall be pledged to the holding of free and unfettered elections as soon as possible on the basis of universal suffrage and secret ballot"; and that the government thus pledged should be recognized forthwith by the three Great Powers without waiting for the elections to be held. The government which after long negotiations was eventually formed and recognized by America and Britain as fulfilling the terms of the Yalta agreement kept a majority of the cabinet seats for ex-members of the Lublin Committee and retained the key ministries of Public Security and Defense—with control of the police and army respectively—in Communist hands, while the Soviet citizen Bierut was left as head of the Polish state.

The elections which were to have been held "as soon as possible" were not held until January 1947, and then they were rigged by the Communists with every conceivable device of violence, intimidation, and fraud. By that time, however, the Polish Communist regime had enjoyed the fruits of *de jure* recognition for a year and a half, and the shameless violation of the pledge on condition of which it had originally been recognized did not cause either the American or the British government to withdraw its ambassador from Warsaw.

It must be emphasized that the Big Three at Yalta did not guarantee free elections in Poland or undertake any responsibility for supervising them; they only required a pledge of free elections from the Polish Communists. In view of the violence and terror which then already prevailed in Poland, it is incredible that any Western statesman or diplomat could seriously have believed that such a pledge was of any value without some machinery for supervision to which Russia would be legally committed. But Russia was not committed to anything. The Polish Communists alone gave the pledge and they alone broke it; the Big Three bore no formal responsibility in the matter.

The agreement on Poland and the effect subsequently given to it deprived of all significance the high-sounding generalizations of the "Declaration on Liberated Europe" which was also signed at Yalta. The principles enunciated in this declaration were admirable, but nobody in Eastern Europe could expect that they would be applied otherwise than according to the precedent of what had been done in Poland. If the Western powers had accepted the accomplished fact of a Soviet puppet regime in Poland without insisting on previous elections or on more than an ineffective minority representation for non-Communist parties in the government, what reason was there to anticipate that they could or would do more for Rumania or Hungary or Czechoslovakia or Bulgaria? The Yalta decisions necessarily broke the back of opposition to Communist rule, not only in Poland, but in every country that had been or was about to be overrun by Russian armies.

What, then, can be urged in justification of the agreement? Why were the Western powers in such a hurry to recognize a new Polish government before elections could be held? It is sometimes argued that, with the war against Hitler still unfinished, the Western Allies could not afford to quarrel with Stalin. But neither could he afford to quarrel with them. He could not simply withdraw from the war, because unless he got his army in Germany, he could not take the war booty and reparations which were to be the spoils of victory. The Western Allies were in sufficient strength on the Rhine to go to Berlin without him if necessary. As far as Europe was concerned, the Big Three could hardly avoid finishing the war together, whatever their diplomatic differences. But Roosevelt may have felt that nothing must be done to annoy Stalin lest it cause him to refuse to join in the war against Japan. If that was the explanation, Poland must be added to the concessions made at Yalta at the expense of China specifically, as the price for Russian aid in the Pacific war.

The section of the Yalta agreement relating to Manchuria has been the most widely criticized of all the Yalta decisions. Like the agreement on Poland, it was a deal between the Big Three to the detriment of a weaker Allied nation and without its consent. But it differed from the Polish "solution" in two important respects. In the first place, whereas Poland was already under Russian occupation, so that the only question was whether an accomplished fact could be altered, the concessions of Chinese sovereign rights to Russia referred to the future and were promised to Russia as a reward for prospective entry into the Pacific war. Second, while in all the negotiations on European questions both Roosevelt and Churchill took part, together with their respective Foreign Ministers, Roosevelt negotiated the agreement for Russia's entry into the Pacific war not only without consulting Churchill (who was only invited to sign it after it had been concluded), but also without the participation of his own Secretary of State.

The exclusion of Stettinius from this transaction is indeed the most extraordinary feature of the whole Yalta conference. The excuse was that the agreement for Russia's entry into the war was purely a military matter in which the State Department was not concerned; Stettinius himself in his memoirs, whether out of loyalty to Roosevelt or to cover up his own humiliation, accepts this version of the matter.

But a treaty involving extensive postwar territorial changes and transfers of sovereign rights is obviously the proper concern of a country's diplomats, not merely of its soldiers.

Moreover, Hopkins and Harriman, who were not military men, were brought into the discussions, though Stettinius and his team of advisers from the State Department were kept out of them. Roosevelt's failure to call on them for information and advice about the extremely complex Far Eastern problems with which he had to deal is all the more strange because he had previously refrained from reading the memoranda which the State Department had prepared for his perusal on the journey to the conference. Byrnes relates in *Speaking Frankly:*

> Not until the day before we landed at Malta did I learn that we had on board a very complete file of studies and recommendations prepared by the State Department. I asked the President if the Department had given him any material and he advised me it was all in the custody of Lieutenant William M. Rigdon. Later, when I saw some of these splendid studies, I greatly regretted they had not been considered on board ship. I am sure the failure to study them while en route was due to the President's illness. And I am sure that only President Roosevelt, with his intimate knowledge of the problems, could have handled the situation so well with so little preparation.

Roosevelt's own knowledge of the problems, however, appears not to have been so intimate as Byrnes would have us believe. The agreement on Manchuria stated that "the former rights of Russia violated by the treacherous attack of Japan in 1904 shall be restored," and afterwards, in verbal justification of the pact, Roosevelt claimed that the Russians were not getting anything new from China but only recovering what the Japanese had taken from them. This indicates that he was unaware that the original leases to Russia of Port Arthur, Dairen, and the South Manchurian Railway had expired twenty years previously and had only been renewed in favor of Japan as a result of the Japanese "Twenty-one Demands" of 1915, while the Russian rights in the Chinese Eastern Railways, as revised by the Sino-Soviet treaty of 1924, had been voluntarily sold by Russia to Japan over China's vehement protest in 1935.

These were historical facts not likely to be known to anyone who was not a specialist in Far Eastern affairs, and a President of the United States could not be expected to discover them by intuition, but if he had been willing to avail himself of the services of the State Department —which kept files and archives for recording such facts—he would have been correctly informed about the past history of the properties which he so lightly made over to Stalin at China's expense. He would have been informed also that these leased territories and railways, whether held by Russia or Japan, had prevented the proper exercise of Chinese sovereignty in Manchuria for half a century, and that at best he was perpetuating what had hitherto proved to be the most dangerous and intractable source of conflict in Far Eastern affairs.

There can be little doubt that Roosevelt avoided consulting Stettinius about this deal for the same reason that he avoided consulting Churchill or Chiang Kai-shek—because he anticipated that they would object. He did not want to read State Department memoranda because they might not fit in with his intentions. Stalin's terms for entering the Pacific war had already been communicated to Roosevelt before Yalta, and he seems to have made up his mind to grant them without giving his official advisers a chance to discuss them—especially in view of the known opinions of Under-Secretary Grew, who had been for ten years Ambassador to Japan and had a great knowledge of Far Eastern problems.

It does not follow, however, that because Roosevelt did not consult the State Department, he did not consult anybody. He had his own executive assistants at the White House, and the one of them specially in charge of Far Eastern affairs was Lauchlin Currie. Currie was mentioned as a fellow-traveler closely connected with the American Communist underground in the list of names given by Whittaker Chambers to Assistant Secretary Adolf Berle in 1940, and was named as a former member of a Soviet spy ring in the recently published FBI report on Communist espionage which was sent to President Truman at the end of 1945. The McCarran Committee also heard considerable testimony about the political activities which Currie is alleged to have carried on in relation to Far Eastern affairs without the knowledge or consent of the State Department. It may be inferred that, if Roosevelt ever asked his advice on what should be conceded to Russia in Manchuria, the advice given would probably not have been to the disadvantage of the Soviet Union.

The stock defense of the Yalta agreement on Manchuria is that the staffs had told Roosevelt that Russia must be brought into the war in order to minimize the American casualties which would be incurred in an invasion of the Japanese homeland. But it was for the President to review this military advice in the light of the basic objectives of American foreign policy. Who was sacrificing American lives and for what end? If Stalin had demanded Alaska as his price for entering the war, most Americans would undoubtedly have considered that it would be better to have a negotiated peace with Japan than buy Russian entry into the war at such a cost.

The surrender of China's sovereign rights was not so different a case, for the United States had in fact got involved in war with Japan precisely because of a policy of opposition to Japanese domination over China, and it was a contradiction of this policy to promote a new domination over China in order to destroy the old one. When Stalin had stated his terms, the question which should have been considered was whether it was possible to have a satisfactory peace with Japan without bringing in Russia at all. In February 1945, Japan was already in fact even more thoroughly defeated than Germany, for the Japanese empire depended entirely on sea communications, and Japanese sea-power had been irretrievably smashed by the battle of the Leyte Gulf in October 1944. According to the testimony of General Bonner Fellers, General MacArthur had already before the Yalta conference communicated to Roosevelt unofficial Japanese peace overtures amounting to acceptance of unconditional surrender but for the reservation that the Japanese monarchy should be preserved (as in the end it was).

If Japan early in 1945 had been encouraged to get out of the war in the way Italy had been, the Japanese would have had to hand over Manchuria, together with other occupied territories in China, directly to the Chinese National Government; Russia would then have had no pretext for invading Manchuria (unless Moscow were to launch an open war of aggression against China), the Chinese Communists would not have been allowed to enter Manchuria and take over the arms stocks of the Japanese army, and it is unlikely that China would be today a Communist country.

The main source of the tragedy of Yalta was an obsession in Roosevelt's mind with the idea of Big Three unity, combined with an increasing disregard of the rights of weaker nations. The Roosevelt of Yalta was no longer the man who had drafted the Atlantic Charter. During the last two years of his life, he fell more and more under the spell of his vision of a world governed arbitrarily for its good by a conclave of three men. In this trend of his thinking there was probably a subtle intoxication of personal power, for the international stage enabled him to gratify that latent appetite for autocracy which he could never indulge in the domestic politics of America.

But it was necessarily Russia, and not the Western powers, that gained by Big Three dictatorship, for it implied principles of an authoritarian, and not of a democratic, order. The democracies can never play the totalitarian game unless they themselves became totalitarian; their interest as democracies lies in a world of independent and freely associated nations large and small. American and British policies over the last few years indicate that this lesson has made an impression. But it cannot be learned too thoroughly.

RUDOLPH A. WINNACKER

Yalta—Another Munich?

The attacks on Yalta produced a strong scholarly reaction. Stung by the more extreme charges, historians sympathetic to Roosevelt tried to remove the Yalta agreements from the context of the Cold War and re-examine them in light of the contemporary wartime situation. They stressed the importance the United States placed on securing Russian entry into the war against Japan and Soviet participation in the projected United Nations. The chief difficulty, they claimed, was not the nature of the agreements signed at Yalta, but rather the subsequent Russian failure to honor them. The debate reached its peak in 1955 with the publication of the Foreign Relations *volume on Yalta and has gradually subsided in the 1960's.*

In an article written early in the Cold War, Rudolph Winnacker, a Defense Department historian, offers a broad defense of American policy. Other articles written from the viewpoint of the Roosevelt administration are W. Averell Harriman, "Our Wartime Relations with the Soviet Union and the Agreements Reached at Yalta," Department of State Bulletin, *XXV (September 3, 1951), 371–379, and Raymond J. Sontag, "Reflections on the Yalta Papers,"* Foreign Affairs, *XXXIII (July 1955), 615–623.*

I

WE ARE a peace-loving people, though we do not shirk a fight which is forced upon us. We do not want war, but all around us we hear talk about war. The tone is sometimes resentful, often surprised, sometimes fearful, never enthusiastic. Most of us feel no personal responsibility for the current sad state of international relations, and with a clear conscience we look for a scapegoat. For many people the decisions reached at the Yalta Conference hold the most prominent place among the causes of the current crisis.

Scapegoat hunting is a difficult indoor sport. The best of historians, after a lifetime of careful and painstaking research and with the best techniques of historical scholarship, have often agreed to disagree on their analysis of the same historical problem. For amateurs the rules are usually not so

Reprinted by permission from the *Virginia Quarterly Review*, XXIV (Autumn 1948), 421–537.

strict. Amateurs may state their prejudices much more blatantly. They may freely ignore evidence without loss of reputation. They may resort to partial quotations and misquotations, or cite newspaper items as expressions of official policy. They may do all this, because their basic aim is to obtain converts for a cause, not to promote the understanding of human affairs. But it does not pay to point this out to them.

The debate about Yalta is being handled largely by amateurs. It is probably too early for scholarly analysis. Too many of the documents are still resting in archives; many memoirs remain to be written; moreover, scholars do not like to commit themselves to judgments until they know the full consequences of a historic event. Still, some considerations on Yalta are in place at the present time. They will not and cannot include a definitive judgment, nor are they intended to influence the debaters. They should, however, contribute to a clearer understanding of the problem and be useful to those who want to discuss, not argue.

II

The criticisms of American policy at the Yalta Conference have been of two types: criticism of the procedures employed in reaching decisions and criticism of the decisions themselves. The first problem need not detain us long. It is true that President Roosevelt's methods of work were not the most systematic—to say the least. His assistants, official and unofficial, found it often difficult, in the absence of clear directives, to discharge their duties efficiently. Many decisions were made off the cuff. In the formulation of some of the most important policies, the people most responsible for their execution were consulted only casually and were finally faced by a firm decision about which they had grave misgivings. At the conferences of the heads of governments, life was especially hectic for conscientious advisers. Sometimes civilians, sometimes the military were ignored. The recollections of Mr. Stimson, Mr. Hull, and other public figures are full of evidence supporting this thesis.

Still, if it is implied by the criticisms made that a more systematic and thorough consideration of problems of state during the Roosevelt Administration would have changed to any great extent the decisions reached, the argument appears of doubtful validity. President Roosevelt had firm, though often not very specific, ideas on basic policy problems that none of his advisers could have combated successfully. He listened to ideas from private as well as official sources, but he kept his own counsel. He was quick to adopt suggestions which fitted his own pattern of thought. He used conferences with his advisers to elaborate his ideas, not to change them. He seldom would sharply disagree with opinions advanced, but inopportune proposals were buried by failure of action on the White House level. In other words, the experience of the entire

Roosevelt era argues against the thesis that, if the President had only consulted Mr. "X" or General "Y" at Yalta, the course of history would have been changed. The Yalta Conference dealt with basic policy problems and on these the President had firm and well-established convictions. The time for revision had not yet come.

The second criticism, that the decisions reached at Yalta during the week from February 4 to 11, 1945, are largely responsible for the disadvantageous political and military situation which we face, requires more detailed examination. In general, the criticism runs as follows: At the Yalta Conference President Roosevelt, already a very sick man, unnecessarily presented the Russian Communists with control over Europe as well as Asia. By the vague agreements on the political future of Eastern European countries he threw the whole of this area into Soviet hands. And even worse, the agreements on the occupation zones of Germany and Austria moved the Russian colossus into Central Europe, where it gained a strategic position from which to threaten, infiltrate, and even control what was left of Western European civilization. All this was without proper regard for or consultation with the peoples involved. In the Far East, the territory of a major ally in the war, China, was bargained away, also without consultation and merely for the needless entry of the Soviet Union into the war against Japan. It would have been preferable to have made no agreements at all. A much stronger attitude should have been taken toward the Soviet Union. Much better conditions would have been obtained by telling the Soviets that the Western Allies would keep on advancing until concrete evidences of Soviet good faith in carrying out its obligations were forthcoming.

The fact that, as a result of World War II, one hundred million people in Eastern Europe are under Soviet domination, the vast majority against their will, is not debatable. The effect of the misery created and the hopes shattered cannot even approximately be measured. Nor can it be disputed that in a world of power politics the Soviet Union has gained tremendous strategic advantages in Europe and the Far East that have enabled her to exert most effective pressure against the Western powers.

Disagreements arise when the discussion turns to the alternative courses of action advocated and their possible consequences, especially when the historic circumstances surrounding Yalta are completely ignored. It is at this point that the greatest caution is advisable. No wishful thinking and no "I said in 1945 . . ." will lessen the seriousness of the problems that were raised at Yalta. Judgments cannot be based on what individuals would have done as individuals; all policies should be evaluated as proposed by a President of the United States, carrying the wide responsibilities this office represents, and answerable to the people for the decisions taken. It is from this point of view that the Yalta Conference must be analyzed.

First, a matter of definition: to make Yalta solely responsible for our so-called surrender to the Soviet Union is, strictly speaking, not correct. Some of the decisions to which the critics object were reached at other times. The zonal occupation of Germany dates back to Teheran in December 1943, and was worked out during 1944 by the European Advisory Commission sitting in London, closely watched, directed, and stymied by the home governments. Much of the future policy toward Germany is implied in the "unconditional surrender" formula announced at Casablanca in January 1943, and spelled out in the Anglo-American agreement on "pastoral Germany" signed at Quebec in September 1944. These policies were in general confirmed by the decisions reached at Yalta and later at Potsdam. The future status of the Western Slavs was discussed at Teheran, where support to Tito was agreed upon, and was a recurring theme in the long debates between the Allies regarding the Mediterranean or the Channel as the major road of invasion. Still, the Yalta Conference represents the logical culmination of our war policy. It was the last conference of the major Allied war leaders, Roosevelt, Churchill, and Stalin. Its agenda included the problem of a United Nations organization, the fate of liberated Europe, and the treatment of Germany as well as of Japan. For these reasons, Yalta may serve as a convenient symbol of American war and postwar policy and will be considered as such in this discussion.

Despite what many people said during the war and repeated after the war, the United States did have a national policy in World War II. The skeptics might not agree with its objectives or assumptions or with the way it was carried out; still, its contents were announced to the world on numerous occasions. Our national objectives were the unconditional surrender of the Axis and the establishment of a new world order of cooperation, based on the principles of the Atlantic Charter and the creation of a United Nations organization. Both of these objectives required the cooperation of the United States with the Soviet Union. Without Soviet help, the defeat of the Axis, especially of Germany, would have been most difficult and costly, if not impossible. Without Soviet participation, a postwar United Nations organization held little promise of success. To obtain Soviet support for these objectives, the United States Government decided to aid the Soviet military effort to the greatest extent possible and to treat Soviet political and territorial demands as those presented by a friendly power and not by the advocates of world revolution. In this way an honest and persevering effort was made in the hope of convincing the Soviet Government of the sincerity of our intentions.

This effort was a failure. There are those who hold the successors of Roosevelt responsible. They claim that the United States Government strayed from the true path of Soviet-American relations after the death of the President and that friendly relations with the Soviet Union are possible, if only we remove Soviet suspicions of our objectives by recognizing the "legitimate" demands of our former ally. Fortunately for the future of our national security, the vast majority of Americans feel differently. They have been convinced by Soviet actions since 1945 that the basic assumption of our national policy during World War II was wrong. The Soviet Union is not willing to become a cooperative member of a free community of nations. Her objectives, as shown by her everyday behavior, include the Communist control of all of Europe and most of Asia. She is not satisfied with a ring of friendly governments around her borders and equal treatment in the council of nations. It matters little whether the Soviet policy is explained as a desire for "security," the inheritance of Tsarist imperialism, or the inevitable clash between Communism and capitalism. The results are the same at the present time.

It seems natural to jump from this analysis to the conclusion that our entire war policy was erroneous. A good many people have done so. Such a conclusion, however, raises some difficult questions, which must be answered fully and fairly before the opinion of the critics can be accepted. Supposing we had taken a firmer attitude toward the Soviet Union at Yalta, how would the results of the Conference have differed? In what areas of the world were we capable of making our concepts prevail? What would have been the effect of a firm, *quasi*-hostile policy on public opinion at home and on the attitude of our Western Allies? Would it have been sufficient just to indicate our displeasure with Soviet demands, or would we have had to back up our point of view by force, and, if so, to what extent? No definite answers can be given to any of these questions, for they are speculative, not factual. Still, measurements of probability can be applied and the reasonableness of solutions can be evaluated.

III

The first step in any discussion of this type consists in clarifying the issue. At the Yalta Conference most of the major war and postwar problems were brought into discussion. On most of these, basic decisions were reached, which have influenced every subsequent international conference. Regarding liberated Europe, it was decided that the United States, Great Britain, and the Soviet Union would jointly aid the liberated countries "to destroy the last vestiges of Nazism and Fascism and to create democratic institutions of their own choice." Interim governmental authorities were to be formed "broadly representative of all democratic elements in the population and pledged to earliest possible establishment through free elections of Governments responsive to the will of the people." For Poland, a Provisional Government of National Unity was prescribed, composed of democratic leaders from Poland itself and from Poles abroad. For Yugoslavia, a similar fusion of exiled of-ficials in London with Partisan leaders at home was advocated. No final action was taken on any territorial settlements, except that Poland was to yield considerable territory along her eastern frontier to the Soviet Union. For her acceptance of the Curzon Line of World War I, Poland was to receive compensation from Germany in the north and west.

Regarding Germany, the principle of joint occupation by the victorious Allies was confirmed. France was invited to become a member of the Allied Control Council and received an occupational zone of her own, formed out of the British and American zones. Reparations in kind by Germany for the losses caused by her aggression were agreed upon and the methods of payment were outlined, but no specific agreement was reached on the total amount to be demanded or on its allocation among the victors.

Regarding Japan, the heads of the three Allied governments agreed that the Soviet Union would enter the war against Japan "two or three months after Germany had surrendered" on condition that the Soviet Union should receive the Kurile Islands from Japan and regain the former rights of Imperial Russia in China, "violated by the treacherous attack of Japan in 1904," and that the allies should recognize the status quo in Outer Mongolia. President Roosevelt was to obtain the concur-rence of Generalissimo Chiang Kai-shek in these conditions, and the Soviet Union indicated her willingness to enter into a pact of friendship and alliance with China.

To cement the friendly relations between the victors, a meeting of Allied and associated powers was called for April 25, 1945, at San Francisco for the purpose of establishing "a general international organ-ization for the maintenance of international peace and security." Soviet adherence to this organization was obtained by the acceptance of the proposal that the permanent members of the Security Council should have the power of veto and that, in addition to the Soviet Union, two Socialist Soviet Republics should be admitted to the original United Nations membership.

These were the major conclusions reached at Yalta, though many other topics were discussed, such as trusteeships, war criminals, Iran, and the Turkish Straits. The objective of all of these was the realization of the concept of "One World" with full participation by the Soviet Union, whose demands for reasonable security were recognized by the establishment of popular-front governments on her western borders and by the restoration of the losses suffered by Tsarist Russia in the Far East.

The dream of "One World" has now been shattered. The Soviet Union has violated the spirit and the letter of the agreements reached at Yalta. This is not just a matter of semantics, of different interpretations of such words as "democratic" or "free." The violations have been continuous and flagrant. Negotiations have been based on the principle of all or nothing. The small concessions made or offered by the Soviet Union have not indicated a basic change in attitude. Our hope now is to contain the Soviet Union within the line drawn at Yalta without the necessity of war.

IV

If we had foreseen this development at Yalta, what would we have done differently? Recognizing the uselessness of Soviet promises, we might have made no agreements regarding liberated Europe, joint control of Germany, and Soviet participation in the Japanese war and in a United Nations organization. And then what? We would have had to face an openly hostile Russia capable of implementing unilaterally the demands we acknowledged at Yalta, with the possible exception of the Kurile Islands and parts of central Germany. At the same time, we would have had to inform a war-weary world that the hope of postwar cooperation between the victors was a mere figment of a deluded imagination. Anybody who takes the trouble to reconstruct the military and political situation in early 1945 must recognize the tremendous difficulties involved in a policy of opposition to the Soviet Union at that time.

At the time of the Yalta Conference, our troops on the Western front had just recovered the ground lost by the Ardennes offensive. We were only a few miles within the German border and quite a few miles from the Middle Rhine. In Italy, we were still bogged down in the Appennines with Germany proper protected by the formidable barriers of the Po River and the Alps. In the East, Soviet troops had just completed a major offensive which had cleared virtually all of Poland and East Prussia, smashed into Germany on a three-hundred-mile front, and reached the Oder River at many points. Soviet troops were only fifty miles from Berlin. Farther south, eastern Czechoslovakia had been overrun, most of Hungary had been liberated, and Yugoslav Partisans, back in their capital of Belgrade since November 1944, were closely following German troops as they withdrew from the country. At the beginning of February 1945, all of Eastern Europe, with the exception of the major portion of Czechoslovakia, was in Soviet hands.

Under these circumstances, the Yalta agreements had considerable merit, even if measured with the benefit of hindsight. In Eastern Europe, where we could do nothing concretely short of war to assist the democratic, non-Communist elements, we obtained promises of equal treatment. These promises were eventually broken, but their violations revealed to the vast majority of citizens in the Western countries the true character of Soviet policy. In Germany, we eventually crossed the Elbe River before Soviet troops had captured Berlin and we finally surrendered to Soviet occupation parts of Central Germany which we had conquered. The Allied Control Council established at Berlin failed to function, but a German peace settlement would be no nearer than it is now if we had faced an openly hostile Soviet Union in 1945. Moreover, no troops could have been redeployed to the Pacific until some agreement had been reached with our former ally. The trouble about Berlin, however, might have been avoided, for most likely that city would have been entirely in Soviet hands.

In the Far East, the Yalta agreements played a similar essential role. We had pierced the outer defenses of the Japanese Empire, but in February 1945, the conquest of Luzon remained to be completed against stubborn resistance and the bloody battles of Iwo Jima and Okinawa were still ahead of us. The Japanese Navy had been sunk in October 1944, in the battle of Leyte Gulf. The blockade of the home islands was becoming more and more effective, and the stage was set for the most devastating air raids of World War II. Victory was in sight, but its ultimate cost was incalculable. A rational enemy would have surrendered, but if the conquest of Guadalcanal, Saipan, and other islands was a precedent, the war would not be won until the enemy's troops had been dug out of each square mile of the Japanese home islands. Moreover, in our drive toward Tokyo we had by-passed some of the strongest Japanese positions; these as well as the formidable forces on the Asiatic mainland remained to be conquered.

Soviet help in the war against Japan was desirable and some Government officials were willing to pay a high price for such assistance. In fact, it mattered little whether it was believed that the Soviets had to be bribed into declaring war or would enter the struggle of their own accord. It was important that in either case the Soviets would be bound by previous agreement to keep out of territory which neither we nor China could defend against a determined Soviet onslaught. Without some agreement, full Communist control in Manchuria and Northern China was to be expected, and the Kuomintang would have had no chance even to attempt the reintegration of these areas into China proper. American troops were unable to establish control over Korea before the Soviets, and the southern half of Sakhalin Island could not have been kept out of Soviet hands, except at the risk of war. Of all the Far Eastern territory yielded at Yalta, only the Kurile Islands might have been occupied ahead of the Soviets.

It is true that eventually we obtained the complete surrender of all Japanese forces in the Pacific as well as in China. This ideal conclusion to the war, however, no responsible expert had been willing to predict in February or even months later. At the beginning of 1945, two main considerations influenced our plans and hopes. In the first place, victory had to be gained as quickly as possible. As long as the Japanese war continued we had no freedom of action in other parts of the world. Moreover, with the inevitable let-down in morale after V-E Day, demands for a negotiated peace were likely to be voiced before long; such talk at home would bring increased resistance abroad. The effects of a prolonged struggle on the economy of the nation had also to be taken into consideration. In other words, the reduction of the time required for victory was one of the main factors to be weighed by our planners. In the second place, we had reached the end of our manpower resources in early 1945. Victory in Europe would give us sufficient combat strength for an assault on the Japanese home islands, but even a preliminary agreement with the Soviet Union on European problems was essential for this redeployment. In any case, fighting on the Asiatic mainland had to be avoided if at all possible. Our striking power might be increased tremendously if the work on the atomic bomb could be carried to a successful conclusion, but until July 16, when the first bomb was exploded in New Mexico, nobody could predict with any degree of certainty whether the atomic bomb would ever work and, if it did, when it would be available. In view of all these considerations, an agreement with even an unfriendly Soviet Union was likely to raise fewer problems than no agreement at all.

Aside from the military situation, strong arguments of a political nature support the policy followed at Yalta. The Soviet Union had gained immense prestige in the United States and in Europe by her successful resistance to the Nazis. Regardless of the official policy pursued, this prestige could not be eradicated overnight. An announcement stating that agreement with the Soviet Union was impossible would have been followed by indignant accusations from millions of sincere citizens, claiming that reactionary elements in the government were preparing, if not provoking, war against our former ally. Even after three years of Soviet violations of the agreements reached at Yalta and other conferences, defenders of the Soviet Union's foreign policy have been able to found a political party in the United States with the main objective of surrendering Europe and Asia to Soviet domination in the hope of starting a new era of good will on earth. It might be regrettable, but it is not disputable, that any less conciliatory policy than that practiced by our government would have divided us much more deeply. In a democracy basic attitudes cannot be changed overnight. The formulation of public opinion on foreign policy requires not only time but also indisputable facts to make an impression on the large number of idealists who refuse to believe that evil can exist in this world.

In less idealistic Europe, the effect of a break between the Allies would probably have been equally disastrous. Communist arguments about American imperialism and neo-fascism would have obtained a sympathetic hearing from many more millions of ordinary war-weary citizens.

Despite the recent sad experience with popular-front governments, left-wing parties of all types, dreading war and reactionary rule more than the dictatorship of the proletariat, would have preferred alliance with the Communists to cooperation with the Right. Throughout the world, the Soviet Union would have had increased opportunities to accomplish her aims by conquest from within, rather than by war from without. As a result of a policy of patience and a prolonged attempt to find a basis for agreement, the Soviet Union now faces an aroused Western world, where only a minority is not convinced that Communism is at least as much of a danger as Nazism ever was. These considerations cannot be lightly tossed aside in a discussion of our national policy during World War II.

V

There are those who claim that a showdown with the Soviets would not have been necessary. A firm stand at Yalta for the rights of the majority in Eastern European countries, for the integrity of China, and for a reasonable settlement in Germany would have made the Soviet Union yield to our demands. This opinion is usually concluded with the terse statement: "I know the Russians!" Most of the listeners, not knowing the Russians intimately, are at a disadvantage in combating such well-documented opinions. Still, if it is true that the Soviets understand only force and are realistic judges of their opponents' strength, it appears extremely doubtful that a mere bluff at Yalta would have worked. It is a fact that the Soviet Union could probably not have faced a war with the Western powers at the time, but at least she was not handicapped by public opinion on this issue. Above all, she was either already in possession of the areas in dispute or prepared to occupy them before the Western powers. Only an aroused United States might have made an impression on the realists in the Kremlin. Even then the probable division among the Western powers and the existence of thousands of Communist-led Partisans along the American lines of communications might have encouraged the Soviet Union to await developments. Nobody can say with certainty that a bluff would or would not have worked, but the painful experience gained since Yalta argues strongly against the success of such a policy.

Some of the critics admit that at Yalta the United States was not in a position to enforce better terms. By that time, it is said, it was too late to remedy the defects of a policy which was wrong from the beginning. The less virulent exponents of this thesis insist that, by adopting a Balkan rather than a Channel strategy, we would have been in a position to contain the Soviet Union within her 1939 boundaries. Prime Minister Churchill is usually mentioned in this connection as a reference and praised for his farsightedness. Unlike our statesmen, he thought of winning the peace as well as the war. There are no reasons why we could not have undertaken such an offensive, but it would have been at the expense of other operations and its final outcome might not have justified the necessary investments. The first price to be paid would have been the abandonment of the invasion of France. As it turned out, this operation was undertaken just in time to prevent a serious dislocation of the British war effort by the Nazi V-bomb attack, launched from sites on the Channel coast. In addition, the Balkan operation itself could hardly be considered very sound strategically. Balkan terrain has been for centuries a nightmare to military strategists. Rugged mountains would have had to be crossed through difficult passes before reaching the Danube plain, and additional mountain ranges protected Germany proper. To accomplish the proposed political objective of liberating the border states in Eastern Europe, final success would have had to be achieved before October 1944. At that time Soviet troops were outside Warsaw and in control of most of Rumania and Bulgaria. It is doubtful that the Western powers could have met this time schedule. Moreover, the most serious military and political problems would have been raised by such an operation if it had been successful. With the most tenuous lines of communications, we would be facing hostile Soviet forces and giving to the whole world the appearance of protecting the Nazis against the justified vengeance of the Russian people and their allies. The principles of singleness of objective and concentration of force are seldom violated with impunity in war or in diplomacy.

The most outspoken critics of our war policy imply that the Communists were always a greater menace to the values we live for than the Nazis and that aid to the Soviet Union was our greatest blunder. Most people find it difficult to make a choice between these two exponents of ruthlessness and persecution. To them a Europe dominated by the Nazis is as great a threat to our security as a Europe under Soviet domination. It happened that in 1941 and 1942 the Nazis were the greater menace of the two. Their own blunders kept them from achieving their conquest of Russia. The possibility of such a victory cannot be written off as of no consequence to the United States on the assumption that the Nazis would have been unable to organize and develop the resources which they had gained. Such arguments have doubtful validity in the twentieth century, with its effective methods of communication and transportation.

Perhaps we should have changed our policy after the Soviet victory at Stalingrad and the first effective Soviet counteroffensives in early 1943. By coming to terms with the Germans, if not the Nazis, we could conceivably have employed their manpower and industrial resources in containing the Soviet Union. Aside from the obvious difficulties in executing such a tortuous policy, it would have been the surest way of alienat-

ing essential friends and losing whatever moral prestige we possess.
Neither the French nor the Italians, neither the Poles nor the Rumanians,
neither the Belgians nor the Dutch love the Russians, but neither do they
like the Germans. The deep and justified hatred for the Nazis and their
supporters existing in Europe is the greatest asset the Soviet Union has.
An Anglo-American-German alliance would have thrown even the most
conservative European patriot into the Soviet camp. In the United States,
the commotion caused by the Darlan incident would have been a minor
rehearsal for the popular revulsion against such an amoral reversal of
alliances. Even full knowledge of what the future held for us would not
have justified or made feasible such a policy.

VI

Our war policy, and especially the Yalta Conference, can be criticized for
many errors of omission and commission. Most of these criticisms are
fully justified, but their bearing on the postwar relations between the
United States and the Soviet Union is debatable. Few will deny that
Lend-Lease to the Soviet Union was loosely administered. Detailed documentation on actual shortages and production rates, as required from
other countries, was never obtained. A more businesslike attitude toward
the Soviets might have improved the morale of our Moscow representatives, produced some savings in Lend-Lease shipments, and led to
favorable action on American requests for the use of airfields and the
travel of military observers. It would probably not, however, have achieved
a change in the Soviet attitude toward the West.

Similarly, the Yalta procedure hardly fitted into the Wilsonian tradition
of open covenants, openly arrived at; though the desirability of this principle cannot be challenged, its effectiveness is another matter. The treatment of China at this Conference can also be subjected to justifiable
criticism. After the decisions on the Far East had been reached at Yalta,
China had very little choice whether to accept or reject the agreements
made without her, and no justification of the decisions can make the
procedure strictly ethical. It is also contradictory, to put it mildly, to
affirm your faith in the Atlantic Charter, including a renunciation of any
"territorial changes that do not accord with the freely expressed wishes
of the people concerned," and agree at the same time to the annexation
of the Kurile Islands by the Soviet Union and to vast changes in the
boundaries of Poland. It will always be one of the greatest tragedies in
history that the hopes and rights of the Eastern European countries
could not have been supported by more substantial guarantees at Yalta,
but to hold the United States, and not the Soviet Union, responsible for
this failure might be considered effective propaganda but hardly a product
of rational analysis. The disapproval felt for these and other decisions
reached at Yalta is probably fully justified. The moral prestige of the

United States was not increased by our participation. Still, the critics face the formidable task of showing that any other course of action would have produced more favorable results.

Whatever alternative policies are suggested, they should not be brushed off by a casual remark that they are based on hindsight. It is a statesman's responsibility to analyze a situation correctly and at no time to make any agreements which, if his estimate was mistaken, would jeopardize the security of his country. It is clear now that our wartime analysis of Soviet intentions was incorrect. How great the chances for the success of our policy were will probably never be known. It might be that, as we are divided between isolationists and internationalists, so the ruling group at Moscow is divided between Russian Communists and World Revolutionaries. The fact remains that the latter group is in control. In carrying out a policy whose basic assumption was not realized, we did not, however, surrender any significant card which it was within our power to withhold. At the same time, we concluded definite agreements whose violation by the Soviet Union made it clear that the Soviets were embarked upon a policy of aggression. Unity at home is the first prerequisite of national security.

It happened that within one decade we encountered two threats to our way of life. We were incapable of meeting both of them simultaneously. We did, however, destroy one, the more dangerous one at the time. We are making progress in containing the other threat. Despite the grave danger to the nation in the recent past and at the present time, we have maintained our basic democratic principles and procedures. This fact is perhaps the scapegoat people are looking for. More arbitrary methods might have provided greater efficiency, flexibility, and possibly even success. But such gains would have been paid for by the destruction of the very values we were and are defending. Fortunately, most of us are unwilling to pay this price.

WILLIAM M. FRANKLIN

Zonal Boundaries
and Access to Berlin

The inability of the wartime Allies to agree on a plan for the post-war treatment of Germany marks the most profound failure of World War II diplomacy. The Big Three discussed the German problem at Teheran and Yalta, but they continually postponed any long-term settlement. For a brief period in 1944 President Roosevelt accepted the Morgenthau Plan for the dismemberment and pastoralization of Germany, but he gradually abandoned it in the face of vehement protests from his military and diplomatic advisers. As a result, temporary arrangements for military occupation set the pattern for the postwar division of Germany.

William M. Franklin, chief historian of the Department of State, describes the casual way in which the Allies agreed on the zones of occupation which placed Berlin deep within Soviet-controlled East Germany and failed to provide secure access to that isolated city. John Snell, Wartime Origins of the East-West Dilemma over Germany *(New Orleans, 1959), and Philip E. Mosely, "The Occupation of Germany,"* Foreign Affairs, *XXVIII (July 1950), 580–604, are important relevant studies. The Morgenthau Plan and the issue of dismemberment are discussed in John L. Chase, "The Development of the Morgenthau Plan Through the Quebec Conference,"* Journal of Politics, *XVI (May 1954), 324–359, and in Philip E. Mosely, "Dismemberment of Germany: Allied Negotiations from Yalta to Potsdam,"* Foreign Affairs, *XXVIII (April 1950), 487–498.*

EVER SINCE THE Berlin blockade of 1948–1949, the author has been asked on a number of occasions to explain how the zonal boundaries in Germany came to be drawn and why Berlin was left as an island in the Communist sea. A brief and simple answer was found to be impossible for several reasons: First, the Department of State does not have all the pertinent records, since the Department was not included in all of the negotiations on this subject. Second, some parts of the story do not seem to be documented adequately in any official records, with the result that certain aspects of the subject are open to controversial interpretations. Third, not only is the story of these negotiations complicated in itself,

Reprinted by permission from *World Politics,* XVI (October 1963), 1–31.

being woven from several separate strands, but it can only be explained in the larger framework of the overall planning for the occupation of Germany. Despite these many limitations and difficulties, the author has felt that he should attempt to set down as complete and objective an answer as he could to the persistent queries which this subject has evoked. The result is the present article.

I. Secretary Hull and Postwar Planning

Cordell Hull remarks acidly in his memoirs that President Roosevelt paid no attention to his suggestion, after Pearl Harbor, that the Secretary of State should participate in the President's war councils, "particularly on those of a combined military and diplomatic nature." [1] Hull was right in pointing out that all the larger military decisions had political implications and that the Secretary of State might have contributed something to these decisions and should, at any rate, have been kept informed of them. But Roosevelt, for reasons of his own, felt that he had to act during the war years as his own Secretary of State as well as the Commander-in-Chief in matters of top-level politico-military importance. This, of course, is every President's prerogative, and when Roosevelt "carried the ball" the Department managed to adjust. Occasionally, however, the President suddenly tossed the ball (as we shall see) to the Secretary of State, who had little idea of what the score was at that particular moment.

The arrangement that emerged early in 1942 was that Roosevelt would work to win the war with Churchill, Chiang, Stalin, and the Joint and Combined Chiefs of Staff, while the Department of State would take care of the more routine foreign relations and would formulate plans for the postwar settlement. The postwar planning task was a major undertaking involving intensive study of hundreds of problems by dozens of experts.[2] This work gained impetus in the spring of 1943 as a result of the rising tide of Allied victories and the visit to Washington of the British Foreign Secretary, Anthony Eden, who came over specifically to talk about postwar problems. The talks at the White House with Eden (most of which were attended by Hull and the President's Special Assistant, Harry Hopkins) ranged widely over a variety of anticipated postwar problems, including the occupation of Germany. The principal conversation on this subject was described by Hopkins as follows:

> We discussed, for some time, the question of precisely what our procedure in Germany during the first 6 months after the collapse of Germany should be.

1. Cordell Hull, *The Memoirs of Cordell Hull* (New York, 1948), II, 1109.
2. See Harley A. Notter, *Postwar Foreign Policy Preparation* (Washington, 1950).

I said I thought there was no understanding between Great Britain, Russia and ourselves as to which armies would be where and what kind of administration should be developed. I said that unless we acted promptly and surely I believed one of two things would happen—either Germany will go Communist or an out and out anarchic state would set in; that, indeed, the same kind of thing might happen in any of the countries in Europe and Italy as well. I said I thought it required some kind of formal agreement and that the State Department should work out the plan with the British and the one agreed upon between the two of us should then be discussed with the Russians. The President agreed that this procedure should be followed. It will, obviously, be a much simpler matter if the British and American armies are heavily in France or Germany at the time of the collapse but we should work out a plan in case Germany collapses before we get to France.[3]

On March 23 Roosevelt followed this up with a note to Hull in which he said:

> Apropos of our conversation the other afternoon, I wish you would explore, with the British, the question of what our plan is to be in Germany and Italy during the first few mónths after Germany's collapse.
>
> I think you had better confer with Stimson about it too.
>
> My thought is, if we get a substantial meeting of the minds with the British, that we should then take it up with the Russians.[4]

But Mr. Hull and his postwar planners were a long way from any "meeting of the minds" even with the President on the fundamentals of policy toward Germany. To begin with, was there to be a single Germany or several little Germanies? This basic question had been raised by Eden with Roosevelt, and the President had indicated a clear preference for dismemberment, although he felt that it should not be done "arbitrarily" à la Clemenceau in 1919.[5] The fact is that Roosevelt, along with Secretary of the Treasury Henry Morgenthau, Jr., and Under Secretary of State Sumner Welles,[6] strongly favored dismemberment, and the President could deny any thought of imposing it only because he was convinced that separatism would really reflect the true desires of the historically divided and culturally differentiated German peoples who had been brought together in the Bismarckian Reich.

3. Robert E. Sherwood, *Roosevelt and Hopkins: An Intimate History* (New York, 1948), 714–15.

4. Hull, II, 1284–85.

5. See Sherwood, 711.

6. See Henry Morgenthau, Jr., *Germany Is Our Problem* (New York, 1945), 1 and map facing 160; Sumner Welles, *The Time for Decision* (New York, 1944), chap. 9.

Mr. Hull and his postwar planners studied the pros and cons of this fundamental problem and came to the conclusion that forcible dismemberment would only sow the seeds of future trouble. If separatist movements with real indigenous strength should develop, this might be something to encourage; otherwise it should be assumed, for planning purposes, that Germany would remain a single state but with a markedly decentralized political and economic structure.[7]

The Quebec Conference of August 1943 (QUADRANT) was the only wartime summit meeting outside the United States that Secretary Hull attended, and even at Quebec he was not included in the meetings of the Anglo-American Combined Chiefs of Staff, although the occupation of Germany was discussed in some detail, as will be subsequently seen. Hull went to Quebec primarily to talk privately with Foreign Secretary Eden about the fundamentals of the German problem, and he was delighted to find that Eden too felt that forcible dismemberment was not the right approach.[8]

Thus encouraged, Hull and his postwar planners proceeded with their elaboration of the corrective and preventive measures that were to be taken in defeated Germany by the victorious powers, and a major paper on this subject was presented by Hull to Eden and to Soviet Foreign Commissar V. M. Molotov at the Moscow Meeting of Foreign Ministers in October 1943. As for the occupational machinery whereby these policies were to be applied, the paper said only that Germany was to be occupied by British, Soviet, and American forces and that there should be an Inter-Allied Control Commission.[9] It is clear from this paper that the Department of State planners were more interested in the long-term goals of Allied policy in Germany than in the mechanism whereby that program would be implemented. The planners had given some attention to occupation procedures but had reached no firm conclusions. Since they did not want to encourage Roosevelt's inclination toward dismemberment, they were hesitant about carving the country into zones of occupation, lest any such boundaries be taken as lines of permanent cleavage or spheres of influence.[10] Furthermore, there was no agreement on what the German frontiers should be after the war, and both Hull and Roosevelt were determined that the frontier question should not be compromised by any "deals" before the final peace settlement. The country committee for Germany (a segment of the Department's postwar planning staff) had recommended in September 1943 against occupation of the entire country: an occupation of "key strategic centers" would suffice. In order

7. See the Department of State policy papers of August and September 1943 on this subject in Notter, 554–60.

8. See Hull, II, 1233.

9. For a summary of this paper, see *ibid.*, 1285–87.

10. See Sir Llewellyn Woodward, *British Foreign Policy in the Second World War* (London, 1962), 441–42.

to maintain the unity of Allied policy, the troops in these occupied centers should be "combined contingents." There should be no separate national zones of occupation. But the organization of military occupation was clearly a subject that would have to be thoroughly discussed with the War Department before any firm decisions could be made. Hence the paper that Secretary Hull presented at Moscow was intentionally vague on this subject.

The American paper that was submitted at Moscow received the general approval of Eden and Molotov. It was obvious, however, that the whole subject would need further study, and for this purpose the Foreign Ministers agreed to establish at London a European Advisory Commission (EAC), which was to come up with agreed recommendations on problems connected with the end of hostilities in Europe, particularly the terms of surrender.[11] Since the American Ambassador at London, John G. Winant, was to be the United States representative on the Commission, his instructions would come from the Department of State; but those instructions would have to be based on decisions agreed to by the Departments of State, War, and Navy. It was, therefore, on the initiative of the Department of State that there was set up in December 1943 the so-called Working Security Committee, a tri-departmental group designed to coordinate policies and produce agreed decisions on these vexing politico-military problems that obviously overflowed the traditional boundaries between State, War, and Navy. It was indeed high time that such a coordinating group was formed, for—unbeknownst to Cordell Hull—the subject of zones of occupation in Germany had already been explored in considerable depth by President Roosevelt, Prime Minister Churchill, and the Combined Chiefs of Staff.

II. Cossac and Rankin

The military planners stumbled into the question of zones of occupation almost by accident. The subject was obviously remote from the urgent task of winning the war, and the very fact that it came up in military circles as early as 1943 is an indication of the difficulty of drawing a sharp line between wartime military problems and postwar political issues.

The military side of this story began in April 1943, when the Combined Chiefs of Staff appointed Lt. Gen. Sir Frederick Morgan as Chief of Staff to the Supreme Allied Commander (COSSAC).[12] The title had an oddly hollow ring, since there was as yet no Supreme Allied Commander and in fact there would be none until General Eisenhower was posted to the spot some nine months later. Meanwhile, General

11. See Lord Strang, *Home and Abroad* (London, 1956), 202.
12. This portion of the story is based largely on Sir Frederick Morgan, *Overture to Overlord* (Garden City, N.Y., 1950).

Morgan was instructed to begin intensive planning for a mammoth cross-Channel attack in 1944, later given the code name OVERLORD. Incidental to this primary assignment, he was also to develop a plan for a quick descent on the Continent in case German power should suddenly collapse before the Western Allies had even crossed the Channel. For this eventuality (which was remote but not unthinkable), the Western Allies needed to have a plan ready to put into immediate operation so that no time would be lost in projecting their forces into Germany and enforcing unconditional surrender.

In working out this emergency plan (code-named RANKIN),[13] General Morgan and his Anglo-American staff ran headlong into the question of whose troops should be sent where in order to occupy Germany quickly and effectively.

In the absence of any political directive, COSSAC started with the given facts of geography and the existing deployment of Allied troops. The build-up of American forces in the British Isles had already begun at bases in Northern Ireland. Additional American troops, mounting to the million mark, were scheduled for camps in Wales and western England. The OVERLORD plan took account of these basic facts by putting American troops on the right flank of British contingents in the projected Channel crossing. When the Allied armies would break out of the coastal foothold and wheel toward the Rhine, the American forces, still on the right flank, would overrun most of northern France, southern Belgium, and all of Luxembourg, and would end up in south-central Germany, while British forces would sweep through northern Belgium and the Netherlands into the north German plain and up into Denmark. Since RANKIN would take the place of OVERLORD if the Nazis suddenly collapsed, General Morgan and his colleagues made the reasonable assumptions: (1) that the troops available for an emergency descent upon the Continent would be those forces, primarily American and British, that were then being built up in the British Isles for the OVERLORD assault, and (2) that the OVERLORD plan for troop deployment and logistic support should be incorporated in the RANKIN plan to the fullest extent possible.

In July 1943, General Morgan received the word that he was to pull his plans together for presentation to the Combined Chiefs of Staff, who would be meeting with the President and the Prime Minister at Quebec in August. The outline of RANKIN as presented to the Combined Chiefs at Quebec provided for the rapid advance of Allied troops into the Rhineland and northwest Germany in order to enforce unconditional

---

13. The exact designation was "RANKIN C." "RANKIN A" and "B" were variations based on a weakening, but not a collapse, of Nazi power. Since these variations received little further consideration, "RANKIN" came to mean "RANKIN C."

surrender. American forces were to assume primary responsibility for France, Belgium, and the Rhine valley from Switzerland to Düsseldorf, drawing their supplies through Antwerp and the French ports. The British were to have primary control over the Netherlands, Denmark, Norway, and northwestern Germany from the Ruhr to Lübeck, with Rotterdam and Hamburg as their main ports of supply.[14]

The COSSAC plan was merely the blueprint for a limited operation, designed to achieve and exploit unconditional surrender. For this purpose, COSSAC felt that it would not be necessary to occupy all of Germany; a Rhineland occupation (in the style of 1919), widened to include the Ruhr and projected northeastward as far as the Kiel Canal, would be sufficient to render Germany impotent. It is interesting to note that the planners in COSSAC, like those in the Department of State, had considered the question of a joint occupation without national zones; but the COSSAC group had abandoned the idea because they knew that in fact the American forces would be driving into southern Germany while the British armies would end up in the north. Separate spheres of responsibility and areas of occupation would thus result, and any alteration of this plan (which was basic for both OVERLORD and RANKIN) would entail logistic complications and political considerations far beyond the competence of COSSAC.

The RANKIN plan said nothing about Berlin or the rest of eastern Germany. Obviously it would not, because COSSAC was only an Anglo-American military planning outfit, with no authorization to deal with the Russians. In order to point up this limitation, the RANKIN outline terminated with the cautionary note that close attention would have to be paid to the question of collaboration with the Soviet Union.

The Combined Chiefs of Staff at Quebec accepted the RANKIN plan in principle but indicated that the size of the forces assigned was somewhat excessive. Roosevelt was not present at the meeting of the Combined Chiefs on August 23 at which RANKIN was discussed, and when the subject came up in the final report of the Combined Chiefs to the President and the Prime Minister, Roosevelt's only comment was that he wanted "United Nations [sic] troops to be ready to get to Berlin as soon as did the Russians." There was no further discussion of the President's suggestion, and apparently nothing was done about it. General Morgan did not personally attend the Quebec Conference, and there is no indication that Roosevelt's thought was ever reported back to him by the COSSAC delegation. From another source, however, there emerged suddenly another plan for the occupation of Germany, a plan that would entail substantial modification of RANKIN shortly after its approval at Quebec.

14. See Maurice Matloff, *Strategic Planning for Coalition Warfare, 1943–1944* (Washington, 1959), 226.

III. The British Plan

Planning in the British government for the postwar occupation of Germany also began intensively in the spring of 1943, after Mr. Eden's return from Washington. On May 25, he presented to the War Cabinet a memorandum suggesting that Germany should be totally occupied and divided into three zones. The members of the Cabinet, however, were not in complete agreement on the need for a total occupation, and the question was referred, later in the summer, to the Armistice and Post-War Committee, chaired by the Deputy Prime Minister, Clement Attlee.[15]

The Attlee Committee studied the whole problem of the occupation of Germany and came up with a confidential report toward the end of the summer of 1943. This report analyzed the arguments for a limited versus a total occupation of Germany and concluded that the whole country would have to be occupied if it was to be effectively disarmed. The report also considered the merits of a joint occupation, as against an occupation with separate national zones, and concluded that Berlin should be under joint occupation but that the rest of Germany should be divided into three zones for occupation by the respective national forces of the major victors.[16]

The three zones, as described in the report, divided Germany roughly into thirds. The northwest zone, designated for the United Kingdom, comprised Schleswig-Holstein, Hannover, Westfalen, Hessen-Nassau, and the Rhein Provinz. The United States was to occupy the southern states of Bavaria, Württemberg, Baden, Hessen-Darmstadt, and the Westmark (Saar and Palatinate). The remainder of Germany (within its frontiers of January 1938) was to be under Soviet occupation, except for Berlin (which was to be jointly occupied) and East Prussia (which it was assumed would be turned over to Poland). The zonal boundaries followed the borders of the German states (*Länder*), except that the huge state of Prussia was divided between the British and Soviet zones. Even this division, however, followed traditional provincial boundaries. The Soviet zone was the largest in area, but the British zone exceeded it in population. Since the American zone was the smallest of all, it was proposed that the United States might take over the occupation of Austria, if it so desired.

It is worth noting that the western boundary of the Soviet zone, as

15. See Woodward, 443–45. For the elaborate but effective committee system through which the British coordinated the thinking of their civilian and military authorities, see also Gen. Sir Leslie Hollis, *One Marine's Tale* (London, 1956), 69.

16. See Strang, 203; Winston S. Churchill, *Triumph and Tragedy* (Boston, 1953), 507–8.

proposed in this British plan, was the boundary eventually accepted. Berlin, as an area under joint occupation, lay 110 miles inside the western boundary of the Soviet zone, but nothing was said about any transit rights to Berlin.

The British plan also took account of the fact that the lines of supply and communication for American and British occupation forces would run across western and northern Europe. For this purpose, France was indicated as being an American "sphere of influence," while Belgium, Luxembourg, Holland, and Denmark would be in the British sphere. The plan thus reflected not only the immediate requirements of troop disposition in OVERLORD and RANKIN but also the perennial British interest in the Low Countries and the "opposite shore" of the North Sea.

This momentous British plan was completed and approved in essential outline by the late summer or early fall of 1943. It does not appear to have been submitted at that time by Churchill or Eden to Roosevelt, Hull, or Winant. It is certain that the State Department planners, who were then hard at work on the German problem, did not hear of it until January 1944.

But General Morgan received a copy of it in draft shortly after the Quebec Conference of August 1943. COSSAC had realized for months that he and his staff needed political guidance in working out the RANKIN plan, but none had been available. Now he had a clear and comprehensive foundation on which he could build. The timing, however, was awkward, for COSSAC's limited RANKIN plan—just approved in outline at Quebec—would now have to be extensively revised. Furthermore, the new occupation plan was of purely British origin: it would need the approval of the American Chiefs of Staff before COSSAC could take it as a basis for combined planning.

It so happened that General Morgan was coming to the United States in October, at the invitation of Gen. George C. Marshall, Army Chief of Staff. Since OVERLORD was the overwhelming concern, Morgan does not appear to have discussed RANKIN with either Marshall or Roosevelt. He brought along, however, a statement indicating how RANKIN would need to be modified and extended in order to make it conform to the British government's more elaborate plan on zones of occupation, and he left a copy of this statement with General Marshall in order to find out whether the American Joint Chiefs of Staff agreed that COSSAC should proceed with the revision of RANKIN along the lines indicated.

General Marshall turned Morgan's paper over to the Joint Chiefs for study. Since it was obvious that this RANKIN business would need political guidance, the Joint Chiefs laid the problem before the President in a memorandum sent via the President's Chief of Staff, Admiral

William D. Leahy.[17] Mr Hull, who was then in Moscow for the conference with Eden and Molotov, apparently heard nothing of this new development, and neither did any of his postwar planners hard at work in the Department of State. There was no machinery for coordinating such politico-military problems, and anyway Roosevelt and the Joint Chiefs were busier than ever, preparing for the crucial conferences to be held at Cairo and Tehran. The memorandum on the proposed revision of RANKIN was taken along when they boarded the U.S.S. *Iowa* on November 11, 1943.

IV. President Roosevelt and the Cairo Conference

Aboard the great battleship, Roosevelt had the opportunity to discuss thoroughly with the United States Chiefs of Staff a number of important problems that were to come up at the forthcoming conferences. In the discussion on November 19, he brought up the subject of RANKIN and proceeded to tie the matter of zones of occupation directly into the question of the permanent dismemberment of the German state, an idea to which he was obviously attached despite the lukewarm reaction of Secretary Hull and the Department's postwar planners. The President told the Joint Chiefs that "practically speaking there should be three German states after the war, possibly five." [18] He thought the zones of occupation ought to conform to these projected lines of dismemberment. He had no serious objections to the British suggestion for a division of Germany into three zones (northwest, south, and east) but he insisted that the northwest zone should extend eastward to include Berlin and that the United States should have *that* zone. He was completely uninterested in the southern zone, even with Austria thrown in. "The United States," he emphasized, "should have Berlin." The President noted that the lines of communication to the south German zone would run through France and he did not want the United States to be involved in "reconstituting France." "France," he said, "is a British 'baby.'" [19]

General Marshall ventured to point out that the basic reason for the COSSAC proposal lay in the accepted fact that the American armies would be on the right (southern) flank of the Allied forces invading Germany. Adm. Ernest J. King, Chief of Naval Operations, supported the General by saying that "the military plans for OVERLORD were so far

17. See *Foreign Relations of the United States: The Conferences at Cairo and Tehran, 1943* (Washington, 1961), 253.

18. Roosevelt never settled on an exact number. At Tehran he proposed five German states plus two internationally controlled regions; at Yalta he argued for "five or seven states." See *ibid.*, 600–2; and *Foreign Relations of The United States: The Conferences at Malta and Yalta, 1945* (Washington, 1955), 614.

19. *Conferences at Cairo and Tehran*, 254.

developed that it would not be practicable to accept any change in
OVERLORD deployment." Roosevelt countered this objection by pointing
out that the army of occupation need not be the same as the forces
assigned to OVERLORD. The bulk of the occupation troops could go direct
from the United States to Germany, around Scotland if necessary. They
would not have to go through France at all. France was going to be a
"headache," with General de Gaulle hoping "to be one mile behind
the troops in taking over the government." Roosevelt did not want
American forces to be tied up in France, particularly since there "would
definitely be a race for Berlin." And he added, "We may have to put
the United States divisions into Berlin as soon as possible." Harry Hopkins echoed the thought by suggesting that "we be ready to put an
airborne division into Berlin two hours after the collapse of Germany."
Admiral Leahy, who was asked by the President to comment "from
the State Department point of view" (sic), bolstered Roosevelt's fear
that there would be civil war in France and urged that United States
troops be gotten out of France as soon as possible.

As the discussion continued, the President warmed up to his subject.
He foresaw that we might have a million troops in Europe—but only
for a year or two. We would not want our forces to become involved
in "local squabbles in such a place as Yugoslavia." There might be civil
war in France. Holland, under Queen Wilhelmina, would be no
problem; but Belgium was a linguistically divided country—maybe
there should be set up a long buffer state between France and Germany
running all the way from Switzerland to the sea through Alsace-Lorraine.
(Shades of Lothair's realm!) If we accepted the COSSAC proposal, said
the President with unusual cynicism, "the British would undercut us in
every move we make in the southern occupational area proposed for
the United States." He added that it was quite evident that British
political considerations were back of this proposal.[20]

At the end of the discussion the President took a handy National
Geographic Society map and drew the zonal boundaries as he thought
they should be.[21] There were roughly the same three zones as in the
British plan, but the northwest zone was enlarged eastward to a line
running from Stettin on the Baltic to the Czech border, thus putting
Berlin and Leipzig in the enormous northwestern (American) zone.

In response to the President's wishes, the United States Chiefs of Staff
drew up a paper on RANKIN (CCS 320/4) which was presented to the
British Chiefs at Cairo on December 4.[22] The paper was an instruction
to COSSAC to reverse his planning by assuming that the United States

20. *Ibid.,* 255–56.
21. The map is reproduced in Matloff, facing 341.
22. The paper, as revised, is printed in *Conferences at Cairo and Tehran,*
786.

would occupy the northwest zone in Germany and that its "sphere" would thus include the Netherlands and Scandinavia. The description of the enlarged northwestern zone specifically included Stettin but excluded Berlin. In view of Roosevelt's earlier insistence on having Berlin, this sudden modification of his thought is difficult to explain. He had, however, discussed the problem at Cairo with Churchill on December 3,[23] and it is possible that the Prime Minister had convinced him that Berlin should be a special area of tripartite responsibility, no matter how the rest of the zonal lines were drawn. This is not apparent from the paper, however, because it dealt only with the American and British zones and said nothing whatever about the Russian zone—for the simple but compelling reason that this paper was a CCS directive to Cossac, who had no connections with the Russians at all.

The British Chiefs of Staff refrained from comment on the size of the zone proposed for American occupation, but they pointed out that this new allotment of zones would entail an unacceptable crossing of American and British forces and their lines of communication and supply as the armies invaded Germany from the west. They blandly agreed, however, that Cossac might be "directed to examine and report on the implications of revising his planning on the basis of the new allocation of spheres of occupation." [24]

As thus significantly amended, the directive went to General Morgan shortly after the Cairo Conference adjourned on December 7. In view of all the previous planning and agreement that had gone into this subject, the General was taken aback. Indeed, by his own account, he thought for a while that he was the victim of a practical joke. When he was assured in all seriousness that the suggestion came from no less than the President of the United States, he promptly put his staff to work. Morgan correctly surmised that the French entanglement was what bothered Roosevelt most of all in Cossac's revised plan, but that plan reflected the troop dispositions in Overlord, and these could not be changed at this stage of the game. From the military point of view, the Cossac staff found untold complications in switching the proposed British and American zones in Germany. General Morgan so reported, and as he says, "No more was ever heard, by us at any rate, of this particular proposition." [25] Other people, however, were to hear a great deal more about it.

V. The European Advisory Commission and the Working Security Committee

The European Advisory Commission, consisting of the American and Soviet Ambassadors, John G. Winant and F. T. Gusev, together

23. *Ibid.*, 674.
24. *Ibid.*, 688, 787.
25. Morgan, 248–50.

with Sir William Strang of the British Foreign Office, met at London
for the first time in mid-December—at the very time when COSSAC,
in another London townhouse, was studying the startling directive from
Cairo. The first formal session of the EAC was held on January 14,
1944, and on the following day the British presented a draft instrument
for German surrender and a memorandum (with map) on the military
occupation of Germany.[26] The memorandum was new to Winant and
Gusev, but it was "old stuff" to Roosevelt, Churchill, COSSAC, and
the Combined Chiefs of Staff. It was essentially the same British plan,
slightly revised in phraseology, that had encountered such vigorous
opposition from Roosevelt at Cairo.[27] Since the proposal was now
being put at the governmental level to the Russians as well as the
Americans, it said nothing, of course, about COSSAC, or the CCS,
or Anglo-American "spheres of influence" in western and northern
Europe. But the proposed zonal boundaries had not been altered. The
British were in the northwest, the Russians in the east, the Americans
in the south. The United States might also occupy Austria if it so
desired. Berlin, 110 miles inside the Soviet zone, was to be occupied
jointly by the three powers.

On February 18, Gusev presented the Soviet draft of surrender terms
for Germany, a terse document of twenty paragraphs, of which the
fifteenth described the proposed zones of occupation. These were identical
with the zones proposed by the British, except that the Soviets prescribed
that East Prussia be counted as in the Soviet zone and that Austria be
occupied by troops of all three powers.[28] When Strang accepted the
Soviet position on East Prussia, the British and Russian proposals on
zonal boundaries in Germany became identical.[29] Winant wired urgently
for instructions.

These developments caught Washington by surprise and precipitated
a flurry of consultation. On February 18 Roosevelt sent the following

26. Strang, 213–14.
27. Winant had attended the Cairo Conference, but he had not been
invited to sit in on the CCS discussions on zones of occupation; see *Conferences at Cairo and Tehran*, 63–64, 301, 352, 688.
28. The three Foreign Ministers at Moscow had announced on November
1, 1943, that Austria was to be liberated from German domination and reestablished as an independent state; for texts of the Anglo-Soviet-American
communiqué and the Declaration on Austria, see *Department of State Bulletin*, IX (November 6, 1943), 307, 310. At Tehran the Big Three had tentatively agreed that most of East Prussia should go to Poland; see *Conferences at Cairo and Tehran*, 594, 603, 604.
29. Gusev either misunderstood or tried to take advantage of an ambiguity
in the British map by claiming that the island of Fehmarn was in the Soviet
zone, but he gave up on this point when Strang insisted that it was part of
Schleswig-Holstein. See Strang, 207; also Strang's article, "New Harsh Language in Diplomacy," *New York Times Magazine*, April 15, 1962.

hasty note to Acting Secretary of State Edward R. Stettinius, Jr.: "What are the zones in the British and Russian drafts and what is the zone we are proposing? I must know this in order that it conform with what I decided on months ago."

This was baffling to the entire Department of State, which had no idea of what Roosevelt had decided on "months ago" and could only guess (erroneously) that it had something to do with the Tehran Conference. Stettinius' reply of the following day described the British and Soviet proposals and explained that no American proposal on zones had been made to date. The memorandum hinted that it would be helpful if Roosevelt sent Hull a set of the Tehran Conference minutes, and it concluded by asking the President for an expression of his views so that the Department could send Winant instructions at an early date.

The President's reply of February 21 said nothing about sending any records of the Tehran Conference to the Department, nor did it explain that the "decision" in question had been expressed not at Tehran but at Cairo and in the framework of the Combined Chiefs of Staff. The memorandum stressed the President's continuing concern that occupation of the southern zone in Germany (together with Austria) would involve the United States in the "postwar burden of reconstituting France, Italy, and the Balkans." This, said the President, "is definitely a British task in which the British are far more vitally interested than we are." [30] He said that there was nothing to the British argument against crisscrossing or "leap-frogging" American and British troops after Germany surrendered; this could readily be arranged. Besides, the American occupation army would have to be supplied across 3,500 miles of water, and this meant that we should use the great north German and Dutch ports. As for the long-range security of Great Britain, that argument had no bearing on the initial occupation period. The United Kingdom could take steps later on with respect to Helgoland, airfields, etc., and by that time, said the President, the Americans "will be only too glad to retire all their military forces from Europe." The President concluded his memorandum with the cryptic remark: "If anything further is needed to justify this disagreement with the British lines of demarcation, I can only add that political considerations in the United States make my decision conclusive."

Although this memorandum did not give the Department a very clear picture of the evolution of this question in the Combined Chiefs of Staff, at least it provided, for the first time, an inkling of where the matter stood and how strongly Roosevelt felt about it. The Department promptly sent the President's remarks to Winant for his guidance.

30. Excerpts from the memorandum are quoted in Hull, ii, 1612, and Matloff, 491.

Meanwhile the Department was trying to reach some agreement on these problems with the Departments of War and Navy through the Working Security Committee that had been set up in December 1943 to bridge the gap between "the military" and "the politicos." (See above, p. 254.) The committee found the gap to be large indeed. The War Department representatives seemed reluctant to participate very actively, on the ground that the whole problem of German surrender, including zones of occupation, was a military matter to be decided in due course by the appropriate military authorities. In response to the arguments of the Department of State, this attitude was relaxed sufficiently to make possible the preparation of an agreed draft instrument for German surrender, but this document said nothing about zones of occupation because this was a subject which the military representatives would not seriously discuss. During January and February they would neither accept nor amend the British or Soviet proposals, nor would they participate in any consideration of an American counterproposal.

It is clear from the account of Philip E. Mosely, one of the Department of State representatives, that he and his civilian colleagues were baffled and irritated by this negative attitude.[31] Some explanation for it can now be made, however. From the Pentagon viewpoint, the subject of zones of occupation was clearly a military matter. It had been worked on by COSSAC and then by the Combined Chiefs of Staff, together with the President and the Prime Minister, at Quebec and Cairo. The question (which was highly classified and unsettled) was still on the agenda of the Combined Chiefs of Staff, and War Department officers at the level of the Working Security Committee had no authority to discuss or share this top-level CCS problem with State Department civilians, who were not even familiar with its background. This awkward dilemma resulted from the fact that the Prime Minister had allowed the subject to be brought up in the European Advisory Commission, while the President (who was never very enthusiastic about the EAC) assumed that the Combined Chiefs of Staff still had sole responsibility in the matter. The lines of authority were now completely fouled. This made little difference on the British side, where the military and civilian elements were closely meshed in the War Cabinet and subordinate committees; but in Washington, with its sharp dichotomy between State Department and Pentagon, the effect was paralyzing. No agreed instruction on zones of occupation could be sent to Winant for weeks and weeks, during which his position became increasingly embarrassing.

31. See Phillip E. Mosely, *The Kremlin and World Politics* (New York, 1960), chap. 6. This is a collection, with additional commentary, of a number of Mosely's articles. Chapter 6 is the article entitled "The Occupation of Germany: New Light on How the Zones Were Drawn," first published in *Foreign Affairs*, XXVIII (July 1950), 580–604.

The Department of State seems to have been willing to accept the British plan; at least it came up with no counterproposal. Mosely has stated that he personally suggested that the boundaries as proposed by the British should be modified by providing a corridor under Western control across Thuringia and Anhalt to Berlin,[32] but there seems to be no documentary evidence that this perceptive thought was ever pushed by the Department of State or was ever formally proposed in the Working Security Committee.

The planning group in the Department of State had considered the alternative of a joint occupation of all Germany without separate national zones. This type of occupation arrangement would tend to hold the occupying powers together by forcing them to formulate and apply uniform policies throughout the entire country, but the difficulties of administering a joint occupation using mixed contingents of British, American, and Russian troops would have been enormous. In view of this difficulty, and because of Roosevelt's vigorous insistence on having the northwest zone and his continued references to dismemberment, the Department of State never seriously advocated the idea of a joint occupation of the whole country.

It is interesting to note, however, that the idea was championed by Gen. Dwight D. Eisenhower, who was in Washington during the first two weeks of January 1944. On the occasion of his visit to the White House, the General was told by Roosevelt about how the British wanted the northwest zone in Germany and how the President had insisted that the United States should have it. Eisenhower expressed objection to dividing Germany into "national sectors," insisting that a joint occupation was desirable and even practicable despite the technical difficulties. If nothing else, said the General, it would "quickly test the possibilities of real 'quadripartite action.' "[33] According to Eisenhower, the President seemed impressed but did not commit himself. There is no indication that Roosevelt ever gave the idea of a joint occupation any serious consideration or that Eisenhower's views were ever reported to the Department of State or the Working Security Committee.

As a matter of fact, not one of these ideas was very negotiable after February 18, 1944, the date on which Gusev, in the Soviet proposal, accepted the boundary of the Soviet zone as presented in the British memorandum of January 15. From this point on, Roosevelt and Churchill might argue about their own zones, but the western boundary of the Soviet zone could be altered only if the United States, acting

32. See *ibid.,* 166.
33. Dwight D. Eisenhower, *Crusade in Europe* (Garden City, N.Y., 1948), 218. The General probably used the word "tripartite" at the time, since the addition of France to the occupation was not seriously considered until the fall of 1944.

alone or with British support, could induce Stalin's representative to accept less than what had been already offered by the United Kingdom. This would have required some hard bargaining and/or considerable compensation. Unfortunately, the plan that Washington finally sent to Winant failed to take account of the realities of the situation.

On February 25, the War Department suddenly came forth with what purported to be the American plan for occupation zones. The letter transmitting this document to the Department of State requested that the enclosed plan be sent to Ambassador Winant for presentation in the European Advisory Commission. The plan was new only to the Department of State, for it was a copy of the paper (CCS 320/4 revised) which had been presented by the United States Chiefs of Staff at the Cairo Conference, outlining a huge northwest zone, claiming this zone for the United States, and instructing COSSAC to report on the logistic implication of such an arrangement. (See above, p. 262.) No explanation of the background of this paper was given to the Department of State, and it is obvious from Mosely's account that he and his colleagues were mystified by the whole procedure. Worded as a directive to COSSAC, the paper could not possibly be submitted, without extensive changes, in the tripartite, political European Advisory Commission. The proposed plan took no account of the British and Soviet proposals pending in the EAC but simply staked out the American claim to a very large northwest zone, a zone which would contain about 51 per cent of the population and 46 per cent of the territory of Germany (excluding Berlin and East Prussia). The paper said nothing about the proposed joint occupation of Berlin, which the Russians had already accepted. The lines as described in the proposal cut crudely across geographic features and administrative boundaries, and since they did not actually meet the German-Czech frontier, there was no clear demarcation between the eastern and southern zones.

When these points were raised in the Working Security Committee, the War Department representatives offered no explanations. Indeed they indicated that none was necessary because this plan had already been approved by the President. This was true (Cairo Conference), but the State Department officials felt that they should be told how this had all come about and they insisted that Winant would certainly need further explanations and instructions if he was to present this plan as an American proposal in the EAC.[34] The War Department representatives, however, did not produce any clarification or explanation; as a matter of fact, they probably could not do so because the plan had come down from such a high level that it was taken as a directive not open to discussion.

On March 8, the Department of State dutifully forwarded the plan

34. Mosely, 172.

to Winant for his consideration. There was no explanation to be given to the Ambassador except that this plan had come from the Joint Chiefs of Staff. The Department did prepare and send to the Ambassador a cartogram showing the differences in the population and territory of the three zones as laid out in the American and British-Soviet proposals. Winant's reaction was a crisp telegram stating that his views on this proposal would be brought to the President and the Secretary of State by George F. Kennan, the Counselor on Winant's staff, who was planning a trip to Washington later that month.

Winant's objections to the plan (as explained by Kennan to Roosevelt on April 3) [35] were the same as those that had occurred to Mosely mittee. The President is reported to have chuckled at this comedy of errors and to have readily admitted that, of course, this plan was now entirely inapplicable for presentation in the EAC. Roosevelt was surprised to learn from Kennan that there was any problem about the Soviet zone—the only problem that the President was concerned about was that the United States should get the northwest zone. Accordingly, he approved the suggestion that Winant be authorized to accept the western boundary of the Soviet zone, as already agreed to by the British and the Russians, while reserving the United States position on the other two zones.

Curiously, the instructions that went to Winant on May 1—approved by the President, the Joint Chiefs, and the Department of State— authorized the Ambassador to accept all the boundaries to which the British and the Russians had agreed but to insist that the United States should have the northwest zone. Winant felt that if Roosevelt wished to continue his argument with Churchill about the zonal allocation, then the United States should not, at this stage, accept the proposed boundary between the northwest and southern zones. In May, Winant himself came to Washington and discussed this with Roosevelt, who expressed his strong desire that Winant should continue to hold out for the northwest zone. Accordingly, when the Ambassador returned to London, he notified the EAC (June 1) of the United States acceptance of only the western boundary of the Soviet zone.

VI. The Roosevelt-Churchill Deadlock

While all this was going on, Roosevelt was trying desperately to straighten the issue out with Churchill, an attempt that resulted in what the Prime Minister later characterized, with masterly understatement, as "a considerable correspondence" between himself and the President.[36] Beginning in early February, Roosevelt sent several cables to the Prime

35. Herbert Feis, *Churchill, Roosevelt, Stalin* (Princeton, 1957), 362.
and other Department of State officers on the Working Security Com-
36. Churchill, 508.

Minister in which he vigorously stressed all the arguments that he had voiced in his memorandum of February 21 to Stettinius. (See above, p. 263.) In his telegram of February 9, F.D.R. struck the jocular tone that he so often used with good effect on "the Prime": " 'Do please don't' ask me to keep any American forces in France. I just cannot do it! I would have to bring them all back home. As I suggested before, I denounce in protest the paternity of Belgium, France, and Italy. You really ought to bring up and discipline your own children. In view of the fact that they may be your bulwark in future days, you should at least pay for the schooling now!" [37]

Churchill was neither amused nor moved. He urged that Cossac's original plan for Anglo-American troop deployment, approved at Quebec, should be adhered to as the basis for putting the British in the north-western zone. It was too late, to alter the position of Anglo-American forces in Overlord, and it would be difficult and dangerous to attempt to switch them in Germany unless and until German resistance had completely collapsed. The Prime Minister felt that Roosevelt's fear of becoming involved for a long period in France, Italy, and the Balkans was quite farfetched. Furthermore, he felt that Norway and the Nether-lands should remain in the British "sphere" in order to facilitate postwar liaison between the three air forces.[38]

Various efforts were made during the spring and summer to break the Roosevelt-Churchill deadlock over the northwest zone. On April 14, Stettinius cabled Hull from London that Eisenhower "was deeply convinced that the British and American zones in Germany should be combined in one Anglo-American zone of occupation." This was a modification of Eisenhower's original suggestion that the entire occupa-tion should be a joint tripartite affair. (See above, p. 265.) In its more limited, bilateral form the General's thought was particularly timely in that it would resolve the immediate deadlock and would preserve into the occupation period the valuable Shaef organization (Supreme Headquarters, Allied Expeditionary Force) for coordinating Anglo-American postwar policies. Secretary Hull, however, felt that Eisen-hower's suggestion (which was repeated to the War Department in May) "had possible political implications that negatived its acceptance." [39]

At the end of July the deadlock took on a more ominous tone, when the Russians indicated that there was little reason for continuing the European Advisory Commission discussions until the British and the Americans came to an agreement on zones. Up to this time, Secretary of War Henry L. Stimson had not intervened in the problem, but now,

37. Matloff, 491.

38. Hull, ɪɪ, 1611–12.

39. *Ibid.*, 1613. See also Forrest C. Pogue, *The Supreme Command* (Wash-ington, 1954), 349–50.

after a briefing by Harry Hopkins, he became concerned. He noted
in his diary that Roosevelt was "hell-bent" on occupying the northwest
zone and that Stettinius and John J. McCloy (then Assistant Secretary
of War) agreed that this was a mistake.[40]

On August 2, Stettinius, as Acting Secretary of State, cabled Roosevelt,
who was then in the Pacific, about the ominous Soviet statement in the
EAC and suggested that the United States should accept the southern
zone, provided that the British (1) would promise to take control, if
necessary, in France, Italy, and the Balkans, and (2) would grant port
facilities in the Low Countries and north Germany to the United
States so that it would not be dependent on French ports. The message
pointed out that the northwestern area would mean "a great many
headaches" in comparison with the southern.[41] The President's reply
of August 3 repeated his contention that "our 3,000 miles of transport"
made it essential that the United States have the north German ports,
and he indicated that he was still awaiting word from Churchill on this
subject.[42]

Stimson noted in his diary that the President's obsession with possible
civil war in France was the basis of his reluctance to accept the
southern zone, and at a luncheon in the White House on August 25
Stimson did his best to dispel Roosevelt's fears on this point.[43] It appears
that Admiral King was also agreeable to accepting the southern zone,
and Eisenhower indicated in August that in the absence of any contrary
decision he was continuing to advance his forces with the British on
the northern flank.[44]

This concerted pressure on Roosevelt was made more effective by
the fact that the French were pulling together better than Roosevelt
had thought possible and by the further fact that the British had indicated
their willingness to carry the major burden in Austria and southeastern Europe.[45] At the Second Quebec Conference (OCTAGON), in
September, the President finally agreed to accept the southern zone
(without Austria), but with certain changes. The sizable province of
Hessen-Nassau, including Oberhessen, was taken out of the northwest

40. Henry L. Stimson and McGeorge Bundy, *On Active Service in Peace
and War* (New York, 1947), 568.

41. Pogue, 350.

42. Hull, II, 1613.

43. Stimson and Bundy, 569, 575.

44. Pogue, 350–51. At some stage of the negotiations Eisenhower also sug-
gested that the Allied headquarters for Germany might be set up, not in
Berlin, but at a "cantonment capital" to be built at the junction of the
American, British, and Soviet zones. The suggestion went unheeded. See
Dwight D. Eisenhower, "My Views on Berlin," *Saturday Evening Post* (De-
cember 9, 1961), 20.

45. See John Ehrman, *Grand Strategy,* v (London, 1956), 516.

zone and added to the southern. On the other hand, a smaller area west of the Rhine, embracing the Saarland and the Palatinate (the West-mark), was added to the British zone, perhaps with the idea that this might later be put under French occupation,[46] perhaps because Roosevelt wanted the British to bear the onus of applying the Morgenthau policy of industrial dismantling in the Saar as well as in the Ruhr.[47] Most important of all, in Roosevelt's view, was the pledge that he got from the British that the ports of Bremen and Bremerhaven would be under American control and that the Americans would have free right of passage between these ports and the American zone.

VII. The Protocol and Its Amendments

The Roosevelt-Churchill deadlock had not prevented the European Advisory Commission from making progress in drawing up at least a tentative document on the occupation of Germany. In March, the EAC decided that the definition of zones should not appear in the surrender document but should take the form of a separate protocol. During the summer, a draft of this protocol was prepared, incorporating the zonal boundaries as described in the British-Soviet proposals. The eastern zone was specifically allocated to the Soviet Union; the allocation of the other two zones was left blank. The area of Greater Berlin, specified as being under joint tripartite control, was divided into three sectors along the lines of existing districts (*Bezirke*), paralleling the zonal arrangements. The eastern sector was explictly assigned to the Soviet Union; the allocation of the northwestern and southern sectors was left blank. In this tentative form the basic protocol was signed ad referendum on September 12, 1944, by Winant, Strang, and Gusev.[48]

The Quebec Conference decisions were then referred to the Commission for incorporation into a formal document. This was easier said than done, for the American and British military authorities were at loggerheads over how to define the American right of control in the ports of Bremen and Bremerhaven and the right of transit across the British zone. By dint of strenuous negotiations, Mosely (who had replaced George Kennan on Winant's staff) succeeded in working out compromise phraseology which was embodied in a tripartite agreement (signed ad referendum on November 14), amending the basic protocol of September 12.[49]

In order to be effective, the protocol and the amending agreement required approval by the signatory governments. The United States

46. See Churchill, 510.

47. For a conjecture on this point, see Feis, 364, citing *Conferences at Malta and Yalta*, 137.

48. For the text, see *Conferences at Malta and Yalta*, 118–21.

49. *Ibid.*, 121–23.

military authorities, however, would not give their approval until they had worked out a very specific agreement with the British on the port and transit problems. After protracted negotiations, involving the Department of State, the Joint Chiefs of Staff, the British Embassy, and the British Staff Mission at Washington, two paragraphs were finally drafted in January 1945 which made Bremen and Bremerhaven an enclave under American control and guaranteed mutual transit rights in very positive terms.[50] The British government had anticipated this happy outcome by registering with the EAC in December its formal approval of the protocol as amended. The Soviet government was obviously waiting for the United States to act, but the U.S. Chiefs of Staff wanted the Bremen settlement to be first formalized in a Combined Chiefs of Staff paper. Further delay was threatened by the fact that the Combined Chiefs of Staff were then on their way to the conferences at Malta and Yalta.

Winant and McCloy were both worried about the implications of additional delay, for American forces, seriously held up by the Battle of the Bulge, were only entering the Rhineland while the Russians were already on the Oder River, some 45 miles from Berlin. Winant's fear, as relayed by Harry Hopkins to Stettinius, was that, if the protocol remained unperfected, "the Russians might reach the border of their zone and then keep on going." [51] Similarly urged by McCloy, Stettinius undertook to straighten this matter out, and in his conversation with Eden at Malta on February 1, 1945, he suggested that they had better prod their military chiefs into agreement, "particularly in view of the fact that the Russians may soon be in Berlin and have views of their own as regards the zones if our two Governments do not approve the carefully negotiated protocol." [52] Eden agreed, and later that same day, after the approval of General Marshall and Field Marshal Alan Brooke was obtained, Stettinius authorized Winant by telegram to register the approval of the United States in the European Advisory Commission.[53] When the formal approval of the Soviet Union was handed in on February 6, the protocol as amended became an effective instrument to go into force after German surrender.

After Stalin reluctantly agreed at the Yalta Conference to admit the French to a zone of occupation in Germany,[54] arrangements were made to carve a French zone in the west and a French sector in Berlin out of the zones and sectors assigned to the Western powers in the

50. *Ibid.,* 198–201.

51. Edward R. Stettinius, *Roosevelt and the Russians: The Yalta Conference* (Garden City, N.Y., 1949), 56.

52. *Conferences at Malta and Yalta,* 201, 498.

53. *Ibid.,* 499.

54. *Ibid.,* 978.

tripartite protocol. This was accomplished only with considerable difficulty and after the Americans had obtained from the French a written pledge of transit rights across the French zone.[55] A final modification of the zonal arrangement in Germany was effected by the Soviet Union when it placed the southern part of East Prussia and the German territory east of the Oder-Neisse River line under Polish administration.[56] But these changes (and a number of small border rectifications that were made later on)[57] did not alter the basic relationship of the Western powers and the Soviet Union as established in the tripartite protocol approved in February 1945, nor did they affect the problem of access to Berlin.

VIII. Access to Berlin

It is a striking fact that during the entire period from January 1944 to February 1945, during which the tripartite protocol was drafted, amended, and finally approved, the question of access to Berlin had never once been raised with the Russians in a forthright manner. In order to understand how this could have happened (or rather not have happened), it is necessary to recall the circumstances in which these negotiations took place.

In the first place, the original British proposal of January 1944—a thoroughly studied Cabinet paper—had drawn Berlin as an island, with no express provision for access or transit rights from the west. This is understandable only in the context of the times, which reflected the almost inescapable wartime assumption of continued cooperation by the victors after the defeat of the common enemy. For most of the leaders in Washington and London, however, this was no blind faith but rather a "hoping against hope," since the alternative was grim indeed. The assumption of at least reasonable cooperation was the foundation for the entire structure of occupation in Germany and Austria; it was not peculiar to the drawing of zonal boundaries. If the assumption had been postwar hostility rather than cooperation, undoubtedly a great many negotiations with the Soviet Union would have been handled differently, including zonal boundaries.

Secondly, it should be noted that the British proposal provided very specifically for the joint occupation of Berlin, so that the need of the Western powers for access to Berlin across the intervening Soviet zone was utterly apparent. Once the Soviet government accepted the right of the Western powers to be in Berlin, it thereby acknowledged the self-

55. For these negotiations, see Mosely, 182–85, and *Foreign Relations of the United States: The Conference of Berlin, 1945* (Washington, 1960), I, 598, 632; II, 1002–6.

56. See *Conference of Berlin*, I, 743; II, 208–9, 1509.

57. See, e.g., a change in the boundary of the U.S.-Soviet zones in *United States Treaties and Other International Agreements*, v, pt. 3, 1954, 2177.

evident corollary of their right to go to Berlin. Transit rights across the British and French zones for the landlocked American Army in south Germany had to be pledged in writing precisely because such rights did not otherwise exist. But the right of the Western powers to be in Berlin was expressly guaranteed in the protocol; so the right of access followed as a matter of course. The logic of this proposition in the circumstances was so compelling that the Soviet government, as we shall see, explicitly accepted it.

Lastly, it should be recalled that the zonal boundaries, while important, were not regarded as of crucial significance at that time, at least by the United States and the United Kingdom. The occupation was envisaged as lasting only a few years, and President Roosevelt, as we have seen, was particularly insistent that large numbers of American troops should not be tied down indefinitely in central Europe when there was still a war to be won in the Pacific. It was anticipated that, even during the initial years of occupation, the Germans would be running their own national administrations (transportation, communication, etc.) under the watchful eye of the Allied Control Council. Germany, it was assumed, would be a "going concern" across zonal boundaries, which were merely for the convenience of the victors in stationing troops.[58] The idea of a possible later dismemberment of Germany was dealt with quite separately from zones of occupation and was in fact disavowed by all three powers by the time of German surrender.[59]

Despite these basic considerations, the unwritten status of the right of access to Berlin was a cause of concern to a number of American officials, from the very outset of the negotiations in the European Advisory Commission. Mosely suggested in the Working Security Committee that the British proposal be modified by drawing a corridor from the western zones to Berlin (see above, p. 265), but this idea was never seriously considered at higher levels in either the State or the War Department. Mosely also states that Winant, when he came to Washington in May 1944, raised the question of access to Berlin with the Pentagon, but that the War Department felt it advisable to leave this problem to be dealt with by the commanding generals through military channels at the appropriate time. Winant apparently made no memoranda of these conversations, and the personal recollections of them are somewhat at variance.[60] This much, however, is clear: Winant received neither instruc-

58. See Strang, *Home and Abroad,* 215.

59. See Mosely's article on "Dismemberment of Germany," *op. cit.,* chap 5; originally published in *Foreign Affairs,* xxviii (April 1950), 487–98.

60. See *ibid.,* 174. See also Albert L. Warner, "Our Secret Deal over Germany," *Saturday Evening Post* (August 2, 1952), 68. John J. McCloy, then Assistant Secretary of War, remembers that he discussed the German surrender problem at this time with Winant but does not recall any discussion of access to Berlin (letter from McCloy to the author).

tions nor encouragement from anyone in Washington to take this matter up with the Russians in the European Advisory Commission at that time. There was, of course, a real question as to when and how this matter should be raised with the Russians. Since the great cross-Channel invasion still lay ahead, it seemed hardly the time to precipitate a hypothetical argument with Gusev in the EAC. Considering the military situation, the British proposal as it stood was farsighted and timely, for it had obtained Russian recognition of the right of the Western powers to be in Berlin on a footing of parity with the Russians, even though the indications were that the Soviet Army would get there first.

The Roosevelt-Churchill deadlock over the northwest zone undoubtedly influenced these considerations of the access problem. As the deadlock dragged on for a half-year, the Russians finally threatened (July 1944) to adjourn the entire negotiation unless progress could be made. Winant apparently concluded that this was no time to raise the question of access but rather to push for signature of the protocol (September 12, 1944) in order to get something down on paper, however tentative and incomplete.[61] Winant's feeling about the primary importance at this time of resolving the Roosevelt-Churchill deadlock was shared, as we have seen, by a number of other high American officials—indeed, by everyone closely concerned with the problem below the presidential level.

The precarious state of the protocol persisted all through the autumn of 1944, as the Americans and British tussled over the Bremen enclave and access thereto from the American zone. Gusev appears to have been irked by the continued delay in completing the protocol, and he urged his Anglo-American colleagues to settle their differences. On November 6, he volunteered the observation that transit arrangements similar to those that the Americans were demanding of the British would be granted by the Soviet Union, giving United States and British forces full access to Berlin across the Soviet zone. This was reassuring, but nothing was done about it at the time, apparently because the Americans and the British were engrossed in their own squabble over Bremen and felt that the matter of transit with the Russians could wait until after the basic protocol was approved by the governments concerned.

Not until the Soviet government approved the protocol on February 6, 1945, were the Western powers assured of their right to be in Berlin, regardless of which army arrived there first. On the same day the planning group of the American Joint Chiefs of Staff completed a paper which they proposed should be sent to the British Chiefs of Staff and the Soviet General Staff. This paper pointed out that United States occupation forces in Berlin would be isolated from the main areas of

61. See the reference to Winant's attitude as reported in Lucius D. Clay, *Decision in Germany* (Garden City, N.Y., 1950), 15.

American occupation, and it proposed that the principle of freedom of transit by road, air, and rail for such American forces should be recognized by the other occupying powers.

The Joint Chiefs of Staff, meeting at Yalta on February 7, considered this proposal and concluded that the paper should be redrafted along broader lines. Consequently this question was not raised with the British or the Russians during the Yalta Conference, but the Joint Staff planners proceeded to revise the paper, broadening it to include Vienna. The reason for this was that the reluctance of the President and the Joint Chiefs of Staff to participate in the occupation of Austria had finally been overcome by Winant and others during 1944, and in January 1945 the United States government had finally agreed to accept a zone of occupation in Austria and to participate in the quadripartite occupation of Vienna. Intensive negotiations were then getting under way in the European Advisory Commission to work out an occupational protocol for Austria similar to the one for Germany. It was already apparent that the Soviet government would claim a substantial zone in eastern Austria, that Vienna (like Berlin) would be surrounded by the Soviet zone, and that in all probability the Red Army would take Vienna and much of Austria long before Western forces could enter the Danube valley.[62]

The revised paper, as approved by the Joint Chiefs of Staff late in February, proposed acceptance of the principle of freedom of transit for American, British, and Soviet forces across all zonal boundaries in Europe, including areas of joint occupation such as Berlin and Vienna. The paper was termed an interim arrangement, pending a more permanent agreement to be worked out in the European Advisory Commission. The British Chiefs of Staff promptly approved this proposal, and a copy was sent to the Soviet General Staff for its concurrence.

The American delegation (and presumably the British) on the European Advisory Commission was informed of this move, and there were discussions as to how to proceed. The feeling was that the military paper would suffice for the immediate future and that the longer-range needs would be met by one of the quadripartite directives that were being drawn up in the EAC for the future guidance of the Allied Control Council for Germany. Unfortunately, no directive embodying the principle of freedom of access to Berlin or Vienna was perfected before German surrender,[63] and as for the Combined Chiefs' communication to the Soviet General Staff—it was never answered.

---

62. These negotiations are briefly but authoritatively recounted in Edgar L. Erickson, "The Zoning of Austria," *Annals of the American Academy of Political and Social Science,* CCLXVII (January, 1950), 106–13.

63. Mosely (p. 186) says that he turned over copies of his drafts on this subject to a SHAEF representative about a week after V-E Day.

One can safely assume that an answer would have been forthcoming soon enough if the Russians had thought it to their advantage. On the other hand, it must be remembered that these were tumultuous weeks in March and April 1945, as the armies pounded toward a meeting in the heart of Germany. Furthermore, a number of subjects suddenly arose that led to the sharpest of exchanges between Roosevelt and Churchill, on the one hand, and Stalin on the other: the treatment of Allied prisoners of war, the implementation of the Yalta agreement on Poland, and the negotiations at Berne for the surrender of German forces in Italy.[64] Stalin's suspicions were further aroused by the fact that the American forces which had driven into Thuringia and Saxony— deep in the Soviet zone—did not seem to be in any hurry to withdraw after V-E Day.[65]

The question of access to Berlin and Vienna was now closely linked to the question of the withdrawal of Allied forces (principally American) from the Soviet zone. Churchill was insistent that there should be no hasty withdrawal, for this would mean "bringing Soviet power into the heart of Western Europe and the descent of an iron curtain between us and everything to the eastward." Before this took place, the Western powers should insist that the Soviets adopt a more cooperative attitude on a number of outstanding problems.[66] President Truman felt that a calculated delay in troop withdrawal might be considered as "going back on our commitments" regarding zonal boundaries, but he joined Churchill in bringing pressure on Stalin to admit an Anglo-American group to Vienna in order to survey the scene so that progress could be made to conclude the protocol on the occupation of Austria.[67] Obviously, any refusal to vacate the designated Soviet zone might have led to a Soviet refusal to admit the Western powers to their designated area of Berlin.

At the suggestion of Hopkins, supported by Winant and others, President Truman decided to link the question of troop withdrawal to the problem of access to Berlin and the establishment of the quadripartite control groups for Germany and Austria. In Churchill's view,

64. See the bitter exchanges in *Correspondence Between the Chairman of the Council of Ministers of the U.S.S.R. and the President of the U.S.A. and Prime Ministers of Great Britain During the Great Patriotic War of 1941– 1945* (Moscow, 1957), I, 306–20; II, 194–214.

65. For the relationship between zonal boundaries and troop movements during the final months of the war, including the decision not to launch an Anglo-American drive on Berlin, see Forrest C. Pogue, "The Decision to Halt at the Elbe," in Kent Roberts Greenfield, ed., *Command Decisions* (Washington, 1960), chap. 22.

66. Churchill, 603.

67. See Harry S. Truman, *Memoirs by Harry S. Truman* (Garden City, N.Y., 1955–1956), I, 298–302.

this was not using the Anglo-American bargaining power to fullest advantage, but he reluctantly assented to the message that Truman then sent to Stalin on June 14. The key sentence of this telegram read as follows: "As to Germany, I am ready to have instructions issued to all American troops to begin withdrawal into their own zone on 21 June in accordance with arrangements between the respective commanders, including in these arrangements simultaneous movement of the national garrisons into Greater Berlin and provision of free access by air, road, and rail from Frankfurt and Bremen to Berlin for U.S. forces." [68] The message also proposed the simultaneous entry of the national garrisons into Vienna and the prompt establishment of the Allied control bodies in both Berlin and Vienna.

Stalin's reply of June 16 was puzzling. He readily agreed to the plan for Western troop movements into Berlin and Austria, suggesting July 1 as a more convenient date than June 21 for the operation. The letter was not unfriendly in tone, but it obviously said nothing explicit about "free access" to Berlin.

Efforts were then made through military channels to pin the Russians down on this point. On June 26, Gen. John Deane, the head of the U.S. Military Mission at Moscow, reported that he had attempted to get confirmation that Soviet commanders had been instructed regarding free access to Berlin and Vienna. "While Lt. General Slavin was unable to give me an immediate reply, from the way he talked I do not anticipate there will be any difficulty in the matter." On June 27, General Deane reported that Marshal Georgi Zhukov would negotiate on the subject with Gen. Lucius Clay, and on the following day Deane added: "It is my opinion that when our representatives meet with Zhukov there will be little difficulty in arranging for free access for our troops to Berlin, and that, if I am correct in this, the same principle will apply to Vienna." [69]

The question of access to Vienna had already arisen in an acute form when the American reconnaissance party reported that the only suitable airports for the Western powers lay in the Soviet zone, outside the city proper. On June 17, Gen. Joseph T. McNarney, the United States Commander in Italy (whose command was engaged in planning for the Austrian occupation), recommended the immediate negotiation of an agreement with the Russians, guaranteeing transit rights across the Soviet zone to Vienna and the joint use of municipal facilities in Vienna proper. This recommendation was promptly sent to Winant for negotiation in the European Advisory Commission.

The protocol on zones of occupation for Austria was now all but

68. *Ibid.,* 303.
69. *Ibid.,* 306–7.

completed, and, like its German counterpart, it contained no specific provision for access to the capital across the Soviet zone. There was, however, one way of achieving the desired result without reopening the protocol to amendments. On June 23, Mosely, with the backing of his British and French colleagues,[70] proposed that the covering report transmitting the protocol to the governments should contain several paragraphs specifically stating that occupation forces, "including those allotted for the occupation of Vienna," would enjoy "freedom of movement and communication throughout Austria" and the equitable use of municipal facilities in the *Innere Stadt* of Vienna.

The ensuing discussion, which stretched over two weeks, was highly illuminating. Gusev and his alternate, G. F. Saksin, opposed the inclusion of these provisions on the grounds that they were so obvious as to go without saying, that no such paragraphs appeared in the occupation protocol for Germany, and that Vienna and Berlin were to be treated the same way. Mosely, René Massigli, and Lord Hood immediately argued that if the principles were obvious there could be no valid objection to stating them in writing. The Soviet representatives insisted that they did not oppose the principles as such; their concern was merely that the implementation should be left to the military commanders on the spot and should not be dictated by the European Advisory Commission sitting in London.

In the continuation of this argument on July 6, Gusev drew the parallel even closer between Berlin and Vienna: "I suggest that we could put off consideration of these principles until the Commanders have had experience in applying these principles in Berlin. The Representatives of the four Governments are in Berlin at the present and they will have many practical questions to settle. Perhaps settling these questions in practice in Berlin will help us to settle the same questions in Vienna."

As a matter of fact, the Berlin problem had already been settled by the agreement which General Clay and his British colleague Gen. Sir Ronald Weeks had concluded with Marshal Zhukov on June 29. Zhukov had been affable and had shown no hesitation about acknowledging the Western powers' right of access to Berlin. It had been readily agreed "that all road, rail and air traffic on authorized routes would be free from border search or control by customs or military authorities." [71] In discussing particular routes there was in fact not much choice, since most transportation lines and facilities had been thoroughly wrecked.

70. The French Provisional Government had been admitted to the European Advisory Commission in November 1944.

71. Report by Ambassador Robert Murphy (U.S. Political Adviser in Germany), in *Conference of Berlin*, I, 136.

Agreement was reached for the Western powers to use the Helmstedt *Autobahn,* the parallel rail line via Magdeburg, and two air corridors, also via Magdeburg.[72]

With agreement thus reached on Berlin, Gusev promptly gave up his opposition to including the principle in the covering report on the Austrian protocol. On July 9 he proposed the following paragraph: "The Allied Council will make the necessary arrangements for transit in Austria by road, rail, air and water for the goods and supplies required by the forces of occupation in Austria, including those forces allotted for the occupation of the City of Vienna and the personnel of the Allied Commission, and likewise for the common use of transport and communication facilities and public utility services in the City of Vienna."

Lord Hood noted that the Soviet draft used the term "transit" rather than "free transit," but there was no use in quibbling further over this point, since the actual meaning of the term had been defined in a mutually satisfactory manner by the Clay-Weeks-Zhukov negotiation. The Western delegates therefore accepted the principle as rephrased by Gusev, and it so appears in the covering report to the Austrian protocol, which was signed the same day.[73] The significance of the paragraph was larger than its actual wording, since by repeated statements the Soviet representatives had asserted that these principles applied to Berlin as well as to Vienna. In this curious fashion the Western negotiators did achieve—at long last—a formal statement of principles on transit rights across the Soviet zone in Austria to Vienna and, by specific analogy, across the Soviet zone in Germany to Berlin.

72. Later in 1945, additional agreements were reached in the Allied Control Council regarding the number of trains per day and the use of the air corridors, the number of the latter being increased to three. See *Department of State Bulletin,* XIV (September 18, 1961), 477.

73. The protocol and the covering report may be found in *Allied Commission for Austria: A Handbook* (Office of the United States High Commissioner for Austria, n.d.). The protocol, signed on July 9, 1945, is No. 1600 in the Treaties and Other International Acts Series (Washington, 1947).

LOUIS GOTTSCHALK

Our Vichy Fumble

Unlike most of the historical controversies arising out of World War II, the dispute over American policy toward France has no Cold War overtones. Instead it reflects an ideological disagreement that developed during the war and lived on to influence subsequent historical writing. The fundamental issue is the wisdom of the American policy of recognizing the Vichy regime in 1941 and working with it at the time of the North African invasion rather than relying on the Free French movement of Charles de Gaulle. Contemporary commentators and later historians have argued that cooperation with a collaborationist regime violated the democratic ideals the United States was fighting for; defenders of the administration counter by claiming that the Vichy policy helped speed the downfall of Nazi Germany.

In this review article, Louis Gottschalk, a specialist in French history, challenges William L. Langer's justification of American policy. Ellen Hammer is equally critical of the administration in "Hindsight on Vichy," Political Science Quarterly, *LXI (June 1946), 175–188. For an interesting discussion of friction with the French later in the war, see Martin Blumenson, "Politics and the Military in the Liberation of Paris,"* Yale Review, *L (Winter 1961), 271–286.*

AMERICAN HISTORIANS seem to be generally agreed upon the *Kriegsschuldfrage* of the Second World War, even though some politicians and writers have tried to raise a controversy regarding the origins of its Japanese-American phase.[1] On the other hand, as Professor William L. Langer declares, in the book under review:[2] "The so-called Vichy policy drew more criticism of the Department of State than almost any other issue of foreign affairs during the war years. In the United States it generated no end of indignation and bitter feeling and led to charges that frequently went beyond the limits of decency and reason" (p.

Reprinted by permission from the *Journal of Modern History*, XX (March 1948), 47–56.

1. Cf. S. F. BEMIS, "First gun of a revisionist historiography for the second World War," *Journal of modern history*, XIX (1947), 55–59.

2. *Our Vichy gamble.* By William L. LANGER, Coolidge professor of history, Harvard University. New York: Alfred A. Knopf, 1947. Pp. 412. $3.75.

382). Already a sort of academic "diplomatic revolution" has been effected by the new *cause célèbre*—with Harry Elmer Barnes [3] lined up on the same side as Langer and Carlton J. H. Hayes.[4]

Sensitive to the severe criticism of his Vichy policy, Secretary of State Cordell Hull asked Langer to make "a detailed and altogether independent study" of it (p. vii). The choice had well-nigh everything to commend it. Langer is undoubtedly, as the publisher's jacket calls him, "one of the most distinguished authorities in the field of modern European history in general and diplomatic history in particular." He also has the rare quality of being able to stand off and look at his own presentation with the eye of an intelligent critic. His "Conclusion" (pp. 382–98) is nearly a masterpiece in this kind of difficult exercise, except for occasional notes of special pleading. In addition, Langer writes a clear and straightforward prose, which, despite some signs of hasty composition, "should," as Admiral William D. Leahy says in a letter reproduced on the jacket, "hold a reader's interest from beginning to end." It does Hull great credit that he chose a historian of recognized honesty and merit to investigate and present his case. Even greater credit is due both men for their "explicit understanding" that Langer should serve "only as a dispassionate scholar, not as an apologist," and that "all relevant materials in the State Department" should be made available to him (p. vii).

These preparations seemed almost perfect for an unbiased study of our Vichy gamble. By showing the stresses that guided our policy-makers, admitting their shortcomings and errors, and indicating the huge part played by the element that in our ignorance we humans call "chance," Langer might have written an account of Franco-American relations from May 1940 to December 1942 with a candor that would have disarmed all unfriendly critics. Unfortunately, despite his earnest efforts to the contrary, his close association with the Office of Strategic Services and the Department of State made him a partisan. Instead of the detached and dispassionate tone that one finds in his studies of diplomacy in the nineteenth century, here he evinces impatience with conflicting points of view and readiness to accept the testimony of witnesses whose judgment is the very core of the dispute.

The impatience is illustrated by Langer's unwillingness to admit that the judgment of censors of the State Department might have had some validity. For example, "liberals" are coupled with "radicals" (pp. 257, 300, and 382)—as if, upon this matter, there were no difference

---

3. *Crucifying the savior of France: France's new Dreyfus case in reverse* (n.p., n.d.).

4. Cf. his review of *Iron out of Calvary: an interpretative history of the second World War* by Walter Phelps Hall (New York, 1947) in the *American historical review*, LII (1947), 709–11.

between them. On one occasion (p. 173, n. 19), it is implied that columnist Samuel Grafton's angry query as to why "Leahy coos and lifts his glass to the ferrets who rule France" is typical of the "uncritical, sensational writing of liberals." Yet Langer also points out that Major George Fielding Eliot (p. 248), Walter Lippmann (p. 298), and 75 per cent of the Americans polled in December 1941 (p. 217) were equally puzzled. It would appear, then, that the coupling of "liberals and conservatives" would have been just as correct as that of "liberals and radicals."

The point would hardly be worth making if it were not directly connected with Langer's conviction that the objections of the opposition were "almost exclusively ideological" (p. 173). "It should be noted, first and foremost," he contends, even in his largely judicious "Conclusion," "that almost all the criticism of the Vichy policy was based on ideological considerations" (pp. 382–83), and, therefore, he implies that this criticism was entirely impractical. This is perhaps not the place to raise the question as to whether victory could possibly have been less glorious or more costly and peace less stable had we conducted a genuinely anti-Fascist, democratic war instead of the opportunistic struggle still in progress. The argument of that question, being largely in the realm of "metahistory," would probably in the end only leave each side more firmly convinced of its own rectitude. Yet it is pertinent that, just as "the Department seems to have underestimated the extent of de Gaulle's following" (p. 394), so it may also have underestimated the strength of the anti-Hitler forces within Germany, its satellites, and its conquests; and, if that were so, a war for ideological objectives like the Atlantic Charter might have saved more American lives than a "day-by-day, hand-to-mouth policy all the way through" (p. 225).

If that point, however, is hard to document either way, no doubt can exist as to *why* certain elements in the United States believed that this was an ideological war. It was because President Franklin D. Roosevelt and the Department of State subscribed to and publicly announced the Atlantic Charter and helped to make it the United Nations Declaration of January 1, 1942. One can easily understand why hard-boiled diplomats might find it expedient to pretend to be ideological while fighting a war first of defense and then of liberation, but, in that case, the historian of their diplomacy should include a frank appraisal of their propaganda technique in his narrative. Langer does not mention lofty pronouncements like the Atlantic Charter. To be sure, he does rebuke those who thought that it might have been expedient to cooperate with General Charles de Gaulle and at the same time to try to maintain formal relations with Marshal Henri Pétain. "That would have been playing both ends against the middle" and was to have been avoided

—not, however, because it would be immoral, but because we would be caught at it (p. 222). Still the Department of State, as we shall see, did not hesitate to play both ends against the middle when it suited its purpose to do so.

If Langer had been less impatient with "liberals," he would have been more willing to recognize the essential difference between them and "radicals." The radicals were anti-Vichy, for one thing, because they were pro-Russian. The liberals were anti-Vichy largely because they were anti-Fascist and assumed that the best way to fight an anti-Fascist war was to unite the anti-Fascist forces (no matter how incompatible these might otherwise be). The radicals could under no circumstances have been induced to see that cooperation with Pétain would be desirable so long as he remained anti-Communist. The liberals, being less doctrinaire and more realistic, might have been willing to support the State Department's policy of collaboration with Vichy if they could have been convinced that Vichy was in fact anti-Fascist.

Indeed, I know some liberals who would have been ready to move bag and baggage to Pennsylvania Avenue if it had been clear that circumstances dictated a policy of opportunism or that ideological considerations would only hinder the success of the war effort. That circumstances so dictated remains unproved, however, even in this book. It, nevertheless, is Langer's thesis. Using chiefly the State Department's files, he shows that Hull and his subordinates went on the assumption that after the fall of France it was better for France and for the Allied cause to recognize Pétain. Until Pétain's meeting with Adolf Hitler at Montoire on October 24, 1940, one frequently encountered liberals who thought likewise. But their arguments in favor of that recognition were not those of the State Department. They argued that since Hitler apparently could not be stopped in Europe, it was better to have some ambivalent personality like Pétain in partial control of part of France than to have a thoroughly antagonistic government in all of it. A few historically minded souls even fondly persuaded themselves that perhaps Pétain would turn out to be a sort of French Baron vom Stein, part tiger, part fox, outwardly conforming to the requirements of the conqueror but secretly organizing his country for a war of liberation. After Montoire and until Pierre Laval came back into power on April 15, 1942, many liberals, both French and American, continued to hope against hope that Vichy was still playing a double game. Admiral Jean Darlan's unabashed hostility to England and Pétain's increasingly obvious weakness gave them pause, but in their ignorance they grasped at their illusion as drowning men grasp at straws.

The State Department, however, had less reason to be ignorant. Even before the United States entered the war, Ambassador Leahy, warning Washington that the government of France was "headed by a feeble, frightened old man, surrounded by self-seeking conspirators," despaired of giving "some semblance of backbone to a jellyfish." [5] Pennsylvania Avenue apparently never was beguiled by the hope that Pétain might turn out to be his country's strong man, but it was inclined to gamble on his patriotism and honesty. Langer's own opinion is: "Pétain remains an enigma. . . . In the autumn of 1940 he probably regarded some measure of collaboration with Germany as unavoidable because he despaired of Britain and the United States. After that he changed his mind once and for all and did what he could to hold collaboration to a minimum" (p. 385).

The State Department's motives, as Langer enumerates them,[6] were:

1. to encourage the "innumerable Frenchmen, mostly nameless, in low positions as well as in high places, who felt they could best serve France by standing behind the venerated figure of the marshal and protecting national interests as best they could" (pp. 386–87);

2. to enable us to exploit "the experience and the connections of many men in the Foreign Ministry" and "the military intelligence service of the French army, which was clandestinely reorganized after defeat" (p. 387);

3. to enable us "to save parts of the French Empire (especially North and West Africa) from falling into the hands of our potential enemies" (p. 389);

4. to keep the French fleet out of Hitler's control (p. 390);

5. "to keep contact with the people of France, to remind them of the past friendship between the two countries, to keep alive the sentiment of liberty and equality, to maintain hope of deliverance, and to stimulate resistance to the conqueror" (p. 391); and

6. to provide "the groundwork of the invasion of North Africa" (p. 395).

In other words, the State Department's purpose was to derive every advantage possible from our recognition of the Vichy government while realizing that we must not count heavily upon the figurehead marshal. If he were with us, so much the better; if he were against us, nevertheless we would use him and his friends as much as circumstances permitted. It was a hard-boiled policy into which ideological considerations could not be permitted to enter. Any suggestion that might render such a policy ineffective by causing Vichy to be unduly suspicious of our sin-

---

5. Leahy to Roosevelt, Nov. 22, 1941, LANGER, p. 194.

6. Cf. Hull's statements of May 5, 1942, *ibid.,* pp. 254–55, and of Nov. 8 and 9, 1942, *ibid.,* pp. 366–67.

cerity was to be spurned. Hence we had to send supplies to North Africa and we dared not support General de Gaulle.

This program, of course, involved working both ends against the middle. A series of secret conversations begun with certain Frenchmen would undoubtedly have been resented by Pétain and his cohorts if they had learned of them. Nevertheless, it must be admitted that if the State Department's purposes had in fact been attained, this policy would have justified itself at least as an expedient one. Those, however, who repudiate ideologies for expedients must be willing to be judged by the results. And what were the results?

Let us leave aside the fact that the State Department seems to have been peculiarly perverse in disregarding the French Resistance. Although certain sources available to the United States government had already reported De Gaulle's popularity inside France (pp. 142, 166, 224–25, 245, and 297–300), and although Langer admits that Washington underestimated the strength of the Free French movement (p. 394), he nevertheless seems to think that the State Department was justified in snubbing De Gaulle up to December 1942.[7] Let us assume, therefore, for the sake of argument, that down to the eve of the invasion of North Africa in November 1942 no satisfactory means existed of rallying Frenchmen and the French Empire to the Allied cause or of exploiting French channels of intelligence other than by subterfuge at Vichy. How well did our collaboration with Vichy enable us to fulfill the purposes of the State Department enumerated above?

In discussing the first-listed purpose, Langer does not tell us how many Frenchmen "felt they could best serve France by standing behind the venerated figure of the marshal." He argues that Pétain was himself fearful of a complete break with the United States and that in spite of our recognition he was constantly confronted with this hazard. But Leahy's "carefully considered" opinion, expressed in his letter to Pétain at the marshal's trial for treason, does not imply that Pétain was noticeably intimidated. Leahy stated: "I must, in all honesty, repeat my opinion as expressed to you at the time that positive refusal to make any concession to Axis demands, while it might have brought immediately increased hardship to your people, would, in the long view, have been advantageous to France." [8] Surely this means that Pétain made concessions to the Axis contrary to Leahy's expressed wishes.

Barnes's booklet (p. 9) also quotes a letter of Leahy to Pétain (June 22, 1945): "During that period (1941–42) you did, on occasion at my request, take action in opposition to the desires of the Axis and favorable to the Allied cause. On every instance when you failed to accept my recommendations to oppose the Axis powers by refusing their de-

7. Cf. *ibid.*, pp. 213–25, 257–68, 300–303, and 394–95.
8. *New York Times,* Aug. 2, 1945, quoted *ibid.*, p. 384.

mands, you stated the reason was that such a positive action by you would result in additional oppression of your people by the invaders." Leahy here testifies, in other words, that Pétain was willing but powerless on the side of the Allies. Leahy's phrase "on occasion at my request" might have been intended to convey the meaning that the marshal did perform certain acts favorable to the Allies *only* because of American representation at Vichy. By itself, however, it does not prove that such was in fact the case.

Indeed, if one contends, as Langer, Barnes, and Leahy do, that Pétain's patriotism was beyond dispute, one may assume that he would, *whenever he could,* have taken "action in opposition to the desires of the Axis and favorable to the Allied cause," no matter how it was suggested. To prove from Leahy's words that our Vichy policy was justified, one would have to argue not only that the actions Pétain took upon our emissaries' requests would not otherwise have been taken but also that they were of sufficient significance to counterbalance the disadvantages of American recognition. Neither Langer nor Barnes has fully established either argument. The fear of a break with the United States, if Leahy is right, does not seem to have had a decisive influence upon Pétain himself, and Langer does not contend that Darlan and Laval were ever seriously worried about the wishes of the United States before the end of 1942.

Langer makes clear that the United States undoubtedly had many supporters among the Vichy bureaucracy, but the only persons that he specifies among "the innumerable patriot Frenchmen" (p. 393) who must have derived aid and comfort from Leahy's presence in Vichy are General Maxime Weygand and his friends in North Africa. Still Leahy, even with the assistance of the Murphy-Weygand agreement, was unable to save Weygand. He was dismissed just about a year before our invasion of Africa and replaced by officers such as Generals Charles Noguès and Alphonse Juin, whose loyalty to Vichy was no less than his and who were still more acceptable to Germany. In the end, they interfered with American plans in North Africa, and they deserted Pétain only after it was clear that he was helpless and that the United States was going to win.

Moreover, "standing behind the venerated figure of the marshal," even if it had provided many Frenchmen with the means of serving France, would not have served the best interests of the United States. For the marshal, no matter how venerated, became more and more a front for stronger figures more fully committed to collaboration with the Axis. The Pétain-Weygand-Laval coalition (named in order of their importance) gave way to the Darlan-Pétain coalition, which in turn yielded to the Laval-Darlan-Pétain coalition. Our efforts to give loyal Frenchmen a rallying-point in the person of Pétain were based upon an obvious miscalculation both of the loyalty of those who rallied around him and of his attractiveness to those others whose loyalty it was to our interest to foster. An O.S.S. correspondent, quoted by Langer himself (p. 245), reported at the time of the Riom trials in March 1942: "Marshal Pétain no longer wields much influence on the great mass of patriots." Surely that was the time, if not earlier, for the State Department to have admitted that the wrong people, if any, had been rallied behind Pétain by appeasement and that therefore it should change its policy. Believing, however, that important figures in North Africa were ready to connive with the United States and that they would be effective at this game, the State Department continued its policy of playing both ends against the middle (provided that neither end was De Gaulle).

The second motive Langer assigns to the State Department was the desire to exploit the opportunities for military information that Vichy afforded. "When the last word is said," he believes, "one can hardly escape the conclusion that for intelligence purposes, if for no others, the Vichy policy was completely justified" (pp. 387–88). This judgment is obviously based upon two assumptions. It is assumed, first, that information from France would have been unavailable if we had not collaborated with Vichy—which probably is a correct judgment, since G2 and other intelligence services were not yet prepared to gather the amount of exploitable information that they are known to have gathered later about other enemy and conquered areas. It is also assumed that the information derived from Vichy sources was correct.

The second assumption is highly dubious. Only rarely does Langer question the good judgment of the American agents within the Vichy empire. Robert D. Murphy, who after the departure of Leahy was our principal representative there, is regularly credited with giving sound opinions and acting wisely. But the record presented by Langer himself raises grave doubts regarding Murphy's wisdom. For example, Murphy was particularly confident that Weygand would insure the United States against German occupation of North Africa and West Africa (p. 179), and yet Weygand readily yielded when Pétain, submitting to German and collaborationist pressure, asked for his resignation. Or again, it was largely on Murphy's insistence that we undertook to send Weygand supplies (p. 189). Langer gives in full the two documents that made up the Murphy-Weygand accord on economic aid to North Africa.[9] The Murphy-Weygand memorandum contains *four* numbered articles, the second of which provided that goods sent to North Africa were not to be re-exported (i.e., to the Germans) and the fourth that, in case of violation of that provision, economic cooperation was automatically to end. Darlan's letter of acceptance, however, confirms only the first three of these propositions, omitting the fourth entirely. Whether Murphy (or anyone else in the State Department, for that matter) noted the omission

9. Murphy to Weygand, Feb. 26, 1941, and Darlan to Murphy, Mar. 10, 1941, *ibid.*, pp. 399–401.

Langer does not show. Except as another, probably unconscious, indication of Murphy's obstinacy in favor of Vichy, the point is unimportant, for events proved that when Vichy violated the agreement and did re-export our goods, our policy gave us no real freedom of action and we did not end the agreement, automatically or otherwise.

It is not astonishing, therefore, that when Murphy encountered some officers and officials in North Africa who "were not wedded to Vichy" (p. 225), he assumed that they were also anti–De Gaulle. The type he met usually were (pp. 306, 312, and 331–32). Yet the Free French claim to have begun their resistance movement in August 1940, and by the end of 1941 they had won important recruits and were gathering information for the American vice-consuls (who thus were not entirely dependent upon Vichy sources) (pp. 228–29). How did Murphy get the impression, then, that in North Africa, De Gaulle had only a negligible following? Because he apparently did not mingle with the Free French, who were especially strong among the lower classes (p. 166), but got his information from ministers and generals. Jacques Lemaigre-Dubreuil and General Charles Mast were among his principal informants (pp. 230, 280–83, 306, 309, 321, and 323–32). Lemaigre had been prominent in French Fascist movements before the war. He was now promoting General Henri Giraud's candidacy as the French leader in North Africa in the event of American invasion. Murphy, believing that Lemaigre's apparent record as a collaborationist in France was studiously deceptive, thought of him as "a courageous, patriotic Frenchman" and used him as a go-between in his dealings with Giraud.[10] Mast was Giraud's representative in North Africa and not only could not be expected to have any friendly feelings toward De Gaulle but also shamefully, if unintentionally, misled Murphy about Giraud's popularity in North Africa (p. 352).

The De Gaullists seem never even to have had a chance to present their case to Murphy. Such information as he picked up about them was likely to be mistaken. At one time he suggested that De Gaulle might "be capable of treachery should the United States undertake military intervention in French North Africa." [11] This caution comes from the very man who did not scruple at beginning our "deal" with Darlan about two months later. At another time he relayed reports of preparations for an "early, large-scale commando operation" by the De Gaullists against Occupied France.[12]

Dispatches from Murphy and his colleagues led Washington to believe that De Gaulle would be received only with hostility in North Africa, while Giraud would be welcomed not only by the French army but per-

10. Murphy to General William J. Donovan, Jan. 11, 1943, *ibid.*, p. 230.
11. *Idem* to *idem*, Sept. 5, 1942, *ibid.*, p. 296.
12. Murphy to Hull, July 21, 1942, *ibid.*, p. 306.

haps also by the French navy.[13] Small wonder, then, that General Dwight D. Eisenhower, having finally taken action on the basis of this information, found that "existing French sentiment in North Africa does not even remotely resemble prior calculations." [14] In all fairness, it should be pointed out that in Eisenhower's estimation the name "to conjure with in North Africa" was neither Giraud nor De Gaulle but Pétain. But of that, more later. Langer has reported enough *mis*intelligence that came from North African Vichyites to raise doubt concerning his conclusion that for intelligence purposes alone our Vichy gamble was completely justified.

Our Vichy policy also proposed, as a third motive, to "save parts of the French Empire from falling into the hands of our potential enemies." Langer himself considers that the State Department's claim to success in this purpose is "at best debatable—though our role was probably a substantial, contributory one" (p. 389). He recognizes that there was nothing we could have done until the end of 1942 to prevent Hitler from taking North Africa had he wished to do so and that, in fact, when Hitler wanted to, he did take Unoccupied France. Incidentally, the author contends that the chief reason for German hesitation to move through Spain to North Africa and to assist the Spanish in reconquering Gibraltar was Hitler's unwillingness to pay General Francisco Franco as much as the *caudillo* asked for cooperation (pp. 91–93, 114, and 126–27). It follows, therefore, that our appeasement of Spain had only minor influence, if any at all, upon Franco's, Hitler's, or Pétain's decisions in that connection.[15] Franco preferred, if he could not get a good price for entering the fight, to remain more or less neutral, picking up whatever chips fell his way. Langer shows that the Spanish authorities, on the one hand, kept silent regarding what they knew about the North African expedition (pp. 240–42), and it is well known that, on the other, they allowed Spanish troops to go (if they did not in fact send them) to fight against Russia.

Despite Franco's prudence, Hitler, in the summer of 1941, might nevertheless have invaded North Africa through Italy and rendered all our collaboration with Weygand futile, had he not preferred to invade Russia instead. Evidently, Hitler's policy of collaboration with those whose ideologies were opposed to his produced, like ours, easy access to misintelligence, and he was led to expect a decisive victory in the east. Afterward, if Hitler chose not to invade North Africa, it was because he preferred to maintain a friendly and cooperative French government

13. Cf. *ibid.*, pp. 306–307; Colonel William A. Eddy to Donovan, Aug. 26, 1942, *ibid.*, p. 309; and Murphy to General George C. Marshall, Oct. 16, 1942, *ibid.*, pp. 323–24.

14. Eisenhower to War Department, Nov. 14, 1942, *ibid.*, p. 357.

15. HAYES (*loc. cit.*, p. 710) does not agree with Langer in this regard.

there rather than to put a new drain on his resources by occupation of a resentful country. Except to the extent that American matériel was furnished to the Germans by a violation of the Murphy-Weygand economic accord, our policy of collaboration with Vichy was not a factor in saving North Africa.

For the same reasons that Hitler did not invade North Africa, he did not invade Unoccupied France. Obviously it was cheaper to have a friendly government in Vichy than to have to suppress an unfriendly people by force. The State Department would perhaps have been wiser, if its purpose really had been to save Unoccupied France and North Africa from invasion, deliberately to encourage the collaborationists. If, however, it encouraged collaborationists, Langer makes clear that it did not do so intentionally. On the other hand, it did intentionally discourage the Free French, although by the summer of 1942 they controlled a large portion of the French Empire.

A fourth part of Langer's analysis of the rationale behind the State Department's policy was that our collaboration with Vichy would help keep the French fleet out of Hitler's hands. That, too, was a gratuitous assumption. We now know (and if our intelligence from our "Vichy friends" had been good, we should have been so persuaded at the time) that if Pétain and Darlan were sincere in anything it was in their declarations that they would rather scuttle the French fleet than surrender it to the Germans. In short, no real need existed to continue recognition of the Vichy government for the purpose of cajoling it into preserving its navy.

The fifth purpose that Langer assigns to the State Department is the wish "to keep contact with the people of France, . . . to maintain hope of deliverance, and to stimulate resistance to the conqueror." A careful study of the Resistance movement inside France will enable us at some future time to determine whether this purpose could have been better achieved by recognizing De Gaulle than by at first refusing to recognize him and then by recognizing him only half-heartedly (down to the end of 1942). The materials for such study are apparently available.[16] It seems reasonable to suppose, however, that the best course to "maintain the hope of deliverance and to stimulate resistance to the conqueror" would have been to have discerned as early as possible the way in which that resistance and deliverance actually would come and to have made that way easy rather than hard. The confusion, conflicts, and doubts that assailed Hull, Under Secretary Sumner Welles, and Murphy can easily be explained, and Langer makes clear that De Gaulle's behavior in the Dakar, Syria, St. Pierre-Miquelon, and other Free French actions caused

16. Cf. Fred L. HADSEL, "Some sources on the Resistance movement in France during the Nazi occupation," *Journal of modern history*, XVIII (1946), 333–40.

perhaps intelligible irritation in Anglo-American diplomatic circles. The historian, however, must avoid assuming that an error that can be explained is therefore justified. When one's criteria of justification eschew the ideological in favor of the expedient, one should be especially careful to shun the appearance of justifying a debatable decision like the preference for Pétain over De Gaulle, for in the end that preference proved to be the less expedient one. It is still harder on a pragmatic basis to justify the choice of Giraud rather than of De Gaulle.

Finally came the North African invasion itself. After the groundwork had been laid by Murphy and his State Department colleagues for collaboration with Vichy-oriented Giraudists, the preparations for the invasion were put under the jurisdiction of the War Department. Although Murphy was appointed Operating Executive Head of the Civil Affairs Section and Adviser for Civil Affairs," [17] he was placed under General Eisenhower, and the State Department nominally passed out of the picture. It was Murphy who arranged the clandestine meeting of General Mark W. Clark with five French conspirators at Cherchell. Among them were General Mast, Henri d'Astier de la Vigerie, "a former Cagoulard" (p. 229), and Lieutenant-Colonel Jousse, a member of the group associated with Lemaigre-Dubreuil (*ibid.*). All of them were apparently among the group that the State Department thought of as French patriots rallied behind Pétain. They agreed that Giraud should be the leader of the French during and after the invasion.

Unfortunately, the conspirators were badly informed about Giraud. When he learned of his selection, he made extraordinary demands (would De Gaulle have demanded as much?) to the effect that he be given supreme command of the Allied forces and that the invasion of continental France should begin simultaneously with, or as soon as possible after, the North African invasion (pp. 330–39). He also proved unable to win any support whatsoever from French army officers in North Africa when finally he consented to go there (p. 352). (De Gaulle would have been able to provide at least the Free French army and navy and would have received some support from Free French elements in Algiers and other cities.) Murphy at one point in the negotiations with Giraud became so panicky about the possible "serious opposition of French Army to our landing" unless Giraud's demands were met that he cabled Eisenhower at Gibraltar that "the invasion of North Africa without favorable High Command will be a catastrophe" and suggested a two weeks' delay (p. 335). Eisenhower thereupon cabled Chief of Staff George C. Marshall: "It is inconceivable that Murphy can recommend such delay with his intimate knowledge of the operation and the present location of troops and convoys afloat. It is likewise inconceivable to me

17. Roosevelt to Murphy, Sept. 22, 1942, LANGER, p. 315.

that our mere failure to concede to such demands as have been made would result in having the French North African Army meet us with serious opposition" (*ibid.*).

Eisenhower was undoubtedly correct, though perhaps not for the reasons he had in mind. If, to paraphrase Montesquieu, the success of the invasion had really been as dependent on a single man as Murphy thought, one would have had to inquire what were the underlying weaknesses in the planning that had made that man so vital. The event proved that Giraud was, in fact, more of a hindrance than a help. Serious opposition from the French North African Army depended on its fighting quality rather than on the preferences of its generals, and that fighting quality was seriously impaired by the lack of equipment and the unwillingness of at least some units to put up more than a token resistance to the Americans.[18]

Langer does not carefully examine the effectiveness of the French North African Army as a fighting force or question whether it really had the will to resist effectively even if it had had the means. Such figures as he gives for French troops and equipment in North and West Africa for 1941 (p. 205) and for Tunisia in 1942 (p. 320) are pitifully low, and if those in North Africa in 1942 were comparable, the French could have put up no real opposition to the Anglo-American invaders. He admits (p. 365) that "French resistance was, at its worst, not too formidable." If it was feared that American lives were at stake, it was only in small part because of the expected French resistance to the American landings in Morocco and Algeria. It was rather because resentment of the Americans might make a mopping-up and occupation necessary, leading therefore to a diversion of strength from, and a delay in, the attack upon Tunisia (pp. 370–71).

Until a careful study is made of the public opinion in North Africa and the attitude of the French forces there, we have to estimate the prevalent spirit from subsequent events. We know that practically all elements of the population of North Africa rallied to the Americans after initial resistance had saved the honor of the French *parole*. The only testimony thereafter of serious difficulty in rallying Frenchmen to the united front came from Darlan, who, upon being put in charge of North Africa, exploited that alleged difficulty as an argument in demanding American support of his ambiguous position (p. 374). He also threw into concentration camps "a large number of those who had been friendly and cooperative with the American enterprise" (p. 378).

Why, then, if resistance was "not too formidable," did the American army put Darlan in charge of North Africa? Part of the answer undoubtedly was the exaggerated but no less real fear that delay of the

18. This statement is based, among other sources, on the oral testimony of a combat officer in the American invasion forces.

attack on Tunisia might result from any resistance whatever in Morocco and Algeria. But the chief reason seems to have been the faulty judgment of several responsible Americans. Murphy, it appears, had miscalculated the degree of support that Giraud would win. He found that Noguès, as resident-general in Morocco, and Juin, as commander of the ground forces in North Africa, hesitated to join in the American plans when first informed of them (before any landing had been effected and before it was clear how big an effort was involved). When Murphy on the eve of invasion went to see Juin, the general stated that "if the matter were entirely in his hands there would be no resistance on his part to the American landing but, as Murphy knew, Admiral Darlan had arrived at Algiers unexpectedly." Langer is satisfied (p. 345) that in fact Darlan's arrival was not prearranged. Juin insisted that, in view of that untoward circumstance, "no matter what decision he himself might take, it would immediately be overruled by Darlan." Thereupon Murphy suggested that Darlan be consulted, and when Darlan arrived, Murphy asked him to join forces with the Americans.

It later developed that both Darlan and Juin were prisoners of French Resistance forces that had already surrounded Juin's house and would allow no one to leave "except a representative of the American consulate." Why was Darlan not arrested and Juin required to proceed without Darlan as he had indicated that he would? Or, if Juin was now considered suspect, why was he not also arrested? Both Frenchmen actually "concluded that they were prisoners." Anyhow, strange as it may seem, Darlan was permitted (in fact, requested) to inform Pétain of what was going on and to ask for "liberty of action."

An American vice-consul was sent with Darlan's message to the French naval officer in charge of the port of Algiers, who was to relay it to Vichy. The vice-consul was allowed by the Resistance volunteers to pass but, naturally, was taken into custody by the French naval authorities. The invasion being off schedule, no American soldiers appeared, and soon the French military came, drove away the volunteers who surrounded Juin's house, and arrested Murphy. When, however, Darlan was convinced that the invasion was real and on a large scale, Juin informed Murphy that the French were ready to cease resistance.[19] All resistance in Algiers in fact ceased at 7 P.M. on November 8, without any promises having been made to Darlan.

Whether Pétain received Darlan's message is not clear. In the same paragraph of his notes (p. 348), Murphy says first (par. 1, l. 2) that he did and later (*ibid.*, ll. 12–13) that it is not clear whether he did. But, however the marshal learned of the invasion, he at once began a double game, which consisted of openly opposing the American maneuver while

19. The story of Murphy's conversations with Juin and Darlan is derived from Murphy's notes, quoted in LANGER, pp. 345–46.

secretly encouraging Darlan to cooperate with it. Meanwhile, resistance continued elsewhere. According to Langer (p. 351), it was "really serious in Morocco," and according to Eisenhower (quoted on the same page), "scattered." Giraud, when he finally arrived on November 9, proved unable to do anything about it and had to go into hiding. When General Clark arrived in Algiers, he decided to confer with Darlan and Juin. Darlan at first temporized, but on November 10 Clark, apparently made of sterner stuff than Murphy and, it must be added, having behind him a more reliable force than a few hundred French Resistance volunteers, gave Darlan half an hour in which to make up his mind or face arrest. Darlan thereupon agreed to issue orders to cease firing everywhere and even to order the French fleet to be ready to move from Toulon if the Germans occupied the whole of France.

So far no commitments had been made to Darlan except, by implication, not to arrest him. He himself, however, "in the name of the marshal," assumed complete control over North Africa. When Pétain (at least outwardly) repudiated his action, Darlan announced that he would rescind his order to cease resistance. Clark replied, "Damned if you do," and Darlan did not, though he "stated that he would have to consider himself under arrest" (pp. 353–54). When all France was occupied, however, he again took control of North Africa, rationalizing that the marshal was helpless as a prisoner of the enemy, and agreed with Giraud and Noguès that he himself should be the political chief while Giraud should command the French troops.

That is how Darlan saved American lives! Whatever lives he saved in the invasion were already saved without any American's having promised him anything but an implied freedom from arrest. The "deal" came afterward in the hope of saving time and lives in the invasion of Tunisia. When Eisenhower arrived in Algiers from Gibraltar on November 13, he accepted the *fait accompli* by Darlan, Giraud, Clark, and Murphy. His reasons for doing so were given in a lengthy dispatch to the War Department on November 14, of which the most comprehensive paragraph (p. 360) read:

> It must be understood that if we repudiate Darlan and attempt from the outside to dictate the personnel of the coalition to run North Africa, the following will be the consequences:
>
> *a.* French armed forces will resist us passively, and in certain instances, actively.
> *b.* The hope of securing cooperation in this area will be lost at great cost to us in stagnation of operations and in requirements for additional troops.
> *c.* The opportunity for gaining some assistance from remaining French naval and military units in North Africa will disappear.

d. The last glimmer of hope with respect to the Toulon Fleet will be gone.

e. Admiral Esteva, in Tunis, will not cooperate and our hope of getting Tunisia quickly will not be attainable. Admittedly, Estava may already be helpless, but there is still a chance of his being able to assist.

Eisenhower did not have the advantage either of Langer's detailed analysis of the events centering around his predicament in Algiers or of the knowledge of events to come, both of which are available to his critics today. Instead, he was surrounded by a group of French officers like Darlan, Giraud, and Noguès, and American civil advisers like Murphy. "From highest to lowest," Eisenhower discovered, "everyone attempts to create the impression that the shadow of the Marshal's figure dominates all his actions and, in fact, his very life." By this time, too, Governor-General Pierre Boisson of West Africa had, in principle, accepted the Darlan-Giraud accord. And so Eisenhower concluded that "the military and naval leaders, as well as the civil governors, agree that only one man has the obvious right to assume the mantle of Pétain and that man is Admiral Darlan" (pp. 357–58).

No doubt, insofar as Eisenhower was able to ascertain the wishes of the people of North Africa, the proper choice seemed to be Darlan. But even if this judgment were right, respect for the wishes of the now conquered North Africans would have been an "ideological" consideration that our hard-boiled military and political leaders should have entertained, by their own standards as described by Langer, only if respect for that consideration had helped to avert the five strategical consequences that Eisenhower feared. But did they? What reason is there now to believe that French armed forces would have continued serious resistance —with all of France occupied by Hitler, with a victorious American army in Morocco and Algiers, with a Free French government in French Equatorial Africa, and with the Germans decisively checked around Stalingrad?

The first of the five "consequences" that Eisenhower feared from a repudiation of Darlan—continued resistance—now seems unfounded. If it is set aside, then apprehension of the second and the third "consequences"—stagnation of operations and loss of assistance from the French forces in North Africa—vanishes with it. As if to prove the unreality of those three "consequences," Darlan was murdered on December 24, only about a month after they were enumerated. (Langer is satisfied that the assassin was either an agent of French royalists or a lone fanatic [p. 379].) None of these three "consequences" followed, however, from Darlan's "repudiation" in this stern fashion. The remaining two "consequences" apprehended from a disavowal of Darlan actually occurred—despite the fact that President Roosevelt accepted Darlan. "The last glimmer of hope with respect to the Toulon Fleet" died when Admiral de Laborde scuttled it; and Admiral Jean Esteva preferred to cooperate with the Germans. Obviously the French admirals had less respect for Darlan than did the American generals. In short, it is questionable whether any of the evils Eisenhower hoped to ward off by his deal with Darlan actually were avoided because of Darlan. Three of them, in all probability, would not have eventuated in any case and two of them did eventuate despite Darlan.

It is hard to see how our North African campaign could have been worse handled on the political side, no matter how brilliantly fought. We refused even to consider as French commander the one leader who had a definite following among French patriots abroad; the man we chose had no efficacious following either at home or abroad; and when we had more or less to discard him, we chose an avowed collaborationist—but only *after* he had already given us practically all the effective aid of which he was capable. Nevertheless, Langer concludes, "Our whole North African policy must be described as an unqualified success, despite the fact that it was never well implemented or exploited to the full" (p. 388). He consoles himself in regard to the scuttling of the Toulon fleet with the thought that "if the Allies failed to get it, so did the Germans" (p. 375). But suppose De Gaulle had accomplished equally little, would Washington have been so easily contented, or would eyebrows have been raised in the direction of "ideologists" who could not deliver the goods? It is hardly conceivable that De Gaulle would have delivered as little as Giraud. It is possible that he might have delivered less than Darlan, but at least he would have saved us from the necessity of a four-hundred-page exposition of our Vichy policy that at times appears to be an apology.

However grievous the necessity for such an exposition, that Langer chose to make it and that he tried to do so in a fair and honest way are reasons for gratitude. He seldom makes assertions for which he has no sources; his arguments, with some exceptions, are delivered with judicial restraint; he nearly always takes into consideration the evidence against his position; and if it is possible to dispute his thesis that we would do the whole thing over again the same way if we had to (p. 397), it is only because he has provided a large part of the necessary information. Until the State Department makes its files generally available, Langer's book will be indispensable to students of Franco-American diplomacy during the second World War, even when they disagree with it.

JOHN K. FAIRBANK

Dilemmas of American Far Eastern Policy

The complicated story of America's wartime relations with China became a matter of public controversy with the victory of the Chinese Communists in 1949. The central issues—the paucity of wartime aid to Chiang Kai-shek, the misreading of the nature and potential of Mao's forces, the refusal to commit American troops in 1945—are clear, but interpretations vary radically. Some see the loss of China as a deliberate betrayal of Chiang; others see a tragic story of lost opportunities; still others see only the inevitable defeat of a corrupt and inefficient Nationalist regime.

In this review article John King Fairbank, a specialist in Chinese history, critically appraises the thesis of Tang Tsou that a bold and persistent American effort to bolster and reform Chiang's government could have saved China from communism. For a defense of Franklin Roosevelt's Asian policy, see Sumner Welles, "Roosevelt and the Far East," Harper's, CCII (February and March 1951), 27–38 and 70–80.

SUGGESTIONS THAT THE government of South Vietnam should hold elections or otherwise pursue "reforms" in order to win back popular support are reminiscent of the United States' predicament in China in the late 1940's. In both cases the provision of American arms did little to endear the recognized government to the populace; the military build-up outstripped the growth of a stable polity; and skillful enemies exploited the resultant imbalance between the armament and the virtue of the ruling regimes. The complexities of Vietnam and China cannot be reduced to formulae, any more than those of Korea—even though American arms have achieved superior firepower and political frustration in all these three areas. South Vietnam in the 1960's, however, makes China in the 1940's all the more fascinating in retrospect, and this lends added interest to a recent study [1] in which a professor of political science at

Reprinted by permission from *Pacific Affairs*, XXXVI (Winter 1963–1964), 430–437.

1. *America's Failure in China, 1941–50* by Tang Tsou with a foreword by Hans J. Morgenthau. Chicago: University of Chicago Press, 1963, 614 pp., $12.50.

the University of Chicago analyzes the disastrous gap between America's wartime aims in China and the means that were used. After a brief survey of the Open Door principles and the "traditional" American China policy, Dr. Tsou offers a narrative and analysis of three main phases—the initial policy and programs, conceived when the American war effort began, "to make China a great power"; the American reaction to China's domestic power struggle as it developed during the war, "to bring about a united and democratic China by peaceful means"; and finally the postwar mediation of General Marshall, which encountered "the limits of a policy of limited assistance." The Korean War and the rise of Communist China form "the ironic fulfillment."

Dr. Tsou achieves a new level of perspective on Chinese and American attitudes both by his comprehensive grasp of the sources and by his analytic acumen. For example, excerpts from Chiang Kai-shek's diary, published by his son Ching-kuo on his seventieth birthday, make plain that he had no idea of the importance of agrarian reform in China and thought primarily in terms of patriotism and political control. On the U.S. side, Dr. Tsou points up American unwillingness either to fight or to relinquish goals obtainable only by fighting—a dilemma inherited from the "traditional" Open Door policy, which demanded the preservation of China's integrity but held that American interests in China were never worth a major war.

America's Failure in China builds upon Herbert Feis's *The China Tangle,* the CBI Theater history in three volumes by Romanus and Sunderland, and on other historical studies to present a systematic discussion of policy alternatives, aims, attitudes, and assumptions during a succession of periods from 1941 to 1950. Since Dr. Tsou sets forth a vigorous and clear-cut thesis with which many students of the subject will probably agree for some time to come, I should like to forgo further praise and rather try to comment on certain major points, as a contribution to further discussion.

1. Whence came the Open Door, with its peculiar and unfortunate combination of demanding China's integrity and yet being unwilling to fight in the Far East? On this point of historical origins, Dr. Tsou seems to overlook the unusual circumstances in which American policy toward China developed during the era of the unequal treaty system, from 1842 down to 1922. I refer to the fact that the treaty system as a particular type of international order was established by British naval power, which backed up the British consular establishment and even, for example, protected foreign trade against Chinese piracy. Thus the whole treaty port system in China and Japan in the nineteenth century was maintained by the obvious presence of gunboats, primarily British. Except for the American use of naval power in Perry's opening of Japan and in the less-publicized American naval fiasco in Korea in 1871, the Americans let

the British take the lead, fight the two wars that set up the system in China, and thereafter underwrite it by force.

Another feature of the treaty system was the high degree of cooperation in it by the Ch'ing government of China, most evident in the Chinese Imperial Maritime Customs Service, which supervised the functioning of the system on its commercial side through a joint Sino-foreign administration. Just as the Open Door notes of 1899 were inspired textually by the views of the Maritime Customs, so the second set of notes in 1900 demanding the preservation of China's territorial integrity may best be understood as an American effort to preserve the treaty system at a time of crisis.

In the end, however, the treaty system was underwritten after 1902 by the Anglo-Japanese alliance. Strangely, Dr. Tsou as a political scientist takes no note of the importance of this international power structure based on the British and Japanese fleets (see pages 14, 16, and 238). Rather than describing the balance of power in the Far East as "maintained by a shifting equilibrium among the conflicting policies and interests of the powers," he might well have analyzed the power structure represented by the Anglo-Japanese alliance, against which no combination of other powers could have availed in the period from 1902 to 1922.

Thus the American consecration of the Open Door idea was a luxury made possible by the fact that the United States could rely upon the stable maintenance of the treaty system in China underwritten by a naval power not its own. Once the Anglo-Japanese alliance was ended in 1922, the stable order of the treaty system, already outmoded by the rise of Chinese nationalism, quickly disintegrated. America's "traditional" Far Eastern policy had been compatible with her military isolationism because the balance of power in the Far East had been maintained, on the whole, by Britain.

2. Dr. Tsou makes one important point that deserves underlining by analogy to Europe. He points out that American political policy in World War II, to make China a great power capable of filling the power vacuum that the defeat of Japan would create in East Asia, required a parallel military policy, which originally aimed to make China the Allied base for the attack on Japan. If China had in fact become the Allied base, with National Government armies trained, supplied, and battle-hardened in victory, the postwar dominance of the National Government could have been unchallengeable and its political and economic health might also have been far more vigorous. The possible analogy with Churchill's "soft underbelly" proposal for military action in southern Europe, which would create a postwar position of non-Communist strength there, may be worth suggesting. Both against Germany and against Japan the American concentration on winning the war, rather than on war-and-politics, led to the logistically more efficient approach

straight at the enemy's heart. I would not attempt to argue with hindsight that this was basically unwise; but certainly it is worth noting that both the Balkans and China—areas which later went Communist and into the Soviet orbit—were given low priority in the Allied military effort. It is often remarked that Communism has spread chiefly where Communist armies have gone; conversely, it might be argued that Communism would not have spread where Allied armies had gone. Specifically, if the Stilwell program for Chinese army training had been been given high priority, the American influence in Free China after 1941 might have contributed to an improvement of the economic situation and of political morale and behavior, as well as to the performance of the Chinese government and its armed forces.

One of Dr. Tsou's main themes is the way in which the program to make China a great power, toward which Stilwell kept working, was dropped because of American strategic concentration on the naval reduction of Japan. Meanwhile Stilwell's efforts in training ground troops were resisted by Chiang Kai-shek as likely to get beyond his control and also by General Chennault as competing with air power. Dr. Tsou makes the further point that this fiasco in American planning was compounded by the imposition of the "Matterhorn" B-29 project for bombing Japan based at Chengtu. The slender Hump tonnage was extensively diverted to this Strategic Air Force project, which aimed with single-minded intensity to hit the enemy, but in the process weakened the China theater. Even when the Japanese offensive in East China in the spring and summer of 1944 had destroyed the advanced American air bases, as Stilwell and Marshall had feared, the B-29's were not diverted to check it until late in the day. This is but one example of many in which the American capacity for fighting and winning the war had the effect of losing the peace. By V-J Day, only one-third of the U.S. equipment of the 39-division army modernization program in China had been delivered, and the Nationalist forces had not been built up as originally hoped.

3. Dr. Tsou is equally eloquent in painting the American dilemma, now familiar to us in Saigon, of trying to support a power-holder and get him to institute "reforms," both at once. The American support of Chiang in World War II was not accompanied by success in the American effort to make him broaden the base of his political power. Rather, U.S. support enabled him to suppress non-Communist political leaders of the very sort whose participation in the National Government might, in the U.S. view, have strengthened it.

Here it seems to me that Dr. Tsou as an American professor of political science suffers from the lack of understanding of Confucian government which has for so long typified his profession. American disappointment in Chiang Kai-shek, Syngman Rhee, and Ngo Dinh Diem, among others, has been so consistent a story of bad luck that we might well assume that something lies behind it other than personality. All these client rulers, holding power in parts of the "Chinese culture area" of East Asia, have been inheritors (as is Mao today) of the great tradition of Confucian government. As latter-day Sons of Heaven, their political behavior harks back to a different world that Western political scientists have only dimly perceived and even then seldom taken seriously.

The following features typify the Confucian ruler in the Chinese tradition. First, he tends to rule for life and pass his power to his offspring in a dynastic succession. Succession was to be arranged in the bedchamber and not by election of constituents or any other show of popular opinion. A Son of Heaven had no terminal facilities by which to get out of the job once he had got in.

Second, he was an autocrat within the institutional limits set by the fact that his government was not a penetrating one but remained rather superficial to the life of the populace in the villages. Within his sphere, the Son of Heaven exercised arbitrary power even though he had to santion it by use of the classical ideology.

Third, the maintenance of his power rested not only on the monopoly of military force but also on his maintenance of his ideological superiority in the established system of political thought. Confucian government had a very high ideological component. It was capable of controlling vast masses of people with a minimum of troops and a maximum of indoctrination—witness, for example, the examination system as only one of its institutional devices.

Fourth, one essential element of the ideology was the concept that the emperor brought men to accept his rule by his virtuous conduct and moral influence. The ruler must therefore be a sage and teacher as well as a commander and administrator, a very powerful executive, raised above the common man and accessible only to the "remonstrance" of officials speaking in terms of the accepted ideology.

In this system, the ruler's prestige was absolutely all-important, not merely as a weather-gauge of his success as a ruler but also as an actual component of his power. Anything which detracted from his prestige, such as direct criticism, was as serious as outright rebellion. The rule of a Son of Heaven was preserved by the official myth that he was a sage and exemplar in his virtuous conduct without exception, not divine but still more-than-human in his abilities for benevolent rule and correct decision.

It follows from this last point that there could be no such thing as a "loyal opposition" in the Confucian government. Since the ruler held his position by his personal qualities and by the theory of Heaven's Mandate given to his family dynasty, there was no way that he could distinguish between his policies of state and his personal rule. Opposition to a policy was opposition to him and struck at the roots of his power. He could never submit his decisions to review or veto by others, least of all by the common herd. He had to take his position and stand upon it as a superior leader, not as a "servant of the people." He was the One Man at the top, carrying the burden of responsibility and decision, and could not delegate it without forfeiting his title to power. Even in the regimes in China today, popular participation is more symbolic than actual in the decision-making process. Communist "democracy" undoubtedly involves the people in the governmental process but certainly not in the position of final arbiters.

From this traditional point of view, the American demand for "democratization" and the broadening of the base of participation by bringing in other leaders can only threaten the position of a Chiang or a Diem. On the contrary, such a man is inclined to feel that he must stand forth as an unshakable and all-wise potentate in form, and rely in fact upon the loyalty of persons who depend upon him for their careers and are not potential rivals. For him, it is "rule or ruin," and so he feels he has everything at stake in resisting the misguided American request. Chiang in Chungking could never see how to share his power and still perform his function as the old-style, monopolistic power-holder. Even later, when protected by the Seventh Fleet in Taiwan, he rejected Dr. Hu Shih's suggestion that the Kuomintang modernize its rule by splitting into two parties, one to be in office and one in opposition. Quite the contrary, when Lei Chen tried to form an opposition party, Western style, in 1960, he was jailed for ten years and the opposition party movement has remained suppressed, just as Diem felt compelled to suppress the Buddhists and all other rivals.

Thus the U.S. policy failure in the "Chinese culture area" has resulted from a conflict between modern Western and traditional Confucian concepts of government. This has been a failure in Americans' intellectual grasp, not merely in the fitting of military means to political ends.

4. Dr. Tsou stresses the point that the American government, assuming an unreal convergence of American and Chinese interests, failed to bargain to secure its own aims in China and turned against Stilwell's policy of seeking a *quid pro quo* for American aid. President Roosevelt sentimentally sought to be a "good neighbor" in China, did not demand contractual arrangements as to Chinese performance in return for American aid, and was even bluffed by Chiang's indirect suggestions of a separate Chinese peace with Japan. In the end Stilwell's policy of bargaining was supported, too late for effect, by Marshall, who eventually succeeded him as the chief American representative and held the same view. The whole story points up the skill of Chiang Kai-shek in manipulating Americans.

American incompetence undoubtedly reached its high point with the performance of Ambassador Hurley, a flamboyant individual who was entirely out of his depth and clung steadfastly, says Dr. Tsou, to three grievous errors: first, that the Soviet Union would follow the American lead in China; second, that the Chinese Communists were not hard-core Communists incapable of compromise; and third, that the Chinese Communists lacked popular support. Against these purblind views, the U.S. Foreign Service officers' estimates of the situation were correct. Dr. Tsou believes they went too far in assuming that the Chinese Communists could "be weaned from Moscow or at least encouraged to follow an independent and nationalistic policy," and this possibility may seem unlikely to most observers in retrospect, despite the big change in Sino-Soviet relations in 1963. However, the assumption was originally made in the context of the stated American effort to make China a great power, and this might conceivably have been carried through by the wartime military program as originally planned. On the other hand, this hopeful view does seem in retrospect to have given too little importance to the Chinese need for ideological orthodoxy, evident in the Confucian tradition mentioned above and in the true-believer dogmatism of Peking recently.

5. Dr. Tsou suggests that the line of "coalition government" may have had a parallel origin on the Chinese Communists' side as a manifestation of the united front concept, but that its announcement was intertwined with the American push in 1944 for Chiang Kai-shek to establish a "war council" and incorporate the Chinese Communists in the war effort against Japan. Thus Ambassador Gauss advocated a war council on August 30, President Roosevelt having first raised it on July 14 in connection with the request that Stilwell take command in China. Chinese Communist representatives in Chungking came out for coalition government first on September 15 in the People's Political Council, and the Party adopted this line formally on October 10, 1944. This parallelism of American and Chinese Communist efforts, each of which has its own background, deserves further study and investigation.

6. While Yalta was a compromise with the Open Door idea, it (and the subsequent Sino-Soviet treaty to which Stalin and Chiang agreed in August 1945) gave the Nationalists a good enough prospect to warrant its being welcomed by them. Russian gains would be limited and Russian support of Chinese unity could be expected on the basis of this settlement, in proportion as the National Government of China remained strong. The Yalta deal became a disaster only because Nationalist and American power in China later deteriorated so rapidly. It was the events *after* Yalta which made it a defeat, not the diplomatic agreement itself.

Ambassador Hurley's misconceived efforts (after the recall of Stilwell in November 1944) included several errors—for example, in the name of coalition, trying to force *both* the minor parties *and* the Chinese

Communists on Chiang Kai-shek, instead of pushing the minor parties and non-Communist figures separately from the Communists. The result was to keep Chiang and his hard-core Kuomintang leaders aligned against all others and push the minor party and non-Communist groups into the Communist position. Later, in September 1945, when the Chinese Communist position had been weakened by the success of the American air-lift of Nationalist troops back to the former Japanese-occupied areas and by the Sino-Soviet treaty between Moscow and Chungking, Hurley failed to press for negotiations in detail. His program of all-out support of Chiang in the name of the war effort discouraged a broadening of the political participation in the National Government. Here, again, the parallel with recent policy in Vietnam is striking. In the China of 1945, as in the South Vietnam of 1963, American policy slipped into the channel of looking upon politics as a means to win a war, not upon warfare as a means to political ends. Since politics are, one hopes, more permanent and pervasive than war, this is an upside-down approach.

7. In the background of General Marshall's mediation, Dr. Tsou points out that American policy was handicapped by a basic belief that "American interests in China were not worth a war," which was reinforced by the fact that the development of the crisis in Europe, and the U.S. confrontation with Soviet power there, made it impossible to contemplate the use of American forces in China. The U.S. demobilization of six million troops in nine months also did not lend support to General Marshall's efforts.

After his almost impeccable display of objectivity, Dr. Tsou's treatment of the Marshall mediation period discloses that he too is human and, as a scholar reconstructing the past, can also be subject to wishful thinking. Repeatedly he lets himself express the hope that the United States could have got a "complete change" in Chinese leadership and that General Marshall by a different policy could have saved the situation (see pages 385–6, 374–5, 389, 399). From all that has gone before, however, the reader is likely to feel that this is most unlikely. Dr. Tsou's discussion of a "program to build up a third force" and reorganize Chinese politics neglects the sadly deteriorating situation of the late 1940's in China as well as the fact that a Chinese regime in power becomes increasingly intent on holding power in proportion as power slips away. How, specifically, might a third force have been supported?

First of all, the rival forces, both Nationalist and Communist, were based on highly articulated and long-standing organizations (both military and administrative), with secret police and a tested inner group of power-holders. In these respects, both the CC clique and the Whampoa military clique under Chiang were rather similar to the

Chinese Communists. Such attributes of organization and power could not by any stretch of the imagination have been achieved in a short time by the so-called "liberals" or even by the "outside generals" in the Nationalist area. It must not be forgotten that Chinese politics were not conducted within any framework of law such as Western political scientists are sometimes wont to assume.

How could an American or Chinese policy-maker in the period 1945–49 have advocated a specifically anti-Chiang program and yet avoided the charge of being pro-Communist, or at least subversive—at worst a knave, at best a fool? Dr. Tsou himself points up the fact of the Nationalists' influence in American politics, where Chiang Kai-shek already had many admirers, particularly in the Republican Party out of power—partly as a result of the American wartime propaganda build-up of his image as Free China's leader.

Was not General Marshall's contribution to the American "failure" mainly that of a doctor receiving a dying patient? *America's Failure in China* vividly portrays his inability to raise the dead. Dr. Tsou, true to his thesis, attributes it to "the two inconsistent elements in the traditional pattern of American policy: the hope to preserve American influence and the incapacity to use force." Perhaps this is over-simple. Granting the doctor's limitations, how about the patient? The situation to be cured was inside the Chinese body politic, largely inaccessible to outsiders. America's failure was only a small aspect of China's general metamorphosis in this period. It must be understood in a broader context than that of the incompatibility of "ends and means" on the American side only. Below this operational level lay the incompatibility of two cultures, which remain incompatible still.

Tang Tsou's judicious summary of the vicissitudes of our China policy in the late 1940's, ending in the final disaster of war in Korea, sets the stage admirably for the study of Sino-American relations as contact-and-conflict between civilizations—an effort that is long overdue and increasingly needed.

IV

Consequences of
World War II

HENRY L. STIMSON

The Decision to Use
the Atomic Bomb

*The use of the atomic bomb to ⟨...⟩
of an extensive debate among histo⟨...⟩
traditional view that President Tr⟨...⟩
good faith, believing that the bomb was the quickest and most effective way to end a bloody war. There is less agreement, however, on the question of whether the bomb was necessary to bring
about the Japanese surrender. Some feel the shock of atomic attack
was vital; others believe that Russian entry into the war and a
tightening naval blockade would have proved equally effective.*

*Secretary of War Henry Stimson, the man upon whom Truman
relied most heavily for advice, gives his personal account of how
the decision was reached. For additional insight into Stimson's role,
see Chapter 32 of the sympathetic biography by Elting E. Morison,*
Turmoil and Tradition *(Boston, 1960). Two important articles are
Louis Morton, "The Decision to Use the Atomic Bomb,"* Foreign
Affairs, *XXXV (January 1957), 334–353, which gives a straightforward summary, and Kazuo Kawai, "Mokusatsu, Japan's Response to the Potsdam Declaration,"* Pacific Historical Review, *XIX
(November 1950), 409–414, which explores the ambiguity of the
Japanese reply to the American demand for unconditional surrender.*

IN RECENT MONTHS there has been much comment about the decision
to use atomic bombs in attacks on the Japanese cities of Hiroshima and
Nagasaki. This decision was one of the gravest made by our government
in recent years, and it is entirely proper that it should be widely discussed. I have therefore decided to record for all who may be interested
my understanding of the events which led up to the attack on Hiroshima
on August 6, 1945, on Nagasaki on August 9, and the Japanese decision
to surrender, on August 10. No single individual can hope to know
exactly what took place in the minds of all of those who had a share
in these events, but what follows is an exact description of our thoughts
and actions as I find them in the records and in my clear recollection.

Plans and Preparations, September 1941–June 1945

It was in the fall of 1941 that the question of atomic energy was first
brought directly to my attention. At that time President Roosevelt ap-

Reprinted by permission from *Harper's*, CXCIV (February 1947), 97–107.

pointed a committee consisting of Vice President Wallace, General Marshall, Dr. Vannevar Bush, Dr. James B. Conant, and myself. The function of this committee was to advise the President on questions of policy relating to the study of nuclear fission which was then proceeding both in this country and in Great Britain. For nearly four years thereafter I was directly connected with all major decisions of policy on the development and use of atomic energy, and from May 1, 1943, until my resignation as Secretary of War on September 21, 1945, I was directly responsible to the President for the administration of the entire undertaking; my chief advisers in this period were General Marshall, Dr. Bush, Dr. Conant, and Major General Leslie R. Groves, the officer in charge of the project. At the same time I was the President's senior adviser on the military employment of atomic energy.

The policy adopted and steadily pursued by President Roosevelt and his advisers was a simple one. It was to spare no effort in securing the earliest possible successful development of an atomic weapon. The reasons for this policy were equally simple. The original experimental achievement of atomic fission had occurred in Germany in 1938, and it was known that the Germans had continued their experiments. In 1941 and 1942 they were believed to be ahead of us, and it was vital that they should not be the first to bring atomic weapons into the field of battle. Furthermore, if we should be the first to develop the weapon, we should have a great new instrument for shortening the war and minimizing destruction. At no time, from 1941 to 1945, did I ever hear it suggested by the President, or by any other responsible member of the government, that atomic energy should not be used in the war. All of us of course understood the terrible responsibility involved in our attempt to unlock the doors to such a devastating weapon; President Roosevelt particularly spoke to me many times of his own awareness of the catastrophic potentialities of our work. But we were at war, and the work must be done. I therefore emphasize that it was our common objective, throughout the war, to be the first to produce an atomic weapon and use it. The possible atomic weapon was considered to be a new and tremendously powerful explosive, as legitimate as any other of the deadly explosive weapons of modern war. The entire purpose was the production of a military weapon; on no other ground could the wartime expenditure of so much time and money have been justified. The exact circumstances in which that weapon might be used were unknown to any of us until the middle of 1945, and when that time came, as we shall presently see, the military use of atomic energy was connected with larger questions of national policy.

The extraordinary story of the successful development of the atomic bomb has been well told elsewhere. As time went on, it became clear that the weapon would not be available in time for use in the European Theater, and the war against Germany was successfully ended by the use of what are now called conventional means. But in the spring of 1945 it became evident that the climax of our prolonged atomic effort was at hand. By the nature of atomic chain reactions, it was impossible to state with certainty that we had succeeded until a bomb had actually exploded in a full-scale experiment; nevertheless, it was considered exceedingly probable that we should by midsummer have successfully detonated the first atomic bomb. This was to be done at the Alamogordo Reservation in New Mexico. It was thus time for detailed consideration of our future plans. What had begun as a well-founded hope was now developing into a reality.

On March 15, 1945, I had my last talk with President Roosevelt. My diary record of this conversation gives a fairly clear picture of the state of our thinking at that time. I have removed the name of the distinguished public servant who was fearful lest the Manhattan (atomic) project be "a lemon"; it was an opinion common among those not fully informed.

> The President . . . had suggested that I come over to lunch today. . . . First I took up with him a memorandum which he sent to me from ———— who had been alarmed at the rumors of extravagance in the Manhattan project. ———— suggested that it might become disastrous and he suggested that we get a body of "outside" scientists to pass upon the project because rumors are going around that Vannevar Bush and Jim Conant have sold the President a lemon on the subject and ought to be checked up on. It was rather a jittery and nervous memorandum and rather silly, and I was prepared for it and I gave the President a list of the scientists who were actually engaged on it to show the very high standing of them and it comprised four Nobel Prize men, and also how practically every physicist of standing was engaged with us in the project. Then I outlined to him the future of it and when it was likely to come off and told him how important it was to get ready. I went over with him the two schools of thought that exist in respect to the future control after the war of this project, in case it is successful, one of them being the secret close-in attempted control of the project by those who control it now, and the other being the international control based upon freedom both of science and of access. I told him that those things must be settled before the first projectile is used and that he must be ready with a statement to come out to the people on it just as soon as that is done. He agreed to that. . . .

This conversation covered the three aspects of the question which were then uppermost in our minds. First, it was always necessary to suppress a lingering doubt that any such titanic undertaking could be successful. Second, we must consider the implications of success in terms of its long-range postwar effect. Third, we must face the problem that would be presented at the time of our first use of the weapon, for with that first use there must be some public statement.

I did not see Franklin Roosevelt again. The next time I went to the White House to discuss atomic energy was April 25, 1945, and I went to explain the nature of the problem to a man whose only previous knowledge of our activities was that of a Senator who had loyally accepted our assurance that the matter must be kept a secret from him. Now he was President and Commander-in-Chief, and the final responsibility in this, as in so many other matters, must be his. President Truman accepted this responsibility with the same fine spirit that Senator Truman had shown before in accepting our refusal to inform him.

I discussed with him the whole history of the project. We had with us General Groves, who explained in detail the progress which had been made and the probable future course of the work. I also discussed with President Truman the broader aspects of the subject, and the memorandum which I used in this discussion is again a fair sample of the state of our thinking at the time.

MEMORANDUM DISCUSSED WITH PRESIDENT TRUMAN
APRIL 25, 1945

1. Within four months we shall in all probability have completed the most terrible weapon ever known in human history, one bomb of which could destroy a whole city.

2. Although we have shared its development with the U.K., physically the U.S. is at present in the position of controlling the resources with which to construct and use it and no other nation could reach this position for some years.

3. Nevertheless it is practically certain that we could not remain in this position indefinitely.

> *a. Various segments of its discovery and production are widely known among many scientists in many countries, although few scientists are now acquainted with the whole process which we have developed.*
>
> *b. Although its construction under present methods requires great scientific and industrial effort and raw materials, which are temporarily mainly within the possession and knowledge of U.S. and*

U.K., *it is extremely probable that much easier and cheaper methods of production will be discovered by scientists in the future, together with the use of materials of much wider distribution. As a result, it is extremely probable that the future will make it possible for atomic bombs to be constructed by smaller nations or even groups, or at least by a larger nation in a much shorter time.*

4. As a result, it is indicated that the future may see a time when such a weapon may be constructed in secret and used suddenly and effectively with devastating power by a willful nation or group against an unsuspecting nation or group of much greater size and material power. With its aid even a very powerful unsuspecting nation might be conquered within a very few days by a very much smaller one. . . .[1]

5. The world in its present state of moral advancement compared with its technical development would be eventually at the mercy of such a weapon. In other words, modern civilization might be completely destroyed.

6. To approach any world peace organization of any pattern now likely to be considered, without an appreciation by the leaders of our country of the power of this new weapon, would seem to be unrealistic. No system of control heretofore considered would be adequate to control this menace. Both inside any particular country and between the nations of the world, the control of this weapon will undoubtedly be a matter of the greatest difficulty and would involve such thoroughgoing rights of inspection and internal controls as we have never heretofore contemplated.

7. Furthermore, in the light of our present position with reference to this weapon, the question of sharing it with other nations and, if so shared, upon what terms, becomes a primary question of our foreign relations. Also our leadership in the war and in the development of this weapon has placed a certain moral responsibility upon us which we cannot shirk without very serious responsibility for any disaster to civilization which it would further.

8. On the other hand, if the problem of the proper use of this weapon can be solved, we would have the opportunity to bring the world into a pattern in which the peace of the world and our civilization can be saved.

9. As stated in General Groves' report, steps are under way looking towards the establishment of a select committee of particular qualifica-tations for recommending action to the executive and legislative branches of our government when secrecy is no longer in full effect. The committee would also recommend the actions to be taken by the War Department prior to that time in anticipation of the postwar problems. All recommendations would of course be first submitted to the President.

1. A brief reference to the estimated capabilities of other nations is here omitted; it in no way affects the course of the argument.

The next step in our preparations was the appointment of the committee referred to in paragraph (9) above. This committee, which was known as the Interim Committee, was charged with the function of advising the President on the various questions raised by our apparently imminent success in developing an atomic weapon. I was its chairman, but the principal labor of guiding its extended deliberations fell to George L. Harrison, who acted as chairman in my absence. It will be useful to consider the work of the committee in some detail. Its members were the following, in addition to Mr. Harrison and myself:

James F. Byrnes (then a private citizen) as personal representative of the President.

Ralph A. Bard, Under Secretary of the Navy.

William L. Clayton, Assistant Secretary of State.

Dr. Vannevar Bush, Director, Office of Scientific Research and Development, and president of the Carnegie Institution of Washington.

Dr. Karl T. Compton, Chief of the Office of Field Service in the Office of Scientific Research and Development, and president of the Massachusetts Institute of Technology.

Dr. James B. Conant, Chairman of the National Defense Research Committee, and president of Harvard University.

The discussions of the committee ranged over the whole field of atomic energy, in its political, military, and scientific aspects. That part of its work which particularly concerns us here relates to its recommendations for the use of atomic energy against Japan, but it should be borne in mind that these recommendations were not made in a vacuum. The committee's work included the drafting of the statements which were published immediately after the first bombs were dropped, the drafting of a bill for the domestic control of atomic energy, and recommendations looking toward the international control of atomic energy. The Interim Committee was assisted in its work by a Scientific Panel whose members were the following: Dr. A. H. Compton, Dr. Enrico Fermi, Dr. E. O. Lawrence, and Dr. J. R. Oppenheimer. All four were nuclear physicists of the first rank; all four had held positions of great importance in the atomic project from its inception At a meeting with the Interim Committee and the Scientific Panel on May 31, 1945, I urged all those present to feel free to express themselves on any phase of the subject, scientific or political. Both General Marshall and I at this meeting expressed the view that atomic energy could not be considered simply in terms of military weapons but must also be considered in terms of a new relationship of man to the universe.

On June 1, after its discussions with the Scientific Panel, the Interim Committee unanimously adopted the following recommendations:

(1) The bomb should be used against Japan as soon as possible;

(2) It should be used on a dual target—that is, a military installation or war plant surrounded by or adjacent to houses and other buildings most susceptible to damage; and

(3) It should be used without prior warning [of the nature of the weapon].

One member of the committee, Mr. Bard, later changed his view and dissented from recommendation (3).

In reaching these conclusions, the Interim Committee carefully considered such alternatives as a detailed advance warning or a demonstration in some uninhabited area. Both of these suggestions were discarded as impractical. They were not regarded as likely to be effective in compelling a surrender of Japan, and both of them involved serious risks. Even the New Mexico test would not give final proof that any given bomb was certain to explode when dropped from an airplane. Quite apart from the generally unfamiliar nature of atomic explosives, there was the whole problem of exploding a bomb at a predetermined height in the air by a complicated mechanism which could not be tested in the static test of New Mexico. Nothing would have been more damaging to our effort to obtain surrender than a warning or a demonstration followed by a dud—and this was a real possibility. Furthermore, we had no bombs to waste. It was vital that a sufficient effect be quickly obtained with the few we had.

The Interim Committee and the Scientific Panel also served as a channel through which suggestions from other scientists working on the atomic project were forwarded to me and to the President. Among the suggestions thus forwarded was one memorandum which questioned using the bomb at all against the enemy. On June 16, 1945, after consideration of that memorandum, the Scientific Panel made a report, from which I quote the following paragraphs:

> The opinions of our scientific colleagues on the initial use of these weapons are not unanimous: they range from the proposal of a purely technical demonstration to that of the military application best designed to induce surrender. Those who advocate a purely technical demonstration would wish to outlaw the use of atomic weapons, and have feared that if we use the weapons now our position in future negotiations will be prejudiced. Others emphasize the opportunity of saving American lives by immediate military use, and believe that such use will improve the international prospects, in that they are more concerned with the prevention of war than with the elimination of this special weapon. We find ourselves closer to these latter views; *we can propose no technical demonstration likely to bring an end to the war; we see no acceptable alternative to direct military use* [italics mine].

With regard to these general aspects of the use of atomic energy, it is clear that we, as scientific men, have no proprietary rights. It is true that we are among the few citizens who have had occasion to give thoughtful consideration to these problems during the past few years. We have, however, no claim to special competence in solving the political, social, and military problems which are presented by the advent of atomic power.

The foregoing discussion presents the reasoning of the Interim Committee and its advisers. I have discussed the work of these gentlemen at length in order to make it clear that we sought the best advice that we could find. The committee's function was, of course, entirely advisory. The ultimate responsibility for the recommendation to the President rested upon me, and I have no desire to veil it. The conclusions of the committee were similar to my own, although I reached mine independently. I felt that to extract a genuine surrender from the Emperor and his military advisers, they must be administered a tremendous shock which would carry convincing proof of our power to destroy the Empire. Such an effective shock would save many times the number of lives, both American and Japanese, that it would cost.

The facts upon which my reasoning was based and steps taken to carry it out now follow.

U.S. Policy Toward Japan in July 1945

The principal political, social, and military objective of the United States in the summer of 1945 was the prompt and complete surrender of Japan. Only the complete destruction of her military power could open the way to lasting peace.

Japan, in July 1945, had been seriously weakened by our increasingly violent attacks. It was known to us that she had gone so far as to make tentative proposals to the Soviet government, hoping to use the Russians as mediators in a negotiated peace. These vague proposals contemplated the retention by Japan of important conquered areas and were therefore not considered seriously. There was as yet no indication of any weakening in the Japanese determination to fight rather than accept unconditional surrender. If she should persist in her fight to the end, she had still a great military force.

In the middle of July 1945, the intelligence section of the War Department General Staff estimated Japanese military strength as follows: in the home islands, slightly under 2,000,000; in Korea, Manchuria, China proper, and Formosa, slightly over 2,000,000; in French Indo-China, Thailand, and Burma, over 200,000; in the East Indies area, including the Philippines, over 500,000; in the by-passed Pacific islands, over 100,-000. The total strength of the Japanese Army was estimated at about

5,000,000 men. These estimates later proved to be in very close agreement with official Japanese figures.

The Japanese Army was in much better condition than the Japanese Navy and Air Force. The Navy had practically ceased to exist except as a harrying force against an invasion fleet. The Air Force had been reduced mainly to reliance upon Kamikaze, or suicide, attacks. These latter, however, had already inflicted serious damage on our seagoing forces, and their possible effectiveness in a last-ditch fight was a matter of real concern to our naval leaders.

As we understood it in July, there was a very strong possibility that the Japanese government might determine upon resistance to the end, in all the areas of the Far East under its control. In such an event, the Allies would be faced with the enormous task of destroying an armed force of five million men and five thousand suicide aircraft, belonging to a race which had already amply demonstrated its ability to fight literally to the death.

The strategic plans of our armed forces for the defeat of Japan, as they stood in July, had been prepared without reliance upon the atomic bomb, which had not yet been tested in New Mexico. We were planning an intensified sea and air blockade, and greatly intensified strategic air bombing, through the summer and early fall, to be followed on November 1 by an invasion of the southern island of Kyushu. This would be followed in turn by an invasion of the main island of Honshu in the spring of 1946. The total U.S. military and naval force involved in this grand design was of the order of 5,000,000 men; if all those indirectly concerned are included, it was larger still.

We estimated that if we should be forced to carry this plan to its conclusion, the major fighting would not end until the latter part of 1946, at the earliest. I was informed that such operations might be expected to cost over a million casualties to American forces alone. Additional large losses might be expected among our Allies, and, of course, if our campaign were successful and if we could judge by previous experience, enemy casualties would be much larger than our own.

It was already clear in July that even before the invasion we should be able to inflict enormously severe damage on the Japanese homeland by the combined application of "conventional" sea and air power. The critical question was whether this kind of action would induce surrender. It therefore became necessary to consider very carefully the probable state of mind of the enemy, and to assess with accuracy the line of conduct which might end his will to resist.

With these considerations in mind, I wrote a memorandum for the President, on July 2, which I believe fairly represents the thinking of the American government as it finally took shape in action. This memorandum was prepared after discussion and general agreement with Joseph C. Grew, Acting Secretary of State, and Secretary of the Navy Forrestal, and when I discussed it with the President, he expressed his general approval.

July 2, 1945

Memorandum for the President.

PROPOSED PROGRAM FOR JAPAN

1. The plans of operation up to and including the first landing have been authorized and the preparations for the operation are now actually going on. This situation was accepted by all members of your conference on Monday, June 18.

2. There is reason to believe that the operation for the occupation of Japan following the landing may be a very long, costly, and arduous struggle on our part. The terrain, much of which I have visited several times, has left the impression on my memory of being one which would be susceptible to a last-ditch defense such as has been made on Iwo Jima and Okinawa and which of course is very much larger than either of those two areas. According to my recollection it will be much more unfavorable with regard to tank maneuvering than either the Philippines or Germany.

3. If we once land on one of the main islands and begin a forceful occupation of Japan, we shall probably have cast the die of last-ditch resistance. The Japanese are highly patriotic and certainly susceptible to calls for fanatical resistance to repel an invasion. Once started in actual invasion, we shall in my opinion have to go through with an even more bitter finish fight than in Germany. We shall incur the losses incident to such a war and we shall have to leave the Japanese islands even more thoroughly destroyed than was the case with Germany. This would be due both to the difference in the Japanese and German personal character and the differences in the size and character of the terrain through which the operations will take place.

4. A question then comes: Is there any alternative to such a forceful occupation of Japan which will secure for us the equivalent of an unconditional surrender of her forces and a permanent destruction of her power again to strike an aggressive blow at the "peace of the Pacific"? I am inclined to think that there is enough such chance to make it well worthwhile our giving them a warning of what is to come and a definite opportunity to capitulate. As above suggested, it should be tried before the actual forceful occupation of the homeland islands is begun and furthermore the warning should be given in ample time to permit a national reaction to set in.

We have the following enormously favorable factors on our side—factors much weightier than those we had against Germany:

Japan has no allies.

Her navy is nearly destroyed and she is vulnerable to a surface and underwater blockade which can deprive her of sufficient food and supplies for her population.

She is terribly vulnerable to our concentrated air attack upon her crowded cities, industrial and food resources.

She has against her not only the Anglo-American forces but the rising forces of China and the ominous threat of Russia.

We have inexhaustible and untouched industrial resources to bring to bear against her diminishing potential.

We have great moral superiority through being the victim of her first sneak attack.

The problem is to translate these advantages into prompt and economical achievement of our objectives. I believe Japan is susceptible to reason in such a crisis to a much greater extent than is indicated by our current press and other current comment. Japan is not a nation-composed wholly of mad fanatics of an entirely different mentality from ours. On the contrary, she has within the past century shown herself to possess extremely intelligent people capable in an unprecedentedly short time of adopting not only the complicated technique of Occidental civilization but to a substantial extent its culture and its political and social ideas. Her advance in all these respects during the short period of sixty or seventy years has been one of the most astounding feats of national progress in history—a leap from the isolated feudalism of centuries into the position of one of the six or seven great powers of the world. She has not only built up powerful armies and navies. She has maintained an honest and effective national finance and respected position in many of the sciences in which we pride ourselves. Prior to the forcible seizure of power over her government by the fanatical military group in 1931, she had for ten years lived a reasonably responsible and respectable international life.

My own opinion is in her favor on the two points involved in this question:

> *a. I think the Japanese nation has the mental intelligence and versatile capacity in such a crisis to recognize the folly of a fight to the finish and to accept the proffer of what will amount to an unconditional surrender; and*

> *b. I think she has within her population enough liberal leaders (although now submerged by the terrorists) to be depended upon for her reconstruction as a responsible member of the family of nations. I think she is better in this last respect than Germany*

*was. Her liberals yielded only at the point of the pistol and, so
far as I am aware, their liberal attitude has not been personally
subverted in the way which was so general in Germany.*

*On the other hand, I think that the attempt to exterminate her armies
and her population by gunfire or other means will tend to produce a
fusion of race solidity and antipathy which has no analogy in the case
of Germany. We have a national interest in creating, if possible, a
condition wherein the Japanese nation may live as a peaceful and useful
member of the future Pacific community.*

*5. It is therefore my conclusion that a carefully timed warning be
given to Japan by the chief representatives of the United States, Great
Britain, China, and, if then a belligerent, Russia by calling upon Japan
to surrender and permit the occupation of her country in order to insure
its complete demilitarization for the sake of the future peace.*

This warning should contain the following elements:

*The varied and overwhelming character of the force we are
about to bring to bear on the islands.*

*The inevitability and completeness of the destruction which the
full application of this force will entail.*

*The determination of the Allies to destroy permanently all
authority and influence of those who have deceived and misled the
country into embarking on world conquest.*

*The determination of the Allies to limit Japanese sovereignty
to her main islands and to render them powerless to mount and
support another war.*

*The disavowal of any attempt to extirpate the Japanese as a
race or to destroy them as a nation.*

*A statement of our readiness, once her economy is purged of
its militaristic influence, to permit the Japanese to maintain such
industries, particularly of a light consumer character, as offer no
threat of aggression against their neighbors, but which can produce
a sustaining economy, and provide a reasonable standard of living.
The statement should indicate our willingness, for this purpose, to
give Japan trade access to external raw materials, but no longer
any control over the sources of supply outside her main islands.
It should also indicate our willingness, in accordance with our
now established foreign trade policy, in due course to enter into
mutually advantageous trade relations with her.*

*The withdrawal from their country as soon as the above objec-
tives of the Allies are accomplished, and as soon as there has
been established a peacefully inclined government, of a character
representative of the masses of the Japanese people. I personally
think that if in saying this we should add that we do not exclude*

a constitutional monarchy under her present dynasty, it would substantially add to the chances of acceptance.

6. *Success of course will depend on the potency of the warning which we give her. She has an extremely sensitive national pride and, as we are now seeing every day, when actually locked with the enemy will fight to the very death. For that reason the warning must be tendered before the actual invasion has occurred and while the impending destruction, though clear beyond peradventure, has not yet reduced her to fanatical despair. If Russia is a part of the threat, the Russian attack, if actual, must not have progressed too far. Our own bombing should be confined to military objectives as far as possible.*

It is important to emphasize the double character of the suggested warning. It was designed to promise destruction if Japan resisted, and hope, if she surrendered.

It will be noted that the atomic bomb is not mentioned in this memorandum. On grounds of secrecy the bomb was never mentioned except when absolutely necessary, and furthermore, it had not yet been tested. It was, of course, well forward in our minds, as the memorandum was written and discussed, that the bomb would be the best possible sanction if our warning were rejected.

The Use of the Bomb

The adoption of the policy outlined in the memorandum of July 2 was a decision of high politics; once it was accepted by the President, the position of the atomic bomb in our planning became quite clear. I find that I stated in my diary, as early as June 19, that "the last chance warning . . . must be given before an actual landing of the ground forces in Japan, and fortunately the plans provide for enough time to bring in the sanctions to our warning in the shape of heavy ordinary bombing attack and an attack of S-1." S-1 was a code name for the atomic bomb.

There was much discussion in Washington about the timing of the warning to Japan. The controlling factor in the end was the date already set for the Potsdam meeting of the Big Three. It was President Truman's decision that such a warning should be solemnly issued by the U.S. and the U.K. from this meeting, with the concurrence of the head of the Chinese government, so that it would be plain that *all* of Japan's principal enemies were in entire unity. This was done in the Potsdam ultimatum of July 26, which very closely followed the above memorandum of July 2, with the exception that it made no mention of the Japanese Emperor.

On July 28, the Premier of Japan, Suzuki, rejected the Potsdam ultimatum by announcing that it was "unworthy of public notice." In the face of this rejection we could only proceed to demonstrate that the ultimatum had meant exactly what it said when it stated that if the Japanese continued the war, "the full application of our military power, backed by our resolve, will mean the inevitable and complete destruction of the Japanese armed forces and just as inevitably the utter devastation of the Japanese homeland."

For such a purpose, the atomic bomb was an eminently suitable weapon. The New Mexico test occurred while we were at Potsdam, on July 16. It was immediately clear that the power of the bomb measured up to our highest estimates. We had developed a weapon of such a revolutionary character that its use against the enemy might well be expected to produce exactly the kind of shock on the Japanese ruling oligarchy which we desired, strengthening the position of those who wished peace, and weakening that of the military party.

Because of the importance of the atomic mission against Japan, the detailed plans were brought to me by the military staff for approval. With President Truman's warm support, I struck off the list of suggested targets the city of Kyoto. Although it was a target of considerable military importance, it had been the ancient capital of Japan and was a shrine of Japanese art and culture. We determined that it should be spared. I approved four other targets, including the cities of Hiroshima and Nagasaki.

Hiroshima was bombed on August 6 and Nagasaki on August 9. These two cities were active working parts of the Japanese war effort. One was an army center, the other was naval and industrial. Hiroshima was the headquarters of the Japanese Army defending southern Japan and was a major military storage and assembly point. Nagasaki was a major seaport, and it contained several large industrial plants of great wartime importance. We believed that our attacks had struck cities which must certainly be important to the Japanese military leaders, both Army and Navy, and we waited for a result. We waited one day.

Many accounts have been written about the Japanese surrender. After a prolonged Japanese cabinet session in which the deadlock was broken by the Emperor himself, the offer to surrender was made on August 10. It was based on the Potsdam terms, with a reservation concerning the sovereignty of the Emperor. While the Allied reply made no promises other than those already given, it implicitly recognized the Emperor's position by prescribing that his power must be subject to the orders of the Allied Supreme Commander. These terms were accepted on August 14 by the Japanese, and the instrument of surrender was formally signed on September 2, in Tokyo Bay. Our great objective was thus achieved, and all the evidence I have seen indicates that the controlling factor in the final Japanese decision to accept our terms of surrender was the atomic bomb.[2]

The two atomic bombs which we had dropped were the only ones we had ready, and our rate of production at the time was very small. Had the war continued until the projected invasion on November 1, additional fire raids of B-29's would have been more destructive of life and property than the very limited number of atomic raids which we could have executed in the same period. But the atomic bomb was more than a weapon of terrible destruction; it was a psychological weapon. In March 1945, our Air Force had launched its first great incendiary raid on the Tokyo area. In this raid more damage was done and more casualties were inflicted than was the case at Hiroshima. Hundreds of bombers took part and hundreds of tons of incendiaries were dropped. Similar successive raids burned out a great part of the urban area of Japan, but the Japanese fought on. On August 6, one B-29 dropped a single atomic bomb on Hiroshima. Three days later a second bomb was dropped on Nagasaki, and the war was over. So far as the Japanese could know, our ability to execute atomic attacks, if necessary by many planes at a time, was unlimited. As Dr. Karl Compton has said, "It was not one atomic bomb, or two, which brought surrender; it was the experience of what an atomic bomb will actually do to a community, *plus the dead of many more,* that was effective."

The bomb thus served exactly the purpose we intended. The peace party was able to take the path of surrender, and the whole weight of the Emperor's prestige was exerted in favor of peace. When the Emperor ordered surrender, and the small but dangerous group of fanatics who opposed him were brought under control, the Japanese became so subdued that the great undertaking of occupation and disarmament was completed with unprecedented ease.

A Personal Summary

In the foregoing pages I have tried to give an accurate account of my own personal observations of the circumstances which led up to the use of the atomic bomb and the reasons which underlay our use of it. To me they have always seemed compelling and clear, and I cannot see how any person vested with such responsibilities as mine could have taken any other course or given any other advice to his chiefs.

Two great nations were approaching contact in a fight to a finish which would begin on November 1, 1945. Our enemy, Japan, com-

2. Report of United States Strategic Bombing Survey, "Japan's Struggle to End the War"; "If the Atomic Bomb Had Not Been Used," by K. T. Compton, *Atlantic Monthly,* December 1946; unpublished material of historical division, War Department Special Staff, June 1946.

manded forces of somewhat over 5,000,000 armed men. Men of these armies had already inflicted upon us, in our breakthrough of the outer perimeter of their defenses, over 300,000 battle casualties. Enemy armies still unbeaten had the strength to cost us a million more. *As long as the Japanese government refused to surrender,* we should be forced to take and hold the ground, and smash the Japanese ground armies, by close-in fighting of the same desperate and costly kind that we had faced in the Pacific islands for nearly four years.

In the light of the formidable problem which thus confronted us, I felt that every possible step should be taken to compel a surrender of the homelands, and a withdrawal of all Japanese troops from the Asiatic mainland and from other positions, before we had commenced an invasion. We held two cards to assist us in such an effort. One was the traditional veneration in which the Japanese Emperor was held by his subjects and the power which was thus vested in him over his loyal troops. It was for this reason that I suggested in my memorandum of July 2 that his dynasty should be continued. The second card was the use of the atomic bomb in the manner best calculated to persuade that Emperor and the counselors about him to submit to our demand for what was essentially unconditional surrender, placing his immense power over his people and his troops subject to our orders.

In order to end the war in the shortest possible time and to avoid the enormous losses of human life which otherwise confronted us, I felt that we must use the Emperor as our instrument to command and compel his people to cease fighting and subject themselves to our authority through him, and that to accomplish this we must give him and his controlling advisers a compelling reason to accede to our demands. This reason furthermore must be of such a nature that his people could understand his decision. The bomb seemed to me to furnish a unique instrument for that purpose.

My chief purpose was to end the war in victory with the least possible cost in the lives of the men in the armies which I had helped to raise. In the light of the alternatives which, on a fair estimate, were open to us, I believe that no man, in our position and subject to our responsibilities, holding in his hands a weapon of such possibilities for accomplishing this purpose and saving those lives, could have failed to use it and afterwards looked his countrymen in the face.

As I read over what I have written, I am aware that much of it, in this year of peace, may have a harsh and unfeeling sound. It would perhaps be possible to say the same things and say them more gently. But I do not think it would be wise. As I look back over the five years of my service as Secretary of War, I see too many stern and heartrending decisions to be willing to pretend that war is anything else than what it is. The face of war is the face of death; death is an inevitable part of every order that a wartime leader gives. The decision to use the atomic bomb was a decision that brought death to over a hundred thousand Japanese. No explanation can change that fact and I do not wish to gloss it over. But this deliberate, premeditated destruction was our least abhorrent choice. The destruction of Hiroshima and Nagasaki put an end to the Japanese war. It stopped the fire raids, and the strangling blockade; it ended the ghastly specter of a clash of great land armies.

In this last great action of the Second World War, we were given final proof that war is death. War in the twentieth century has grown steadily more barbarous, more destructive, more debased in all its aspects. Now, with the release of atomic energy, man's ability to destroy himself is very nearly complete. The bombs dropped on Hiroshima and Nagasaki ended a war. They also made it wholly clear that we must never have another war. This is the lesson men and leaders everywhere must learn, and I believe that when they learn it they will find a way to lasting peace. There is no other choice.

WILLIAM APPLEMAN WILLIAMS

A New Vision
of American Omnipotence

*A growing number of historians have challenged the prevailing
justification for the use of the atomic bomb. Disturbed by evidence
that Japan would probably have surrendered without the attacks
on Hiroshima and Nagasaki, they have explored the possibility that
postwar political considerations, not overpowering military needs,
influenced the Truman administration. They couple the decision
to use the bomb with the breakup of the Grand Alliance in the
spring of 1945, and suggest that Truman and his advisers were
intent on demonstrating the awesome new weapon in order to
force the Soviet Union into a more compliant mood. The crucial
confrontation, according to this view, came at Potsdam, the final
summit conference of the war which convened just after the first
successful atomic explosion at Alamogordo on July 16.*

*William A. Williams explores the relationship between the
atomic bomb and Truman's diplomacy at Potsdam in this selection,
taken from Chapter Six of* The Tragedy of American Diplomacy
*(2nd ed., New York, 1962). In using the term "Open Door,"
Professor Williams has in mind a broader concept than the traditional American policy in China. He conceives of the Open Door
policy as a conscious American strategy to "establish the conditions
under which predominant American economic power would extend
the American system throughout the world without the embarrass-
ment and inefficiency of traditional colonialism." Gar Alperovitz,
"The Trump Card,"* New York Review of Books, *VIII (June 15,
1967), 6–12, is an important restatement of the "atomic blackmail" thesis.*

FOLLOWING UPON President Roosevelt's clear expression of a desire
to retain "complete freedom of action," the United States Government
under President Truman initiated and sustained a vigorous drive to
undercut the Stalin-Churchill agreement of October 1944, concerning
eastern Europe, and to replace it with the Open Door Policy. Churchill
supported that determined effort to subvert the understanding which

Reprinted by permission from William Appleman Williams, *The Tragedy of
American Diplomacy* (2nd ed., New York, 1962), pp. 244–257.

he himself had originally and voluntarily written out and pushed across the table to Stalin. Truman and Churchill undertook that course, moreover, in the full knowledge and open acknowledgment that Stalin had honored his part of the bargain in Greece.

This insistence upon applying the Open Door Policy to eastern Europe (and, of course, to Asia) was decided upon before anyone knew for sure that the atomic bomb would work.[1] Along with the feeling among American policy-makers that Russia's war-caused weakness would enable them to secure major concessions from Moscow, that consideration must be kept constantly in mind when following the sequence of events after the defeat of Germany. The success of the bomb strengthened an existing attitude and a traditional strategy—it did not call forth a new approach.

Stimson's diary entry covering a conversation with Truman on June 6, 1945, indicates that American leaders were conscious of the relationship between the bomb and their general strategy at an early date. Truman "said that he had been thinking of that," Stimson noted, "and mentioned the same things that I was thinking of, namely the settlement of the Polish, Rumanian, Yugoslavian, and Manchurian problems." By the end of the month, in preparation for the Potsdam Conference, the American position concerning the countries of eastern Europe had become clear and firm. The United States planned "to insist on the re-organization of the present governments or the holding of free general elections." The broad objective was phrased in the classic terms of the Open Door Policy: "To permit American nationals to enter, move about freely and carry on commercial and government operations un-molested in the countries in question."

The goal was "access, on equal terms, to such trade, raw materials and industry" as existed and developed. In the meantime, such access was sought "to modify existing arrangements." As part of that general effort, American officials planned to demand unrestricted movement for American newspapermen so that "the spotlight [can be] trained on these areas." And finally, the United States emphasized the specific objective

1. This account of the Potsdam and London conferences, which took place between July and November 1945, is based upon a wide selection of primary and secondary materials. The reader without recourse to manuscript collections can find the main elements of the story, and most of the quotations used here, in these published volumes: J. F. Byrnes, *Speaking Frankly* and *All in One Lifetime* (New York: Harper and Bros., 1947 and 1958); W. S. Churchill, *Triumph and Tragedy* (Boston: Houghton Mifflin, 1953); H. L. Stimson and M. Bundy, *On Active Service in Peace and War* (New York: Harper & Bros., 1948); *Memoirs by Harry S. Truman* (Garden City, N.Y.: Doubleday, 1955–56); and the most illuminating two volumes, *Foreign Relations: The Conference of Berlin (The Potsdam Conference), 1945* (Washington: Gvt. Printing Office, 1960), which also print revealing excerpts from Stimson's Diary.

of internationalizing the commercial waterways of the Danube River system with a Western majority on the board of control.

Similar stress was laid on guaranteeing the Open Door Policy in Asia. American leaders seem to have entertained a particularly vivid hope that the defeat of Japan would turn the clock back to 1903–1904, a maneuver that would enable the United States to step back on the mainland of Asia at the moment of its greatest success in Manchuria with the expectation that this time it would not be frustrated as before. The Russians posed the only danger to this idyllic picture. On the eve of the first general session at Potsdam, for example, Stimson seems to have set himself the role of special tutor to Truman and Byrnes on the importance of the Open Door Policy in the Far East. Even though the lessons had apparently been going on for some time, Stimson saw Truman again on July 14, 1945. "[I] went over [it] with him carefully," Stimson wrote in his diary, "again and again warning him to be absolutely sure that the Russians did not block off our trade."

Still concerned, Stimson wrote the President a special letter on July 16. Concentrating on "our clear and growing interests in the Orient," the Secretary all but hammered the words through the page in the course of his pounding on the crucial importance of the Open Door Policy. Ideally, of course, Russia should not have anything to say about handling Japan or the general problems of the Far East. At most, and only if it became absolutely necessary in the face of Soviet complaints, some kind of "token occupation" would be arranged.

Stimson next had a briefing session with Byrnes on July 17. The subject had not changed. Neither had the dedication of the tutor. "I impressed on him," Stimson recorded, "the importance of the Open Door Policy." A series of special reports made the same point. Harriman, for example, prepared one which placed—even in that context—a noticeable emphasis on "the development of commerce and trade of the United States." Perhaps his service as an artillery officer in World War I had inured him to such bombardments, for Truman seemed never to blink at the hammering on the same point. Obviously pleased, Stimson reported on July 18, 1945, that the President "was confident of sustaining the Open Door Policy."

Stalin arrived in Potsdam with a noticeably different set of priorities. He was still concerned about Russia's frontiers in Europe, about preventing Germany from trying it all over in another 25 years, and about a major economic transfusion for the Soviet Union's battered economy. Apparently shrewd enough to realize that he had but little chance to obtain a large loan from the United States, and in any event unable to plan on that basis in the summer of 1945, Stalin laid immediate and heavy emphasis on being treated as an equal and upon obtaining massive reparations from Germany and its former allies.

"This Council," Stalin remarked in explaining the Soviet view of the conference at its first general session, "will deal with reparations and will give an indication of the day when the Peace Conference should meet." The primary political issue, he continued, was that of dealing with Germany and its former allies. That was "high policy. The purpose of such a policy was to separate these countries from Germany as a great force." Recurring often to the "many difficulties and sacrifices" brought upon Russia by those Axis partners, Stalin argued that the proper strategy was "to detach them once and for all from Germany." As for reparations, Russia would if necessary "compel" such deliveries.

The American response on reparations was crucial to the outcome of the Potsdam Conference, and also, very probably, to the whole course of subsequent events. "Reparations," Byrnes told Molotov on July 20, "do not seem to the United States to be an immediate problem." He then added that "the United States does not intend to make advances to any country in order that reparations may be paid by them." "We do not intend, as we did after the last war, to provide the money for the payment of reparations." The full significance of those remarks by Byrnes cannot be grasped without understanding both the background of each of them, and the interrelationship between them. It seems wise, therefore, to discuss them separately before putting them together.

First of all, and as revealed in Byrnes's remark about loans, American policy-makers had misread the history of their experience with reparations after World War I. They concluded that American loans to Germany had simply ended up as reparations to England and France, who themselves had not repaid their debts to the United States. In the American view, therefore, the United States had been twice played the fool. The vigorous assertion by Byrnes reflected a determination not to fall into the same trap still another time.

That reaction was based on a seriously distorted interpretation of the World War I experience. It neglected, on the one hand, the creative role of American loans and the harmful effects of having actually collected money from England and France. On the other hand, and regardless of the estimate made of those and similar factors, the World War I situation blinded American leaders to the vastly different one that existed at the end of World War II. It was not so much that they had learned no lesson from history but rather that they had become almost obsessed with the wrong lesson.

The real point was that the capital for reconstruction at the end of World War II had to come from some place. Alternative sources were available. Either it could come from the United States under more relevant conditions and terms than had been arranged at the end of World War I, or it could come in the form of reparations taken by Russia—reparations which could be stopped only by recourse to another war. American policy-makers had used history to block their view of the present.

In order to avoid the second alternative, American leaders would obviously have had to negotiate a loan to Russia in conjunction with their discussion and settlement of other issues. But that approach was never even initiated, let alone put into sustained operation. The contradiction involved can be explained, however, by reference to the atom bomb. *Byrnes knew, when he told Molotov on July 20 that reparations were not "an immediate problem," that the atom bomb was a success.* The first news reached Potsdam on July 18. And as Stimson noted in his diary, Truman and other American leaders were "highly delighted" and "very greatly reinforced." It seems very likely, therefore, that the information on the bomb (even though the first dispatches were not complete accounts) served to convince the United States that it could hold the line on reparations and bargain from a position of formidable power.

But this reaction actually served, in a deeply ironic way, to close both the intellectual and the psychological jaws of the trap that American policy-makers had set for themselves. For in fact it left the United States with no moderate, flexible policy. It hardened both the feeling that the Russians would have to come to terms and the reading of history to the point that no loans should be granted if they would end up as reparations. That attitude left the United States with no choice but to acquiesce or use the bomb if the Russians refused to give way and accept American conditions for economic aid.

The extent to which this analysis explains American policy can be seen by the response to further news about the bomb test. Truman had already indicated, in a private conference with Churchill, that he was very favorably inclined toward the old Roosevelt idea of an Anglo-American entente. He was also aware of the understanding between Churchill and Roosevelt of September 18, 1944, concerning the bomb: "The suggestion that the world should be informed . . . with a view to an international agreement regarding its control and use," the two had agreed, "is not accepted."

Churchill seems to have insinuated in his masterful way that the secret might be kept from Stalin. This was by no means a novel idea. It had, after all, been kept from him up to that point. And Stimson records that he and others were very "doubtful" about sharing the news of the test bomb. However it evolved, and Truman appears to have refused to consider saying nothing to the Russians, the final compromise was to tell Stalin in a brief, casual way that the United States had developed a new weapon. Much has been made of the fact that Stalin already knew about the bomb through espionage. That is of course true, but he probably learned more of direct importance in observing how the news of the successful test firing affected the attitude and manner of Truman and Byrnes at the next session of the Potsdam Conference.

Stimson reports that Truman was "immensely pleased" and "tremendously pepped up by it." The President "said it gave him an entirely new feeling of confidence." This change is apparent even in reading the third-person stenographic account of the meeting with Stalin on July 21, 1945. One of the first questions to arise concerned the governments in eastern Europe, and this is the official account.

> PRESIDENT TRUMAN: The American Government was unable to recognize the governments of the other satellite countries [besides Italy]. When these countries were established on a proper basis, the United States would recognize them and not before. The President stated that the meeting would proceed and that this question would be passed over.

After he returned to England, Churchill told the House of Commons that "we possessed powers which were irresistible." His comments to Stimson at the time, in Potsdam, are perhaps even more revealing. "He [Truman] stood up to the Russians in a most emphatic and decisive manner, telling them as to certain demands that they absolutely could not have and that the United States was entirely against them. . . . He told the Russians just where they got off and generally bossed the whole meeting."

Truman bossed the meeting but he did not change American policy on reparations. That oversight served to subvert the power of the bomb. An astute American observer warned on the next day, July 22, that the Russian position on reparations should not be discounted. It was backed by "intense popular feeling and fresh experience." But the old block against loans, when combined with the new vision of omnipotence, led the United States into a dead end. In order to avoid financing Russian reparations through loans to Germany, Italy, or other former Axis partners, and with the myopic confidence induced by the news of the bomb, Byrnes proposed to Molotov on July 23 that "each country tak[e] reparations from its own zone."

Now the fascinating thing is that the Russians fought that proposal for one whole week—from July 23 to July 31—before Stalin finally agreed to it. Even then, he remarked very sharply that it was "the opposite of liberal." [2]

Those two sentences have been set apart, and even further emphasized, for two reasons. First: the Byrnes offer to Molotov of July 23 clearly meant that the Russians would have a free hand in their zone of Germany and throughout eastern Europe. The freedom to

2. Italics added to the material quoted, as well as to my words.

control economics implied—demanded—political control. Assistant Secretary of State Clayton understood this point and commented on it with great perception in a memorandum of August 16, 1945, after the offer had been accepted by the Soviets. Although he was formally denying the point he was raising, the tone of his remarks needs no comment. "There appears to be," he noted ruefully, "an unfortunate tendency to interpret the reparations operating agreement as an indication of complete abandonment of four power treatment of Germany. This is not stated in the texts and should not be accepted as a necessary conclusion. . . ." But whether accepted or not, that was the meaning of the final arrangement.

To argue that the Russians did not understand the implications of the Byrnes offer of July 23 even though Clayton did is to argue that they were fools. To argue that they did understand it and still acted as they did is to argue that they played Byrnes and Truman and Stimson along for one entire week as a matter of private amusement. Those positions can be held and defended as viable explanations of Russian behavior. But the evidence indicates that the Russians very deeply wanted a firm commitment on reparations in the form of heavy industrial equipment from the restored production of the Ruhr Valley more than they wanted anything else. Such reparations would not only provide crucial help at home, but the agreement providing for them would be based on an Allied control of German industry that would in turn limit Germany's ability to start another war. Clayton himself, certainly as conservative and hard-headed an operator as the United States had produced, concluded in a memorandum of July 27, 1945, that this was the correct analysis. Molotov's behavior between July 23 and July 31 further supports that interpretation.

Molotov connected the issues of reparations and German war potential very simply: "The question of reparations was even more urgent because unless this was settled there could be no progress on economic matters" involving the future strength of German industry. Hence the Soviets wanted "clear replies to the questions." Byrnes gave them one by suddenly remarking that the United States now considered the Yalta figure of 10 billions for Russia to be "impractical." Molotov then shot back that the Soviets were "entitled to a clear answer" on what figure the United States did find acceptable. Failing to obtain one, Molotov then raised—very directly and without any frills—the central implication of the proposal that Byrnes had offered on July 23.

> MR. MOLOTOV: My understanding, Secretary Byrnes, is that you have in mind the proposal that each country should take reparations from its own zone. If we fail to reach an agreement the result will be the same. . . .

THE SECRETARY [BYRNES]: Yes. . . .

MR. MOLOTOV: said would not the Secretary's suggestion mean that each country would have a free hand in their own zone and would act entirely independently of the others?

THE SECRETARY [BYRNES]: said that was true in substance. . . .

In spite of those candid and revealing remarks by Byrnes, the Soviet Union nevertheless continued its efforts to reach an agreement involving all of Germany. Molotov was still "anxious" about the issue on June 29 and 30. He wanted "a fixed sum or quantity agreed upon," including materials from the Ruhr, because the Soviets feared "they would be left with very little equipment as reparations in spite of the fact that the Germans had destroyed Soviet industries. They needed agricultural machinery and [goods] to rehabilitate their railroads." They also wanted to settle what Stalin had on the first day of the conference referred to as the issue of "high policy"—preventing Germany from attacking Russia in another 25 years.

Finally, in the face of continued American refusal to discuss the issues in that related way, Stalin accepted the Byrnes proposal of July 23, 1945. He then extended it in a way that clearly foreshadowed the division of Europe. The specific issue involved the assignment of German assets in other European countries, but the discussion immediately picked up overtones of a far broader nature.

PREMIER STALIN: . . . with regard to shares and foreign investments, perhaps the demarcation lines between the Soviet and Western zones of occupation should be taken as the dividing lines and everything west of that line would go to the Allies and everything east of that line to the Russians.

THE PRESIDENT [TRUMAN] inquired if he meant a line running from the Baltic to the Adriatic.

PREMIER STALIN replied in the affirmative. . . .

[BRITISH FOREIGN SECRETARY] BEVIN said he agreed and asked if Greece would belong to Britain. . . .

PREMIER STALIN suggested that the Allies take Yugoslavia and Austria would be divided into zones. . . .

MR. BYRNES said he thought it was important to have a meeting of minds. Mr. Bevin's question was whether the Russians' claim was limited to the zone occupied by the Russian Army. To that he understood Mr. Stalin to say "yes." If that were so he was prepared to agree.

PREMIER STALIN replied in the affirmative. . . .

THE PRESIDENT [TRUMAN] said that he agreed with the Soviet proposal.

The American decision to give the Russians a free hand on reparations throughout eastern Europe can in the end be explained only in one of three ways. The first would be to assert that the United States knowingly handed eastern Europe over to the Soviet Union. This is absurd on the face of it. It is also belied by Truman's actions during the conference and by his blunt public remarks after the meeting was over. The eastern European countries, he announced on August 9, 1945, were "not to be spheres of influence of any one power." The Open Door Policy was thereby reaffirmed. A second explanation would be based on the idea that the United States made the reparations deal without understanding its political implications. But that interpretation is undercut by the analyses prepared by Clayton and other American officials who did see those possibilities.

The third explanation is supported by direct and indirect evidence. It is, simply, that the United States—confident in its vast economic and military superiority over Russia—made the reparations agreement to avoid any indirect financing of Soviet recovery. American leaders were certain that the bomb, and Russia's great recovery needs, provided them with the leverage to re-establish the Open Door, and pro-Western governments, in eastern Europe.

This vision of omnipotence was apparent in Truman's remarks of August 11, 1945. "We must constitute ourselves," he explained, "trustees of this new force to prevent its misuse." As for the possibility that the Soviets would construct their own bomb, Byrnes recalled that "no one seemed too alarmed at the prospect." But perhaps the best evidence of the American attitude came in connection with the use of the bomb against Japan. Byrnes later remarked that American leaders had eastern Europe as well as Asia in mind when they reached the decision to use the weapon as soon as possible.

That recollection is borne out by the evidence of the time. The decision to bomb Japan as quickly as possible was made during the Potsdam Conference, and at the very time of the toughest discussions about eastern Europe. In a very candid meeting on July 23, 1945, Truman, General George C. Marshall, Stimson, and others generally agreed that the Russians were no longer needed in the war against Japan. They also talked very directly of using the bomb before the Russians could enter that conflict. Actually, however, that was not a new approach. Stimson had recommended as early as July 2, 1945, that the bomb should be dropped at a time when "the Russian attack, if actual, must not have progressed too far." And once it had proved out in the test, Truman was "intensely pleased" with the chance of using it before the Russians even entered the war.

This sense of urgency about using the bomb makes it possible to advance beyond the question of whether the United States dropped the bomb to end the war against Japan, or whether it did so in order to check the Russians. The evidence provided by the government archives and private American leaders converges on one explanation: The United States dropped the bomb to end the war against Japan *and thereby stop the Russians in Asia, and to give them sober pause in eastern Europe.*

Once it was known to work, the atomic offensive against Japan could have been delayed as much as a month or six weeks—if all that had been at stake was the saving of American lives which might be lost in the invasion of Kyushu that was projected for the fall. By that time, for example, the United States would have had a small arsenal of the weapons, so that it would have made little difference if the first drop during a demonstration had misfired or otherwise failed. As for the saving of lives, they would still have been spared by using the weapon in September. But the bomb had to be used quickly, and if necessary repeatedly, if the war was to be ended before the Russians honored their promise to attack within three months after Germany was defeated.

Secretary of State Byrnes has offered this very explanation of the dropping of the bomb—and with equal directness. Indeed, he has done so twice. He was asked in 1960, on the fifteenth anniversary of the bomb, whether there was "any urgency to end the war in the Pacific before the Russians became too deeply involved?" "There certainly was on my part," Byrnes replied. "We wanted to get through with the Japanese phase of the war before the Russians came in." [3] Even earlier, in 1958, Byrnes revealed how the United States encouraged Chiang Kai-shek to drag out his negotiations with Stalin over their arrangements in Manchuria.[4] Referring to an American dispatch to Chiang of July 23, 1945, Byrnes explained the meaning and importance of a particular sentence. "The second sentence was to encourage the Chinese to continue negotiations after the adjournment of the Potsdam Conference. . . . If Stalin and Chiang were still negotiating, it might delay Soviet entrance and the Japanese might surrender. The President was in accord with that view."

American leaders were becoming so enthusiastic and confident over the power of the bomb that Secretary of War Stimson undertook a very courageous and searching review of the existing attitude. Even before Roosevelt died, Stimson was somewhat disturbed over the way various members of the government were reacting to the progress reports on the weapon. True enough, he felt that the bomb should be used against

---

3. J. F. Byrnes, "We Were Anxious to Get the War Over," *U.S. News and World Report* (August 15, 1960). See also the remarks of Leo Szilard in the same issue for further evidence on the point.

4. J. F. Byrnes, *All in One Lifetime,* 291–99; Truman's *Memoirs,* 315–19, 423–25; and *Foreign Relations. The Conference at Potsdam,* II, 276.

Japan and kept from the Russians until safeguards had been established; but he also fretted that the attitude of the majority of American leaders would lead to neither peace nor prosperity. During the next five months, Stimson grew progressively more convinced that the American attitude and policy concerning the bomb were leading into another armament race, and perhaps even to a horrible war with Russia. On the eve of the Potsdam Conference, for example, he cautioned Truman that war would become inevitable if the United States took the position that all differences with the Soviet Union were irreconcilable. The Secretary's increasing concern was very probably caused by the interaction of four factors: the strong line taken by Truman and Byrnes at Potsdam; the awful destruction caused by the bombs at Hiroshima and Nagasaki; the clear evidence that Byrnes and the President had been encouraged by the bomb to maintain and even increase their pressure on Russia at the upcoming foreign ministers' conference scheduled for September in London; and his own searching thought and reflection on the problem, which were certainly provoked in part by his own great responsibility in recommending the use of the weapon.

The evidence suggests very strongly that Stimson devoted most of his intellectual and moral energy to the problem of the bomb from the end of the Potsdam Conference through the time when he received reports on the havoc caused in Japan. The result was a performance very similar, though of course more courageous and dramatic, to the one resulting from his experience in the late 1920's with armed intervention in Latin America. In that instance he concluded he had been wrong and set about to bring the Marines home from Nicaragua and to change the basic policy.

Stimson decided in the late summer of 1945 that the United States "was on the wrong path" in handling Russia in connection with the bomb. Having made that judgment, he undertook a brave, serious effort to persuade Truman and Byrnes to change their policy. He saw Byrnes on September 4, 1945, only to discover that the Secretary of State "was very much against any attempt to co-operate with Russia." Stimson noted that Byrnes was "full of his problems with the coming meeting of the foreign ministers and he looks to having the presence of the bomb in his pocket, so to speak, as a great weapon."

Byrnes left for London on September 5, unmoved by Stimson's arguments. Deeply concerned, and aware that his long government service was coming to an end, Stimson took his case directly to the President. His formal letter and memorandum to Truman, dated September 11, 1945, made two crucial points. The first involved his conclusion, based on a careful evaluation and analysis of all the evidence he could obtain, that American efforts to force the pace, or determine the nature, of internal relaxation or liberalization in Russia by applying pressure "would be so resented that it would make the objective we have in view less probable." It followed from that estimate that the most vital issue of American foreign affairs concerned the way the United States dealt with Russia in connection with the bomb. Stimson outlined the consequences of the then existing attitude and policy of Truman and Byrnes with a degree of accuracy that seems almost eerie in view of subsequent developments. "Unless the Soviets are voluntarily invited into the [nuclear] partnership upon a basis of co-operation and trust, we are going to maintain the Anglo-Saxon bloc over against the Soviet in the possession of this weapon. Such a condition will almost certainly stimulate feverish activity on the part of the Soviet toward the development of this bomb in what will in effect be a secret armament race of a rather desperate character. There is evidence to indicate that such activity may have already commenced."

He continued in a passage so important that he italicized it when making the document public in 1948. *"Those relations may be perhaps irretrievably embittered by the way in which we approach the solution of the bomb with Russia. For if we fail to approach them now and merely continue to negotiate with them, having this weapon rather ostentatiously on our hip, their suspicions and their distrust of our purposes and motives will increase."*

In conclusion, Stimson stressed the need for a direct approach *"to* Russia." *"I emphasize perhaps beyond all other considerations,"* he wrote, *"the importance of taking this action with Russia as . . . peculiarly the proposal of the United States. Action of any international group of nations, including many small nations who have not demonstrated their potential power or responsibility in this war would not, in my opinion, be taken seriously by the Soviets."*

Stimson's powerful argument may have caused Truman to pause, and perhaps momentarily to reconsider the militant anti-Soviet policy he had laid down on April 23, 1945. If so, the second thoughts were quickly set aside. Byrnes arrived in London determined to apply the strategy of the Open Door Policy in every area of the world. On the question of Axis colonies, for example, the American proposal was to place them under a trusteeship guaranteeing the Open Door principle. And as far as Japan and the Asia settlement were concerned, the United States took its control so much for granted that Byrnes was truly and literally "surprised" when the Russians asked for some share in making the decisions.

GAR ALPEROVITZ

How Did the Cold War Begin?

The response of historians to the Cold War paralleled that of the American people. While the diplomatic conflict with Russia was being waged intensely, scholars accepted and reinforced their government's official position. They stressed the postwar aggressive tendencies of the Soviet Union, the forebearance of the United States, and the belated but firm response with the adoption of the containment policy in 1947. But with the thaw that developed in the 1960's, historians began to look at the origins of the Cold War from a new perspective. Gradually a revisionist school emerged to suggest that the United States was as responsible as Russia—or more so—for the breakup of the wartime partnership and the resulting two decades of international tension.

Gar Alperovitz presents the major revisionist themes in his review of Marvin F. Herz, Beginnings of the Cold War *(Bloomington, Ind., 1966). Other articles in this same vein are Gar Alperovitz, "The Double Dealer,"* New York Review of Books, *VII (September 8, 1966), 3–4, a critical review of Allen W. Dulles,* The Secret Surrender *(New York, 1966); and John Bagguley, "The World War and the Cold War," in David Horowitz, ed.,* Containment and Revolution *(Boston, 1967), pp. 76–124.*

WRITING AS "MR. X," George Kennan suggested twenty years ago that the mechanism of Soviet diplomacy "moves inexorably along the prescribed path, like a persistent toy automobile wound up and headed in a given direction, stopping only when it meets with some unanswerable force." [1] A generation of Americans quickly embraced Kennan's view as an explanation of the tension, danger, and waste of the Cold War. But was his theory of inexorable Soviet expansion—and its matching recommendation of "containment"—correct? A cautious but important book, *Beginnings of the Cold War,* suggests we might well have been more critical of so mechanistic an idea of the way Great Powers act and how the Cold War began.

Martin F. Herz is currently a United States diplomat serving in

Reprinted by permission from the *New York Review of Books,* VIII (March 23, 1967), 6–12.
1. *Foreign Affairs,* July 1947.

Teheran. His book is mainly concerned with the few months between the 1945 Yalta and Potsdam Conferences. It is well-documented and contains no polemic; indeed, as he says, "the author expresses few views of his own. . . ." The book begins by recapitulating the main issues in dispute when Truman became President: Poland, German reparations, lend-lease aid. It moves from the Polish issue to a broader discussion of spheres of influence, and from reparations and lend-lease to a general analysis of aid to Russia and its relation to other diplomatic considerations. The two issues are integrated in a brief concluding discussion of how the "die was cast" in 1945, and the Cold War began.

Any examination of the very earliest postwar period forces us to think about developments *before* 1947 when it was decided to contain the Soviet Union by "unanswerable force." Herz's study is important because it makes two serious judgments about this period: first, that in 1945 Soviet policy was by no means inexorably prescribed and expansionist; second, that mistakes made by American officials just after the war may well have prevented the kind of compromise and accommodation which is just beginning to emerge in Europe today.

These suggestions recall Walter Lippmann's *The Cold War,* published in 1947, which also argued—with greater candor and less detail—that the Russians might have been willing to accept a negotiated settlement in 1945 and 1946, but that US policy ignored opportunities to meet them halfway. Lippmann's now little-remembered book offered a powerful critique of Kennan's theory of Soviet expansion and American containment. If Herz's view is correct, accepted interpretations of American-Russian relations are called into question. And if Lippmann was right in saying that American policy helped to prevent an accommodation in 1945 and 1946, the Cold War itself must be regarded, at least in part, as the result of fundamental errors of American diplomacy. These are startling conclusions, but anyone willing to bring an open mind to Herz's book or to Lippmann's will find that they have exposed many weaknesses in the usual explanations of early events in the Cold War.

No one, of course, can be certain of "what might have been." But Herz refutes at least one accepted myth. Contrary to current historical reconstructions, there is abundant evidence that American leaders in 1945 were not much worried about the expansion of communism into *Western* Europe. That worry came later. In the days just after the war, most Communists in Italy, France, and elsewhere were cooperating with bourgeois governments. At Potsdam, in 1945, Truman regarded the Russians' desires for concessions beyond their area of occupation as largely bluff. The major issues in dispute were all in Eastern Europe, deep within the zone of Soviet military occupation. The real expansion of Soviet power, we are reminded, took place in Poland, Hungary,

Bulgaria, Rumania, Czechoslovakia, and the eastern regions of Germany and Austria.

The US in 1945 wanted Russia to give up the control and influence the Red Army had gained in the battle against Hitler. American demands may have been motivated by an idealistic desire to foster democracy, but Herz's main point is that in countries like Rumania and Bulgaria they were about as realistic as would be Soviet demands for changes in, say, Mexico. Any such parallel has obvious limits, the most significant of which is not that democracy and communism cannot easily be compared, but that Eastern Europe is of far greater importance to Soviet security than is Mexico to American security: from the time of Napoleon—and twice in the lifetime of millions of present-day Russians —bloody invasions have swept through the area to their "Middle West."

In the early spring of 1945, negotiations concerning one border state—Poland—brought the main issue into the open. At Yalta and immediately thereafter, the US had mainly mediated between Stalin and Churchill on Poland; Roosevelt had warned Churchill that to make extreme demands would doom the negotiations. A month later, in the faltering last days of Roosevelt's life, the US itself adopted a new tough line, demanding that pro-Western and openly anti-Russian Polish politicians be given more influence in negotiations to set up a new government for Poland. As was predicted, the Russians balked at the idea of such an expansion of anti-Soviet influence in a country so important to their security, and the negotiations ground to a halt.[2] Moreover, at this precise moment, Russian suspicions about the West deepened with Allen Dulles' concurrent but unrelated secret negotiations with Nazi generals in Switzerland.[3] The result was a violent quarrel which shook the entire structure of American-Soviet relations. But this was only the beginning. The demands on the Polish question reflected the ideas of the men who were to surround the new President; led by Joseph Grew and James F. Byrnes, they soon convinced Truman to attempt to make stronger demands elsewhere in Eastern Europe.

2. The details of this history are often greatly misunderstood. Herz also vacillates in describing Roosevelt's Polish policy. See Appendix I of my *Atomic Diplomacy: Hiroshima and Potsdam* for a discussion of this question. Documentation for other facts and quotations not specifically given in this review can also be found here.

3. See *The New York Review*, October 8, 1965. The only important new information in Cornelius Ryan's popularized history, *The Last Battle* (Simon and Schuster, 1966, 571 pp., $7.50), suggests that Stalin was so aroused by Dulles' negotiations and the West's blatant denial they were taking place) that he suspiciously concluded other Western statements at this time were also lies. According to Ryan, when Eisenhower informed Stalin he did not intend to capture Berlin, Stalin thought this was another Western attempt to deceive him. On this basis he, in turn, lied to Eisenhower, misleading him about the timing of the Red Army's own thrust to take the city.

For most of the war Roosevelt had been highly ambivalent toward such matters. By late 1944, however (in spite of wavering on the politically sensitive Polish issue in his dying days), Roosevelt concluded it would be a fundamental error to put too much pressure on Russia over other regions vital to her security. In September and October 1944, and in early January 1945, he gave form to his conclusion by entering into armistice agreements with Britain and Russia, which gave the Soviet military almost complete control of internal politics in each Eastern European ex-Nazi satellite. It was understood, for instance, that the Soviets would have authority to issue orders to the Rumanian government, and that, specifically, the Allied Control Commission would be "under the general direction of the Allied (Soviet) High Command acting on behalf of the Allied Powers." The Rumanian accords, and the similar but slightly less severe Bulgarian and Hungarian armistice agreements, served to formalize the famous Churchill-Stalin spheres-of-influence arrangement which, without FDR's agreement, had previously given the Russians "90 per cent" influence in Rumania, "80 per cent" influence in Bulgaria, and "75 per cent" influence in Hungary, in exchange for "90 per cent" British influence in Greece and a "50-50" split of influence in Yugoslavia. The armistice accords were also modeled after a previous understanding which had contained Soviet endorsement of dominant American-British influence in Italy. The Eastern European armistice agreements have been available to the public for years, but have been successfully buried, or avoided by most scholars. Herz has exhumed them, and he shows that they contain American endorsement of dominant Soviet influence in the ex-Nazi satellites.

At Yalta, in early February 1945, Roosevelt pasted over these specific texts the vague and idealistic rhetoric of the famous Declaration on Liberated Europe. The President apparently wished to use the Declaration mainly to appease certain politically important ethnic groups in America; he devoted only a few minutes to the matter at the Yalta Conference, and the familiar rhetoric promising democracy was almost devoid of practical meaning. For example, who was to decide in given instances between the American and Soviet definitions of common but vague terms like "democratic"? Much more important, as Herz shows, in the broad language of the Declaration the Allies agreed merely to "consult" about matters within the liberated countries, not to "act," and they authorized consultations only when all parties agreed they were necessary. Thus the United States itself confirmed the Russians' right to refuse to talk about the ex-Nazi satellites. The State Department knew this and, in fact, had tried to insert operative clauses into the Declaration. But Roosevelt, having just signed the armistice agreements, rejected this unrealistic proposal. Moreover, when the Soviets after Yalta crudely tossed out a Rumanian government they did not like, the President, though unhappy that he had not been consulted, reaffirmed his basic position by refusing to intervene.

Ironically, Herz's book lends credence to the old Republican charge that Roosevelt accepted a compromise at Yalta which bolstered Stalin's position in Eastern Europe. The charge, while correct in essentials, was silly in assuming that much else, short of war, could have been done while the Red Army occupied the area. The Republican politicians also ignored the fact that at Yalta Roosevelt could not expect a continued American military presence in Europe for very long after the war. This not only deprived him of leverage, it made an accommodation with Russia much more desirable for another reason: Red Army help became essential as a guarantee that Germany would not rise from defeat to start yet a third World War. Stalin also needed American help, as he too made clear, to hold down the Germans. Hence, underlying the American-Soviet plans for peace at Yalta was not "faith" but a common interest—the German threat—which had cemented the World War II alliance. From this 1945 perspective the crucial portion of the Yalta agreement was not the Declaration on Liberated Europe, nor even the provisions on Poland, but rather the understanding that the United States and Russia (with Britain and France as minor partners) would work together to control Germany. This meant, among other things, joint action to reduce Germany's physical power by extracting reparations from Germany industry.

Although Herz tends to play down the German issue, he does take up important economic matters that relate to it. He understands that Moscow was in a cruel dilemma which, had the US been shrewd enough, might have been resolved to the benefit of both American diplomacy and the economic health of Europe. The Russians were greatly in need of aid for their huge postwar reconstruction program. Importing industrial equipment from Eastern Europe was a possible solution, though a doubtful one, for taking this equipment would inevitably cause political problems. Reparations from Germany were another, but the key industrial sectors were in American hands. Finally, the United States itself was a potential source. Herz argues (as did Ambassadors Harriman and Winant at the time) that a US reconstruction loan for Russia would have been wise; it would have given US diplomacy strong leverage in a variety of negotiations. (Without other sources of reconstruction to aid, the Russians were almost inevitably reduced to extracting industrial goods from either Germany or Eastern Europe.) American officials seriously considered such a loan, but, as Herz shows, they did not actively pursue it with the Russians—though one or two crude attempts were made to use a loan as a bludgeon in negotiations. With a future US troop commitment unlikely, and a large loan ruled out, the United States had no real bargaining power. Hence its attempts at intervention in Eastern Europe amounted to little more than bluster. The State Department wanted to have it both ways: it wanted to hold the Russians to the vague promises of the Yalta Declaration; it also wanted to avoid the specific texts of the armistice agreements. But the Republicans, and even Secretary Byrnes in his later writings, understood the weakness of this position. The Republicans, for their part, also wanted to have it both ways. They wanted to argue both that Roosevelt gave the Russians all the authority they needed for their actions *and* that the Russians broke their agreements.

The Republican attack on Yalta came late in the Cold War, and was combined with a new demand that the US "roll back" Soviet influence. Few now realize how unoriginal the demand was, for a "roll back" effort —without its latter-day label—was, in fact, at the center of Harry Truman's first postwar policy. The President, we now know, made this effort in a spurt of confidence derived from the new atomic bomb. But the policy failed in its continuing attempt to reduce Soviet control by expanding Western influence in Poland. It also failed in its bold follow-up effort to force the Russians to change the Bulgarian and Rumanian governments. Nevertheless, these opening moves of the post-war period helped to set the tone of the new Administration's attitude toward Russia. Truman, although publicly proclaiming his adherence to Roosevelt's policy of cooperation, seems to have understood that his approach differed fundamentally from his predecessor's. (In private, as Secretary of State Stettinius has written, he complained that the intervention in Poland rested on rather shaky diplomatic ground.) Indeed, by September 1945, the basic change in US policy was so clearly defined that, as Secretary of State Byrnes later wrote, the Russian complaint that Roosevelt's policy had been abandoned was "understandable." [4]

What was the result? Like Herz, John Foster Dulles (who assisted Byrnes at the time) also believed that the Cold War began in 1945. Dulles emphasized in his book *War or Peace* (1950) that a new tough line of US policy was adopted at this time over dimly remembered issues deep within the Soviet-controlled Balkans. Herz prints almost the full text of the crucial 1945 Hopkins-Stalin talks, which reveal the equally important point that, in Russia, the change in American policy produced what Stalin termed "a certain alarm." A few thoughtful US officials recognized the significance of these developments. Secretary of War Henry L. Stimson, for example, tried to block the campaign to engage American prestige in Eastern Europe. In White House discussions he argued, first, that the demand for more Western influence

---

4. *Speaking Frankly,* Harper, 1947.

in Poland was a mistake: "The Russians perhaps were being more realistic than we were in regard to their own security. . . ." He then tried to cut short efforts to intervene elsewhere, reminding Truman, as Stimson's diary shows, that "we have made up our minds on the broad policy that it was not wise to get into the Balkan mess even if the thing seemed to be disruptive of policies which the State Department thought were wise." Stimson pointed out that "we have taken that policy right from the beginning, Mr. Roosevelt having done it himself or having been a party to it himself."

When Stimson failed in his conservative effort to limit American objectives, the stage was set for one of the great tragedies of the Cold War. As Stimson understood, the Russians, though extremely touchy about the buffer area, were not impossible to deal with. Had their security requirements been met, there is evidence that their domination of Eastern Europe might have been much different from what it turned out to be. Churchill, too, thought the Russians were approachable. Obviously, conditions in Eastern Europe would not meet Western ideals; but Churchill judged, in late 1944 and early 1945, that Moscow was convinced it would be much easier to secure its objectives through moderate policies. In Greece at this time, as Churchill was to stress in *Triumph and Tragedy*, Stalin was "strictly and faithfully" holding to his agreement *not* to aid the Greek Communists. Even in much of the border area, the Russians seemed willing to accept substantial capitalism and some form of democracy—with the crucial proviso that the Eastern European governments had to be "friendly" to Russia in defense and foreign policies. Finland serves as a rough model of a successful border state. Here, too, the armistice made the Soviets supreme, giving rights parallel to the Bulgarian and Rumanian accords plus the right to maintain Soviet military installations. However, the US made no independent effort to intervene: Finland maintained a foreign policy "friendly" to Russia; and the Russians were—as they still seem to be—prepared to accept a moderate government.

Although it is often forgotten, a modified application of the Finnish formula seemed to be shaping up elsewhere in 1945 and much of 1946. In Hungary, Soviet-sponsored free elections routed the Communist party in 1945. In Bulgaria, a country with rather weak democratic traditions, the 1945 elections were complicated by competition for Great Power support among the various internal factions. Certainly the results were not perfect, but most Western observers (except the State Department) felt they should have been accepted. In Austria, the Communists were swamped in Soviet-run free elections in their zone in 1945, and, after a hesitant start, a free democratic government emerged for the entire country. In Czechoslovakia, from which the Red

Army withdrew in December of 1945, democracy was so clearly accept-able to Soviet policy that the US had little to protest at the time.[5]

Almost all of this was to change, of course. The freedoms in Hungary were to end in 1947. The initial pattern in Czechoslovakia was to be reversed in 1948. But writers who focus only on the brutal period of totalitarian control after 1947 and 1948 often ignore what happened earlier. The few who try to account for the known facts of the 1945–46 interlude usually do so in passing, either to suggest that the demo-cratic governments "must have been" more smoke screens, formed while Moscow waited for the US to leave the Continent; or that the Russians "must have been" secretly planning to take full control, but were methodically using the early period to prepare the groundwork for what came later. (Communists, too, like to ignore the 1945–46 period, for it suggests the possibility that Soviet Russia was more interested in an old-fashioned *modus vivendi* with the capitalists than in spreading World Communism. This was the essence of Tito's bitter complaint that Stalin tried to turn back the Yugoslav revolution.)

The Russians have displayed so much duplicity, brutality, and intran-sigence that it is easy to imagine the 1945–46 interlude as a mere smoke screen. But they also have a long history of protecting "socialism in one country" in a rather conservative, nationalistic way: the moder-ation of the 1945–46 interlude can be viewed as a logical extension of this tradition. That at least two quite different interpretations of their 1945–46 policy are conceivable is now rarely admitted, and the relative merits of each have not been seriously examined. Herz's study calls for a careful reappraisal of early postwar Soviet objectives.[6] If the Russians were secretly harboring plans for an ultimate takeover, they certainly were preparing a lot of trouble for themselves by sponsoring free politics, by pulling out the Red Army (it is not particularly shrewd to have to *re*-introduce foreign troops), by ripping up the Red Army's main rail connections across Poland—as they did in the fall of 1945. As

5. W. H. McNeill's *America, Britain and Russia* provides a good general survey of this period. Note that early in 1946 the Red Army also withdrew from control of two other border areas: Northern Iran and Manchuria.

6. Today most writers simply take the mechanistic theory of Soviet expan-sion for granted. An example of what this can lead to is John Toland's *The Last 100 Days* (Random House, 1965), an account of the closing months of World War II which assumes that the Russians were inevitably evil and ex-pansionistic, and that therefore the "good" Germans had to be used to help contain them. Toland dwells on details of the Western Front. He devotes much less attention to the Eastern Front, taking much of his material from German sources. Accordingly, the book popularizes a one-sided caricature of Russians as pillaging sadists and irrepressible rapists. (As for the Germans, it is only the rare Nazi camp guard who is a brutal exception to the rule of "the other guards, who generally treated the prisoners well"!)

well informed an observer as Averell Harriman believed, as he once testified to Congress, that Soviet policy in 1945 was ambivalent, that it could have become either more moderate within a framework of security and understanding with the West, or that it could have become hard-line and totalitarian, within the framework of insecurity and conflict. Harriman, though puzzled by the ultimate Russian decision in favor of the iron-fisted policy, clearly saw that Soviet expansion was neither inexorable nor inevitable.

At least one reason for Russia's shift to a tough line may be traced to mistakes made by US officials. As Stimson argued—and as history later showed—the demand for more influence in Soviet-controlled areas was almost certainly doomed from the start. This basic miscalculation stemmed, finally, from an attempt to overextend *American* diplomatic sway. Lippmann was, I believe, correct in seeing that the other error was the failure of US policy-makers to turn their energies to an early solution of the crucial German problem. Bolstered by the atomic bomb, which eliminated the threat that had been Roosevelt's central concern, American leaders dallied over Germany. Moreover, by refusing to hold to Roosevelt's agreement that a specific target for German reparations would be set (July 1945), by permitting France to hamstring the German Control Commission (fall, 1945), by halting German reparations shipments (spring, 1946)—US policy suggested the very prospect Russia feared most: the abandonment of economic and political controls and the possibility that a new and powerful Germany would rise from the ashes of Nazism to become the bastion of Western capitalistic aggression in Europe. The United States had no such aggressive intent. Nonetheless, the US chose not to negotiate seriously on Germany until a full year-and-a-half after the war's end. Especially after Secretary Byrnes's tough speech in Stuttgart in the fall of 1946, American policy was shortsighted enough to suggest a threat to Russia at the very time it was attempting to weaken Soviet control in the vital area which lay —protectively or threateningly—between German power and the Russian heartland. The Russians, who had no nuclear weapons, were far less casual about the question of security; their grip seemed to tighten in the buffer area month by month, as their worst fears about Germany seemed to come true.

The Russians were not easy to deal with, either in Germany or elsewhere. Nevertheless, if the hypothesis suggested by Lippmann's book is correct—and Herz's study indirectly supports it—there are reasons to believe that US policy itself may have to share responsibility for the imposition of totalitarian control in Eastern Europe, and possibly also for the subsequent expanding Communist agitation in Western Europe. The *addition* of increased insecurity to known Soviet paranoid tendencies may explain the rigidity which Soviet leaders displayed in their satellite policy after 1946. The first pattern seemed crudely similar to the Finnish or Austrian models. Would it have been reversed had the US seriously tried from the first to resolve the European security problem—as Lippmann urged? That Soviet actions may have been in part reactions to their judgments of American intentions may also help to explain why sustained Communist opposition developed in the West only *after* the clear breakdown of German control arrangements. It was not in 1945, but late in 1946 and in 1947, that the Italian and French Communists began to reverse their initial policy of cooperation with bourgeois governments. Was the changed focus of Communist politics part of the inexorable plan? Or was it primarily a rather shortsighted response to American policy itself?

Once the Communists became active in Western Europe, of course, the United States was faced with quite another set of issues. Disputes with Russia moved out of the border regions. The threat some officials had anticipated while reading Marx and listening to Communist propaganda began to become a political reality. In 1947, those who proposed a mechanical theory of Soviet expansion had to deal with expanding Communist political activity in the West. And it was in July of that year, precisely two years after Truman faced Stalin in his first Potsdam showdown over Eastern Europe, that Kennan's containment recommendation was publicly offered.

We do not yet have answers to all the questions about postwar American-Russian relations, but we know enough to consider afresh whether either of the Great Powers ever really did move inexorably, like a wound-up toy automobile, as "Mr. X" argued. Herz's sturdy little book suggests they did not, and is at least the beginning of a more subtle explanation of the complex sequence of interacting events which produced the Cold War.

ARTHUR M. SCHLESINGER, JR.

Origins of the Cold War

The revisionist explanation of how the Cold War began has opened up a historical debate which may prove to be as vigorous and long-lived as the dispute over American entry into World War II. So far, the debate turns largely on events in 1945, especially the decision to use the bomb and American opposition to Soviet domination of Poland and Eastern Europe. The continued publication of the Foreign Relations *volumes and the opening of State Department files for 1946 and 1947 within the next few years will provide historians with an opportunity to examine such crucial episodes as the conflict over Iran, the Baruch plan for international control of atomic energy, and the Greek crisis which gave birth to the Truman Doctrine. Even with this new evidence, however, historical judgments will still probably turn on such intangible factors as Truman's attitude toward the Soviet Union, the precise motivation behind Russian expansion, and the relationship between ideology and the national interest in Moscow and Washington.*

Arthur Schlesinger, Jr., deals with these intangibles in this article which he wrote in 1967 as a rebuttal to the revisionists. For a more sympathetic appraisal of the historiographical debate, see Christopher Lasch, "The Cold War, Revisited and Re-Visioned," New York Times Magazine *(January 14, 1968), pp. 26–27, 44–59.*

I

THE COLD WAR in its original form was a presumably mortal antagonism, arising in the wake of the Second World War, between two rigidly hostile blocs, one led by the Soviet Union, the other by the United States. For nearly two somber and dangerous decades this antagonism dominated the fears of mankind; it may even, on occasion, have come close to blowing up the planet. In recent years, however, the once implacable struggle has lost its familiar clarity of outline. With the passing of old issues and the emergence of new conflicts and contestants, there is a natural tendency, especially on the part of the generation which grew up during the Cold War, to take a fresh look at the causes of the great contention between Russia and America.

Some exercises in reappraisal have merely elaborated the orthodoxies promulgated in Washington or Moscow during the boom years of the Cold War. But others, especially in the United States (there are no

Reprinted by permission from *Foreign Affairs*, XLVI (October 1967), 22–52.

signs, alas, of this in the Soviet Union), represent what American historians call "revisionism"—that is, a readiness to challenge official explanations. No one should be surprised by this phenomenon. Every war in American history has been followed in due course by skeptical reassessments of supposedly sacred assumptions. So the War of 1812, fought at the time for the freedom of the seas, was in later years ascribed to the expansionist ambitions of Congressional war hawks; so the Mexican War became a slaveholders' conspiracy. So the Civil War has been pronounced a "needless war," and Lincoln has even been accused of maneuvering the rebel attack on Fort Sumter. So too the Spanish-American War and the First and Second World Wars have, each in its turn, undergone revisionist critiques. It is not to be supposed that the Cold War would remain exempt.

In the case of the Cold War, special factors reinforce the predictable historiographical rhythm. The outburst of polycentrism in the Communist empire has made people wonder whether communism was ever so monolithic as official theories of the Cold War supposed. A generation with no vivid memories of Stalinism may see the Russia of the forties in the image of the relatively mild, seedy, and irresolute Russia of the sixties. And for this same generation the American course of widening the war in Viet Nam—which even non-revisionists can easily regard as folly—has unquestionably stirred doubts about the wisdom of American foreign policy in the sixties which younger historians may have begun to read back into the forties.

It is useful to remember that, on the whole, past exercises in revisionism have failed to stick. Few historians today believe that the war hawks caused the War of 1812 or the slaveholders the Mexican War, or that the Civil War was needless, or that the House of Morgan brought America into the First World War or that Franklin Roosevelt schemed to produce the attack on Pearl Harbor. But this does not mean that one should deplore the rise of Cold War revisionism.[1] For revisionism is an essential part of the process by which history, through the posing of new problems and the investigation of new possibilities, enlarges its perspectives and enriches its insights.

More than this, in the present context, revisionism expresses a deep, legitimate, and tragic apprehension. As the Cold War has begun to lose its purity of definition, as the moral absolutes of the fifties become the moralistic clichés of the sixties, some have begun to ask whether the appalling risks which humanity ran during the Cold War were, after all, necessary and inevitable; whether more restrained and rational policies might not have guided the energies of man from the perils of conflict into the potentialities of collaboration. The fact that such questions are

1. As this writer somewhat intemperately did in a letter to *The New York Review of Books,* October 20, 1966.

in their nature unanswerable does not mean that it is not right and useful to raise them. Nor does it mean that our sons and daughters are not entitled to an accounting from the generation of Russians and Americans who produced the Cold War.

II

The orthodox American view, as originally set forth by the American government and as reaffirmed until recently by most American scholars, has been that the Cold War was the brave and essential response of free men to Communist aggression. Some have gone back well before the Second World War to lay open the sources of Russian expansionism. Geopoliticians traced the Cold War to imperial Russian strategic ambitions which in the nineteenth century led to the Crimean War, to Russian penetration of the Balkans and the Middle East, and to Russian pressure on Britain's "lifeline" to India. Ideologists traced it to the Communist Manifesto of 1848 ("the violent overthrow of the bourgeoisie lays the foundation for the sway of the proletariat"). Thoughtful observers (a phrase meant to exclude those who speak in Dullesese about the unlimited evil of godless, atheistic, militant communism) concluded that classical Russian imperialism and Pan-Slavism, compounded after 1917 by Leninist messianism, confronted the West at the end of the Second World War with an inexorable drive for domination.[2]

The revisionist thesis is very different.[3] In its extreme form, it

2. Every student of the Cold War must acknowledge his debt to W. H. McNeill's remarkable account, *America, Britain and Russia: Their Cooperation and Conflict, 1941-1946* (New York, 1953) and to the brilliant and indispensable series by Herbert Feis: *Churchill, Roosevelt, Stalin: The War They Waged and the Peace They Sought* (Princeton, 1957); *Between War and Peace: The Potsdam Conference* (Princeton, 1960); and *The Atomic Bomb and the End of World War II* (Princeton, 1966). Useful recent analyses include André Fontaine, *Histoire de la Guerre Froide* (2 v., Paris, 1965, 1967); N. A. Graebner, *Cold War Diplomacy, 1945-1960* (Princeton, 1962); L. J. Halle *The Cold War as History* (London, 1967); M. F. Herz, *Beginnings of the Cold War* (Bloomington, 1966); and W. L. Neumann, *After Victory: Churchill, Roosevelt, Stalin and the Making of the Peace* (New York, 1967).

3. The fullest statement of this case is to be found in D. F. Fleming's voluminous "The Cold War and Its Origins" (New York, 1961). For a shorter version of this argument, see David Horowitz, *The Free World Colossus* (New York, 1965); the most subtle and ingenious statements come in W. A. Williams' *The Tragedy of American Diplomacy* (rev. ed., New York, 1962) and in Gar Alperowitz's *Atomic Diplomacy: Hiroshima and Potsdam* (New York, 1965) and in subsequent articles and reviews by Mr. Alperowitz in *The New York Review of Books*. The fact that in some aspects the revisionist thesis parallels the official Soviet argument must not, of course, prevent consideration of the case on its merits, nor raise questions about the motives of the writers, all of whom, so far as I know, are independent-minded scholars.

is that, after the death of Franklin Roosevelt and the end of the Second World War, the United States deliberately abandoned the wartime policy of collaboration and, exhilarated by the possession of the atomic bomb, undertook a course of aggression of its own designed to expel all Russian influence from Eastern Europe and to establish democratic-capitalist states on the very border of the Soviet Union. As the revisionists see it, this radically new American policy—or rather this resumption by Truman of the pre-Roosevelt policy of insensate anticommunism—left Moscow no alternative but to take measures in defense of its own borders. The result was the Cold War.

These two views, of course, could not be more starkly contrasting. It is therefore not unreasonable to look again at the half-dozen critical years between June 22, 1941, when Hitler attacked Russia, and July 2, 1947, when the Russians walked out of the Marshall Plan meeting in Paris. Several things should be borne in mind as this reexamination is made. For one thing, we have thought a great deal more in recent years, in part because of writers like Roberta Wohlstetter and T. C. Schelling, about the problems of communication in diplomacy—the signals which one nation, by word or by deed, gives, inadvertently or intentionally, to another. Any honest reappraisal of the origins of the Cold War requires the imaginative leap—which should in any case

---

I might further add that all these books, in spite of their ostentatious display of scholarly apparatus, must be used with caution. Professor Fleming, for example, relies heavily on newspaper articles and even columnists. While Mr. Alperowitz bases his case on official documents or authoritative reminiscences, he sometimes twists his material in a most unscholarly way. For example, in describing Ambassador Harriman's talk with President Truman on April 20, 1945, Mr. Alperowitz writes, "He argued that a reconsideration of Roosevelt's policy was necessary" pp. 22, repeated on p. 24). The citation is to pp. 70–72 in President Truman's *Years of Decision*. What President Truman reported Harriman as saying was the exact opposite: "Before leaving, Harriman took me aside and said, 'Frankly, one of the reasons that made me rush back to Washington was the fear that you did not understand, as I had seen Roosevelt understand, that Stalin is breaking his agreements.'" Similarly, in an appendix (p. 271), Mr. Alperowitz writes that the Hopkins and Davies missions of May 1945 "were opposed by the 'firm' advisers." Actually the Hopkins mission was proposed by Harriman and Charles E. Bohlen, who Mr. Alperowitz elsewhere suggests were the firmest of the firm—and was proposed by them precisely to impress on Stalin the continuity of American policy from Roosevelt to Truman. While the idea that Truman reversed Roosevelt's policy is tempting dramatically, it is a myth. See, for example, the testimony of Anna Rosenberg Hoffman, who lunched with Roosevelt on March 24, 1945, the last day he spent in Washington. After luncheon, Roosevelt was handed a cable. "He read it and became quite angry. He banged his fists on the arms of his wheelchair and said, 'Averell is right; we can't do business with Stalin. He has broken every one of the promises he made at Yalta.' He was very upset and continued in the same vein on the subject."

be as instinctive for the historian as it is prudent for the statesman—into the adversary's viewpoint. We must strive to see how, given Soviet perspectives, the Russians might conceivably have misread our signals as we must reconsider how intelligently we read theirs.

For another, the historian must not overindulge the man of power in the illusion cherished by those in office that high position carries with it the easy ability to shape history. Violating the statesman's creed, Lincoln once blurted out the truth in his letter of 1864 to A. G. Hodges: "I claim not to have controlled events, but confess plainly that events have controlled me." He was not asserting Tolstoyan fatalism but rather suggesting how greatly events limit the capacity of the statesman to bend history to his will. The physical course of the Second World War —the military operations undertaken, the position of the respective armies at the war's end, the momentum generated by victory, and the vacuums created by defeat—all these determined the future as much as the character of individual leaders and the substance of national ideology and purpose.

Nor can the historian forget the conditions under which decisions are made, especially in a time like the Second World War. These were tired, overworked, aging men: in 1945, Churchill was 71 years old, Stalin had governed his country for 17 exacting years, Roosevelt his for 12 years nearly as exacting. During the war, moreover, the importunities of military operations had shoved postwar questions to the margins of their minds. All—even Stalin, behind his screen of ideology—had become addicts of improvisation, relying on authority and virtuosity to conceal the fact that they were constantly surprised by developments. Like Eliza, they leaped from one cake of ice to the next in the effort to reach the other side of the river. None showed great tactical consistency, or cared much about it; all employed a certain ambiguity to preserve their power to decide big issues; and it is hard to know how to interpret anything any one of them said on any specific occasion. This was partly because, like all princes, they designed their expressions to have particular effects on particular audiences; partly because the entirely genuine intellectual difficulty of the questions they faced made a degree of vacillation and mind-changing eminently reasonable. If historians cannot solve their problems in retrospect, who are they to blame Roosevelt, Stalin, and Churchill for not having solved them at the time?

III

Peacemaking after the Second World War was not so much a tapestry as it was a hopelessly raveled and knotted mess of yarn. Yet, for purposes of clarity, it is essential to follow certain threads. One theme indispensable to an understanding of the Cold War is the contrast between two clashing views of world order: the "universalist" view, by which all nations shared a common interest in all the affairs of the world, and the "sphere-of-influence" view, by which each great power would be assured by the other great powers of an acknowledged predominance in its own area of special interest. The universalist view assumed that national security would be guaranteed by an international organization. The sphere-of-interest view assumed that national security would be guaranteed by the balance of power. While in practice these views have by no means been incompatible (indeed, our shaky peace has been based on a combination of the two), in the abstract they involved sharp contradictions.

The tradition of American thought in these matters was universalist— i.e., Wilsonian. Roosevelt had been a member of Wilson's subcabinet; in 1920, as candidate for Vice President, he had campaigned for the League of Nations. It is true that, within Roosevelt's infinitely complex mind, Wilsonianism warred with the perception of vital strategic interests he had imbibed from Mahan. Moreover, his temperamental inclination to settle things with fellow princes around the conference table led him to regard the Big Three—or Four—as trustees for the rest of the world. On occasion, as this narrative will show, he was beguiled into flirtation with the sphere-of-influence heresy. But in principle he believed in joint action and remained a Wilsonian. His hope for Yalta, as he told the Congress on his return, was that it would "spell the end of the system of unilateral action, the exclusive alliances, the spheres of influence, the balances of power, and all the other expedients that have been tried for centuries—and have always failed."

Whenever Roosevelt backslid, he had at his side that Wilsonian fundamentalist, Secretary of State Cordell Hull, to recall him to the pure faith. After his visit to Moscow in 1943, Hull characteristically said that, with the Declaration of Four Nations on General Security (in which America, Russia, Britain, and China pledged "united action . . . for the organization and maintenance of peace and security"), "there will no longer be need for spheres of influence, for alliances, for balance of power, or any other of the special arrangements through which, in the unhappy past, the nations strove to safeguard their security or to promote their interests."

Remembering the corruption of the Wilsonian vision by the secret treaties of the First World War, Hull was determined to prevent any sphere-of-influence nonsense after the Second World War. He therefore fought all proposals to settle border questions while the war was still on and, excluded as he largely was from wartime diplomacy, poured his not inconsiderable moral energy and frustration into the promulgation of virtuous and spacious general principles.

In adopting the universalist view, Roosevelt and Hull were not indulging personal hobbies. Sumner Welles, Adolf Berle, Averell Harriman,

Charles Bohlen—all, if with a variety of nuances, opposed the sphere-of-influence approach. And here the State Department was expressing what seems clearly to have been the predominant mood of the American people, so long mistrustful of European power politics. The Republicans shared the true faith. John Foster Dulles argued that the great threat to peace after the war would lie in the revival of sphere-of-influence thinking. The United States, he said, must not permit Britain and Russia to revert to these bad old ways; it must therefore insist on American participation in all policy decisions for all territories in the world. Dulles wrote pessimistically in January 1945, "The three great powers which at Moscow agreed upon the 'closest cooperation' about European questions have shifted to a practice of separate, regional responsibility."

It is true that critics, and even friends, of the United States sometimes noted a discrepancy between the American passion for universalism when it applied to territory far from American shores and the pre-eminence the United States accorded its own interests near home. Churchill, seeking Washington's blessing for a sphere-of-influence initiative in Eastern Europe, could not forbear reminding the Americans, "We follow the lead of the United States in South America;" nor did any universalist of record propose the abolition of the Monroe Doctrine. But a convenient myopia prevented such inconsistencies from qualifying the ardency of the universalist faith.

There seem only to have been three officials in the United States Government who dissented. One was the Secretary of War, Henry L. Stimson, a classical balance-of-power man, who in 1944 opposed the creation of a vacuum in Central Europe by the pastoralization of Germany and in 1945 urged "the settlement of all territorial acquisitions in the shape of defense posts which each of these four powers may deem to be necessary for thir own safety" in advance of any effort to establish a peacetime United Nations. Stimson considered the claim of Russia to a preferred position in Eastern Europe as not unreasonable: as he told President Truman, "he thought the Russians perhaps were being more realistic than we were in regard to their own security." Such a position for Russia seemed to him comparable to the preferred American position in Latin America; he even spoke of "our respective orbits." Stimson was therefore skeptical of what he regarded as the prevailing tendency "to hang on to exaggerated views of the Monroe Doctrine and at the same time butt into every question that comes up in Central Europe." Acceptance of spheres of influence seemed to him the way to avoid "a head-on collision."

A second official opponent of universalism was George Kennan, an eloquent advocate from the American Embassy in Moscow of "a prompt and clear recognition of the division of Europe into spheres of influence and of a policy based on the fact of such division." Kennan argued that nothing we could do would possibly alter the course of events in Eastern Europe; that we were deceiving ourselves by supposing that these countries had any future but Russian domination; that we should therefore relinquish Eastern Europe to the Soviet Union and avoid anything which would make things easier for the Russians by giving them economic assistance or by sharing moral responsibility for their actions.

A third voice within the government against universalism was (at least after the war) Henry A. Wallace. As Secretary of Commerce, he stated the sphere-of-influence case with trenchancy in the famous Madison Square Garden speech of September 1946 which led to his dismissal by President Truman:

> On our part, we should recognize that we have no more business in the *political* affairs of Eastern Europe than Russia has in the *political* affairs of Latin America, Western Europe, and the United States. . . . Whether we like it or not, the Russians will try to socialize their sphere of influence just as we try to democratize our sphere of influence. . . . The Russians have no more business stirring up native Communists to political activity in Western Europe, Latin America, and the United States than we have in interfering with the politics of Eastern Europe and Russia.

Stimson, Kennan, and Wallace seem to have been alone in the government, however, in taking these views. They were very much minority voices. Meanwhile universalism, rooted in the American legal and moral tradition, overwhelmingly backed by contemporary opinion, received successive enshrinements in the Atlantic Charter of 1941, in the Declaration of the United Nations in 1942, and in the Moscow Declaration of 1943.

IV

The Kremlin, on the other hand, thought *only* of spheres of interest; above all, the Russians were determined to protect their frontiers, and especially their border to the west, crossed so often and so bloodily in the dark course of their history. These western frontiers lacked natural means of defense—no great oceans, rugged mountains, steaming swamps, or impenetrable jungles. The history of Russia had been the history of invasion, the last of which was by now horribly killing up to twenty million of its people. The protocol of Russia therefore meant the enlargement of the area of Russian influence. Kennan himself wrote (in May 1944), "Behind Russia's stubborn expansion lies only the age-old sense of insecurity of a sedentary people reared on an exposed plain in the neighborhood of fierce nomadic peoples," and he called this "urge" a "permanent feature of Russian psychology."

In earlier times the "urge" had produced the tsarist search for buffer states and maritime outlets. In 1939 the Soviet-Nazi pact and its secret protocol had enabled Russia to begin to satisfy in the Baltic states, Karelian Finland, and Poland, part of what it conceived as its security requirements in Eastern Europe. But the "urge" persisted, causing the friction between Russia and Germany in 1940 as each jostled for position in the area which separated them. Later it led to Molotov's new demands on Hitler in November 1940—a free hand in Finland, Soviet predominance in Rumania and Bulgaria, bases in the Dardanelles—the demands which convinced Hitler that he had no choice but to attack Russia. Now Stalin hoped to gain from the West what Hitler, a closer neighbor, had not dared yield him.

It is true that, so long as Russian survival appeared to require a second front to relieve the Nazi pressure, Moscow's demand for Eastern Europe was a little muffled. Thus the Soviet government adhered to the Atlantic Charter (though with a significant if obscure reservation about adapting its principles to "the circumstances, needs, and historic peculiarities of particular countries"). Thus it also adhered to the Moscow Declaration of 1943, and Molotov then, with his easy mendacity, even denied that Russia had any desire to divide Europe into spheres of influence. But this was guff, which the Russians were perfectly willing to ladle out if it would keep the Americans, and especially Secretary Hull (who made a strong personal impression at the Moscow conference), happy. "A declaration," as Stalin once observed to Eden, "I regard as algebra, but an agreement as practical arithmetic. I do not wish to decry algebra, but I prefer practical arithmetic."

The more consistent Russian purpose was revealed when Stalin offered the British a straight sphere-of-influence deal at the end of 1941. Britain, he suggested, should recognize the Russian absorption of the Baltic states, part of Finland, eastern Poland, and Bessarabia; in return, Russia would support any special British need for bases or security arrangements in Western Europe. There was nothing specifically Communist about these ambitions. If Stalin achieved them, he would be fulfilling an age-old dream of the tsars. The British reaction was mixed. "Soviet policy is amoral," Anthony Eden noted at the time; "United States policy is exaggeratedly moral, at least where non-American interests are concerned." If Roosevelt was a universalist with occasional leanings toward spheres of influence and Stalin was a sphere-of-influence man with occasional gestures toward universalism, Churchill seemed evenly poised between the familiar realism of the balance of power, which he had so long recorded as a historian and manipulated as a statesman, and the hope that there must be some better way of doing things. His 1943 proposal of a world organization divided into regional councils represented an effort to blend universalist and sphere-of-interest conceptions. His initial rejection of Stalin's proposal in December 1941 as "directly contrary to the first, second and third articles of the Atlantic Charter" thus did not spring entirely from a desire to propitiate the United States. On the other hand, he had himself already reinterpreted the Atlantic Charter as applying only to Europe (and thus not to the British Empire), and he was, above all, an empiricist who never believed in sacrificing reality on the altar of doctrine.

So in April 1942 he wrote Roosevelt that "the increasing gravity of the war" had led him to feel that the Charter "ought not to be constructed so as to deny Russia the frontiers she occupied when Germany attacked her." Hull, however, remained fiercely hostile to the inclusion of territorial provisions in the Anglo-Russian treaty; the American position, Eden noted, "chilled me with Wilsonian memories." Though Stalin complained that it looked "as if the Atlantic Charter was directed against the U.S.S.R.," it was the Russian season of military adversity in the spring of 1942, and he dropped his demands.

He did not, however, change his intentions. A year later Ambassador Standley could cable Washington from Moscow: "In 1918 Western Europe attempted to set up a *cordon sanitaire* to protect it from the influence of bolshevism. Might not now the Kremlin envisage the formation of a belt of pro-Soviet states to protect it from the influences of the West?" It well might; and that purpose became increasingly clear as the war approached its end. Indeed, it derived sustenance from Western policy in the first area of liberation.

The unconditional surrender of Italy in July 1943 created the first major test of the Western devotion to universalism. America and Britain, having won the Italian war, handled the capitulation, keeping Moscow informed at a distance. Stalin complained:

> The United States and Great Britain made agreements but the Soviet Union received information about the results . . . just as a passive third observer. I have to tell you that it is impossible to tolerate the situation any longer. I propose that the [tripartite military-political commission] be established and that Sicily be assigned . . . as its place of residence.

Roosevelt, who had no intention of sharing the control of Italy with the Russians, suavely replied with the suggestion that Stalin send an officer "to General Eisenhower's headquarters in connection with the commission." Unimpressed, Stalin continued to press for a tripartite body; but his Western Allies were adamant in keeping the Soviet Union off the Control Commission for Italy, and the Russians in the end had to be satisfied with a seat, along with minor Allied states, on a meaningless Inter-Allied Advisory Council. Their acquiescence in this was doubtless not unconnected with a desire to establish precedents for Eastern Europe.

Teheran in December 1943 marked the high point of three-power collaboration. Still, when Churchill asked about Russian territorial interests, Stalin replied a little ominously, "There is no need to speak at the present time about any Soviet desires, but when the time comes we will speak." In the next weeks, there were increasing indications of a Soviet determination to deal unilaterally with Eastern Europe—so much so that in early February 1944 Hull cabled Harriman in Moscow:

> Matters are rapidly approaching the point where the Soviet Government will have to choose between the development and extension of the foundation of international cooperation as the guiding principle of the postwar world as against the continuance of a unilateral and arbitrary method of dealing with its special problems even though these problems are admittedly of more direct interest to the Soviet Union than to other great powers.

As against this approach, however, Churchill, more tolerant of sphere-of-influence deviations, soon proposed that, with the impending liberation of the Balkans, Russia should run things in Rumania and Britain in Greece. Hull strongly opposed this suggestion but made the mistake of leaving Washington for a few days; and Roosevelt, momentarily free from his Wilsonian conscience, yielded to Churchill's plea for a three-months' trial. Hull resumed the fight on his return, and Churchill postponed the matter.

The Red Army continued its advance into Eastern Europe. In August the Polish Home Army, urged on by Polish-language broadcasts from Moscow, rose up against the Nazis in Warsaw. For 63 terrible days, the Poles fought valiantly on, while the Red Army halted on the banks of the Vistula a few miles away, and in Moscow Stalin for more than half this time declined to cooperate with the Western effort to drop supplies to the Warsaw Resistance. It appeared a calculated Soviet decision to let the Nazis slaughter the anti-Soviet Polish underground; and, indeed, the result was to destroy any substantial alternative to a Soviet solution in Poland. The agony of Warsaw caused the most deep and genuine moral shock in Britain and America and provoked dark forebodings about Soviet postwar purposes.

Again history enjoins the imaginative leap in order to see things for a moment from Moscow's viewpoint. The Polish question, Churchill would say at Yalta, was for Britain a question of honor. "It is not only a question of honor for Russia," Stalin replied, "but one of life and death. . . . Throughout history Poland had been the corridor for attack on Russia." A top postwar priority for any Russian régime must be to close that corridor. The Home Army was led by anti-Communists. It clearly hoped by its action to forestall the Soviet occupation of Warsaw and, in Russian eyes, to prepare the way for an anti-Russian Poland. In addition, the uprising from a strictly operational viewpoint was premature. The Russians, it is evident in retrospect, had real military problems at the Vistula. The Soviet attempt in September to send Polish units from the Red Army across the river to join forces with the Home Army was a disaster. Heavy German shelling thereafter prevented the ferrying of tanks necessary for an assault on the German position. The Red Army itself did not take Warsaw for another three months. Nonetheless, Stalin's indifference to the human tragedy, his effort to blackmail the London Poles during the ordeal, his sanctimonious opposition during five precious weeks to aerial resupply, the invariable coldness of his explanations ("the Soviet command has come to the conclusion that it must dissociate itself from the Warsaw adventure"), and the obvious political benefit to the Soviet Union from the destruction of the Home Army—all these had the effect of suddenly dropping the mask of wartime comradeship and displaying to the West the hard face of Soviet policy. In now pursuing what he grimly regarded as the minimal requirements for the postwar security of his country, Stalin was inadvertently showing the irreconcilability of both his means and his ends with the Anglo-American conception of the peace.

Meanwhile Eastern Europe presented the Alliance with still another crisis that same September. Bulgaria, which was not at war with Russia, decided to surrender to the Western Allies while it still could; and the English and Americans at Cairo began to discuss armistice terms with Bulgarian envoys. Moscow, challenged by what it plainly saw as a Western intrusion into its own zone of vital interest, promptly declared war on Bulgaria, took over the surrender negotiations, and, invoking the Italian precedent, denied its Western Allies any role in the Bulgarian Control Commission. In a long and thoughtful cable, Ambassador Harriman meditated on the problems of communication with the Soviet Union. "Words," he reflected, "have a different connotation to the Soviets than they have to us. When they speak of insisting on 'friendly governments' in their neighboring countries, they have in mind something quite different from what we would mean." The Russians, he surmised, really believed that Washington accepted "their position that although they would keep us informed they had the right to settle their problems with their western neighbors unilaterally." But the Soviet position was still in flux: "the Soviet Government is not one mind." The problem, as Harriman had earlier told Harry Hopkins, was "to strengthen the hands of those around Stalin who want to play the game along our lines." The way to do this, he now told Hull, was to be understanding of their sensitivity, meet them much more than half way, encourage them and support them wherever we can, and yet oppose them promptly with the greatest of firmness where we see them going wrong. . . . The only way we can eventually come to an understanding with the Soviet Union on the question of non-interference in the internal affairs of other countries is for us to take a definite interest in the solution of the problems of each individual country as they arise.

As against Harriman's sophisticated universalist strategy, however, Churchill, increasingly fearful of the consequences of unrestrained competition in Eastern Europe, decided in early October to carry his sphere-of-influence proposal directly to Moscow. Roosevelt was at first content to have Churchill speak for him too and even prepared a cable to that effect. But Hopkins, a more rigorous universalist, took it upon himself to stop the cable and warn Roosevelt of its possible implications. Eventually Roosevelt sent a message to Harriman in Moscow emphasizing that he expected to "retain complete freedom of action after this conference is over." It was now that Churchill quickly proposed —and Stalin as quickly accepted—the celebrated division of southeastern Europe: ending (after further haggling between Eden and Molotov) with 90 percent Soviet predominance in Rumania, 80 percent in Bulgaria and Hungary, fifty-fifty in Jugoslavia, 90 percent British predominance in Greece.

Churchill in discussing this with Harriman used the phrase "spheres of influence." But he insisted that these were only "immediate wartime arrangements" and received a highly general blessing from Roosevelt. Yet, whatever Churchill intended, there is reason to believe that Stalin construed the percentages as an agreement, not a declaration; as practical arithmetic, not algebra. For Stalin, it should be understood, the sphere-of-influence idea did not mean that he would abandon all efforts to spread communism in some other nation's sphere; it did mean that, if he tried this and the other side cracked down, he could not feel he had serious cause for complaint. As Kennan wrote to Harriman at the end of 1944:

> As far as border states are concerned the Soviet government has never ceased to think in terms of spheres of interest. They expect us to support them in whatever action they wish to take in those regions, regardless of whether that action seems to us or to the rest of the world to be right or wrong. . . . I have no doubt that this position is honestly maintained on their part, and that they would be equally prepared to reserve moral judgment on any actions which we might wish to carry out, i.e., in the Caribbean area.

In any case, the matter was already under test a good deal closer to Moscow than the Caribbean. The Communist-dominated resistance movement in Greece was in open revolt against the effort of the Papandreou government to disarm and disband the guerrillas (the same Papandreou whom the Greek colonels have recently arrested on the claim that he is a tool of the Communists). Churchill now called in British Army units to crush the insurrection. This action produced a storm of criticism in his own country and in the United States; the American Government even publicly dissociated itself from the intervention, thereby emphasizing its detachment from the sphere-of-influence deal. But Stalin, Churchill later claimed, "adhered strictly and faithfully to our agreement of October, and during all the long weeks of fighting the Communists in the streets of Athens not one word of reproach came from *Pravda* or *Izvestia*," though there is no evidence that he tried to call off the Greek Communists. Still, when the Communist rebellion later broke out again in Greece, Stalin told Kardelj and Djilas of Jugoslavia in 1948, "The uprising in Greece must be stopped, and as quickly as possible."

No one, of course, can know what really was in the minds of the Russian leaders. The Kremlin archives are locked; of the primary actors, only Molotov survives, and he has not yet indicated any desire to collaborate with the Columbia Oral History Project. We do know that Stalin did not wholly surrender to sentimental illusion about his new friends. In June 1944, on the night before the landings in Normandy, he told Djilas that the English "find nothing sweeter than to trick their allies. . . . And Churchill? Churchill is the kind who, if you don't watch him, will slip a kopeck out of your pocket. Yes, a kopeck out of your pocket! . . . Roosevelt is not like that. He dips in his hand only for bigger coins." But whatever his views of his colleagues it is not unreasonable to suppose that Stalin would have been satisfied at the end of the war to secure what Kennan has called "a protective glacis along Russia's western border," and that, in exchange for a free hand in Eastern Europe, he was prepared to give the British and Americans equally free hands in their zones of vital interest, including in nations as close to Russia as Greece (for the British) and, very probably—or at least so the Jugoslavs believe—China (for the United States). In other words, his initial objectives were very probably not world conquest but Russian security.

V

It is now pertinent to inquire why the United States rejected the idea of stabilizing the world by division into spheres of influence and insisted on an East European strategy. One should warn against rushing to the conclusion that it was all a row between hard-nosed, balance-of-power realists and starry-eyed Wilsonians. Roosevelt, Hopkins, Welles, Harriman, Bohlen, Berle, Dulles, and other universalists were tough and serious men. Why, then, did they rebuff the sphere-of-influence solution?

The first reason is that they regarded this solution as containing within itself the seeds of a third world war. The balance-of-power idea seemed inherently unstable. It had always broken down in the past. It held out to each power the permanent temptation to try to alter the balance in its own favor, and it built this temptation into the international order. It would turn the great powers of 1945 away from the objective of concerting common policies toward competition for postwar advantage. As Hopkins told Molotov at Teheran, "The President feels it essential to world peace that Russia, Great Britain and the United States work out this control question in a manner which will not start each of the three powers arming against the others." "The greatest likelihood of eventual conflict," said the Joint Chiefs of Staff in 1944 (the only conflict which the J.C.S., in its wisdom, could then glimpse "in the fore-seeable future" was between Britain and Russia), ". . . would seem to grow out of either nation initiating attempts to build up its strength, by seeking to attach to herself parts of Europe to the disadvantage and possible danger of her potential adversary." The Americans were perfectly ready to acknowledge that Russia was entitled to convincing assurance of her national security—but not this way. "I could sympathize fully with Stalin's desire to protect his western borders from future attack," as Hull put it. "But I felt that this security could best be obtained through a strong postwar peace organization."

Hull's remark suggests the second objection: that the sphere-of-influence approach would, in the words of the State Department in 1945, "militate against the establishment and effective functioning of a broader system of general security in which all countries will have their part." The United Nations, in short, was seen as the alternative to the balance of power. Nor did the universalists see any necessary incompatibility between the Russian desire for "friendly governments" on its frontier and the American desire for self-determination in Eastern Europe. Before Yalta the State Department judged the general mood of Europe as "to the left and strongly in favor of far-reaching economic and social reforms, but not, however, in favor of a left-wing totalitarian regime to achieve these reforms." Governments in Eastern Europe could be sufficiently to the left "to allay Soviet suspicions" but sufficiently representative "of the center and *petit bourgeois* elements" not to seem a prelude to Communist dictatorship. The American criteria were there-fore that the government "should be dedicated to the preservation of civil liberties" and "should favor social and economic reforms." A string of New Deal states—of Finlands and Czechoslovakias—seemed a reasonable compromise solution.

Third, the universalists feared that the sphere-of-interest approach would be what Hull termed "a haven for the isolationists," who would advocate America's participation in Western Hemisphere affairs on condition that it did not participate in European or Asian affairs. Hull also feared that spheres of interest would lead to "closed trade areas or discriminatory systems" and thus defeat his cherished dream of a low-tariff, freely trading world.

Fourth, the sphere-of-interest solution meant the betrayal of the principles for which the Second World War was being fought—the Atlantic Charter, the Four Freedoms, the Declaration of the United Nations. Poland summed up the problem. Britain, having gone to war to defend the independence of Poland from the Germans, could not easily conclude the war by surrendering the independence of Poland to the Russians. Thus, as Hopkins told Stalin after Roosevelt's death in 1945, Poland had "become the symbol of our ability to work out problems with the Soviet Union." Nor could American liberals in general watch with equanimity while the police state spread into countries which, if they had mostly not been real democracies, had mostly not been tyrannies either. The execution in 1943 of Ehrlich and Alter, the Polish socialist trade union leaders, excited deep concern. "I have particularly in mind," Harriman cabled in 1944, "objection to the institution of secret police who may become involved in the persecution of persons of truly democratic convictions who may not be willing to conform to Soviet methods."

Fifth, the sphere-of-influence solution would create difficult domestic problems in American politics. Roosevelt was aware of the six million or more Polish votes in the 1944 election; even more acutely, he was aware of the broader and deeper attack which would follow if, after going to war to stop the Nazi conquest of Europe, he permitted the war to end with the Communist conquest of Eastern Europe. As Archibald MacLeish, then Assistant Secretary of State for Public Affairs, warned in January 1945, "The wave of disillusionment which has distressed us in the last several weeks will be increased if the impression is permitted to get abroad that potentially totalitarian provisional governments are to be set up without adequate safeguards as to the holding of free elections and the realization of the principles of the Atlantic Charter." Roosevelt believed that no administration could survive which did not try everything short of war to save Eastern Europe, and he was the supreme American politician of the century.

Sixth, if the Russians were allowed to overrun Eastern Europe without argument, would that satisfy them? Even Kennan, in a dispatch of May 1944, admitted that the "urge" had dreadful potentialities: "If initially successful, will it know where to stop? Will it not be inexorably carried forward, by its very nature, in a struggle to reach the whole —to attain complete mastery of the shores of the Atlantic and the

Pacific?" His own answer was that there were inherent limits to the Russian capacity to expand—"that Russia will not have an easy time in maintaining the power which it has seized over other people in Eastern and Central Europe unless it receives both moral and material assistance from the West." Subsequent developments have vindicated Kennan's argument. By the late forties, Jugoslavia and Albania, the two East European states farthest from the Soviet Union and the two in which communism was imposed from within rather than from without, had declared their independence of Moscow. But, given Russia's success in maintaining centralized control over the international Communist movement for a quarter of a century, who in 1944 could have had much confidence in the idea of Communist revolts against Moscow?

Most of those involved therefore rejected Kennan's answer and stayed with his question. If the West turned its back on Eastern Europe, the higher probability, in their view, was that the Russians would use their security zone, not just for defensive purposes, but as a springboard from which to mount an attack on Western Europe, now shattered by war, a vacuum of power awaiting its master. "If the policy is accepted that the Soviet Union has a right to penetrate her immediate neighbors for security," Harriman said in 1944, "penetration of the next immediate neighbors becomes at a certain time equally logical." If a row with Russia were inevitable, every consideration of prudence dictated that it should take place in Eastern rather than Western Europe.

Thus idealism and realism joined in opposition to the sphere-of-influence solution. The consequence was a determination to assert an American interest in the postwar destiny of all nations, including those of Eastern Europe. In the message which Roosevelt and Hopkins drafted after Hopkins had stopped Roosevelt's initial cable authorizing Churchill to speak for the United States at the Moscow meeting of October 1944, Roosevelt now said, "There is in this global war literally no question, either military or political, in which the United States is not interested." After Roosevelt's death Hopkins repeated the point to Stalin: "The cardinal basis of President Roosevelt's policy which the American people had fully supported had been the concept that the interests of the U.S. were worldwide and not confined to North and South America and the Pacific Ocean."

VI

For better or worse, this was the American position. It is now necessary to attempt the imaginative leap and consider the impact of this position on the leaders of the Soviet Union who, also for better or for worse, had reached the bitter conclusion that the survival of their country depended on their unchallenged control of the corridors through which enemies had so often invaded their homeland. They could claim to have been keeping their own side of the sphere-of-influence bargain. Of course, they were working to capture the resistance movements of Western Europe; indeed, with the appointment of Oumansky as Ambassador to Mexico they were even beginning to enlarge underground operations in the Western Hemisphere. But, from their viewpoint, if the West permitted this, the more fools they; and, if the West stopped it, it was within their right to do so. In overt political matters the Russians were scrupulously playing the game. They had watched in silence while the British shot down Communists in Greece. In Jugoslavia Stalin was urging Tito (as Djilas later revealed) to keep King Peter. They had not only acknowledged Western preeminence in Italy but had recognized the Badoglio régime; the Italian Comunists had even voted (against the Socialists and the Liberals) for the renewal of the Lateran Pacts.

They would not regard anti-Communist action in a Western zone as a *casus belli;* and they expected reciprocal license to assert their own authority in the East. But the principle of self-determination was carrying the United States into a deeper entanglement in Eastern Europe than the Soviet Union claimed as a right (whatever it was doing underground) in the affairs of Italy, Greece, or China. When the Russians now exercised in Eastern Europe the same brutal control they were prepared to have Washington exercise in the American sphere of influence, the American protests, given the paranoia produced alike by Russian history and Leninist ideology, no doubt seemed not only an act of hypocrisy but a threat to security. To the Russians, a stroll into the neighborhood easily became a plot to burn down the house: when, for example, damaged American planes made emergency landings in Poland and Hungary, Moscow took this as attempts to organize the local resistance. It is not unusual to suspect one's adversary of doing what one is already doing oneself. At the same time, the cruelty with which the Russians executed their idea of spheres of influence—in a sense, perhaps, an unwitting cruelty, since Stalin treated the East Europeans no worse than he had treated the Russians in the thirties—discouraged the West from accepting the equation (for example, Italy = Rumania) which seemed so self-evident to the Kremlin.

So Moscow very probably, and not unnaturally, perceived the emphasis on self-determination as a systematic and deliberate pressure on Russia's western frontiers. Moreover, the restoration of capitalism to countries freed at frightful cost by the Red Army no doubt struck the Russians as the betrayal of the principles for which *they* were fighting. "That they, the victors," Isaac Deutscher has suggested, "should now preserve an order from which they had experienced nothing but hostility, and could expect nothing but hostility . . . would have been the most miserable anti-climax to their great 'war of liberation.'" By 1944 Poland was the critical issue; Harriman later said that "under instructions from President Roosevelt, I talked about Poland with Stalin more frequently than any other subject." While the West saw the point of Stalin's demand for a "friendly government" in Warsaw, the American insistence on the sovereign virtues of free elections (ironically in the spirit of the 1917 Bolshevik decree of peace, which affirmed "the right" of a nation "to decide the forms of its state existence by a free vote, taken after the complete evacuation of the incorporating or, generally, of the stronger nation") created an insoluble problem in those countries, like Poland (and Rumania), where free elections would almost certainly produce anti-Soviet governments.

The Russians thus may well have estimated the Western pressures as calculated to encourage their enemies in Eastern Europe and to defeat their own minimum objective of a protective glacis. Everything still hung, however, on the course of military operations. The wartime collaboration had been created by one thing, and one thing alone: the threat of Nazi victory. So long as this threat was real, so was the collaboration. In late December 1944, von Rundstedt launched his counter-offensive in the Ardennes. A few weeks later, when Roosevelt, Churchill, and Stalin gathered in the Crimea, it was in the shadow of this last considerable explosion of German power. The meeting at Yalta was still dominated by the mood of war.

Yalta remains something of a historical perplexity—less, from the perspective of 1967, because of a mythical American deference to the sphere-of-influence thesis than because of the documentable Russian deference to the universalist thesis. Why should Stalin in 1945 have accepted the Declaration on Liberated Europe and an agreement on Poland pledging that "the three governments will jointly" act to assure "free elections of governments responsive to the will of the people"? There are several probable answers: that the war was not over and the Russians still wanted the Americans to intensify their military effort in the West; that one clause in the Declaration premised action on "the opinion of the three governments" and thus implied a Soviet veto, though the Polish agreement was more definite; most of all that the universalist algebra of the Declaration was plainly in Stalin's mind to be construed in terms of the practical arithmetic of his sphere-of-influence agreement with Churchill the previous October. Stalin's assurance to Churchill at Yalta that a proposed Russian amendment to the Declaration would not apply to Greece makes it clear that Roosevelt's pieties did not, in Stalin's mind, nullify Churchill's percentages. He could well have been strengthened in this supposition by the fact that *after* Yalta, Churchill himself repeatedly reasserted the terms of the October agreement as if he regarded it, despite Yalta, as controlling.

Harriman still had the feeling before Yalta that the Kremlin had "two approaches to their postwar policies" and that Stalin himself was "of two minds." One approach emphasized the internal reconstruction and development of Russia; the other its external expansion. But in the meantime the fact which dominated all political decisions—that is, the war against Germany—was moving into its final phase. In the weeks after Yalta, the military situation changed with great rapidity. As the Nazi threat declined, so too did the need for cooperation. The Soviet Union, feeling itself menaced by the American idea of self-determination and the borderlands diplomacy to which it was leading, skeptical whether the United Nations would protect its frontiers as reliably as its own domination in Eastern Europe, began to fulfill its security requirements unilaterally.

In March Stalin expressed his evaluation of the United Nations by rejecting Roosevelt's plea that Molotov come to the San Francisco conference, if only for the opening sessions. In the next weeks the Russians emphatically and crudely worked their will in Eastern Europe, above all in the test country of Poland. They were ignoring the Declaration on Liberated Europe, ignoring the Atlantic Charter, self-determination, human freedom, and everything else the Americans considered essential for a stable peace. "We must clearly recognize," Harriman wired Washington a few days before Roosevelt's death, "that the Soviet program is the establishment of totalitarianism, ending personal liberty and democracy as we know and respect it."

At the same time, the Russians also began to mobilize Communist resources in the United States itself to block American universalism. In April 1945 Jacques Duclos, who had been the Comintern official responsible for the Western Communist parties, launched in *Cahiers du Communisme* an uncompromising attack on the policy of the American Communist Party. Duclos sharply condemned the revisionism of Earl Browder, the American Communist leader, as "expressed in the concept of a long-term class peace in the United States, of the possibility of the suppression of the class struggle in the postwar period and of establishment of harmony between labor and capital." Browder was specifically rebuked for favoring the "self-determination" of Europe "west of the Soviet Union" on a bourgeois-democratic basis. The excommunication of Browderism was plainly the Politburo's considered reaction to the impending defeat of Germany; it was a signal to the Communist parties of the West that they should recover their identity; it was Moscow's alert to Communists everywhere that they should prepare for new policies in the postwar world.

The Duclos piece obviously could not have been planned and written much later than the Yalta conference—that is, well before a number of events which revisionists now cite in order to demonstrate American responsibility for the Cold War: before Allen Dulles, for example, began to negotiate the surrender of the German armies in Italy (the episode which provoked Stalin to charge Roosevelt with seeking a separate peace and provoked Roosevelt to denounce the "vile misrepresentations" of Stalin's informants); well before Roosevelt died; many months before the testing of the atomic bomb; even more months before Truman ordered that the bomb be dropped on Japan. William Z. Foster, who soon replaced Browder as the leader of the American Communist Party and embodied the new Moscow line, later boasted of having said in January 1944, "A post-war Roosevelt administration would continue to be, as it is now, an imperialist government." With ancient suspicions revived by the American insistence on universalism, this was no doubt the conclusion which the Russians were reaching at the same time. The Soviet's canonization of Roosevelt (like their present-day canonization of Kennedy) took place after the American President's death.

The atmosphere of mutual suspicion was beginning to rise. In January 1945 Molotov formally proposed that the United States grant Russia a $6 billion credit for postwar reconstruction. With characteristic tact he explained that he was doing this as a favor to save America from a postwar depression. The proposal seems to have been diffidently made and diffidently received. Roosevelt requested that the matter "not be pressed further" on the American side until he had a chance to talk with Stalin; but the Russians did not follow it up either at Yalta in February (save for a single glancing reference) or during the Stalin-Hopkins talks in May or at Potsdam. Finally the proposal was renewed in the very different political atmosphere of August. This time Washington inexplicably mislaid the request during the transfer of the records of the Foreign Economic Administration to the State Department. It did not turn up again until March 1946. Of course this was impossible for the Russians to believe; it is hard enough even for those acquainted with the capacity of the American government for incompetence to believe; and it only strengthened Soviet suspicions of American purposes.

The American credit was one conceivable form of Western contribution to Russian reconstruction. Another was lend-lease, and the possibility of reconstruction aid under the lend-lease protocol had already been discussed in 1944. But in May 1945 Russia, like Britain, suffered from Truman's abrupt termination of lend-lease shipments—"unfortunate and even brutal," Stalin told Hopkins, adding that, if it was "designed as pressure on the Russians in order to soften them up, then it was a fundamental mistake." A third form was German reparations. Here Stalin in demanding $10 billion in reparations for the Soviet Union made his strongest fight at Yalta. Roosevelt, while agreeing essentially with Churchill's opposition, tried to postpone the matter by accepting the Soviet figure as a "basis for discussion"—a formula which led to future misunderstanding. In short, the Russian hope for major Western assistance in postwar reconstruction foundered on three events which the Kremlin could well have interpreted respectively as deliberate sabotage (the loan request), blackmail (lend-lease cancellation), and pro-Germanism (reparations).

Actually the American attempt to settle the fourth lend-lease protocol was generous and the Russians for their own reasons declined to come to an agreement. It is not clear, though, that satisfying Moscow on any of these financial scores would have made much essential difference. It might have persuaded some doves in the Kremlin that the U.S. government was genuinely friendly; it might have persuaded some hawks that the American anxiety for Soviet friendship was such that Moscow could do as it wished without inviting challenge from the United States. It would, in short, merely have reinforced both sides of the Kremlin debate; it would hardly have reversed deeper tendencies toward the deterioration of political relationships. Economic deals were surely subordinate to the quality of mutual political confidence; and here, in the months after Yalta, the decay was steady.

The Cold War had now begun. It was the product not of a decision but of a dilemma. Each side felt compelled to adopt policies which the other could not but regard as a threat to the principles of the peace. Each then felt compelled to undertake defensive measures. Thus the Russians saw no choice but to consolidate their security in Eastern Europe. The Americans, regarding Eastern Europe as the first step toward Western Europe, responded by asserting their interest in the zone the Russians deemed vital to their security. The Russians concluded that the West was resuming its old course of capitalist encirclement; that it was purposefully laying the foundation for anti-Soviet régimes in the area defined by the blood of centuries as crucial to Russian survival. Each side believed with passion that future international stability depended on the success of its own conception of world order. Each side, in pursuing its own clearly indicated and deeply cherished principles, was only confirming the fear of the other that it was bent on aggression.

Very soon the process began to acquire a cumulative momentum. The impending collapse of Germany thus provoked new troubles: the Russians, for example, sincerely feared that the West was planning a separate surrender of the German armies in Italy in a way which would release troops for Hitler's eastern front, as they subsequently feared that the Nazis might succeed in surrendering Berlin to the West. This was the context in which the atomic bomb now appeared. Though the revisionist argument that Truman dropped the bomb less to defeat Japan than to intimidate Russia is not convincing, this thought unquestionably appealed to some in Washington as at least an advantageous side-effect of Hiroshima.

So the machinery of suspicion and counter-suspicion, action and counter-action, was set in motion. But, given relations among traditional national states, there was still no reason, even with all the postwar jostling, why this should not have remained a manageable situation. What made it unmanageable, what caused the rapid escalation of the Cold War and in another two years completed the division of Europe, was a set of considerations which this account has thus far excluded.

VII

Up to this point, the discussion has considered the schism within the wartime coalition as if it were entirely the result of disagreements among national states. Assuming this framework, there was unquestionably a failure of communication between America and Russia, a misperception of signals, and, as time went on, a mounting tendency to ascribe ominous motives to the other side. It seems hard, for example, to deny that American postwar policy created genuine difficulties for the Russians and even assumed a threatening aspect for them. All this the revisionists have rightly and usefully emphasized.

But the great omission of the revisionists—and also the fundamental explanation of the speed with which the Cold War escalated—lies precisely in the fact that the Soviet Union was *not* a traditional national state.[4] This is where the "mirror image," invoked by some psychologists, falls down. For the Soviet Union was a phenomenon very different from America or Britain: it was a totalitarian state, endowed with an all-explanatory, all-consuming ideology, committed to the infallibility of government and party, still in a somewhat messianic mood, equating dissent with treason, and ruled by a dictator who, for all his quite extraordinary abilities, had his paranoid moments.

Marxism-Leninism gave the Russian leaders a view of the world according to which all societies were inexorably destined to proceed along appointed roads by appointed stages until they achieved the classless nirvana. Moreover, given the resistance of the capitalists to this development, the existence of any non-Communist state was *by definition* a threat to the Soviet Union. "As long as capitalism and socialism exist," Lenin wrote, "we cannot live in peace: in the end, one or the other will triumph—a funeral dirge will be sung either over the Soviet Republic or over world capitalism."

Stalin and his associates, whatever Roosevelt or Truman did or

4. This is the classical revisionist fallacy—the assumption of the rationality, or at least of the traditionalism, of states where ideology and social organization have created a different range of motives. So the Second World War revisionists omit the totalitarian dynamism of Nazism and the fanaticism of Hitler, as the Civil War revisionists omit the fact that the slavery system was producing a doctrinaire closed society in the American South. For a consideration of some of these issues, see "The Causes of the Civil War: A Note on Historical Sentimentalism" in my *The Politics of Hope* (Boston, 1963).

failed to do, were bound to regard the United States as the enemy, not because of this deed or that, but because of the primordial fact that America was the leading capitalist power and thus, by Leninist syllogism, unappeasably hostile, driven by the logic of its system to oppose, encircle, and destroy Soviet Russia. Nothing the United States could have done in 1944–45 would have abolished this mistrust, required and sanctified as it was by Marxist gospel—nothing short of the conversion of the United States into a Stalinist despotism; and even this would not have sufficed, as the experience of Jugoslavia and China soon showed, unless it were accompanied by total subservience to Moscow. So long as the United States remained a capitalist democracy, no American policy, given Moscow's theology, could hope to win basic Soviet confidence, and every American action was poisoned from the source. So long as the Soviet Union remained a messianic state, ideology compelled a steady expansion of Communist power.

It is easy, of course, to exaggerate the capacity of ideology to control events. The tension of acting according to revolutionary abstractions is too much for most nations to sustain over a long period: that is why Mao Tse-tung has launched his Cultural Revolution, hoping thereby to create a permanent revolutionary mood and save Chinese communism from the degeneration which, in his view, has overtaken Russian communism. Still, as any revolution grows older, normal human and social motives will increasingly reassert themselves. In due course, we can be sure, Leninism will be about as effective in governing the daily lives of Russians as Christianity is in governing the daily lives of Americans. Like the Ten Commandments and the Sermon on the Mount, the Leninist verities will increasingly become platitudes for ritual observance, not guides to secular decision. There can be no worse fallacy (even if respectable people practiced it diligently for a season in the United States) than that of drawing from a nation's ideology permanent conclusions about its behavior.

A temporary recession of ideology was already taking place during the Second World War when Stalin, to rally his people against the invader, had to replace the appeal of Marxism by that of nationalism. ("We are under no illusions that they are fighting for us," Stalin once said to Harriman. "They are fighting for Mother Russia.") But this was still taking place within the strictest limitations. The Soviet Union remained as much a police state as ever; the régime was as infallible as ever; foreigners and their ideas were as suspect as ever. "Never, except possibly during my later experience as ambassador in Moscow," Kennan has written, "did the insistence of the Soviet authorities on isolation of the diplomatic corps weigh more heavily on me . . . than in these first weeks following my return to Russia in the final months of the war. . . . [We were] treated as though we were the bearers of some species of the plague"—which, of course, from the Soviet viewpoint, they were: the plague of skepticism.

Paradoxically, of the forces capable of bringing about a modification of ideology, the most practical and effective was the Soviet dictatorship itself. If Stalin was an ideologist, he was also a pragmatist. If he saw everything through the lenses of Marxism-Leninism, he also, as the infallible expositor of the faith, could reinterpret Marxism-Leninism to justify anything he wanted to do at any given moment. No doubt Roosevelt's ignorance of Marxism-Leninism was inexcusable and led to grievous miscalculations. But Roosevelt's efforts to work on and through Stalin were not so hopelessly naïve as it used to be fashionable to think. With the extraordinary instinct of a great political leader, Roosevelt intuitively understood that Stalin was the *only* lever available to the West against the Leninist ideology and the Soviet system. If Stalin could be reached, then alone was there a chance of getting the Russians to act contrary to the prescriptions of their faith. The best evidence is that Roosevelt retained a certain capacity to influence Stalin to the end; the nominal Soviet acquiescence in American universalism as late as Yalta was perhaps an indication of that. It is in this way that the death of Roosevelt was crucial—not in the vulgar sense that his policy was then reversed by his successor, which did not happen, but in the sense that no other American could hope to have the restraining impact on Stalin which Roosevelt might for a while have had.

Stalin alone could have made any difference. Yet Stalin, in spite of the impression of sobriety and realism he made on Westerners who saw him during the Second World War, was plainly a man of deep and morbid obsessions and compulsions. When he was still a young man, Lenin had criticized his rude and arbitrary ways. A reasonably authoritative observer (N. S. Khrushchev) later commented, "These negative characteristics of his developed steadily and during the last years acquired an absolutely insufferable character." His paranoia, probably set off by the suicide of his wife in 1932, led to the terrible purges of the mid-thirties and the wanton murder of thousands of his Bolshevik comrades. "Everywhere and in everything," Khrushchev says of this period, "he saw 'enemies,' 'double-dealers' and 'spies.' " The crisis of war evidently steadied him in some way, though Khrushchev speaks of his "nervousness and hysteria . . . even after the war began." The madness, so rigidly controlled for a time, burst out with new and shocking intensity in the postwar years. "After the war," Khrushchev testifies,

> the situation became even more complicated. Stalin became even more capricious, irritable and brutal; in particular, his suspicion grew. His persecution mania reached unbelievable dimensions. . . . He decided everything, without any consideration for anyone or anything.

Stalin's wilfulness showed itself . . . also in the international relations of the Soviet Union. . . . He had completely lost a sense of reality; he demonstrated his suspicion and haughtiness not only in relation to individuals in the USSR, but in relation to whole parties and nations.

A revisionist fallacy has been to treat Stalin as just another Realpolitik statesman, as Second World War revisionists see Hitler as just another Stresemann or Bismarck. But the record makes it clear that in the end nothing could satisfy Stalin's paranoia. His own associates failed. Why does anyone suppose that any conceivable American policy would have succeeded?

An analysis of the origins of the Cold War which leaves out these factors—the intransigence of Leninist ideology, the sinister dynamics of a totalitarian society, and the madness of Stalin—is obviously incomplete. It was these factors which made it hard for the West to accept the thesis that Russia was moved only by a desire to protect its security and would be satisfied by the control of Eastern Europe; it was these factors which charged the debate between universalism and spheres of influence with apocalyptic potentiality.

Leninism and totalitarianism created a structure of thought and behavior which made postwar collaboration between Russia and America—in any normal sense of civilized intercourse between national states—inherently impossible. The Soviet dictatorship of 1945 simply could not have survived such a collaboration. Indeed, nearly a quarter-century later, the Soviet régime, though it has meanwhile moved a good distance, could still hardly survive it without risking the release inside Russia of energies profoundly opposed to Communist despotism. As for Stalin, he may have represented the only force in 1945 capable of overcoming Stalinism, but the very traits which enabled him to win absolute power expressed terrifying instabilities of mind and temperament and hardly offered a solid foundation for a peaceful world.

VIII

The difference between America and Russia in 1945 was that some Americans fundamentally believed that, over a long run, a modus vivendi with Russia was possible; while the Russians, so far as one can tell, believed in no more than a short-run modus vivendi with the United States.

Harriman and Kennan, this narrative has made clear, took the lead in warning Washington about the difficulties of short-run dealings with the Soviet Union. But both argued that, if the United States developed a rational policy and stuck to it, there would be, after long and rough passages, the prospect of eventual clearing. "I am, as you know," Harriman cabled Washington in early April, "a most earnest advocate of the closest possible understanding with the Soviet Union so that what I am saying relates only to how best to attain such understanding." Kennan has similarly made it clear that the function of his containment policy was "to tide us over a difficult time and bring us to the point where we could discuss effectively with the Russians the dangers and drawbacks this status quo involved, and to arrange with them for its peaceful replacement by a better and sounder one." The subsequent careers of both men attest to the honesty of these statements.

There is no corresponding evidence on the Russian side that anyone seriously sought a modus vivendi in these terms. Stalin's choice was whether his long-term ideological and national interests would be better served by a short-run truce with the West or by an immediate resumption of pressure. In October 1945 Stalin indicated to Harriman at Sochi that he planned to adopt the second course—that the Soviet Union was going isolationist. No doubt the succession of problems with the United States contributed to this decision, but the basic causes most probably lay elsewhere: in the developing situations in Eastern Europe, in Western Europe, and in the United States.

In Eastern Europe, Stalin was still for a moment experimenting with techniques of control. But he must by now have begun to conclude that he had underestimated the hostility of the people to Russian dominion. The Hungarian elections in November would finally convince him that the Yalta formula was a road to anti-Soviet governments. At the same time, he was feeling more strongly than ever a sense of his opportunities in Western Europe. The other half of the Continent lay unexpectedly before him, politically demoralized, economically prostrate, militarily defenseless. The hunting would be better and safer than he had anticipated. As for the United States, the alacrity of postwar demobilization must have recalled Roosevelt's offhand remark at Yalta that "two years would be the limit" for keeping American troops in Europe. And, despite Dr. Eugene Varga's doubts about the imminence of American economic breakdown, Marxist theology assured Stalin that the United States was heading into a bitter postwar depression and would be consumed with its own problems. If the condition of Eastern Europe made unilateral action seem essential in the interests of Russian security, the condition of Western Europe and the United States offered new temptations for Communist expansion. The Cold War was now in full swing.

It still had its year of modulations and accommodations. Secretary Byrnes conducted his long and fruitless campaign to persuade the Russians that America only sought governments in Eastern Europe "both friendly to the Soviet Union and representative of all the democratic elements of the country." Crises were surmounted in Trieste and Iran. Secretary Marshall evidently did not give up hope of a modus vivendi until the Moscow conference of foreign secretaries of March

1947. Even then, the Soviet Union was invited to participate in the Marshall Plan.

The point of no return came on July 2, 1947, when Molotov, after bringing 89 technical specialists with him to Paris and evincing initial interest in the project for European reconstruction, received the hot flash from the Kremlin, denounced the whole idea, and walked out of the conference. For the next fifteen years the Cold War raged unabated, passing out of historical ambiguity into the realm of good versus evil and breeding on both sides simplifications, stereotypes, and self-serving absolutes, often couched in interchangeable phrases. Under the pressure even America, for a deplorable decade, forsook its pragmatic and pluralist traditions, posed as God's appointed messenger to ignorant and sinful man, and followed the Soviet example in looking to a world remade in its own image.

In retrospect, if it is impossible to see the Cold War as a case of American aggression and Russian response, it is also hard to see it as a pure case of Russian aggression and American response. "In what is truly tragic," wrote Hegel, "there must be valid moral powers on both the sides which come into collision. . . . Both suffer loss and yet both are mutually justified." In this sense, the Cold War had its tragic elements. The question remains whether it was an instance of Greek tragedy—as Auden has called it, "the tragedy of necessity," where the feeling aroused in the spectator is "What a pity it had to be this way" —or of Christian tragedy, "the tragedy of possibility," where the feeling aroused is "What a pity it was this way when it might have been otherwise."

Once something has happened, the historian is tempted to assume that it had to happen; but this may often be a highly unphilosophical assumption. The Cold War could have been avoided only if the Soviet Union had not been possessed by convictions both of the infallibility of the Communist word and of the inevitability of a Communist world. These convictions transformed an impasse between national states into a religious war, a tragedy of possibility into one of necessity. One might wish that America had preserved the poise and proportion of the first years of the Cold War and had not in time succumbed to its own forms of self-righteousness. But the most rational of American policies could hardly have averted the Cold War. Only today, as Russia begins to recede from its messianic mission and to accept, in practice if not yet in principle, the permanence of the world of diversity, only now can the hope flicker that this long, dreary, costly contest may at last be taking on forms less dramatic, less obsessive, and less dangerous to the future of mankind.